ARCHAEOLOGICAL THEORY IN EUROPE

MATERIAL CULTURES

Series editors: Daniel Miller, *Department of Anthropology, University College, London;* Michael Rowlands, *Department of Anthropology, University College, London;* Christopher Tilley, *Department of Archaeology, St David's University College, Wales.*

The Material Cultures series crosses the traditional subject boundaries of archaeology, history, and anthropology to consider human society in terms of its production, consumption, and social structures. This approach breaks down the narrow compartmentalisation which has until now obscured understanding of past and present societies and offers a more broadly-based (and coherent) set of explanations.

The series editors draw upon the expert knowledge of specialists in many fields, and in almost every continent; but it is a requirement that each title in the series should address issues which transcend the limits imposed by existing subject categories.

Forthcoming titles

THEORY AND PRACTICE IN ARCHAEOLOGY
Ian Hodder

MATERIAL CULTURE AND TEXT
Christopher Tilley

ARCHAEOLOGICAL THEORY IN EUROPE

The last three decades

Edited by

Ian Hodder

London and New York

First published in 1991
by Routledge
11 New Fetter Lane, London EC4P 4EE

Simultaneously published in the USA and Canada
by Routledge
a division of Routledge, Chapman and Hall Inc.
29 West 35th Street, New York, NY 10001

© 1991 Ian Hodder

Phototypeset in 10/12pt Garamond by
Intype, London
Printed in Great Britain by
T J Press (Padstow) Ltd, Padstow, Cornwall

British Library Cataloguing in Publication Data
Archaeological theory in Europe : the last three decades. –
(Material cultures)
I. Hodder, Ian II. Series
930.101

Library of Congress Cataloging in Publication Data
Archaeological theory in Europe : the last three decades / edited by
Ian Hodder.
p. cm. -- (Material cultures)
Includes bibliographical references and index.
1. Archaeology--Europe--Philosophy--History--20th century. 2.
Europe--Intellectual life--20th century. I. Hodder, Ian. II. Series.
CC101.E85A73 1991
930.1'01--dc20   90-22339

ISBN 0–415–06521–6

CONTENTS

CONTENTS

PREFACE

In the 1960s and early 1970s, theoretical writing in western archaeology was dominated by a particular Anglo-American perspective often termed New Archaeology. These 'New' ideas, mainly deriving from the USA, had varying influences in European countries. Indeed, the failure of the New Archaeology to take an equally firm hold throughout Europe suggests the possible existence of European perspectives in archaeological theory which are diverse and different from the North American view.

It might be argued that European archaeology was simply 'left behind', 'out of date' and generally atheoretical. Its traditional authority structures perhaps prevented discussion of new ideas and it would in the end catch up with the positivist, processual Anglo-American ideas. But, on the other hand, it can be argued that the European rejection of theory derived from the particular historical context of the recent political manipulation of history and prehistory, and from a theoretical perspective that was deeply historical. The first concern of the chapters in this volume is to evaluate the distinctively national and European characteristics of archaeology in European countries in the 1960s and 1970s. More specifically, the chapters consider the developments of archaeological theory in each country in the 1960s and 1970s in relation to the positivist and anthropological perspectives being espoused in the USA. The incorporation of ecology, adaptation and the natural science model for archaeology will be discussed. It is clear from the experiences of each country that these external sources had only minimal impact. The main source of inspiration for European archaeology was an intellectual milieu dominated by writers such as Marx, Gramsci, Hegel, Croce, Lévi-Strauss, Dumezil, Eliade, Braudel, Wittgenstein, Feyerabend and Habermas.

The second concern of the volume is to consider the emerging characteristics of a distinctively European and non-positivist archaeology. By the late 1970s and early 1980s it was beginning to become clear that few Anglo-American archaeologists would any longer call themselves New Archaeologists and that there was a breakdown in the unity and confidence of archaeology as a discipline. During the 1980s in the USA, the reaction seems to have been mainly to retreat from broader theoretical discussion and to concentrate on the mechanics of site formation processes, middle-range theory and hunter-gathering optimising strategies. In Europe, on the other hand, the 1980s saw a rising tide of theoretical debate and it is now possible to argue that theoretical writing in western archaeology is dominated by European perspectives. This new theoretical discussion has not simply involved a catching up with Anglo-American archaeology but has gone along different paths. Thus, the second aim of each chapter in the volume is to evaluate the development of archaeological theory in the different European countries in the 1980s and to assess future directions. As Bjørn Myhre notes in his chapter on Scandinavian archaeology, there is no longer one archaeology or one prehistory, but many. The debate incorporates a wide range of ideologies and perspectives. It is often strongly focused on non-positivist philosophies, Marxism and the critique of structuralism. It is concerned with linking history and anthropology. It is involved in the socio-politics of archaeology. The overall impression from reading this book is that European archaeology, in contrast to archaeology in North America or elsewhere, is fundamentally historical in emphasis, is strongly Marxist in orientation, and is undeniably social in construction.

A third and related point made in this book concerns the recent history of theoretical argument in European archaeology. In much Anglo-American archaeology a development sequence is often described from culture-historical to processual to post-processual approaches, and the same sequence is assumed for Europe as a whole. But this book demonstrates that most countries in Europe have witnessed quite different patterns of development. For example, Greek archaeology has long been dominated by a nationalism and isolationism resulting from a claimed diachronic continuity with the great achievements of the Classical world. This heavy ideological use of the past led to a Marxist reaction in the 1980s. In Italy there has been a long Marxist historicist tradition in

PREFACE

intellectual, political and cultural life, which has produced a distinctively Marxist archaeology. In Spain, the continuation of fascist government into the mid 1970s meant that the recent awakening of theoretical Marxist debate has had to be linked to fundamental methodological concerns about the rigour of excavation and survey. Marxism has been joined to positivism – an alliance which many in Anglo-American archaeology would see as unholy. In France, the institutional neglect and intellectual marginalisation of prehistoric and proto-historic archaeology over several centuries produced a situation in which archaeology became increasingly unable to enter into theoretical dialogue. So in the era of 'soixante-huit' and more recently, the intellectual ferment associated with Sartre, Althusser, Foucault, Lévi-Strauss, Bourdieu and Derrida has been met with an archaeological discussion in France of typology, formalisation and documentation systems. Only recently is there some indication of a wider debate. Examples of these regional traditions can be multiplied by moving from chapter to chapter.

A fourth point concerns an eastern parallel with the links between the USA and Western Europe. In Eastern Europe, the recent development of archaeological theory cannot be understood without reference to the practical conditions set by Soviet domination and the intellectual traditions set by Marxism. Recent political changes in Eastern Europe are already leading to an open re-evaluation of the perspectives engendered under Soviet rule. This volume seeks to explore the way in which archaeologists in Eastern Europe have their own traditions and are exploring new directions which incorporate but transform old dogmas. I have therefore explicitly excluded the Soviet Union from my definition of Europe for the purposes of this volume, since I wanted to examine the nature of archaeological theory in the area between the two old superpowers. Undoubtedly, however, it will be of interest to see how archaeological discussion develops in the various European republics of the Soviet Union.

A fifth point deals with the need for theory in European archaeology. One of the dangers in the Europe of the 1990s is that ethnic unrest may create a new instability as liberalisation occurs, especially in Eastern Europe. There is a great danger that archaeology may be used once again, as it was used prior to the last war, to justify these regional claims. One of the most important aspects of an emphasis on archaeological theory is that it focuses our attention on concepts and taken-for-granteds used in the construction of the past – including past ethnicities. There is a need for a continual critique of reconstructions of the past as ideological. Nationalist and ethnic uses of archaeology to justify conflict need to be counteracted, as far as they can, with a wary and critical theoretical eye.

In fact it was precisely the uncritical link between archaeological theory and nationalist claims which led to an inhibited theoretical discussion in many parts of Europe until recent years. It is a paradox that much European archaeology has seen little theoretical discussion within an intellectual milieu rich in debate – a milieu characterised by writers such as Marx, Weber, Croce, Lévi-Strauss. Why was archaeology so particularly inhibited? Perhaps the answer is partly that it was a young science which in many areas still provides too few data for interpretation and analysis. Perhaps, too, in many countries archaeology was and is a marginal discipline within hierarchical university systems which discourage young innovators (although not all disciplines were equally lacking in innovative debate). But perhaps the most important factor is that few archaeologists in Europe can work without the shadow of the misuse of the past for nationalist purposes during the Third Reich. German archaeology and the German school of ancient history have had a strong influence in many parts of Europe from Spain and Portugal to Austria. The example of the uncritical use of the past within the Germanic tradition led many into an atheoretical refuge. A more adequate response is to celebrate theory in archaeology but within a critical mode. Indeed, it is from the standpoint of theoretical discussion that the way we construct the past can be opened to debate.

This volume grew out of a session at the annual conference of the Institute of Field Archaeologists in Birmingham in April 1987, although it bears little resemblance to the original event. All the papers were changed for the volume, others in the session were not included here and new ones were added. The source for the volume is thus rather broader than the Birmingham conference. Changes in the European community as 1992 approaches and the transformation of Eastern Europe in the Gorbachev era have encouraged increased contact and debate among European archaeologists. In addition, several countries have seen a rapid expansion of archaeology over recent decades. This volume tries to capture some of the new movement and debate. Although all the chapters were written before the events of 1989 and before the reunification of Germany, most were revised to incorporate these changes.

It was not possible to include all European countries in a single volume. My choice was largely arbitrary, dependent on personal contacts, but I tried to cover a range of countries north and south, east and west. I have tried to mention some of the developments in other countries in my introductory chapter. Equally arbitrary was the choice of authors for each country. No author can be seen as representative of a national or regional tradition, and different authors would have produced a different book. As far as possible, I selected people who would be able to identify national trends that were distinctive and intellectually challenging. As a result the book celebrates diversity rather than uniformity.

It might have been possible to find authors who could discuss archaeological theory in Europe thematically. Instead I have found myself forced into editing a country-by-country account. As is noted in Chapter 1, the regional differences within European experiences of archaeology are historically contingent, and closely linked to national traditions. It would have been difficult and unsatisfactory to break up these different traditions and to force them into general themes or trends. It is the regional diversity of developments in European archaeological theory which makes that theory distinctive.

I am grateful to João Zilhão for the account of nationalist uses of the past in Portugal in Chapter 1, and to S. Milisauskas, S. Stoddart, D. Bailey, T. Taylor, M. Navarette, F. Audouze and other anonymous reviewers for their advice and comments.

1

ARCHAEOLOGICAL THEORY IN CONTEMPORARY EUROPEAN SOCIETIES: THE EMERGENCE OF COMPETING TRADITIONS

Ian Hodder

As I took the book down from the shelf in the library a slight shiver went through me. It was a slim, old book. The excitement that I felt was not the thrill of handling for the first time a great masterpiece that had shaped the course of scholarship, although it is true that this book had indeed had a formative influence on the long-term development of European archaeology through its definition of archaeological 'cultures'. Rather, my shiver was closer to fear and to a feeling of terror that books such as this had contributed to, or had been used to justify, acts of the greatest barbarism that Europe and the world have seen.

The book was Gustaf Kossinna's *Die Herkunft der Germanen*, published in 1920. It is only recently, as for example German artists such as Anselm Kiefer and Jörg Immendorf have begun to incorporate the Nazi past into their work, that archaeologists have begun to evaluate the role of archaeology under the Third Reich as an example of the social and political nature of archaeology (e.g. Veit 1989). Kossinna used his settlement-archaeology method to show the descent of a Nordic, Aryan, German race from Indo-Germans and to demonstrate the outward movement of influences from this superior core area. He used archaeological finds to argue that parts of Poland had in fact been Germanic since the Iron Age. But it was mainly after his death, in the Third Reich, that Kossinna's ideas and methods were used to develop most fully the 'master race' ideology. In 1935 Himmler founded the *Deutsches*

Ahnenerbe (German Forefathers' Heritage) which conducted arch-aeological excavations from 1938 (McCann 1989). Here Kossinna's methods were obligatory. Excavations were carried out by SS men under scientific control, sometimes to a high standard and directed by excellent scholars (McCann 1988). Every SS unit stationed within the territory of the Reich was supposed to have a Germanic excavation in the area to act as a cultural focus of 'German great-ness'. The purpose of the excavations was educational, and to provide scientific support for the National Socialist view concern-ing the superiority of the Germanic races.

One example of the interpretations offered dates from 1941 when Himmler remarked on the steatopygic form of the palaeo-lithic figurines from Vestonice and Willendorf (McCann 1988). Since the women of 'savage peoples' such as the Hottentots were seen as having similar figures, it was argued that perhaps these people had been driven out of Europe by a combination of factors including the Nordic races. Himmler asked the *Ahnenerbe* to provide evidence for this theory, and the ethnographer Bruno Beger extended the hypothesis to propose that since Jewesses had similar forms the Jews and Hottentots were racially related. He suggested that the Race and Settlement Office could examine and take photos of Jewesses in an unclothed state (McCann 1988).

I have started this book with this account and with my own reaction to handling Kossinna's book because it is impossible to understand the development of archaeological theory in post-war Europe without comprehending the Nazi use of the past and the reaction to it. In addition, the Nazi link between ethnogenesis and archaeology has a wider context in Europe. In one form or another ethnogenetic uses of the culture-historical method have played an important political role in many European countries. Poles and Germans have long disputed their territories in terms of Slavs and Germanic tribes. In the immediate post-war years Poland responded to the theory of Germanic origins with attempts to justify its presence in the 'Regained Territories', such as Silesia, Pomerania or the Lubusz lands. The highest emotions in Poland were triggered by the problem of the origins of the Slavs, including the ethnic origin of the Lusatian culture (personal communication from Arkadiusz Marciniak of the Institute of Prehistory, Poznan). For Hungary the peace negotiations following the First World War did not produce political boundaries which coincided with ethnic boundaries, thus giving rise to arguments concerning the archaeological identification of Slavic or Hungarian populations. Ethnic issues have been important in, for example, Bulgaria, Albania, Greece, Czechoslovakia, France, Britain and Norway, and the debates have concerned the archaeological recognition of Indo-Europeans, Celts, Scythians, Slavs, Thracians, Dacians, Germans, Lusitanians and so on.

A further example of the particular link between fascism and ethnogenesis, albeit with less fearful results, is seen in Portugal from 1926 to 1974 (personal communication from João Zilhão of the Institute of Archaeology, Lisbon). The ideology of the regime was based to a large extent on the glorification of the past, and on the identification with those same 'glorious' traditions. Even the prehistoric past was used to justify the independent existence of the Portuguese state. A central role was played by the 'myth-ification' of Variathus, a military leader of the late Iron Age in west-central Iberia in the Roman wars. National consciousness was said to have been born as a result of the resistance against the Roman armies, and the twelfth-century Portuguese state was considered as the final outcome of the growth of national consciousness. The roots of this nationalism were extended beyond Variathus' Lusitanians to more remote periods. It was argued that there was a cultural distinctiveness to the populations living in the Portuguese territory as early as the neolithic period and that there was a racial continuity between the modern Portuguese and the neolithic peoples of western Iberia. Archaeologists promoting these investigations were also, to a large extent, influential members of the ruling elite. As an example, Professor Mendes Correia, an internationally acclaimed anthropologist and archaeologist, organiser of the 1930 Oporto 'Congrès International d'Anthropologie et d'Archéologie Préhistorique', was between 1936 and 1956 mayor of Oporto, member of the Corporative Chamber and deputy in the National Assembly.

I stood between the racks in the library and flipped through the pages of Kossinna's book. The maps looked familiar. Indeed I had spent much time myself producing and analysing similar distribution maps of artefact types in prehistoric northern Europe. Aspects of Kossinna's settlement-archaeology method are still used today as a routine part of archaeological enquiry. His ideas were the basis for Childe's formulation of the idea of archaeological cultures (Childe 1925) which is perhaps the single most significant building block of European prehistory. We are told today that

3

such culture-historical and mapping procedures are neutral and objective. This objectivity, this archaeology-at-arm's-length, that we so often claim is partly a reaction against the perversions of the past wrought by fascist regimes in Europe. But the European experience of archaeology is undeniably social and historical. I have already begun to show that it was not only Germany in the 1930s and 1940s that saw politically motivated uses of archaeology. Any historical review of the development of archaeology in Europe cannot avoid the links to nationalism and to ethnicity. So, to what extent can it be argued that our present scientific enterprise in archaeology is not also socially constituted? Does not the familiarity of Kossinna's maps force us to question whether our own methods are, in perhaps different ways, motivated?

From Archaeological Theory to Theoretical Archaeology

I returned to my seat in the library and began reading Kossinna's book. I was struck by the lack of extensive discussion of theoretical issues. This was above all a pragmatic methodology for charting the origins and development of Germanic culture. Of course, theoretical discussions, dangerous ones, were involved in linking distribution maps to cultures and races (see. e.g. Veit 1989). Distributions of artefacts and practices in the Bronze Age were identified with Germans, Celts and North Illyrians. But there was no lengthy discussion of why these correlations could be made, no elaborate account of norms, traditions, symbols, transmission, socialisation, sharing of cultural traits and so on.

It can more generally be claimed that culture history is a methodology rather than a theory although of course it contains theoretical assumptions. But the main aim of culture-historical reconstructions of the design and dispersal of cultural traits and entities was the pragmatic ordering of the 'history' of Europe and its divisions. For the inhabitants of Europe the past was and is immediately relevant. The objects, monuments and sequences are in themselves of interest. They did not have to be passed through a theoretical filter before consumption. In the main periods of culture-historical reconstruction up to the 1960s and 1970s, theory was closely linked to concrete questions and in such a context the main emphasis was placed on collecting more data rather than on developing abstract theory. The dominance of ethnogenetic questions drew attention away from the need to develop theoretical discussion.

One of the main reasons for the retention of an empirical and descriptive approach in European archaeology after the war was repulsion at the use made of archaeology by the Third Reich. This blatant misuse of archaeology had a long-lasting impact on the willingness of archaeologists, particularly in those countries most influenced by the Germanic tradition, to move beyond culture-historical accounts. The Soviet model for the organisation of scientific research had a similar inhibiting effect in Eastern Europe. An obligatory Marxism became defined in the form of a dogmatic vulgar Marxism. Engels was often the main source, and the growth of the productive forces was seen as the main determinant of historical development. For a number of reasons, the result of forcing this perspective on to Eastern European archaeology was a still greater commitment to empirical description. Archaeologists found the Marxist theory difficult to apply and they retreated into the culture-historical framework in which they had been trained, albeit with the obligatory Marxist introductory and closing words. In any case many scholars resented the external pressures on their work and concentrated on what was possible – chronological and empirical documentation.

In addition to the Kossinna syndrome and Soviet domination, underlying structural factors contributed to the empiricist emphasis in European archaeology. Most important of these were the traditional authority structures in European universities and academies. These inhibited innovation by the young who underwent long apprenticeships under the patronage of aged professors in their 'cathedral' chairs. In addition, particularly in Eastern Europe, archaeologists had difficulty maintaining contact with colleagues in other countries and had little access to western archaeological journals, conferences and so on. There were severe pragmatic impediments on breaking out of an atheoretical culture history.

It is often said that the Anglo-American New Archaeology of the 1960s and 1970s which began what is now termed processual archaeology (Binford 1962; Flannery 1967; Clarke 1973) was primarily methodological. Of course, like culture history, it had theoretical components derived in this case from anthropology, culture ecology and evolutionary theories, and considerable emphasis was placed on the generation of hypotheses. But much of the theory was and is explicitly 'middle range' (see Schiffer

1988 for a review of the concept of middle-range theory in North America). Bogucki (1985) summarises recent processual archaeology in Europe as being concerned with palaeoeconomy, ecology, geographic models, demographic and exchange models and social archaeology. The main contribution of processual archaeology was to our ability to reconstruct economic and subsistence strategies, exchange distributions, social organisation from burial and settlement data and so on. Apart from general accounts of systems, adaptations, ecology and evolution, the impact of processual archaeology, closely linked chronologically to the expansion of the use of scientific techniques from radiocarbon dating to subsurface prospecting, was largely methodological.

I do not mean to imply that archaeology up to the 1980s lacked theoretical discussion. Many archaeological theories were developed or borrowed from adjacent disciplines. As I will argue, archaeologists in Europe were early included in theoretical debates about, for example, history, Marxism and inference. But archaeology primarily developed pragmatically to assist in the understanding of the origins of Europe and its nation states. Even as the link between culture history and ethnogenesis became weakened in the post-war era, the Kossinna syndrome and a range of political factors entrenched most European archaeologists in a descriptive and methodological mode.

It is only recently that it has become possible to argue for the emergence from archaeological theory of a theoretical archaeology (Bogucki 1985). Already by 1973 David Clarke had argued that archaeology would develop as a discipline not through the mere collection of data but through the elaboration of theoretical discussion. Many processual archaeologists embraced the aim of developing laws or generalisations not linked to time and place. It was recognised that archaeology needed to develop its own distinctive body of theory. Theoretical archaeology, concerned with abstract issues apparently unrelatd to particular practical issues, has been supported by, for example, Theoretical Archaeology Group meetings in Britain and Scandinavia. Books such as those by Shanks and Tilley (1987a, 1987b), while prefigured by Clarke's (1968) *Analytical Archaeology* or Taylor's (1948) *A Study of Archaeology*, reinforce the trend in the 1980s for fuller theoretical debate of a wider range of issues. As the scope, level and quantity of archaeological theory expands, so the potential for creating a new 'subdiscipline' of theoretical archaeology grows.

Many of the chapters in this volume identify a new, younger generation of archaeologists in Europe concerned with discussing a wider range of theoretical issues from various forms of Marxism to structuralism and hermeneutics.

But of course all theory is to some degree socially embedded and pragmatic, and it is important to try and identify the conditions within which the current expansion of theoretical discussion in European archaeology is taking place. There are a number of relevant strands. First, several of the countries experiencing an expansion of archaeological theory are also undergoing a heritage boom in which there are wider intrests in interpretative issues. As field archaeology, sometimes developer-funded, expands in order to protect and save the archaeological heritage, university-based archaeology emphasises intellectual concerns while at the same time trying to maintain its involvement in the new areas of expansion and funding. For example, in Britain the topics and participants in Theoretical Archaeology Group conferences have differed radically from those in the annual conference of the professional Institute of Field Archaeologists. Second, as archaeology has expanded over recent decades it has increasingly been able to define itself as a discipline independent of history and Classical studies. In order to establish a professional institute or a university department of archaeology it is important to be able to demonstrate distinctive methods, bodies of data and bodies of theory. Clarke (1973) argued that to lose its innocence and gain maturity as an independent discipline archaeology needed to develop many different types and levels of theory. Third, as a corollary of the attempt successfully being made to gain disciplinary recognition and to define the boundaries of its resource unit, archaeology has to identify itself and gain esteem in relation to other disciplines. The concern is to show that archaeology is not cut off, left out of intellectual debate, that it can deal in the same currency. In this context, the contribution of abstract theory is enhanced by its common value. Rather than being concerned largely with pragmatic issues of 'where we come from', modern archaeological pragmatism, at least in parts of the community, centres on general debates about systems theory, Marxism, structuralism, critical theory and the like. Theoretical archaeology enhances the discipline's contribution and standing by engaging in a wider debate.

However, perhaps the main reasons for the recent awakening of interest in archaeological theory in Europe are political. The ending of the Franco and Salazar regimes has produced a new openness to ideas in Spain and Portugal. Several university systems underwent transformation in the 1960s and 1970s. West German society is increasingly dealing with its Nazi past and the Kossinna syndrome is being overcome (Veit 1989). The decline and collapse of Soviet oppression in Eastern Europe is leading to a fervour of interchange and interest in new ideas. In fact, the impact on archaeology of the events leading up to the 1989 transformation of Eastern Europe is still difficult to evaluate. Certainly we might expect a greater movement of scholars, ideas, publications and fieldwork opportunities but some of the changes may have negative effects. Most East European countries now face economic decline and perhaps a decrease in the number of archaeologists that can be supported (Milisauskas 1990), and financial difficulties might restrain travel and the purchase of periodicals and books. Nevertheless, it is to be hoped that the decrease in centralised control will lead to the appearance of numerous younger archaeologists and, at least in the long run, a wider theoretical debate.

While the growth of theoretical archaeology may well be linked to a changing historical setting, it remains a minority concern. While most archaeologists are involved in reconstruction and heritage management, the number of papers, conferences and posts devoted to purely theoretical discussion always has been, and remains, small. And in many countries the main participants in theoretical discussion are marginal and subordinate rather than forming a central elite. On the other hand, definitions of general principles can be argued to be important for the definition of any academic discipline. In addition, the very generality of theoretical discussion often ensures it greater visibility (and potential significance) than specific site or artefact reports.

The pragmatic interest in the past for its own sake, which derives from the direct historical links between past and present and from the immediacy of ethnic and regional differences, remains the primary motivating force for most European archaeology. But I have argued above that social changes in recent decades which have included a significant expansion of archaeology in universities have been associated with an increasing intellectualisation of the discipline.

Similar developments have been occurring on the other side of the Atlantic. Indeed it has been claimed by Bogucki (1985: 780) that 'the explicit consideration of theoretical issues is considerably rarer in European archaeology than it is in North America'. This statement is difficult to uphold for the 1980s since on the one hand North American archaeology has been held back by the dominance of the methodological concerns of processual archaeology while on the other hand many, although by no means all, countries in Europe have seen a rapid expansion of theoretical discussion recently. It is easier to agree with Renfrew's (1982: 142) view regarding the British response to the New Archaeology that 'the intellectual scene, as far as archaeology is concerned, seems in some ways more lively than in America'.

History as theory

The European theoretical archaeological scene may be increasingly lively but it is also based on different assumptions from North American processual archaeology. These differences will be examined further in the following section. For the moment it is important to recognise that an adequate understanding of archaeological theory in Europe must acknowledge that history has a theoretical component (Trigger 1989). In the archaeological context it is perhaps useful to make a distinction between cultural history which involves study of the spatial and temporal relations of cultures and styles, and history which involves the understanding of cultural change. As we have seen, European archaeology has long been dominated by ethnogenetic questions which required little theoretical discussion beyond the methodologies of culture-historical reconstruction. But the presumption of historical links with the past also encouraged concern with wider historical questions with a clear theoretical component.

The latter point is evident in the broader interest with European origins. Rowlands (1984, 1987) has shown that a concern with understanding the uniqueness of European experience has been the leitmotif of social and philosophical thought in Europe since the eighteenth century. The concern was to show how capitalism 'evolved' and to emphasise the universality and progressive nature of the changes that Europe had been going through. Although the concern was particularly to explain the distinctiveness of Europe that led to modern capitalism, the endeavour sought a universal legitimation in a general theory and it dealt with long-term, broadscale and often comparative issues. It therefore was associated with theoretical discussion within a historical framework as seen in the work of Marx and Weber. Childe, whose ideas built on those of Montesquieu, Hegel and Marx (Rowlands 1984), saw the origins of a distinctively European society in the Bronze Age. But his comparison with Asian societies and his wider intellectual background placed these culture-historical aims within a broader theoretical perspective. Kossinna and Marx were conjoined in Childe. It is through Marxism in particular that the historical emphasis in European archaeology achieves an abstract theoretical and generalising character. The debate between a vulgar Marxism which looks at history in terms only of productive forces and versions in which such determinism is variously transformed is central to theoretical development in Europe.

Beyond Marx, there are many other important writers in Europe who created the intellectual milieu in which archaeologists work and who gave that milieu a strongly historical character. Weber, Dumezil, Eliade, Gramsci, Hegel, Braudel and Croce were all historians but they were none the less theoretical for that. The opposition between history and theory claimed by North American processual archaeologists has little relevance in Europe (see Trigger 1989).

A further aspect of history which has led to heightened theoretical awareness in Europe is the history of research. I will below (p. 20) outline some of the ways in which archaeological research has developed in the different countries of Europe. Each age, in each country, writes its own history and its own archaeology. As a result of these changes and differences, and as a result of the engrained social and political uses and misuses of archaeology in the European context, it is difficult to remain blind to the theoretical construction of archaeological objects, difficult not to see archaeologists transforming reality and difficult not to recognise artefacts as products rather than records. These points are made in the chapters in this volume. The overall impact of the ever-present social history of archaeological research is to 'problematise' archaeological data, method and theory, and to open them to debate.

Throughout Europe, archaeology's closest intellectual ties are with history. This is not only because of factors including origin and ethnogenesis but also because prehistory is everywhere linked to history via proto-history (the latter describing phases in which 'prehistoric' societies are written about by Classical Mediterranean authors). It is therefore always possible to argue that the prehistoric past can be interpreted with the aid of historical texts. Even where ethnography has influenced the development of archaeology, it is defined in terms of the ethnography (folk culture and history) of Europe's own peoples, as in Poland and Hungary.

It is possible that an underlying belief in the superiority of European culture encouraged the use of history rather than anthropology in order to understand the European past (Veit 1989: 49). Childe, for example, held negative attitudes towards ethnographic parallels, as did many of his contemporaries in Britain and Europe. It was historical theory which was embraced in preference to anthropological theory.

Some general trends in the recent development of European archaeological theories

Because of the social and historical nature of archaeology each country has its own distinctive history of research. The diversity is remarkable and is discussed later in this chapter (p. 20). There is a danger, then, in trying to identify general trends. A number of authors (e.g. Bogucki 1985; Hodder 1986; Shennan 1987) have described a linear development of archaeological theory from culture history to processual archaeology to post-processual approaches. I have already identified some of the difficulties with this scheme such as the predominantly methodological concerns of culture history and processual archaeology and the long involvement of European archaeology in historical and other theories. Following Kuhn (1962), Patterson (1986) notes that to present the history of archaeology as cumulative and linear is to support one group at the expense of another. Certainly the scheme of development as normally presented favours the Anglo-American view at the expense of the varieties of archaeological experience in Europe. Shennan (1987: 365) goes so far as to argue that the new theoretical ferment of the decade from 1977 to 1987 was largely restricted to English-speaking archaeologists in Britain and Scandinavia.

This book demonstrates a rather different view – that many countries in Europe have been undergoing theoretical ferment within their own traditions of archaeological research. Many European countries did not go through a processual phase. Processual ideas were often adopted selectively. Many would reject post-processual archaeology (see below, p. 16). The recent history of

11

theoretical archaeology in Europe reflects two types of evolution, whatever the theoretical issues (east or west). In some countries a debate developed on local grounds, enriched by external influences. In other countries, external traditions provided the main source of debate although translation into local forms gradually occurred. An example of the first type of evolution is provided by Italy, and of the second by Spain, with an intermediary form illustrated by Scandinavian countries. In fact all countries fall somewhere on a continuum between local and external sources of theoretical debate.

Diversity in the evolution of theory in archaeology in the different countries is one of three further general characteristics of theoretical debate in Europe, beyond the distinctive dependence on historical and particularly Marxist theories which has already been discussed. It is on these three additional themes that I will focus the remaining sections of this chapter. The themes are: first, a general rejection of processual approaches but incorporation of processual methodologies within history; second, an awareness and celebration of theoretical diversity; and third, an interest in the social construction of archaeological knowledge.

Processual methodologies in history

I have already noted the long tradition, alongside culture-historical methods for the establishment of 'time-space systematics', of a strong historical and often Marxist perspective in European archaeology. A common European complaint against processual archaeology was that it was ahistorical. This was a widely accepted evaluation of Anglo-American discussions in the 1960s and 1970s. Functionalist and systemic arguments were regarded with suspicion as being too synchronic and anthropological.

The long use of historical theories and methods meant that many European archaeologists remained somewhat bemused by the excitement in the 1960s and 1970s on the other side of the Atlantic. This was particularly true of the ecological, economic and settlement archaeology approaches and methods. Such ideas had developed early within historical perspectives in Italy, Scandinavia and Britain and in all the countries influenced by the Germanic tradition. In many other study areas, too, the dominant European response was 'we've seen it all before'. As European archaeologists stood on their western shores watching the small ripples caused by those distant New Archaeological rumblings, the waves did indeed seem very small and very familiar and not contradictory to a historical approach.

Some other examples of this sense of *déjà vu* can be provided. The distinctions made by Labuda in 1957 (see Kobyliński, this volume, Chapter 9) between ergotechnic, sociotechnic and psychotechnic are similar to those made later by Binford (technomic, sociotechnic and ideotechnic). Myhre (Chapter 7) notes that a debate in the *Norwegian Archaeological Review* in 1968–9 between Malmer and Bakka foreshadows the discussion between Binford and Gould in *American Antiquity* in 1985. An area of methodology in which the older European tradition had already made inroads is behavioural archaeology and site formation processes. In Europe this aspect of methodology was subsumed within source criticism which, deriving from historical method, defined the range of special factors which had to be taken into account when making inferences or 'reading' from the archaeological record. Conditions of survival, retrieval and sampling had to be studied. Eggers's distinctions in the 1950s between living culture, dead culture and retrieved culture (see Chapter 8) previewed the distinctions made in the 1970s by Clarke (1973) and Schiffer (1976). But in Europe the rather narrow concerns of North American behavioural archaeology are placed within the broader context of cultural and historical meanings, for example concerning the symbolism of discard (e.g. Richards and Thomas 1984; Sommer 1990).

The problem that 'we've seen it all before' was compounded by the realisation that examples of the application of New Archaeology often demonstrated a superficial knowledge of the data. For example, the high-quality multi-disciplinary projects in Germany which integrated a wide range of environmental and scientific techniques and in which students were expected to 'know the material well' contrasted favourably with the narrower hypothesis testing, tunnel-vision approach often engendered by processual archaeology.

On the other hand, it was and is undoubtedly the case that historical theories in Europe were not aligned to a sophisticated methodological armoury. I have shown why European archaeologists were often sceptical of the anthropological theories espoused by the processual archaeologists. But there was a need for processual methodologies. European archaeology had seen little methodological discussion beyond culture history. The long retention of a culture-historical, empirical and descriptive method stifled the introduction of new scientific methods. The centralised and hierarchical university systems inhibited new research designs and sampling procedures in many countries. Even Renfrew's (1983) important and clear demonstration of the relevance of new approaches to dating, exchange and inference have taken a long time to persuade the old guard, despite their attraction to younger scholars.

In many European countries the major breakthrough that is sought is not so much the exchange of processual for historical theories but a methodological revolution. Archaeologists in most European countries are gradually embracing the new scientific methods and techniques. The advent of radiocarbon dating, sampling methods and systematic excavation techniques has begun to transform archaeological practices in many countries. For example, Spanish archaeology witnessed a technological revolution in the post-Franco era in which palaeoeconomic, spatial and scientific techniques were introduced. In France in the 1960s and 1970s excavation and physical science methods were introduced, and archaeometry and information processing for a time played a dominant role. In Scandinavia and Hungary new survey and computer techniques were applied.

In general the methodological changes did not lead to theoretical or conceptual change. Indeed in France, they had a stagnating effect (see Chapter 5). Elsewhere the methods were integrated into culture-historical approaches. Even in Scandinavia where the techniques were linked to deductive reasoning, hypothesis testing and model building, theory did not change fundamentally (see Chapter 7). European archaeology had always claimed to be scientific in a general sense and as far back at least as Schliemann at Troy, it had used hypothesis testing procedures. Despite the challenge of unexpected radiocarbon dates, many of the palaeoeconomic and settlement archaeology concerns were familiar in Europe. Certainly the positivism of the New Archaeology was not remarkable in an intellectual community long accustomed to debates about the Vienna school.

In Anglo-American archaeology it is customary to link methodological claims of the New Archaeology with positivism and with systemic, processual, ecological and behavioural approaches. Europe provides an interesting contrast to this view. Not only are the new techniques and methods integrated into traditional culture-historical concerns, but they often become the handmaiden of Marxist archaeology. To many on the Anglo-American scene, positivism and Marxism may seem strange bed-fellows, since Marxism is often linked to critical approaches in which the separation of fact and theory, and the neutral, asocial nature of archaeological scientific method, are denied. While such views are found in Britain and Scandinavia, elsewhere Marxist archaeology is often linked to a strong commitment to objective scientific procedures. Alternatively, the more sophisticated Marxist theoretical positions, as found in Spain, claim a methodology which overcomes the opposition of objectivity and subjectivity (Marcen and Risch 1990; Nocete and Ruiz 1990).

The materialism inherent in most Marxist traditions in Europe, reminiscent of the strongly materialist American processual archaeology, coupled with the evolutionary views of the New Archaeology which themselves had Marxist affiliations, allowed a close association between the two perspectives. In addition, perhaps because of its political context in Europe, Marxist archaeology had remained theoretically dogmatic rather than methodologically creative. In most countries, at least until recently, methodological and epistemological issues in archaeology had simply not been raised in relation to Marxism. Here was a vacuum into which the methodologies of the New Archaeology could easily be sucked.

For example, in Greece, the techniques of the New Archaeology were introduced in order to operationalise Marxism (see Chapter 4). The common materialism and rejection of particularism underlay this marriage. In both Poland and Czechoslovakia, the new methods could be integrated with the problem-orientation provided by Marxism (see Chapters 9 and 10).

Through time, as I will argue below (p. 16), a range of different Marxist perspectives developed in European archaeology and many of these rejected the positivism of processual archaeology. Complex dialectical and critical positions are now widely found. But it is of interest that at least initially Marxism, positivism and scientific methodology were often linked. While in North American archaeology Marxism is frequently viewed with suspicion as being dogmatic and closed to scientific testing, perhaps partly because of the association of Marxism with the Soviet Union and China, in the European middle between the eagle and the bear, positivism, science and Marxism are often conjoined.

15

Theoretical diversity

Many countries in Europe would reject Anglo-American post-processual archaeology precisely because it is insufficiently wedded to objective, neutral scientific techniques and therefore appears to take archaeology back to older traditional approaches. In addition, the use of the term post-processual assumes a process-ual phase which many countries in Europe have not experienced. In Spain, for example, there has not been a strong New Archaeolo-gical or processual phase and culture history still dominates. Those archaeologists in Spain who wish to use further rigorous scientific, environmental and physical methods fear that a post-processual approach will detract from their task and will give support to the historical particularism from which they wish to escape. In my view there is a confusion here between the use of certain scientific methods of analysis (which I believe all post-processual archaeol-ogists and historical theorists would embrace) and processual the-ories and epistemologies (which post-processual archaeologists with their more committed historical perspectives would reject). Nevertheless, it is undoubtedly the case that post-processual archaeology, despite its European base, may not be of immediate value in countries on the continent in which a culture-historical method has become indistinguishable from historical theory and in which the desire for positivist rigour derives from a traditional empiricism. It is my impression, on the other hand, that in Poland, for example, the debate over Marxist and other historical theories will allow a discussion of post-processual archaeology alongside the introduction of analytical methods.

In any case, the definition of post-processual archaeology which I would prefer (Hodder 1986) emphasises the opening up of theor-etical debate to a wider range of issues including Marxism and post-positivism. In this respect the current scene in European archaeology contributes to post-processual archaeology through the great diversity of theoretical positions which it currently embraces.

For example, I have already discussed the widespread domi-nance of Marxist theoretical positions and their internal variety. Some Marxist approaches remain relatively 'vulgar' and materialist, often linked to a positivist and natural science methodology. Marx-ist approaches influenced by Althusser, on the other hand, are found in Britain, France, Greece, Scandinavia and Italy. In these structural Marxist perspectives which use the anthropological writings of Terray, Godelier and Friedman, the materialist emphasis is often replaced by the dominance of the social relations of production. The resulting analyses have much in common with social processual archaeology (e.g. Renfrew and Shennan 1982), and often fall short of problematising the nature of the archaeological record and material culture.

Critical perspectives are, however, found in Britain, France, Poland and Spain. Indeed, there is a widely accepted view in Europe that archaeological theory consists of conceptual systems that 'represent' rather than 'reconstruct' the past. They try to adhere to reality but they, and reality itself, are at the same time conditioned by historical and scientific development. Thus archaeology is scientific but science is itself situated. For example, the influence of Wittgenstein and Feyerabend in Scandinavian archaeology in the early 1970s led to a view that archaeology is not an objective science but is social and political (see Chapter 7). For Poland, Kobyliński (see Chapter 9) argues that the logical correctness of explanatory procedures is dependent on an understanding of archaeology as a particular historical form of study. Theory and practice must always be linked to the questions being asked and, in contrast to North American New Archaeology, where our questions and theories come from does matter. There is not only one valid type of science. Such concerns frame the emphasis on source criticism and the source creation process – how we create the archaeological record – which has often been of interest in Europe (see p. 13). In some extensions of this type of work, as in Poland (see Chapter 9), source criticism has involved definition of the ontological characteristics of archaeological evidence, considerations of the role of the archaeologists in creating evidence, and problems of biases inherent in the archaeological record. The discussion in Poland has been linked to the critique of positivism. Such interests give a new twist to the notion of 'site formation' processes because the archaeologist participates in the formation of the site.

The theoretical diversity in Europe extends beyond Marxism, neo-Marxism and critical theory. For example, the concerns with material culture meanings and with the social embeddedness of archaeological theory and practice have often led to discussion of hermeneutics and critical hermeneutics. The attempt to embed material events within the whole framework of meaning in which they were once situated clearly involves the analyst in a double hermeneutic in which 'their' and 'our' understandings are gradually accommodated in a moving double circle. This process of double reading has to be critically aware (Hodder 1986; Shanks and Tilley 1987a). Such issues are discussed in Britain, Scandinavia and Poland.

In many countries, semiotics and structuralism have played significant roles, at times allied with science and positivism and at other times leading to deconstruction and critique of processual archaeology. In Spain, for example, some structuralist analysis is linked to materialist and functional arguments and to hypothesis testing and nomological-deductive approaches (see Chapter 2). Criado Boada (1989) on the other hand uses structuralism and semiotics in an analysis of megalithic burial in Spain which is decidedly post-positivist (see also Criado Boada and Fabregas Valcarce 1989). In Britain, Scandinavia and Poland, the impetus derived initially from Lévi-Strauss and from Soviet models, but other influences elsewhere in Europe have included Dumezil and Eliade. Indeed, most structuralist analysis in European archaeology is strongly tied to historical questions rather than to the universal structures of the human mind sought by Lévi-Strauss. For example, in Bulgaria Marazov (1988) studied a grave in the Copper Age Varna cemetery which has objects, a mask and ornaments arranged around an absent body. Marazov conducts a semiotic analysis in which the cenotaph is seen as a ritual text which 'wrote' the form of a symbolically 'dead' 'king', and in which right:left::male:female are organising principles. These observations are related to the structuring of the mythologies of the Greek, Hittite and Indo-European worlds. In Britain there is an increasing concern to identify 'structured deposition' of animal bones, pottery and flint, whether in ritual monuments (Richards and Thomas 1984) or in the discard patterns of occupational refuse (Wait 1985).

Other theoretical directions are also beginning to appear on the horizon. Post-structuralism, and especially the work of Derrida, Foucault and Barthes, is emerging as an important component of social theory, particularly in relation to deconstruction (Bapty and Yates 1990; Tilley 1990). Scandinavian archaeology, especially in Norway, has developed a strong tradition of feminist and gender studies, and similar developments can now be seen in Britain. The Annales School has had some influence in Italy and in Britain, particularly through the work of Braudel (Hodder 1988), but increasingly through the ideas of Duby, Le Goff and Ladurie.

The idea of a unified science of archaeology, still held to in North America and briefly glimpsed in Scandinavia and Britain in the mid 1970s, is now in total disarray in Europe. The notion that archaeology should have unified theory, method and aims is widely rejected. Today European archaeology is redefining itself in relation to two traditionally dominant external authorities to its west and east. In comparison with the dogmatism of both North American processual archaeology and Soviet-style Marxim, European archaeology is increasingly characterised by a diversity and openness of theoretical and methodological debate. But from where does this diversity derive?

Archaeology as a social and historical product

I have tried to identify some general trends in the recent development of archaeological theory in Europe. The main themes have been the overall dominance of historical perspectives, the evaluation of new methodologies for dealing with European questions about the archaeological past, and the emergence of diverse theoretical positions. For many Anglo-American processual archaeologists, the dominance of history and the diversity of scientific approaches are seen as anti-science heresy. The idea that there is more than one way of doing science is often seen as unacceptable. Even more so, the notion that archaeological science is socially constructed destroys the very basis of processual archaeology's belief system. But it is precisely the social nature of archaeological enquiry which explains the diversity of theoretical argument in Europe.

It is difficult to be a European archaeologist and remain unaware of the ways in which historical and social conditions have shaped the way excavations, analysis and interpretation are carried out. We have already seen how an emphasis on source criticism has at times led to a reflexive discussion. The political use of the past is hard to ignore in a Europe ravaged by a Nazi history. In any case, the very diversity of archaeological traditions in Europe undermines notions of a universal and neutral objectivity. The general characteristics which I have outlined for recent European archaeology account for only a small portion of the total variability. The trends describe a thin veneer which fails to mask the different ways in which archaeological theory has developed in each country, or within smaller regions within Europe. The full nature of this diversity can only be appreciated by reading the individual chapters in this volume. But I wish here to relate the local differences to particular social, economic and political circumstances. The past is undeniably social, as is the practice of archaeology.

Take Greece, for example, where the overpowering pressure of the achievements of the distant past became linked to nationalism and an inward- and backward-looking isolationism in intellectual and archaeological circles. The diachronic continuity with the Classical past impeded not only prehistoric but also theoretical archaeology. It led to a rejection of ahistorical processual archaeology. When the reaction to culture-historical approaches came it derived its impetus not from the New Archaeology, but from a historically situated critique. The blatant political and ideological uses of the continuity argument produced Marxist and neo-Marxist critiques. These seemed appropriate in a context in which the past was an ideological construct.

Or take Italy where, despite some recent applications of processual archaeology, much work has remained faithful to a long Marxist historical tradition in intellectual, political and cultural life. Or Spain, where the all-too-recent decline of fascism has encouraged a flourishing Marxist perspective and has at the same time produced a need to link such a perspective with a very late transformation of field and analytical methodologies. As a result Marxism is closely allied to positivist and natural science approaches. Or France, where the institutional neglect and intellectual marginalisation of prehistoric and proto-historic archaeology over several centuries of research produced a situation in which archaeology became increasingly unable to enter into theoretical dialogue. In contrast to wider developments in France in the humanities, French archaeology opposed the work of writers from Lévi-Strauss to Barthes and Derrida with problems of typology and formalisation. So when the intellectual and political case for reform was made in the late 1960s, the response of French prehistoric and proto-historic archaeology, true to its historical tradition, was to move into documentation, culminating in the work of Gardin (e.g. 1979) and inhibiting theoretical debate. Even the more recent growth of French archaeology in the late 1970s and 1980s has concentrated on a theme with a long pedigree in France, the anthropology of technical systems.

The examples can be multiplied. In Eastern Europe, the recent development of archaeological theory cannot be understood without reference to the practical conditions set by Soviet domination and the intellectual traditions set by Marxism, although the latter vary from country to country. The development of the 'History of Material Culture' concept in the 1930s in the Soviet Union had a strong impact in Poland and Czechoslovakia in the post-war years. But while some countries in Eastern Europe submitted to the strong Marxist influence in the social sciences, in Czechoslovakia the organisation of archaeological studies (including training in philosophy) provided a basis for critical theoretical debate. In Scandinavia, the growth of anthropology and sociology in Norway in the 1950s and 1960s provided a historical context which prejudiced Norwegian archaeology in favour of an early acceptance of Anglo-American New Archaeology. The ability to accept the external ideas derived from the internal influence of social anthropology, human geography and ecology which created a new platform for development. The early growth of feminist, Marxist and critical perspectives can also be linked to social and political conditions in Scandinavia.

Conclusion

As I placed Kossinna's book back on the shelf I felt more able to see it in a broader context. His ideas and their later use are only extreme examples of a general European experience in which archaeology is actively embedded in social life. Even the reaction against ideological misuses of the past and the retreat into descriptive culture-historical accounts can be seen to be historically contextual. As Cleuziou *et al.* note in Chapter 5, the history of theories used in archaeology cannot be separated from the concrete conditions of practical research or from the social functions of archaeology in society.

The European experience also shows that we can accept that the past and archaeology are socially embedded while retaining a commitment to scientific methodological rigour. It offers a range of hermeneutic and critical perspectives which allow the linkage between society and science to be followed. We do not need, as archaeologists, to feel that the only alternative to positivist processual archaeology is a hopeless slide towards relativity and chaos. European traditions demonstrate a range of satisfactory possibilities between the two extremes. Thus I would disagree with Shanks and Tilley's (1987a) view that archaeological data represent no more than a 'network of resistances' against which our socially constituted minds deploy. Rather, the experience of archaeological data and the patterning observed in the past do more than resist our ideas; they help create them. The antiquity of human activity in Europe, the sequences of change through time, the contrasts between European, Near Eastern and other regions, have all contributed to our understanding of ourselves. If the data had been different we would understand ourselves differently. The continuities we claim with the past have in part been created by that past. Archaeological science involves a dialectical relationship between past and present. The hermeneutic circle is not a vicious one.

My dominant impression as a result of editing this volume is that archaeology is always socially engaged. This is a different perspective from that which prevails in North America. It also implies that we cannot write the history of European archaeology in simple culture-history – processual – post-processual terms. Most countries in Europe with their varied institutional and political contexts have followed quite different trajectories which emphasise Marxism or history or both. Indeed my two main further impressions of European archaeology concern the overall acceptance of the centrality of historical enquiry and the widespread incorporation of Marxist theory. In these two ways again European archaeological theory differs from its North American counterpart. Because of these various characteristics, European archaeology has a distinctive role to play in wider theoretical debates.

References

Bapty, I. and Yates, T. (1990) *Archaeology after Structuralism: Archaeological Discourse and the Strategies of Post-Structuralism*, London: Routledge.

Binford, L. R. (1962) 'Archaeology as anthropology', *American Antiquity* 28: 217–25.

Bogucki, P. (1985) 'Theoretical directions in European archaeology', *American Antiquity* 50: 780–8.

Childe, V. G. (1925) *The Dawn of European Civilisation*, London: Kegan Paul.

Clarke, D. L. (1968) *Analytical Archaeology*, London: Methuen.

—— (1973) 'Archaeology: the loss of innocence', *Antiquity* 47: 6–18.

Criado Boada, F. (1989) 'We, the post-megalithic people . . .', in I. Hodder (ed.) *The Meanings of Things*, London: Unwin Hyman.

Criado Boada, F. and Fabregas Valcarce, R. (1989) 'The megalithic phenomenon of northwest Spain: main trends', *Antiquity* 63: 682–96.

Flannery, K. V. (1967) 'Culture history v. culture process: a debate in American archaeology', *Scientific American* 217: 119–22.

Gardin, J.-C. (1979) *Archaeological Constructs*, Cambridge, Cambridge University Press.

Hodder, I. (1986) *Reading the Past*, Cambridge: Cambridge University Press.

—— (1988) *Archaeology as Long Term history*, Cambridge: Cambridge University Press.

Kossinna, G. (1920) *Die Herkunft der Germanen*, Leipzig: Kabitzsch.

Kuhn, T. S. (1962) *The Structure of Scientific Revolutions*, Chicago: University of Chicago Press.

McCann, B. (1988) 'The Nationalist Socialist perversion of archaeology', *World Archaeological Bulletin* 2: 51–4.

—— (1989) ' "Volk und Germanentum": the presentation of the past in Nazi Germany', in P. Gathercole and D. Lowenthal (eds) *The Politics of the Past*, London: Unwin Hyman.

Marazov, I. (1988) 'Grave No. 36 from the Chalcolithic necropolis in Varna – myth, ritual and attributes', Paper delivered to Saarbrucken Conference.

Marcen, P. G. and Risch, R. (1990) 'Archaeology and historical materialism: outsiders' reflections on theoretical discussions in British archaeology', in F. Baker and J. Thomas (eds) *Writing the Past in the Present*, Lampeter: St David's University College.

Milisauskas, S. (1990) 'People's revolutions of 1989 and archaeology in Eastern Europe', *Antiquity* 64: 283–5.

Nocete, F. and Ruiz, A. (1990) 'The dialectic of the present and the past in the construction of a scientific archaeology', in F. Baker and J. Thomas (eds) *Writing the Past in the Present*, Lampeter: St David's University College.

Patterson, T. C. (1986) 'The last sixty years: toward a social history of Americanist archaeology in the United States', *American Anthropologist* 88: 7–26.

Renfrew, A. C. (1982) 'Discussion: contrasting paradigms', in A. C. Renfrew and S. Shennan (eds) *Ranking, Resource and Exchange*, Cambridge: Cambridge University Press.

—— (1983) 'Divided we stand: aspects of archaeology and information', *American Antiquity* 48: 3–16.

Renfrew, A. C. and Shennan, S. (1982) *Ranking, Resource and Exchange*, Cambridge: Cambridge University Press.

Richards, C. and Thomas, J. (1984) 'Ritual activity and structured deposition in later neolithic Wessex', in R. Bradley and J. Gardiner (eds)

Neolithic Studies: a Review of Some Current Research, British Archaeological Report 133, Oxford.

Rowlands, M. J. (1984) 'Conceptualising the European Bronze and early Iron Age', in J. Bintliff *European Social Evolution*, Bradford: University of Bradford.

—— (1987) ' "Europe in prehistory": a unique form of primitive capitalism?', *Culture and History* 1: 63–78.

Schiffer, M. (1976) *Behavioural Archaeology*, New York: Academic Press.

—— (1988) 'The structure of archaeological theory', *American Antiquity* 53: 461–85.

Shanks, M. and Tilley, C. (1987a) *Re-constructing Archaeology*, Cambridge: Cambridge University Press.

—— (1987b) *Social Theory and Archaeology*, Cambridge: Polity Press.

Shennan, S. J. (1987) 'Trends in the study of later European prehistory', *Annual Review of Anthropology* 16: 365–82.

Sommer, U. (1990) 'Dirt theory, or archaeological sites seen as rubbish heaps', *Journal of Theoretical Archaeology* 1: 47–60.

Taylor, W. (1948) *A Study of Archaeology*, Memoirs of the American Anthropological Association 69.

Tilley, C. (1990) *Reading Material Culture*, Oxford: Blackwell.

Trigger, B. (1989) *A History of Archaeological Thought*, Cambridge: Cambridge University Press.

Veit, U. (1989) 'Ethnic concepts in German prehistory: a case study on the relationship between cultural identity and archaeological objectivity', in S. Shennan (ed.) *Archaeological Approaches to Cultural Identity*, London: Unwin Hyman.

Wait, G. A. (1985) *Ritual and Religion in Iron Age Britain*, British Archaeological Report 149, Oxford.

2

THEORY IN SPANISH ARCHAEOLOGY SINCE 1960

J. M. Vázquez Varela and R. Risch[1]

Introduction

J. M. Vázquez Varela

In Spain, as in other West European countries, archaeological theory and methodology have undergone important and at times very rapid changes since 1960. Various socio-political, economic, academic, geographical and cultural factors in Spain have nevertheless meant that the pace and pattern of this evolution have been somewhat different from elswehere. The archaeological literature published in Spain during these years (consisting of over 10,000 articles and books) reveals both constant trends and certain very sudden changes. In general, a very traditional attitude to archaeology was maintained throughout the 1960s and the first half of the 1970s, but this was followed by a highly complex situation in which a variety of schools and tendencies coexisted, not always peacefully. This second period gradually generated a fruitful process of dynamic reappraisal that has gone beyond the mere imitation of foreign models.

One of the main influences on the dynamics of archaeological thought in Spain during the last thirty years has been the country's political situation. Under the regime headed by General Franco, which lasted until 1975, certain attitudes were frowned upon by the authorities, who thus blocked the introduction of alien theories and the development of models (especially Marxist) that went against official ideology. Related to this political environment, the prevailing university system, based on deference to the authority of the academic establishment, favoured certain kinds of traditional, routine research rather than theoretical innovation, epistemological analysis and methodological creativity. This tendency was exacerbated by archaeology's academic classification among the humanities, which preserved it from the influence of the natural sciences. Furthermore, at a time when the trend in the rest of the world was for prehistoric studies to court the natural sciences and anthropology, the subject of prehistory was divorced in Spain from ethnology, with which it had hitherto been associated in history faculties. Other factors tending to sustain traditional archaeology have included economic limitations in the fields of education and research (a chronic problem shared by other disciplines), which have prevented investigation on a scale that would do justice to the enormous archaeological wealth of a country whose geographical structure has favoured the development of such an intricate cultural mosaic. In addition, geographical proximity to France, which had traditionally strongly influenced Spanish culture (twenty years ago, French was taught in all Spanish schools and universities, English in practically none), aided the introduction of theories and methods originating in French centres of learning.

Although some of these factors are still at work, traditional archaeology has been increasingly challenged over the last decade by a more vigorous, innovative and stimulating way of thought that entered Spain by two main routes: Spanish studies of American archaeology, which inevitably involved exposure to – and discussion and appraisal of – English and American influences, especially that of the New Archaeology; and the presence in Spain of many foreign researchers attracted by the country's archaeological wealth. European scholars have indeed long been visiting Spain to study questions of interest for Western Europe as a whole, to the extent that in Madrid there is a permanent centre (the German Archaeological Institute) for German archaeologists, most of whom have concentrated on proto-history and the Classical period. The French have also carried out many studies here, especially on the palaeolithic. In recent years, however, the Europeans have been joined in Spain by Americans investigating the middle palaeolithic, the Cantabrian upper palaeolithic and south-eastern Spanish proto-history. This influx of archaeologists representative of a wide variety of different schools (American New Archaeology, the German tradition, and various strains of French thought) has naturally had a great influence on the archaeology practised and preached by the Spanish themselves. Together with the development of American anthropology and the introduction

26

of anthropology as a distinct academic specialism in Spanish universities, it has allowed the continued presence of traditional archaeology to be accompanied by the growth of an 'anthropological archaeology' defined largely in terms of scientific method rather than anthropological theory. This new approach was for a long time based somewhat slavishly on the New Archaeology, but is now beginning to develop theories and methods of its own that testify to its increasing maturity.

The exploitation of the sources of intellectual inspiration mentioned above has been encouraged and aided by the great changes in Spanish society in recent years. In particular, the advent of democracy has brought with it numerous advantages for scientific research: a climate of political and ideological freedom tolerating debate; a reform of the university system that aims to promote research and accepts the authority of individual academics within their fields; the provision of more funds for research; an improvement in the social status of all kinds of research activity; and greater interest in things Anglo-American, from life-styles and language to scientific methods and theories. All this has allowed the birth of anthropological archaeology (in the sense defined above of scientific methodology) alongside traditional archaeology, which though remaining faithful to its original postulates is itself beginning to undergo an apparent metamorphosis so as to adapt to the new intellectual climate. The coexistence of traditional archaeology and anthropological archaeology is not without its tensions, with traditionalists scorning anthropologists as 'theorisers' and anthropologists disparaging traditionalists as 'potologists' (cacharrólogos). Add to this the traditional rivalries between different universities and regions (Spain has seventeen semi-autonomous territories) and it is possible to get some idea of how dynamic (some would say chaotic) the current situation is. In this simmering melting-pot of schools and approaches, the reappraisal of methods and theories in the light of the great variety of topics tackled has begun to result in the appearance of a number of studies with a peculiarly Spanish stamp.

Spanish Archaeology from 1960 to the 1970s

At the first congress of Spanish Anthropologists, held in Seville in January 1973, J. Alcina-Franch presented a paper in which he analysed the current situation of Spanish archaeology and its

27

development during the previous decades (Alcina-Franch 1975). As characteristics of Spanish archaeology between 1940 and 1970 he listed the following:

(1) an almost complete lack of theoretical orientation;
(2) lack of any coherent programme of research;
(3) the ubiquitous adherence to a descriptive, or 'archaeographic', style;
(4) the absence of all but historicist interpretations;
(5) deficient consideration of environmental factors;
(6) the absence of interdisciplinary or multi-disciplinary studies.

With regard to the first of these points, it was suggested that Spanish archaeology in the period 1940–70 was open to exactly the same criticisms as Walter Taylor made of pre-war American archaeology in 1948 (Taylor 1948). Alcina considered the cause of this situation to be the habit of treating archaeology within a historicist framework, which made for essentially descriptive, unprogrammatic research. A survey of the latest volumes of five of the most important Spanish archaeological and prehistorical journals (*Ampurias* and *Pyrenae*, published in Barcelona; *Archivo de Prehistoria Levantina*, published in Valencia; *Cesaraugusta*, published in Saragossa; and *Trabajos de Prehistoria*, published in Madrid) showed that of a total of 172 articles considered, 63 per cent were merely descriptive (reports of archaeological material recovered by excavation or studies of collections or individual pieces), with no attempt at greater generalisation than the analysis of a few typological series; 12 per cent were studies of collections of coins, inscriptions, etc.; and only 10 per cent were historiographic or concerned with historical interpretation. The articles reporting excavations or prospections exhibited a total lack of theoretical orientation 'even from the historical point of view, the only one that most Spanish archaeologists, in principle, recognise as being of interest' (Alcina-Franch 1975).

The acceptance of only the historical viewpoint, i.e. the interpretation of archaeological data within an exclusively historical or culture-history framework, meant that archaeology was in fact used simply to illustrate historical research on high cultures, the study of pre- or proto-historic cultures being forced into a similar historical mould distinguished only by a concern for determining sequences, contacts and typological or stylistic variations that were often explained using a diffusionist model. For

28

Alcina, the cause of this situation was the isolation of traditional archaeology from the natural sciences and the academic anti-Marxism attributable to the then current political regime. The only signs of reform that he detected in Spain were positive responses to the works of Gordon Childe, while other English and American theorists were unknown.

As a reaction against the situation described above, Alcina proposed the use of the models that were originally the basis of the New Archaeology; also that Spanish archaeology, while encouraging interdisciplinary work and scientific co-operation in general, should rest firmly on an anthropological basis, since only anthropology would be able to provide the theoretical framework so sadly lacking in Spanish traditional archaeology. These principles he recognised as already having been put into effect in the little anthropological archaeology then practised in Spain, most of it on American themes. Finally, Alcina expressed his confidence that the intellectual evolution and critical capacity of the new generations of undergraduates, together with the expansion of anthropological studies, would eventually overcome resistance to this kind of approach and achieve highly positive results.

Because of its swingeing criticisms, Alcina's paper, which appeared both in the proceedings of the congress and as a chapter in a book of theoretical reflections on archaeology, history and anthropology (Alcina 1975), kindled considerable polemic, but it proved prophetic as regards the growth of anthropological archaeology, which indeed owes much to his efforts and those of his disciples. His description of the situation in 1973 was quite accurate on the whole, but it would be unfair not to mention here a number of precursors. Theoretical meditations on the nature of archaeology as a discipline had already been published by Esteva (1959) and Alonso del Real (1961), with the conclusion that its objectives, programme and methods should be brought increasingly into line with those of anthropology. Interesting contributions to anthropological archaeology had also been made during the 1940s within the culture-history approach of the Viennese school, especially by specialists in the proto-historic peoples of the Iberian peninsula. However, the standard-bearer of anthropological archaeology in Spain was, and still is, the *Revista Española de Antropología Americana*, which since its foundation in the mid 1960s has served to divulge the successive waves of the New Archaeology, while classical work in the New Archaeology has since 1970 been made available to a wider university public in the *Cuadernos de Antropología Social y Etnología.*

Not without difficulties (as Alcina had foreseen), anthropological archaeology thus began to emerge beside traditional archaeology as the result of its discussion by the Americanists, the penetration of a variety of French tendencies, and the arrival of numerous American researchers wishing to apply their theories, methods and programmes to the quantitatively and qualitatively rich archaeological material available in Spain and so test them against the theories and methods of other schools. At the same time, the installation of palynological laboratories and C14 equipment, and greater familiarity with and facilities for the application of physical, chemical, biological and mathematical techniques, allowed the use of more rigorous methodologies in keeping with the theoretical progress. Traditional archaeology nevertheless continued to be the dominant tendency, as is shown by inspection of the literature listed in the *Repertorio de Arqueología Española* for these years; for in spite of the apparently impeccable presentation of many reports of excavations or other investigations, with their initial enunciation of rigorous working hypotheses, their detailed explanation of the methods employed and their painstaking description of the material recovered (not forgetting lengthy appendices listing the results of analysing the finds by physical or chemical techniques, etc.), this rigour is often but a thin disguise covering what is basically a neo-positivist historicist approach. The basic position of traditional archaeology continued to be that described by Alcina in 1973.

The 1980s have seen an acceleration of change in Spanish archaeology, for alongside a traditional archaeology that is increasingly rigorous in its methods but unforgiving as regards its lack of critical acumen and engrained historicism, a minority group has been increasingly active and influential wherever the new generation has attained posts of responsibility as researchers or in the lecture halls. As a result, contributions have appeared that are no longer slavish imitations of imported models or fashions, but instead include an increasing amount of original thought: theoretical papers reviewing archaeology as a discipline, epistemological essays and numerous articles reporting advances in methods of prospection, excavation, physical, chemical and palaeontological analysis, and the application of mathematical tools and computer techniques. Indeed, the effervescence of Spanish archaeology in these years has meant that these studies have often combined a wide variety of theoretical attitudes.

It should be emphasised, however (personal communication from M. I. Martinez Navarrete of the Centre for Historical Studies, Madrid), that the revival of archaeological debate in the 1980s was largely independent of the discussions around 1975. The initial interest in anthropological archaeology had been less towards processual, adaptive and evolutionary theories and more towards scientific methods, environmental studies and the like. In the new context of the 1980s, the dichotomy which emerged was not between history and anthropology but between a traditional descriptive empiricism on the one hand and, on the other, historical materialism and other explanations using a scientific methodology. The latter was seen as non-arbitrary and hence as liberating and radical. In such a context the term 'anthropological archaeology' came to have little relevance, and the contribution of processual archaeology continued to be largely methodological or technical.

Theory and Method in Spanish archaeology during the 1980s

R. Risch

In general one can say that theoretical awareness in Spanish archaeology started developing at the beginning of the 1980s, mainly among a younger generation of archaeologists. This must also be understood in relation to social and political changes in Spain at that time. These can very broadly be characterised by the political instability of the young democracy (in early 1981 the Spanish Congress was occupied by military forces, and in October 1982 the last of a series of military insurrections failed), economic difficulties and the strong political awareness and commitment of large parts of society (mainly among those social classes and groups that most strongly resisted the dictatorship, that is the working class, the peasants, national groups like Basques and Catalans, and certain intellectuals).

The sense of creating a new state was expressed in the progressive nature of parts of the Spanish universities, and surely influenced questions about the future of archaeology in society and in the new Spain. The theoretical and methodological foundations of the discipline were discussed, with the aim of developing an epistemological framework in which a more scientific and socially relevant archaeology could be undertaken.

Traditional archaeology was thoroughly analysed on the one hand (e.g. Martinez Navarrete and Vicent 1983), while on the other hand the influence of perspectives from the USA and England promoted the beginning of alternative views (e.g. Estévez *et al.* 1981). It is interesting that the influences on Spanish archaeology thus shifted from Central Europe, predominantly Germany, towards the English-speaking countries. Traditional archaeology, which had hitherto dominated at the institutional level, had developed from the foundations of German archaeology, mainly concerned with the improvement of excavation techniques and the establishment of typological sequences for the prehistoric cultures of the Iberian peninsula. An interesting account of what was, and still to a certain extent is, 'traditional' archaeology can be seen in the recent book by Antonio Beltrán *Ser arqueologo*, 'To be an archaeologist' (1988). A younger generation of archaeologists, at that time mostly still graduate students, considered this approach insufficient for their aim of understanding prehistoric societies, and started looking for new perspectives.

The beginning of this development took place in an atmosphere hostile to theoretical discussion, which was considered irrelevant to archaeology and was frequently seen as the result of left-wing propaganda. An example of this is the 'reactions' produced by the appearance of Lull's *La 'cultura' de El Argar*, the subtitle of which may be translated 'A model for the study of prehistoric socioeconomic formations' (1983) (on the influence of this work, see also Martinez Navarrete 1989). The marginal position of the theoretical debate can be recognised in, for example, the 'peripheral' character of the universities (peripheral not in a pejorative sense, but in relation to economic resources and the numbers of teaching staff) that have organised congresses on theoretical issues: Cáceres (*Actas* 1985), Teruel 1984 and 1986 (Burillo 1984, 1986), Murcia 1986 (Jornadas 1986). A more recent theoretical congress, although taking place in Barcelona in late 1986, was organised by archaeology students under serious infrastructural difficulties (see Ballestín *et al.* 1988a: 149–51). These examples show that the discourse was struggling not only with the difficulties of the subject but also with an often intolerant and unproductive environment. Also, and this is an important feature of the evolution of theoretical perspectives in Spain, there was a general lack of trends in the discussions other than a generalised apathy and rejection of theory. Theoretical awareness was only shown by isolated individuals, or by small and marginal groups spread throughout Spain. Thus one cannot talk of one centre of theoretical debate in Spain, but only of individuals and groups. Nor do I think that one can even speak of 'theoretical debate', understood as the development of ideas through propositions, critique and replies; at least this does not appear in published form. Few of the synthetic works which have recently appeared on theory and method cite Spanish contributions, let alone offer any deeper discussion of them (Fernández Martínez 1989; Alcina-Frank 1989). The reasons for this lack, or conscious avoidance, of an open scientific discussion may lie in the sphere of the micro-politics of our subject or in the bad theoretical training of most archaeologists.

Nevertheless, the situation has definitely been changing over recent years. The creation of a large number of working places and departments of archaeology in universities, regional and city councils, etc., has opened the possibility for 'institutionalising' the concept of theory, and giving it continuity in the country. The sudden increase of publications and conferences on theory and method at the present time signals a new situation. What are the reasons behind this change, and has real 'progress' taken place? Although 'traditional' anti-theoretical archaeology still controls large parts of the power structures in archaeology, to discuss theoretical aspects no longer constitutes an act of radical critique. What Lull (1990) called the 'clandestine' atmosphere of the early years has gone. Yet this does not mean that archaeology has become more 'progressive', since the power structures and unequal distribution of resources and employment, as well as the reproduction of a conservative and elite discourse, are guaranteed. 'Theory' has been integrated and is now used by the old system. This shows that in just ten years a rather complex development has taken place in Spanish archaeology which should be analysed more deeply.

Research programmes and areas of interest

The major change in Spanish archaeology of the 1980s took place in the field of research methods and techniques, as a result of what Vicent (1984) called the 'technological revolution'. Influenced by processual archaeology and the palaeoeconomic school of

Cambridge, researchers have shown an increasing interest in applying scientific techniques, rather than merely concentrating on the recovery of objects and architectural structures. The new methods mainly concern the analysis of organic materials, metal objects or stone implements, the recording of intrasite distribution patterns and systematic field surveying. Nevertheless, these new archaeological techniques are often used in an uncritical way, and are not related to any specific questions or theoretical frame for the reconstruction of prehistoric societies. The traditional approach remains unchanged; only the archaeological record has been extended to include new sorts of materials.

However, an increasing number of research programmes are now working with explicit hypotheses on the environment, economy and society, as well as with social theories of historical change. Examples include the works on palaeolithic cave sites in northern Spain (e.g. Gomez 1983; Bernaldo de Quiros 1980; Vila i Mitja *et al.* 1985). In Galicia, Criado *et al.* (1986) have been working on the spatial distribution patterns of megalithic monuments and settlements from a perspective that attempts to relate environment, culture and symbols (see also Bello *et al.* 1987). Specific research on the socio-economic formations of Copper and Bronze Age societies has been undertaken by a team from Barcelona in south-east Spain in collaboration with an English team (Chapman *et al.* 1987), and there is a similar project in Mallorca (Gasull *et al.* 1984). Other interesting research is being undertaken on the Iberic settlement of the Lower Aragón (Burillo and Peña 1984), also using a spatial approach.

Moving from this level of specific research programmes towards a more general perspective, we can observe an improvement in the discussion of specific aspects within archaeological theory. In this respect the area of spatial archaeology has received most attention, thanks to two congresses organised by Burillo and his team in Teruel (Burillo 1984, 1986). Although the discussion was centred on very general principles, the importance of these congresses is reflected in the growing awareness of spatial aspects in the understanding of prehistoric societies.

The so-called 'archaeology of death' has also been a focus of Spanish archaeological theory (e.g. Ruiz-Zapatero and Chapa 1988). After a critique of processual archaeology's approaches to the understanding of burial practices, Lull and Picazo (1989) have developed an alternative based on historical materialism. The func-

34

tionalist idea of an economic time of labour, separate from a social time of labour, is rejected. Instead, tombs and their contents have to be related to social cost and relative social value respectively, which themselves are conditioned by the general social relations of production. Invested labour cannot in their view be defined only in terms of effort or energy invested, as labour has an implicit social value. Following the same direction, Lull and Estevez (1986) developed a statistical analysis that made it possible to establish hypotheses about the social structures of the Bronze Age, using burial complexes.

Theoretical perspectives

Apart from these specific examples of archaeological theory, the discussion of a 'general theory' for archaeology received close attention during the 1980s. The congress of Soria in 1981 (*Primeras Jornadas* 1984) on 'Methods in archaeology' can be considered as the first time that theoretical issues were discussed on a broad basis. Although the general level of discussion was very basic compared to what was going on at the same time in, for example, England, Mexico or the USA, its fundamental importance lies in the fact that it represents a starting point for Spanish theoretical archaeology. Some years later the 'Seminar on new tendencies in archaeological methodology', organised in Madrid in 1985 (unpublished), had a strong influence on the Spanish archaeological debate. The congress organised in Barcelona in December 1986, 'Theoretical tendencies in archaeology', mentioned on p. 32, is the most important event so far, as it was the first time that epistomological issues were discussed in monograph form (Ballestín *et al.* 1988a). It illustrates the progression in ideas since the first positions taken up in Soria in 1981. Archaeologists and social anthropologists analysed from different perspectives the problem of archaeological theory and epistemology, archaeology's role in the social sciences, and its present political and social implications and difficulties in Spain.

Today, many works include some consideration of aspects of general theory and epistemology. I would mention three main currents explicitly developed in this respect, using as criteria their relevance to the debate, their specific attention to theoretical problems, and their originality in relation to the general development of archaeological theory in Europe and America. In this sense, I follow a similar selection to Martinez Navarrete (1989) in her recent review of the Spanish theoretical debate.

(1) Marxist ideas have played an important role ever since the beginning of theoretical discussions in Spanish archaeology. The socio-political situation of Spain during recent decades has been relevant in this respect. Marxism has been discussed on a political as well as an academic level, for example, by the Communist Party in Spain and it must be remembered that as recently as 1979 the now ruling Spanish Socialist Party still included 'Marxism' on their political agenda. This awareness of Marxism in society and in the social sciences has mainly been represented in archaeology by two working teams, one at the 'Autonomous University' of Barcelona, the other at the University of Jaen. Marxist debates in other countries also influenced the new discussions in Spanish archaeology. Thus, neo-Marxist perspectives in French anthropology were important. An interesting critique of French neo-Marxism was conducted by Catalan archaeologists (Ballestín et al. 1988b). But considering themselves historians rather than anthropologists, both the Barcelona and Jaen teams are more associated with Latin American archaeological Marxism on the one hand, and Italian on the other. Latin America, with such archaeologists as Bate, Lumbreras and Muntané, possibly has the most important Marxist tradition in archaeology in the western world. In Italy the work of Bianchi Bandinelli and his scholar Carandini (see Chapter 3 of this book) is also relevant to the developments in Spain. Of course the work of Gordon Childe is of great importance too in this respect.

(2) J. Vicent, from the Department of Prehistory of the Centre for Historical Studies (CSIC) in Madrid, has carried out a critical revision of the present state of archaeological theory. He has introduced the concepts of the Frankfurt School into archaeology, and in this way also uses related to a Marxist approach. His initial proposal comprises the development of archaeological theory through the notion of 'language', understood in an epistemological sense.

(3) A different direction has been taken by C. Martín de Guzmán, from the Department of Prehistory of the Universidad Complutense of Madrid. His aim is the formation of an archaeological theory through structuralism, but from a different

approach to the one taken by British archaeology in the last years.

Conceptualising archaeology

In the early stages of the development of an archaeological theory one of the central questions was to find an adequate definition of the subject and its object of study.

In 1981 the group from Barcelona, which was one of the first to approach these questions, outlined the need for a more scientific archaeology, concentrating on the history and evolution of socio-economic formations, the level of development of the productive forces and the complexity of their relations of production as seen in material remains (Estévez et al. 1981: 24, 1984: 28). It is important that the Marxist groups emphasise the fact that archaeology is a science related to history (Estévez et al. 1984: 22; Ruiz et al. 1986a: 10).

Lull (1988a, 1988b, 1989), who continued the early theoretical work of the group from Barcelona, has centred his work on the conceptualisation of what the object of archaeology is. He criticises the definition of archaeology as the science that studies the material remains which societies in all times and places have created for their production and reproduction, since it implies that the objects of study of archaeology are the material remains themselves. This is considered to be wrong because: first, not all archaeological materials are of the same order and therefore cannot be grouped into the same categories; second, the media of information and the object of study of a science cannot be identical; it implies that things have meaning in themselves, which in turn implicitly defends a descriptive and positivist archaeology. Rather, the real 'object of study of archaeology is to propose coherent representations which, by means of validating theories through empirical support, explain the historical meaning of the nature, properties and presence of archaeological materials' (Lull 1988b: 74).

For Vicent (1982: 64), following in this case a more anthropological perspective, prehistory and archaeology should be considered as two different disciplines, which both aim towards the same formal object: culture. Archaeology represents the basis for the deductions developed by prehistory, in order to understand culture in a synthetic way at a general scale (Vicent 1982: 66).

Both disciplines have to develop different methodologies. Prehistory should mainly be concerned with coherent models in the field of the social sciences, and archaeology with the method of correspondence between the theoretical model and the empirical evidence.

Martín de Guzmán (1984: 40), on the other hand, claims that the knowledge of prehistory has to refer to the 'meaning' and the 'structural position' of the material object, seen as the product of past societies. Again, this can only be achieved through the building of a 'scientific' archaeology, which means a discipline with a particular theoretical frame (Martín de Guzmán 1988: 27). Its aim is to formulate 'logical representations' of past social and cultural facts (Martín de Guzmán 1984: 53). But in order to achieve this true scientific knowledge, archaeology will need a specific paradigm, understood as the model *par excellence* of a discipline (Martín de Guzmán 1988: 56). This paradigm is urgently needed where the empiricist, particularist and inductivist positions still dominate, and where the archaeological object is admired and fetishised (Martín de Guzmán 1988: 36f.).

The 'paradigm' proposed by Martín de Guzmán (1984) for the object of archaeology is a 'structural model' with two levels. On the first level the model will be concerned with the typology and function of the object. On the second level the typological-functional context becomes a category of contexts, which expresses structural relations and which will be verified by the mode of study. 'To each material expression of the culture (signifier) corresponds, at least, one intentional component (signified)' (Martín de Guzmán 1984: 53). This relation between 'signification' and 'significant' in the artefact allows the object to be considered as a sign. These signs tend to imply connotations that transform them into 'symptoms' – because of their reiterative frequency in the discourse – or into 'symbols' with a metaphorical or metonymical change sanctioned by the social tradition, and incorporated into institutional levels (Martín de Guzmán 1984: 48).

An important part of the analysis of this 'discourse of the object' is the 'non-verbal syntax', as adapted for example by Leach to anthropology. The main problem that arises is that one object may contain more than one cultural 'meaning', the so-called 'polysemy of the object'. Only the contextual relations of the objects can help to replace them in a cultural structure. The object conceived as a message would consist of a semantic value which implies a direct meaning (e.g. ashes, flakes, bones), and an associated value which arises from its contextual relations, a functional incidence and 'meaning' (Martín de Guzmán 1984: 50f.). The aim of the discursive analysis (logical and theoretical) is to define the dimensions of structural complexities, as well as significant and regular patterns in the archaeological register, in order to reveal their structural function. Thus, established 'chains of equivalences' allow the definition of structural categories, providing an economic and social meaning. It is important to note that this linguistic-structuralist approach, presented around 1982 (Lull 1990), goes in a similar direction to the cognitive and contextual archaeology in England which was unknown in Spanish archaeology.

The group of Jaen has offered a different method of conceptualising the archaeological object, by creating a contextual theoretical matrix in which the artefact is seen as a 'product' (Ruiz et al. 1986b). For the development of an operational theory of the 'product' in archaeology, they start from Clarke's analytical approach, rejecting Binford's neo-functional view of the artefact. The artefact, seen in its context of disposition and deposition, becomes a product. This allows us to study the technical relations of production: 'The technology as part of the economic structure, transforms the artefact into the effect of a process of labour, and consequently into a product whose use value has to be distinguished' (Ruiz et al. 1986b: 67). What follows is a development of spatial categories in relation to the theory of the artefact: areas of production, consumption and exchange. Yet this relation between space and object should not result in a typology of products in the way Clarke proposed, because the same artefacts can appear at different levels (consumer good, object of exchange), and because a typology would not help to reconstruct the socioeconomic processes. Therefore it is important to propose a 'theory of the means of production' as well as a 'theory of the product'. The first would be, as Carandini considered, more related to a technological level, the second more to social relations.

A 'macro' level of spatial analysis gives rise to the historical concept of the socio-economic formation as a political and economic territory, which is the state (Ruiz et al. 1986a: 59). As such it has to be explained by a double theory, on the one hand in spatial terms, and on the other in political terms.

An important feature of these early critical approaches is the emphasis on using analytical categories for the description of the archaeological record in order to avoid the impressionist character of descriptive traditional archaeology. In this respect Clarke's work was very influential, and his analytical concepts were also the basis for the development of the new archaeological terminology (Estevez *et al.* 1981, 1984: 26).

Methodology

According to the initial definition of archaeology as a 'science', it was of prime importance to develop a methodology, and to discuss the epistemological foundations of archaeology. The agreement of all the authors in this respect must be seen in the light of the dominating view of archaeology as a catalogue (Vicent 1988) and of its complete lack of explicit methodological foundations.

As their theoretical 'manifesto', 'Reflections from a non-innocent archaeological project' implies, the team in Jaén centre their critique on traditional positivism which regards data as innocent, and value-free science as possible (Ruiz *et al.* 1986a: 9).

For Vicent (1984), epistemological research involves comparing an existing project with a possible one which is better adapted to the formal and theoretical objective of the discipline. The definition of both 'real' and 'possible archaeology' is undertaken at a twofold level. A 'general level' will mainly work out a meta-language with which we can describe and compare different theoretical and methodological problems of prehistory. This possibility of developing a rational reconstruction aims to make explicit the logical determinations of our discourse (Vicent 1984: 73f.). A 'restricted level' involves the discussion of the specific epistemological problems of the discipline and the self-correction of its research programmes. As a result of the problems arising from both levels, it appears that in a programme of epistemological research the 'general level' can only be used as a frame of reference for the 'restricted level', which has to determine, at least partially, our meta-language (Vicent 1984: 79). Also on the 'restricted level' problems arise from the lack of explicitness of our discipline.

More recently, Vicent has attempted to show the possibility of developing this alternative philosophy of archaeology on the basis of 'Critical Theory'. 'Scientific knowledge appears before us as a social product, whose sense depends on its relation to non-cognitive interests of the social praxis' (Vicent 1988). Such a 'critical philosophy of archaeology' is based on the concept of the 'negative dialectic' as conceived by Adorno, that is the implicit negation of a global sense of archaeological praxis beyond the subjective and objective conditions in which it develops (Vicent 1988: 4). The aim is to reveal the 'false consciousness' of archaeological praxis that arises between the perception of archaeological activity and the implications in reality. This 'false consciousness' appears in the New Archaeology as the acceptance of the unquestioned absolute of a normative epistemology within a model of scientific rationality.

Lull (1988b) gives to the concept of 'representation' a key role in the development of an epistemology suitable to archaeology. Scientific representations should be formal and systemic models with factual implications, which establish the dialectic relation between the fact and its scientific comprehension. In such a model there should be no contradictions between the logical bases which sustain it (formal sphere) and the archaeological patterns (factual sphere), the whole procedure being legalised through the methodology (Lull 1988b: 71). The representation should establish the causes of the structural relations between subject and object through a definition of the world that considers the dialectic between them both. The 'representations' we generate about the past are objective models formulated in the present, in order to understand the past. They are strongly influenced by the context in which they are being produced and, therefore, do not imply truthfulness, even if their internal structure is coherent. On the other hand, theory does not only try to understand reality, but also to transform it; this means that it is important to distinguish between theory and method. Ideology may be the motor of scientific theories, but the method itself, through which ideas are tested, must be independent (Lull 1989: 23). Often in archaeology, hypotheses are verified not through their empirical implications but through other hypotheses. The result is that rather than scientific discussions, ideological debates take place in the discipline. For Lull, the solution to these problems can only emerge through the use of a 'dialectical methodology'. Knowledge is understood as the dialectical process between what we think about reality and reality itself. Therefore what has to be formalised is the dialectic relation between theory and practice, which is the actual process of knowledge (Lull 1989: 16). The aim should be to show the relation perception–idea–reasoning. Finally there is an emphasis on the ethical condition of archaeology, that we should make our theories, and the method used, explicit.

Martín de Guzmán (1984) tries to link the idea of culture as language with the nomological-deductive method. Valid explanations require that, first, the 'principle of relevance' and, second, constrastability should be fulfilled. Nevertheless, the 'notion of grammar' appears as a method which is better suited to cultural phenomena (Martín de Guzmán 1984: 56), because of the differences between the social and the natural sciences, and their different concepts of 'objectivity'. The latter results from the difficulties of using 'experiments' in the social sciences, as well as from the implications of social scientists working in their own cultural context.

> In synthesis it would seem legitimate to base an epistemology of archaeological models on the systematic study of the correspondences between syntactic and semantic concepts. These contain or imply the contexts (and the relations) certified by means of *excavation directed* through a previous plan where the important cultural, economic, institutional, environmental, etc. issues are being questioned.
>
> (Martín de Guzmán 1988: 35)

Reaction to external debate

Finally, it is important to study the reaction of archaeological theory in Spain towards the theoretical debates in Britain and the USA, mainly concerning 'processualism' and 'post-processualism'. The theoretical debate in Spain started late, basically when the 'paradigm' (Martín de Guzmán 1988) of processual archaeology was being revised in its countries of origin as well as in Latin America (see e.g. Gándara 1982). But it is interesting to realise that when Spanish archaeology became aware of the theoretical debates, it developed them in a plurality of directions. Approaches coming from the English-speaking world have been criticised and improved, as in the case of Clarke's analytical categories, rather than just adapted as fixed models to Spanish archaeology.

In 'Archaeology as archaeology', also presented at the Theoretical Archaeology Group (TAG) Conference in Britain in 1983, the Barcelona group (Estévez *et al.* 1984) emphasised the status of archaeology as a science in its own right, clearly distancing themselves from the anthropological perspective of the New Archaeology. Binford's divisions of a society into economic, social and ideological levels were rejected (Estévez *et al.* 1984: 26) in favour of hierarchically interrelated levels in a given socio-economic formation. The idea of 'spatial archaeology' was criticised as unable to explain the synchronic/diachronic relations of an object (which depended on the socio-economic formation in which it was produced), and as unrelated to a social theory.

Vicent severely criticised processual archaeology on an epistemological level, as well as through its application to prehistory. Processualism has insufficiently discussed the relation between a general epistemology and prehistory, accepting in an unreflecting way the concepts of 'philosophy of science' as developed for the physical sciences which are mainly based on 'laws' and on normative methodological procedures. For Vicent it would first be necessary to find a language in which 'laws' are a significant grammatical category (Vicent 1984: 84ff.). Instead, New Archaeology has not considered that the hypothetico-deductive programme represents a speculative and analytical conception of a reality which can only manifest itself phenomenologically. As a meta-theory developed for physical systems, all models proposed for the social sciences 'would be mechanical, and are therefore, and here lies the fundamental question, deterministic' (Vicent 1982: 48). The scientific rationality on which processualism is based was never questioned, and the idea of science was simply equated to the adoption of the hypothetico-deductive method. Philosophical discussion in archaeology is reduced to propositions concerning the interpretation of hypothetico-deductive categories in archaeological terms. Yet culture cannot be understood as a mechanical system because its explanation is possible neither in terms of physical facts, nor in terms of causality. Culture, for Vicent, can only be comprehended. Lull's (1988b) development of a 'theory of representation' in archaeology has also to be seen in relation to the critique of the 'hypothetico-deductive' method sustained by processualism.

Nevertheless, the 'critical learning process' of Spanish theoretical discussion has not followed the lines of English 'post-processual' archaeology either. Even the structural approach of Martín de Guzmán, which shows conceptual similarities, clearly differs in questions of methodology. Vicent, who proposed to conceptualise cultural phenomena through the notion of 'language' from an epistemological perspective, understands this in the German tradition of 'Critical Theory' rather than in the sense of French structuralism from which it was introduced into English post-processualism.

Recently an increasing number of rather critical commentaries on post-processual archaeology have appeared. For Vicent, Hodder's (e.g. 1986) theoretical construction is

> directly based on the idealist tradition of historical particularism. Hodder seems to ignore the fact that a restoration of subjectivism, based on concepts such as 'empathy' and other allusions to a knowledge of history 'from the inside' etc., requires the supposition of models of rationality opposed to a radical perspective of the critique of archaeological knowledge. By transforming the subjectivity of the individual, its 'empathetic' capacity, into the final reference of archaeological knowledge and its validation, the knowledge is directly under the control of all the interests that form the subject as a social individual.
>
> (Vicent 1988)

For this author processualism and post-processualism are two competing versions of the same conservative tradition in the social sciences (Vicent 1990). Through processualism a new version of positivism became the dominant paradigm, and with Hodder a renewed post-modern form of the old relativist and idealist discourse is presented. Other criticism of post-processualism (Ruiz et al. 1988) has concerned its lack of a coherent and explicit theoretical body, its methodological anarchy, rejection of objective knowledge, and the acceptance of idealism as an ontological position and as the epistomological base of theory.

One of the weaknesses of these criticisms is that post-processualism is too much identified with Hodder's work (translated and better known in Spain than that of other authors who use this approach), which itself has been changing rapidly, without too much regard to variations in position. But however accurate these criticisms are, they express scepticism towards something which in the English theoretical debate might be 'radical', but which in the Spanish context can be integrated in such a way as to revive the 'traditional' subjective archaeology. Fernández Martínez (1989: 267), thinking in scientific circles, even suggests that post-processualism is returning to pre-processualist positions.

A critical outlook

A theory implies 'radicalism' or 'conservatism' not just in itself but in relation to the political and social context in which it is produced, as well as to the scientific and political praxis it demands.

While in the situation of the early 1980s practically any theoretical proposal would have supposed a challenge to the traditional archaeological community, today the terminology 'hypothesis', 'verification', 'deduction', etc., is of common use. Although the idea of 'theory', even in a Marxist version, has been integrated into archaeology, its conservative character has not changed in general. This implies that something which is exposed as 'critical' within a former frame of reference may no longer be so. In this sense the revisions of post-processualism through other critical positions are superficial because they do not take into account this new situation.

Especially where archaeological praxis is concerned, little has changed since the 1970s and early 1980s. The number of excavations has increased, but the results and the specific process of research remain in the private domain of many archaeologists. On the other hand, in the last ten to twenty years, 'treasure hunting' has increased rapidly in connection with international networks of clandestine – or not so clandestine – trade in antiquities. With the growth of industrial activities as well, many sites have already been destroyed and official protection in fact is normally non-existent. But 'professional archaeology' remains mostly indifferent and shows no sign of taking a committed attitude in order to force the official institutions to take measures. Finally, and not unrelated to the previous points, one should mention the absence of communication between archaeology and the rest of society. The archaeological community generally remains more interested in the maintenance of its elitist positions and the reproduction of its privileges than in the social relevance it could claim by offering a critical view of the past in relation to the present. On a political level, the archaeological institutions have returned to their entrenched positions after the short period between the end of the dictatorship and the mid 1980s. This process corresponds to the general political evolution of what was formerly an alternative left-wing party but which now supports the government.

While from a 'reformist' perspective it is difficult to doubt that the overall situation of archaeology (jobs, finances, etc.) has improved, basically because Spain has become a richer country and wants to reach the 'European standard', it should also be clear that the initial dynamism has decreased. Some recent publications even give the impression that the consequence is a retrogression or impoverishment of theoretical development in Spanish archaeology: while the early publications, however open they may be to criticism, contained original approaches moving in a plurality of directions, the recent works (e.g. Fernández Martínez 1989) are superficial copies of the 'knowledge' that circulates in archaeology in England and the USA, with few original contributions to the Spanish or English theoretical debate.

This new situation for theory should lead, in my view, to a different approach to post-processual archaeology, one which includes elements of non-conformity towards the dominating structures. Also the fact that the recent changes in Eastern Europe are resulting in a general shift towards more conservative positions in the social sciences should induce us to reconsider our route to a critical and committed Spanish archaeology. This would be more constructive than limiting the discussion to problems of theoretical and methodological inconsistencies. On the other hand there are plenty of possibilities for developing a 'radical' discourse: economic orthodoxy still dominates most archaeological models; although Spain has important ecological problems with historical origin, environmental studies are still descriptive approaches and no socio-economic ecological perspective has been developed; the cultural heritage and the problem of what to do with it have not been considered from an alternative position; but feminist archaeology is starting to develop (Picazo and Sanahuja 1989) as well as discussions on the role of education in archaeology (Bardavio Novi 1990). These are just some examples of the alternatives which exist and are possible. It does not mean that the classical radical approaches, mainly Marxist, have lost their revolutionary potential, only that it will be necessary to question their present form and context of application. Finally Spanish, and more widely Mediterranean (also including North African) and Latin American social thought has produced a marginal and critical tradition sufficient to develop its own approaches, rather than just to reproduce out of context the models of the English-speaking world which are now so much in fashion. The aim should be to widen and diversify international communication, which is still very poor and controlled by particular 'bosses', while 'capital' finds it ever easier to cross borders.

The development of Spanish archaeology shows that 'radicalness' or 'marginality', and what is considered as such, has to be questioned continually. But questioning does not mean wholesale rejection of valuable approaches. A specific feature of the Spanish marginal discussion has been its emphasis on the epistemology and coherence of archaeological models, and a critical attitude towards archaeology in general. Inside the country even though the idea of theory may have become integrated, archaeology resists thorough revision. Outside, and especially in the context of post-processualism, the Spanish discussion on theory can suppose an interesting contribution to a critical discourse whose main weakness has been its method. I therefore think that the present conditions should lead us to use and adapt all the possibilities we still have for the development of critical or radical approaches in archaeology; this can only take place through communication and discussion on an international scale.

Note

1. The first part of this chapter, by J. M. Vázquez Varela, was translated by I. C. Coleman of the Translation Service, Instituto de Idiomas, University of Santiago de Compostela, Spain.

The author of the second part, R. Risch, wants to thank V. Lull, M. Martínez Navarrete and M. Ruiz Parra for their helpful and interesting comments on the original text, and the bibliographic information provided. Many thanks also to I. Hodder, M. Shackle and A. Walker, who corrected the English, and to Juan Vicent for information on his research. As ever, sole responsibility for faults and confusion lies with the author.

References

Actas de las II Jornadas de Metodología y Didáctica de la Historia, Prehistoria y Arqueologia 1981 (1985), Cáceres.

Alcina-Franch, J. (1975) 'La arqueología antropológica en España: situación actual y perspectivas', in *Primera reunión de Ántropólogos españoles – Sevilla 1973*, Seville.

Alcina Franch, J. (1989) *Arqueología antropológica*, Madrid: Akal.

Alonso del Real, C. (1961) *Sociología pre y protohistórica*, Madrid: Instituto de Estudios Políticos.

Ballestín, X., *et al.* (eds) (1988a) *Corrents teòrics en arqueologia – Actes del colloqui celebrat a la Facultat de Geografia i Història de la Universitat de Barcelona els dies 11, 12 i 13 de 1986*, Barcelona: Columna.

Ballestín, X., González Marcén, P. and Lluró, J. M. (1988b) 'Marxisme i Antropología – els límits de la teoría', in X. Ballestín *et al. Corrents teòrics en arqueologigia – Actes del colloqui a la Facultat de Geografia i Història de la Universitat de Barcelona els dies 11, 12 i 13 de 1986*, Barcelona: Columna.

Bardavio Novi, A. (1990) 'Els coneixements en arqueología, per a qui?, per a que?', *Arqueocrítica* 2:5–10.

Bello, J. M., Criado, F. and Vázquez, J. M. (1987) *La cultura megalítica de la Provincia de La Coruña y sus relaciones con el marco natural – implicaciones socioeconómicas*, La Coruña.

Beltrán, A. (1988) *Ser arqueologo*, Madrid: Fundación Universidad-Empresa.

Bernaldo de Quiros, F. (1980) *Notas sobre la economía del Paleolítico Superior*, Madrid: Centro de investigación y Museo de Altamira.

Burillo, F. (ed.) (1984) *Arqueologia Espacial – Coloquio sobre distribución y relación entre los asentamientos, 27–29.9.1984, Teruel*, vols 1–6, Teruel: Seminario de Arqueología y Etnologia Turolense.

—— (1986) *Arqueología Espacial – Coloquio sobre el microespacio (2), 15–17.9.1986, Teruel*, vols 7–11, Teruel: Seminario de Arqueología Etnología Turolense.

Burillo, F. and Peña, J. L. (1984) 'Modificaciones por factores geomorfológicos en el tamaño y ubicación de los asentamientos primitivos', in F. Burillo (ed.) *Arqueología Espacial – Coloquio sobre distribución y relación entre los asentamientos, 27–29.9.1984, Teruel*, Teruel: Seminario de Arqueología y Ethnología Turolense.

Chapa, T. (1988) 'Perspectivas actuales de la arqueología española', *Revista de Occidente* 81: 135–42.

Chapman, R., Lull, V., Picazo, M. and Sanahuja, E. (eds) (1987) *El Proyecto Gatas: Sociedad y Economía en el sudeste de España, 2500–800 a.n.e. – 1. La Prospección Arqueológica*, British Archeologists Reports, International Series 348, Oxford.

Criado, F., Aira Rodriguez, M. J. and Díaz-Fierros, F. (1986) *La construcción del paisaje: Megalitismo y ecología en la Sierra de Barbanza (Galicia)*, Santiago: Dirección Xeneral do Patrimonio Artistico e Monumental.

Esteva, C. (1959) 'Sobre el método de la arqueología', *Revista de Indias* 75: 89–106.

Estévez, J., Gasull, J., Lull, V., Sanahuja, E. and Vila, A. (1981) 'La investigación en prehistoria: estado de la cuestión', in *Estudios sobre historia de España (Homenaje a Tuñon de Lara)*, vol. 1, Madrid: Universidad Internacional Menendez Pelayo.

—— (1984) 'Arqueología como arqueología: propuesta para una terminología operativa', in *Primeras Jornadas de Methodologia de Investigación Prehistorica, Soria, 1981*, Madrid.

Fernández Martínez, V. M. (1989) *Teoría y método de la arquelogía*, Madrid: Sintesis.

Gándara, M. (1982) 'La vieja "nueva arqueología" (primera parte and segunda parte)', in *Teorías métodos y técnicas en arqueología: reimpresiones de anthropología Americana*, Mexico: Instituto Panamericano de Geografía e Història.

Gasull, J., Lull, V. and Sanahuja, E. (1984) *Son Fornes l: La fase talayótica – Ensayo de reconstrucción de una comunidad prehistórica de la isla de Mallorca*. B.A.R. Int. Ser. 209, Oxford.

Gómez, A. (1983) *Formas economicas del Paleolítico Superior Cantábrico l, Tito Bustillo*, Salamanca: Ediciones Universidad de Salamanca.

Hodder, I. (1986) *Reading the Past*, Cambridge: Cambridge University Press.

'Jornadas sobre metodología arqueológica, October 1986', Murcia (typed manuscript).

Lull, V. (1983) *La 'cultura' de El Argar: un modelo para el estudio de las formaciones económico-sociales prehistoricas*, Madrid: Akal.

—— (1988a) 'Per una definició materialista de l'arqueología', in X. Ballestín, *et al. Corrents Teòrics en Arqueología – Actes del colloqui celebrat a la Facultat de Geografia i Història de la Universitat de Barcelona els dies 11, 12 i 13 de 1986*, Barcelona: Columna.

—— (1988b) 'Hacía una teoría de la representación en arqueologígía', *Revista de Occidente* 81:62–76.

—— (1989) 'El procedimiento científico en arqueología: la fragilidad del método hipotético-deductivo', *Revista del Instituto de Conservación y Restauración de Bienes Culturales* 1.

—— (1990) *La prehistoria de la teoría arqueológica en el estado español* (in press).

Lull, V. and Estévez, J. (1986) 'Propuesta metodológica para el estudio de las necrópolis argáricas', in *Homenaje a Luis Siret 1934–1984*, Seville.

Lull, V. and Picazo, M. (1989) 'Arqueología de la muerte y estructura social', *Archivo español de arqueología* 62: 5–20.

Martín de Guzmán, C. (1984) 'Nociones epistemológicas y Arqueología Prehistórica', in *Primeras Jornadas de Metodología de Investigación Prehistórica, Soria 1981*, Madrid.

—— (1988) 'Arqueología y paradigma: tendencias y resistencias', *Revista de Occidente* 81: 27–46.

Martínez Navarrete, M. I. (1989) *Una revisión crítica de la prehistoria española: la Edad del Bronce como paradigma, Siglo XXI*, Madrid.

Martínez Navarrete, M. I. and Vicent, J. (1983) 'La periodización: un análisis histórico-crítico', in *Homenaje al Prof. Martin Almagro Basch*, Madrid: Ministerio de Cultura.

Nocete, F. (1984a) 'Elementos para un estudio del patrón de asentamiento en las campiñas occidentales del Alto Guadalquivir durante la Edad del Cobre', in F. Burillo (ed.) *Arqueología Espacial – Coloquio sobre la distribución y relación entre los asentamientos, 27–29.9.1984, Teruel*, Teruel: Seminario de Arqueología y Etnología Turolense.

—— (1984b) 'Jefaturas y territorio: Una revisión critica,' *Cuadernos de Prehistoria de Granada* 9: 289–304.

—— (1986) 'Una història agraria: El proceso de consolidación de la economía de producción', in A. Ruiz *et al.* (eds) *Arqueología en Jaén: Reflecciones desde un proyecto no inocente*, Jaén: Diputación Provincial de Jaén.

Picazo, M. (1988) 'La arqueología de la muerte y los estudios clásicos', in *Simposium sobre dependencia en la Antiguedad*, Madrid.

Picazo, M. and Sanahuja, E. (1989) 'Los estudios de la mujer a lo largo de la Prehistoria y en la Antiguedad Clásica', in *Arqueocrítica*, Barcelona.

Primeras Jornadas de Metodología de Investigación Prehistórica – Soria 1981 (1984), Madrid.

Ruiz, A. (1978) 'Elementos para un análisis de la fase asiática de transición', in *Primeras sociedades de clase y modo de producción asiático*, Madrid: Akal.

—— (1980) 'Los pueblos íberos del Alto Guadalquivir – Análisis de un proceso de transición', *Cuadernos de Prehistoria de Granada* 3: 255–84.

Ruiz, A., Chapa, T. and Ruiz-Zapatero, G. (1988) 'La arqueología contextual: una revisíon crítica', *Trabajos de Prehistoria* 45: 11–17.

Ruiz, A. and Molinos, M. (1984) 'Elementos para un estudio del patrón de asentamiento en las campiñas del Alto Guadalquivir durante el horizonte Pleno Iberico – un caso de sociedad agrícola con estado', in F. Burillo (ed.) *Arqueología Espacial – Coloquio sobre la distribución y relación entre los asentamientos, 27–29.9.1984, Teruel*, Teruel: Seminario de Arqueología y Etnología Turolense.

Ruiz, A., Molinos, M. and Hornos, F. (eds) (1986a) *Arqueología en Jaén: Reflexiones desde un proyecto no inocente*, Jaén: Diputación Provincial de Jaén.

Ruiz, A., Molinos, M., Nocete, F. and Castro, M. (1986b) 'Concepto de producto en arqueología', in F. Burillo (ed.) *Arqueología Espacial – Coloquio sobre el microespacio (2), 15–17.9.1986. Teruel*, Teruel: Seminario de Arqueología y Etnología Turolense.

Ruiz-Zapatero, G. and Chapa, T. (1988) 'La arqueología de la muerte – perspectivas teórico-metodológicas', in *Congreso sobre las necrópolis celtibéricas*, Zaragoza-Daroca: Institución Fernando el Católico.

Vicent, J. (1982) 'Las tendencias metodologicas en prehistoria', *Trabajos de Prehistoria* 39: 9–54.

—— (1984) 'Fundamentos para una investigación epistemológica sobre la prehistoria', in *Primeras Jornadas de Metodología de Investigación Prehistórica, Soria, 1981*, Madrid.

—— (1985) 'Un concepto de Metodología: Hacia una definición epistemológica de prehistoria y arqueología', in *Actas de las II Jornadas de Metodología y Didáctica de la Història, Prehistòria y Arqueología 1981*, Cáceres.

—— (1988) 'Filosofía y arqueología hacia una conciencia critica', in *Primera Reunión hispano-mejicana de Arqueología. Las Navas del Marquez, Avila, Mayo 1988*, Madrid.

—— (1990) *El debat post-processual: algunes observacións 'radicals' sobre una arqueología 'conservadora'*, Barcelona: Cotazero.

Vila i Mitja, A. *et al.* (1985) *El Cingle Vermell – Assentament de Caçadors-Recollectors del Xè milleni B.P., Barcelona.*

3

THE ITALIAN PERSPECTIVE ON THEORETICAL ARCHAEOLOGY

Bruno d'Agostino[1]

At the beginning of the twentieth century Italian culture was dominated by positivist thought which saw the experimental method as the only valid approach to scientific research. The epistemological basis of the human sciences appeared no different from that of the natural sciences, and a lively interest was taken in ascertaining the possible correlations between these two fields. Within the archaeological arena, this situation hindered the establishment of a rigid division between prehistory and proto-history on the one hand and Classical archaeology on the other, to the clear advantage of the latter. In fact, studies of prehistory paid more attention to ecological problems, to the collection of those excavation data which could cast light on the relationship between humans and their natural environment. It was customary for that relationship to be deduced from analyses of human bones and of animal and vegetable remains. Besides, even though field research often left much to be desired, there was a clear understanding of the stratigraphical method which constituted an obligatory standard of reference.

In this climate of opinion it seemed natural that an archaeologist could move freely from prehistory to the Classical period, and, among the more informed proponents, that the archaeological method could legitimately be applied to everything investigable by means of excavation.

The most significant figure in this picture is Giacomo Boni. Director of the excavations in the Roman Forum and on the Palatine from 1902, he undertook the excavations of the proto-historical cemetery of the Forum, accurately documenting all aspects of the burial place, from the shape of the grave to the appearance of the wooden casing, from the position of the accompanying grave goods to the nature of the human, vegetable and animal remains. He began to apply a rigorous stratigraphical method to the complex archaeological stratification which had continued without interruption from the tenth century BC to the time of the Renaissance. In the Palatine excavation he paid equal attention to the frescoed Roman houses under the *Domus Flavia* as to the Renaissance layout of the Farnese Gardens.

This conception of archaeology did not last long, yet it left an important mark. For example, many of Giacomo Boni's characteristics came together in the person of P. Orsi, another great archaeologist who dominated the scene in southern Italy and Sicily during the first three decades of the twentieth century. Nevertheless, the situation began to change very quickly, for two main reasons. The first can be attributed to a profound alteration in the cultural climate. Since the first decade of the twentieth century, the influence of idealist thought from the Hegelian tradition had begun to make itself powerfully felt through the works of Benedetto Croce.

Crocean idealism, which was characterised by a strongly historicist sense, conceived of history as the history of ideas and therefore coincident with philosophy: history, inasmuch as it is a product of the spirit, could alone be the basis of true knowledge. From this derived the primacy of the human sciences, following a tradition which had both a Hegelian matrix and deep-seated roots in the Italian philosophical tradition, particularly in the thought of G.B. Vico. Thus a strict division was created between the natural and the human sciences. Besides, there hung over the latter the fierce Crocean prejudice against sociology, which was considered to be a farrago of generalisations without intellectual validity. So the way was barred to any possible encounter between the study of the ancient world and sociology: a union which had rendered the French cultural tradition so productive under the impetus of sociologists such as E. Durkheim and M. Mauss, and of ancient historians such as G. Glotz and L. Gernet.

It is undeniable that the influence of Croce had negative effects on archaeology. Prehistory was the first area to be damaged, being unable to justify its reconstructions through the study of ancient literary sources: it came to be seen as the illiterates' way to science. This prejudice caused a rigid separation between prehistory and Classical archaeology: the underlying prejudice against empirical research and the experimental method was reflected in the poor quality of field research.

Nevertheless, it would be unjust to regard the Crocean experience on balance as a purely negative one. The historicist conception put an end to evolutionary determinism, typical of positivism, and opened a wide conceptual door to an understanding of different cultures and artistic expressions foreign to Classical culture. Here, the Crocean aesthetic, which defined art as a prelogical intuition expressed in a directly mediated way in the form of a poetic fragment, had an extraordinary importance.

It is difficult to say at what point archaeology, a discipline little inclined in Italy to reflection upon method, directly experienced the influence of Crocean thought. It certainly felt the cultural influences of the contemporary bourgeoisie, who found a higher and more systematic expression in Croce's thought.

As a result of this new climate, prehistory and Classical archaeology took two completely different paths. While the former strengthened its ties with the natural sciences, Classical archaeology increasingly tended to identify itself with the history of ancient art, understood as the history of great personalities and of masterpieces viewed outside their context. Thus it ultimately ignored the fundamental aspects of Crocean historicism, by lapsing into an evolutionary view which recognised abstract perfection in the art of Periclean Athens.

The changes in the cultural climate were accompanied by important historical events. From the beginning of the second decade of this century Italy became involved in colonial ventures, which reached their peak in the fascist era with the creation of the 'empire'. The task of colonial archaeology became that of demonstrating the 'Roman spirit' of conquered regions, by way of monumental excavations at Leptis Magna, Sabratha, etc. The measure of worth was quantity, to the total exclusion of quality: scientific interest gave way to propaganda. The rhetoric of ancient Rome and its imperial eagles conferred on archaeology the character of an ostentatious display. The archaeological activity in the colonies also exercised a deleterious influence on much that was going on in Italy.

In this situation, for instance, a decision was taken at the end of 1938 to carry out high-speed excavations in ancient Ostia in preparation for the 1942 Universal Exhibition, which in fact was never held because of the Second World War. The same circumstances made possible the creation of the Via dell'Impero, which involved digging up the Imperial Forums and demolishing an entire district of Renaissance Rome. All this allowed 'the decisive union of ancient Rome with modern Rome, the resurrection of the ruins and their new symbolic participation in the life of the state' in the words of the director of the German Archaeological Institute, L. Curtius.

It must be said that not all archaeology accommodated itself to the new standards of working, nor did all archaeologists submit to serving fascism. At least one shining example upheld the scientific and moral standard of the discipline, namely U. Zanotti Bianco, doctor and sociologist before he became an archaeologist, who was sentenced in 1934 to police confinement at Paestum. In this situation, together with P. Zancani Montuoro, he dedicated himself to investigating the celebrated Sanctuary of Hera at the mouth of the Sele river. Their excavation of the sanctuary, conducted with the same methodological rigour as in the great European excavatory operations, served to redeem the image of Italian archaeology during those years of provincialism and domination by rhetoric.

The downfall of fascism came about in a climate of strong ideological tension: yet the old guard of archaeologists loyal to the regime succeeded in extricating themselves completely unscathed, still retaining uncontested control of the positions of power. The figure of R. Bianchi Bandinelli dominated in this disheartening scene. Trained in Central Europe, he had begun his scientific career at the beginning of the fascist period. However, his European cultural dimension, and continued interest in what was developing in the capitals of international culture, had enormously extended his own range of observation, thus placing him at the heart of the cultural debate.

Bianchi Bandinelli had no desire to be a theoretician of culture, nor would he have accepted being identified with one particular school or rigid philosophical position. Yet in the immediate postwar period he decided to join the Italian Communist Party, feeling the necessity to make clear the eminently practical character of this choice. Perhaps precisely because he was a free spirit Bianchi Bandinelli always proved ready to understand and try out new approaches in so far as they appeared useful in illuminating the problems he encountered. This interest in what was new enabled him to mediate not only between archaeology and the other human sciences, but also between the Italian experience and the most profitable ideas emerging in the European arena. His training, which was of a Central European type, had as its point of reference the School of Vienna and the thought of A. Riegl. In this environment artistic expression was seen as an aspect of general culture. Interest centred on the complex relationship between artistic expression and the taste of an environment and an era. The concept of taste (*Kunstwollen*) relativised artistic expression since the latter could assume very different forms according to the society which gave rise to it. This conception, which Riegl had tested in the study of artistic craftsmanship of late antiquity, enabled Bianchi Bandinelli to understand forms of artistic expression regarded until then as 'marginal' and inferior to Classical art, for example the art of archaic Greece and Italic art.

In the study of artistic expression in the Italic world, the archaeological culture of the 1930s oscillated between two extreme positions, both of which were incorrect: according to Classical culture of an academic stamp, it consisted of infantile creations without formal dignity. On the other hand, the archaeology of the regime, in its search for 'national roots', exalted Italic art as an expression of an original and 'anti-Classical' taste. It was to Bianchi Bandinelli's credit that he opposed both these simplifications in order to investigate thoroughly the complex relationship between Etruscan and Italic art on the one hand and the figurative culture of the Greek world on the other. His most important work, a collection of essays written before the Second World War, was *Storicità dell'arte classica*. This title had a twofold significance. First, it emphasised the historical character of ancient art and its formal changes consonant with the deep-seated processes of the transformation of society. And second, it signified that the artistic production of the Greek and Roman world was founded upon a tradition which formed the element of continuity and solid *humus* in which all innovations took root. This continuity differentiated Greek from Italic art; the latter had, from time to time, devised expressive new modes, but never managed to organise them into coherent language.

The encounter with the aesthetic of Croce, coming at the beginning of the 1930s, was like a bolt from the blue, but not unproblematic. With its romantic stance and exaltation of poetry as a lyrical intuition situated outside time, the Crocean aesthetic was unable to satisfy for long the desire to discover through the work of art the complexities and tensions of the society of the time.

Even more important was the encounter with Marxist thought. This had ancient roots in Italy, and since the beginning of the century had given birth to a tradition endowed with its own particular physiognomy. However, the influence of Marxist thought on Italian intellectuals after the Second World War was particularly significant, due primarily to the writings of Antonio Gramsci. This Sardinian political theorist distilled his philosophical speculations and reflections on Italian culture and society above all into his *Prison Notebooks*. Fortunately, these were rescued from fascist censorship and published in 1947. If the Marxist *vulgata* was inclined to present history as a produce of economics, Gramsci regarded the link between economics and culture, and between structure and superstructure, as dialectical. If it is not possible to ignore socio-economic analyses in the study of cultural phenomena, it is also true that culture itself often anticipates and modifies processes which are current in actual society. In the historical field Gramsci united this ability to rethink the Marxist tradition with a strong interest in traditions and popular culture. He directed his attention to the existence of diverse levels of culture and expression which operated in specific ways within a particular society. Although the culture of the ruling classes was certainly the official one, it lived in continual tension with other languages specific to the subordinate classes. This conception turned out to be extremely productive in the study of Roman and Italic art, and permitted Bianchi Bandinelli to place its foundations on a new intellectual footing, while recognising an ever stronger bond between society and culture. Bandinelli died on 17 January 1975, having demonstrated in his most recent contributions a new concern for structuralist method as a complement to historical analysis.

A variety of experiences enriched his methodological armoury, but Bianchi Bandinelli remained, and always wished to remain, an art historian. His aim was to show the articulations and transformations of society through the analysis of figurative language. Economic and social history, which formed the background to his research, became the principal topics of interest for many of his students during the 1960s (e.g. F. Coarelli, A. Carandini, M. Torelli, N.F. Parise). Italy had emerged decisively from the tunnel of post-war reconstruction, and, as in other European countries, was in the process of building up an affluent capitalist society. A deep dissatisfaction, ethical even more than political, drove young intellectuals towards Marxism. At first, the new climate was felt to be a reaction against divisions betwen disciplines, and a lively interest was shown in the reconstruction of those aspects of the ancient world such as its economic and social history which traditional archaeology and even ancient sources left in obscurity. Even in the study of the ancient world, Marx's conception of the forms of production assumed a central role. The essential task appeared to be that of establishing those connections which, in any specified economic and social structure, related the producers and the means of production. At first, the attitude was one of rigid orthodoxy, with more or less explicit recourse to the succession of forms of production as described in Marxist texts, and a strong emphasis on economic processes.

These ideas were particularly apparent in the sphere of influence of the journal *Dialoghi di Archeologia* founded in 1967 following an agreement between Bianchi Bandinelli and a group of young people, many his former students. The journal constituted a unique phenomenon in the Italian archaeological scene. The members of the editorial board were in fact elected and responsible to a group of young 'friends of the journal'. In addition to its scientific contributions, the journal contained a political section, written by the 'friends'. In this way the rules of the consortia came to be challenged, by opening up for discussion the formation of laws, the distribution of finances, and irregularities in the organisation both of archaeological training and of the tutelage of the Cultural Properties.

Particularly important in the history of the journal was the conference on the beginnings of the Greek colonisation of the west. This took place at Ischia in 1968 and resulted in a rapprochement between Classical archaeologists and scholars of proto-history (e.g. R. Peroni) drawn together in a productive collaboration with historians of the ancient world (e.g. E. Lepore). This was not a one-off collaboration but had strong motivations which ensured its survival. An interest in the socio-economic aspects of the ancient world had brought Classical archaeologists to a new conception of archaeology as the history not so much of ancient art as of material culture. In this way Classical archaeologists rediscovered the importance of typology, and of the techniques of seriation of handmade artefacts in everyday use. Thus the work of the Classical archaeologist became similar to that of the scholar of prehistory or medieval archaeology. It seemed as if the barricades erected during the first decades of this century had at last been broken down. This situation was doubtless favoured by the activity of such scholars as R. Peroni, who aimed at superseding the typological-definitory approach in order to historicise prehistory. Historians of antiquity such as E. Lepore must be given credit for the acceptance among archaeologists of the anthropological method.

The concept of material culture was new to Italian archaeologists, even though it had long been part of the culture of other countries, such as East European countries. A. Carandini can be credited with introducing this new concept of archaeology into Italy in a pamphlet which appeared in 1975. This was the first book to reflect upon the archaeological situation and its significance in a country in which traditionally no love had been lost between archaeology and theory.

The new interest in material culture necessitated a drastic reappraisal of the significance and techniques of archaeolgical excavation. In this field indeed there had been no attempt at valid theoretical reflection in Italy since the writings of G. Boni at the beginning of the century. The routine procedures of the Superintendencies (central government archaeological authorities) lacked scientific foundation most of the time. Carandini is responsible for introducing into Italy the *open area* method, which in Great Britain had for some time usefully replaced Wheeler's method. The appearance of Caradini's treatise on the technique of excavation, and the translation in the next few years of the principal contributions to the subject from abroad, profoundly altered the Italian archaeological scene, bringing significant improvement in the average quality of operations, even in the troubled area of rescue excavations.

Before discussing the latest developments in Italian archaeology, it is necessary to say something about what happened in the area of prehistory after the Second World War, since here also current developments have their roots in that period.

The tradition of G. Boni and P. Orsi, who rejected the separation between prehistory and the Classical world, was carried on by L. Bernabò Brea, who had dominated the Italian scientific scene from the 1940s to the present. In the field of prehistory he has been responsible for such fundamentally important excavations as the cave of the Arene Candide near Finale Ligure, those at Lipari, and the scientific systematisation of the excavations at Poliochni (Lemnos). As a result of these fundamental operations and others too numerous to mention, this Genoese scholar has resystematised the prehistory of Italy, Sicily and the Aegean. His excavations and publications relating to Sicily and the Magna Graecia of the Classical era have been equally important. Essential to Bernabò Brea's stance is the rejection of every cultural fashion. So also is the use of whatever heuristic tools seem appropriate for the reconstruction of the historical picture, from the arguments provided by diffusionism to the use of typology as an instrument for defining the *facies* and their succession in time. For him it is important constantly to compare the data documented by archaeology with the traditions about ancient peoples handed down by Greek and Roman writers, in the attempt to historicise prehistory.

Very different is the approach of S.M. Puglisi. For a long time he occupied the chair of prehistory in the University of Rome, accumulating an outstanding group of students. He also has ranged freely over a wide geographical and cultural area, from Italy to Africa and the Anatolian plateau. Puglisi, however, has been less inclined to grand systematic syntheses and more interested in problems connected with the interpretation of archaeological evidence. His work shows traces of the ideas which in those years were being developed by V. Gordon Childe. For Puglisi also, the characterisation of a culture cannot be limited to the simple definition of a typological repertory of handmade artefacts: culture is primarily the way in which a human group organises its economic behaviour and its relationship to the environment. In this respect, the definition of a *facies* on the grounds of the typology of handmade artefacts is of secondary interest. A typological inventory is the product of a specified economic and social structure, and can recur over a long period where the structural conditions remain unaltered. Thus it is not possible to establish *tout court* chronological equations between similar *facies*. On these grounds he believed, for example, that the typical *facies* of the Bronze Age persisted in Puglia well after the threshold of the first millennium, preserving unchanged the formal repertory of the second. In a volume published in 1959 Puglisi expressed more fully his ideas about the Bronze Age culture which developed over many centuries throughout a large part of the Italian peninsula. He proposed a global reconstruction of this civilisation, in its cultural, economic and productive aspects, as well as in its process of formation, which he sought to explain, not in terms of diffusion, but on the basis of what was then known of preceding local *facies*. His attempts at reinterpreting each class of handmade artefact in relation to the prevailing mode of production was also important, thus correcting the symbolico-religious interpretations which were then prevalent. Using these new interpretative models he showed how archaeology could make a valid contribution to the reconstruction of the economic basis of an ancient society.

In essence, Puglisi's approach was inspired by an orthodox Marxism in line with that of Childe. His attention to problems of methodology became an effective stimulus in an archaeological scene little inclined to concern itself with theory. This became even more explicit, and to some extent dominant, in his students, who have retained his essential characteristics (e.g. M. Tosi, A. Palmieri, A. Cazzella). Their presence on the cultural scene has had a marked impact in recent years; this brings us to the last fifteen years.

In this period, in line with a world-wide trend, the most progressive branch of Italian archaeology has been entirely dominated by anthropology. The divisions within anthropology have become more marked, and so in this respect the story of *Dialoghi di Archeologia* is typical.

This journal, in the sphere of proto-history, was first engaged in the attempt at a global reconstruction of the life of ancient communities by some very interesting experiments, particularly those relating to Rome and Latium. Interest in bio-archaeology has favoured the study of the complex relationship between human communities and their environment; at the same time the attention to settlement strategies and multicausal processes gave greater breadth to attempts at historical reconstruction. Behind these new directions in research are the pioneering studies by H. Mueller Karpe and R. Peroni on the political and social structuring processes within proto-historic communities. These scholars undertook the analysis of the necropolises with methods based on typology and the seriation of contexts. These methods, which nowadays would be hastily dismissed as 'Monteliusian', facilitated a new approach to proto-history. Adherence to the models of the New Archaeology matured at the same time as it began to lose its momentum in the United States and the most advanced European culture. The result was a kind of closure against any life still remaining in the Italian post-war cultural tradition. The necropolises which provide fundamental and controlling evidence for the studies of proto-history are now examined by the use of quantitative criteria and mathematical formulations, seeking in them a direct mirroring of actual society. In spite of these reservations, there is no doubt that this kind of research is contributing to a period of considerable methodological reflection, which imposes a new rigour on the treatment of data and on the verification of models for the study of ancient communities.

A different conception of the anthropology of the ancient world was maturing slowly in the sphere of influence of the *Dialoghi di Archeologia* from the end of the second half of the 1960s. N.F. Parise had initiated this conception by his reading of Mauss and Polanyi, who enabled him to see the problems of the origin and significance of coins in the ancient world in a new light. A specific stimulus in this direction had come from ancient historians. Also, at that time, the culture of the Left in Italy, as in France, was undergoing an important process of methodological revision: at the centre of the debate were Marx's writings on precapitalist economic structures. In French anthropology, this led to the conclusion that economics should not necessarily be regarded as the immediate driving-force of the social dynamic in pre-capitalist societies. To be sure, even simple communities are affected by economic factors, but these are mediated through other mental categories such as religion or family relationships. This reformulation of Marxist thought, due principally to M. Godelier but clearly inspired by Louis Althusser, made it possible to enlarge the field of enquiry considerably, by attempting a reconstruction of ancient societies, including even those aspects which had been relegated to the superstructure. This was the context of a meeting of scholars working in the *Centre des recherches comparées sur les sociétés anciennes*, directed by J.P. Vernant. The study of the ancient mentality is carried out here according to procedures outlined in the 1930s by L. Gernet. These were developed in original ways by a very diverse range of scientists, each with a strong individuality, such as Vernant himself, P. Vidal Naquet, N. Loraux, A. Schnapp and others. The inspiration of the sociological tradition of Durkheim and Mauss, and of the psychology of history of Meyerson, was combined with the Lévi-Strauss's structuralism which was particularly alive in scholars like M. Detienne. Most stimulating for archaeologists was the realisation that, by studying the ancient mentality and changes in the conception of reality, it was possible to get a feel for the great socio-political and structural transformations. For the scholars of the Centre, as already for L. Gernet, interest focuses on the moment of birth of the Greek *polis* and the great changes which accompany it, in religion and law, in philosophical and scientific thought, in art and in literature.

For the archaeologist, this engagement with the study of ancient societies opened a new field of enquiry, alternative to that of the material culture proposed by Carandini. The latter had correctly put forward as evidence the 'unintentional testimony' appropriate to archaeological documentation. This definition was adequate for the 'everyday refuse' contained in the strata which cover an ancient settlement. But alongside this kind of evidence, there is another, which, by contrast, is invested with the maximum of intentionality. For example, in necropolises and tombs, each element, from the arrangement of the burial-places to their shape, from the funerary rites to the choice and disposition of the grave goods, has been considered and arranged in advance for the moment of highest social performance in the ancient world, i.e. death. Studying a group of tombs or a necropolis involves the reassembling of a system of structured signs which represent the society of the living in its social and functional hierarchy. It is not, however, a mechanical type of mirroring; rather the representation is organised according to its own rules. These can reflect relationships to the real, or render them in a reversed way, transformed, so that, between the real and its representation, there is established a metaphorical type of relationship. In reconstructing the system and understanding its relationship with the real, what counts is the analysis of qualitative differences. It would be illusory to rely upon quantitative criteria and statistics as if they reflected *tout court* the articulations of actual society.

The stimulus provided by the study of the ancient mentality has led, in Italy as in France, to the pursuit of iconographic and iconological research. In this connection, there existed in Italy the important tradition of research associated with the name of Bianchi Bandinelli, also responsible for publicising in Italy the methods of research employed by the school of Vienna and the followers of A. Warburg. An important contribution in this direction has been made by M. Taddei with his iconological studies of Indian art. A new field has been opened up in the study of the figurative cycles of Greek and Italic tombs by A. Pontrandolfo and A. Rouveret. By applying the semiological method to this kind of evidence, they identified various systems of funerary representations which have complex implications for social and cultural history. This current in Italian anthropology, which is keeping an attentive but critical eye on the experiments of the New Archaeology, has remained substantially faithful to the Italian Marxist historicist tradition. It emphasises both the synchronic and diachronic dimensions in the search for a point of equilibrium between structure and history.

Note

This chapter was translated into English by Margaret A. Wilson.

References

Bianchi Bandinelli, R. (1974) *AA.BB.AA e BC. L'Italia storica e artistica allo sbaraglio*, Bari.
Carandini, A. (1975) 'Archeologia e Cultura materiale', Bari.
Manacorda, D. (1982) 'Cento anni di ricerche archeologiche italiane: il dibattito sul metodo', *Quaderni di Storia* 16: 8ff.
—— (1982) 'Per una indagine sull'archeologia italiana durante il ventennio fascista', *Archeologia Medievale* 9: 443ff.
d' Agostino, B. (1984) '*Italy*', in H. Cleere (ed.) *Approaches to the Archaeological Heritage*, Cambridge.
—— (1985) 'Le strutture antiche del territorio', *Annali della Storia d'Italia* vol. VIII, Rome: Einaudi.

4

THE POWERFUL PAST: THEORETICAL TRENDS IN GREEK ARCHAEOLOGY

Kostas Kotsakis[1]

Introduction: A Historical Perspective

For a small country like Greece, archaeology has always had a much more central role than in other European countries. Even though European archaeology had constantly identified itself with the reconstruction of a European past (Leone 1982a; Trigger 1984), in Greece this past had at a very early stage acquired a social and political significance of a very high order (Skopetea 1984). This concern with the past – 'our past', as most of the Greek scholars of the nineteenth century would have it – was not only a central theme of the Greek intellectual background at the end of the eighteenth century (Dimaras 1985) but also a firm political issue with obvious links with national patriotic aspirations.

Archaeological monuments were soon to become the very emblems of the new Greek state which emerged after the struggle against Ottoman rule in 1821. One of the symbolic acts which vividly describes this close relationship was the restoration of a Parthenon column drum to welcome King Otto, the Bavarian prince who was assigned to the throne of Greece, to his new capital Athens in 1835 (Skopetea 1984: 179). But even before this symbolic act of ideological unity between the classicist ideas and the expression of state power, the emerging Greek state had already announced its determination to ensure the protection of its 'antiquities' – which in the terms of the period meant exclusively monuments of the Classical Greek past – through concrete administrative measures (Kokkou 1977: 39–46; Petrakos 1982: 16–19). State patronage was thus officially introduced into Greek archaeology.

Greece was clearly not the only European country to fetishise its past in order to add the necessary colouring to the dominant ideology. The post-Napoleonic era in the early nineteenth century witnessed, throughout Europe, a marked increase in nationalistic sentiments backed by the romanticism prevalent at the time (Trigger 1984: 358). Archaeology was very soon enlisted into the service of the glorification of the past and a very definite patriotic content was included. However, what is perhaps unique in the case of Greek archaeology is that this ideological use of the past had at least two distinctive aspects: one is the upsurge of nationalistic feeling which turned the focus of interest to the monuments and history and also a whole set of cultural phenomena (Politis 1984); the other is an active international concern for the Classical Greek past, stemming this time not from an ethnic relation but from a conception of a definite cultural descent. So, to use Trigger's terms (1984), archaeology practised in Greece by Greeks and foreigners was from the beginning nationalist and imperialist respectively. As a consequence, there was very little room left for any original approach which would escape this dichotomous impasse.

It is not at all my intention here to discuss the complicated problems of the formation of Greek national consciousness, especially in relation to attitudes concerning the integration of the past in the political and ethnic models of the nineteenth century (Skopetea 1984). It seems, however, that for certain social strata of the emerging Greek society at the beginning of the century the realisation of the ideological potential of a glorious past was not exclusively linked to the European romantic movement. Rather, the romantic movement found fertile ground in an already existing, albeit somewhat loosely compiled, set of ideas claiming links with the ancient Greeks. Thus, in contrast to the romantic movement, this attitude did not refer to Greece as described by the classicism of the time, but as a part of a long tradition stemming from the final centuries of the Byzantine era and established during the long dark period before the nineteenth century (Svoronos 1981: 58; Dimaras 1985: 124–36; *contra* Mango 1965, 1984). What perhaps romanticism made more explicit was the need to operationalise this tradition by bringing in concrete factual evidence.

At the turn of the century the picture of Greek archaeology was therefore fairly complex. The dominant ideology (Leone *et al.* 1987) projected from the new Greek kingdom was modelled on a direct kinship with the past. Within this ideology one can find expressions of conflicting social groups: that of the emerging middle class as well as the administrative elite with roots in the eighteenth century was one element (Svoronos 1981: 31–64, 92–4; 1987: 218–36), but there was also, though at times suppressed, the almost spontaneous prescientific conception of care for antiquities. This deeply embedded folk consciousness is presumably a partial result of the tradition implied above (Skopetea 1984: 180–81). On the other hand, the concern of the European centres of archaeology with Greece emphasises a definite split in this historically structured set of ideas by introducing the scientific standards of the time. For a considerable number of active Greek archaeologists, this simply meant nothing other than provincialisation, which would inevitably result in an even more introverted and ethnocentric scientific attitude (Skopetea 1984: 182). So in the case of Greek archaeology – as well as history and folklore studies – the dominant ideology, under the banner of national identity, reinforced both directly and indirectly by the foreign interest in Greek antiquities and taking advantage of the positive disposition of the people, emerged as a belief in diachronic continuity in Greek history, a unity in space and time, showing minimum interest in any other aspect of it (Kyriakidou-Nestoros 1978: 44–6).

There was indeed very little chance of including in this strict ideological model anything that would not establish a direct continuity with the Classical Greek past, since anything else was either disregarded or seen as an unnecessary complication. The Middle Ages in Greece provide such an example: only late in the nineteenth century was their significance generally recognised among scholars and intellectuals (Dimaras 1985: 398–400; Skopetea 1984: 166–9) while official interest in the fate of the monuments of the period had to wait until the foundation of the Byzantine Museum in Athens in 1914 (Kokkou 1977: 283–6). The fate of prehistoric archaeology was similar, with the possible exception of the part which could either be related to proto-history through legends and the Homeric poems, or seen as a prelude to the Classical civilisation (Tsountas 1928). The discussion by Tsountas, the founder of Greek prehistoric archaeology (1909: 390–5), of the close relationship between the neolithic 'megaron' and the Classical doric temple is particularly enlightening in this respect. It proved that the quest for continuity could be extended both ways, forwards and backwards from the Classical pivot.

Even more serious consequences for the development of Greek archaeology can be discerned in the power and self-sufficiency of this ethnocentric ideological construct. Being a solid paradigm for research, it literally legitimised the absence of any theoretical discussion. The focus of research was sufficiently well defined: diachronic continuity, which after a certain stage became commonplace enough not to require proof, at least not in archaeology. Continuity had more or less become normal science in the Kuhnian sense (Kuhn 1970), and was therefore considered self-evident. Instead, it was sufficient to treat these cultural traces as though they had some important content, immediately useful and relevant to modern Greeks for a variety of reasons (see e.g. Karouzos 1967; Romaios 1955). Most often this concern was sought in a history of art (Karouzos 1961) based on the Hegelian German tradition of Riegl and Wölflin (Whitley 1987).

From this point of view there was no particular urge for Greek archaeologists to follow European theoretical orientations. There was no universal application to begin with. Archaeology simply did not seem to be concerned with abstract human activity on a world-wide scale or with abstract historical process. Human history, a central theme in countries like England with a leading international political role at the time (Trigger 1984: 364), was of no concern to Greek history. Greek archaeology was in fact defining itself and its audience with much more modest limits in mind. The idea of progress, closely related to the middle classes (Trigger 1981), social evolutionism and its negative image – diffusionism – prevalent in Europe (Daniel 1963; Trigger 1978, 1980), the environmental determinism of Ratzel (Earle and Preucel 1987), the historical particularism of Boas (Harris 1968) in its archaeological aspect, left Greek archaeology almost completely unaffected. Some more or less remote echoes of these shifting paradigms are barely recognisable in Greek anthropology no earlier than the first quarter of the twentieth century (Kyriakidou-Nestoros 1978: 99–120). In the case of archaeology, one had to wait even longer.

I will not attempt to deal further with the historical formation of the body of beliefs and ideas that constitute Greek archaeology and its interpretative apparatus. It would require much more extensive treatment and documentation of the impact the political history of modern Greece had had on the position of Greek archaeologists in Greek pre- and post-war society, the role of Greece itself in relation to the hegemony of foreign countries, even the consequences of the defeat of the left-wing movement in the civil war of 1946–9, to name but a few. Last but not least, this attempt would require a survey of the degree to which differing groups of individuals accept the dominant interpretation of the past (Hodder 1986: 167), in other words an evaluation of the reliability of the dominant ideology itself.

This introductory discussion is meant to show that what has often been described as the lack of theory in Greek archaeology (Chourmouziadis 1978; 1986) is not simply the result of Greece being outside the centres of theoretical innovation. It is also – and perhaps most importantly – the concrete result of historical processes that from a very early date have tied the reconstruction of the past to a specific political programme. It is interesting to note in this respect that similar orientations in archaeology have been developed in other Balkan countries as well, under the concept of ethnogenesis (Davis 1983: 419).

We are nowadays much better prepared theoretically to accept the ideological content of our reconstructions of the past and place them in their context (Rowlands 1984), although this critique has more or less always been part of the standard Marxian discourse (Goldman 1969). The elaboration of this argument will take us back to 'Feuerbach' and *The German Ideology* (Marx 1976) or even to dichotomies like science versus consciousness which do not seem welcome any more in certain post-processual quarters (Hodder 1987b). The awareness achieved nevertheless is largely related to the recent specific affirmation that the reconstruction of the past has considerable potential for revealing the deeper logic of archaeological interpretations (Hodder 1984; Shennan 1986; Shanks and Tilley 1987) or – in its Marxist version (Leone 1982a, 1982b; Leone et al. 1987) – for '[helping] those who write or dig the history to become aware of the ideological notions that generate modern everyday life' (Leone 1982b: 754). In what follows, I will try to trace this trail of Greek prehistoric archaeology, not aiming at a 'history' of the discipline, but rather at the critical evaluation of its theoretical background. This discussion will not include Classical archaeology. The reasons are twofold: on the one hand, Classical archaeology has developed into a separate, more or less closed system with minimal rapport with developments in Anglo-American archaeology (Cartledge 1986; Snodgrass

1987). On the other hand, partly as a result of this theoretical isolation, prehistoric archaeology is rapidly diverging from an accord with the unchanging concepts and practices of Classical archaeology (Snodgrass 1987: 2–3). Thus, even in the specific case of Greece, where this confined affinity was operative until fairly recently, it would no longer be feasible, and would indeed be misleading, to discuss them as a single theoretical field.

The first paradigms in Greek prehistory

We cannot really speak of the introduction of theoretical paradigms in Greek prehistoric archaeology until after the Second World War. The first half of the twentieth century, spurred on by the discovery of the Mycenaean and Minoan civilisations (Sherratt 1980: 136–43), was largely characterised by the quest for establishing the prehistory of the Greeks. The formal discussion was initiated from the well-known article of Haley and Blegen (1928) and culminated as late as 1970 in a Colloquium on Bronze Age Migrations held in Sheffield (Crossland and Birchall 1973). Only one Greek archaeologist took part in the colloquium, S. Marinatos (Marinatos 1973a, 1973b). This was probably the last official expression of this long argument, which revolved around migrationism and diffusionism in a Montelian fashion, and, interestingly enough, it was decisively undermined by a model of indigenous neolithic development presented there by Renfrew (1973b).

Perhaps the most striking development during this period was precisely the assertion of a central role for the identity of prehistoric Greeks. This of course was not surprising in view of the ideological horizon which, as described above, had already been formed, even though it now often reached the ultimate limits of absurdity and inadvertently deflected interest from other sources of information. For most Greek archaeologists of this period, acting within an administrative structure which did not really separate prehistoric from Classical archaeology, bringing the Greeks into prehistory was not even a question of diffusion or migration, but rather of showing once again the continuity of a charismatic culture. In doing this they stated their belief in a unified archaeological field based on common objectives. This trend was certainly reinforced by studies such as Nilsson's *The Mycenaean Origins of Greek Mythology* (1932); but reading on

to Bronze Age artefacts – of which very little was actually understood – myths and legends surviving in the Homeric poems or in
the Classical literature was hardly justified fifty years or more
after Schliemann's idiosyncratic contribution to Aegean archaeology. Yet it was a practice which died very hard (see e.g. Marinatos 1971).

Needless to say, during this same period there were archaeologists who were pursuing more modest aims, producing nevertheless much more concrete and sound results. A whole body of
archaeological data was compiled during this period and published
both then and later (e.g. Mylonas 1928, 1929; Platon 1965). I will
mention only A. Keramopoullos as a case of remarkable ingenuity
and inventiveness who nevertheless did not find any followers, a
telling example of discontinuities apparent in a discipline with an
atheoretical structure, as discussed above. There is no evidence
that Keramopoullos was familiar with the works of O. G. S.
Crawford (1912) or Cyril Fox (1922), but his survey work on
west Macedonia (1932, 1933) clearly included a diachronic and
geographical aspect which was without precedent in Greek archaeology at that time. It took almost fifty years before similar work
was produced, as a result not of the influence of Keramopoullos
but rather of the survey activities of the foreign archaeological
schools in Greece.

Moving away from the domination of these quasi-historical
interpretations and towards the emancipation of prehistory in
Greece from its heavy ideological burden was obviously a very
long process. In an ambitious multi-volumed collective edition
which appeared as late as 1970 under the title *Istoria tou Ellinikou
Ethnous* ('History of the Greek Nation') (Christopoulos *et al.*
1970) one reads in the programmatic statements in the preface (p.
4):

> This continuous march of man on the Greek land through
> millennia, from the first settlements of the Stone Age up to
> the present day, is followed by the history of the Greek
> Nation. It presents the documented continuity of the Greek
> World, its cultural unity and the internal integrity of Greek
> culture.[2]

And further on (p. 9):

> just as today the annexation of the Creto-Mycenaean World

71

to Greek History is considered natural, so tomorrow every-
one will accept a truth which is already visible, that the basic
roots of the Greek Nation and the main components of the
Greek Spirit are laid in Prehistory!

Almost 150 years after the romantic *Volksgeist*, a call to an ach-
ronic Greek Spirit as an expression of an apolitical Greek Nation
strikes one as definitely misplaced in time.

The 'History of the Greek Nation' is notable, however, for
another reason, that is for bringing together all the active Greek
prehistorians of the time. Among them D. R. Theocharis, who
already had a long career in archaeology, was responsible for the
chapters on the neolithic and the Early Bronze Age (Theocharis
1970: 32–79, 88–97). With the work of D. R. Theocharis prehistoric archaeology took a considerable step towards recognition as
a separate and respectable discipline, and not simply as a necessary
stage preceding the study of the Classical period. His archaeological activity coincided with the post-war period. In many ways this
was a period of tremendous new possibilities for Greek prehistory,
although it was also a time of rapid transformation of a society
which emerged from a ten-year war with countless losses. Fast
rates of urbanisation and extensive mechanisation of agriculture
were among the main symptoms of this transformation. They are
not unknown elsewhere, in both industrialised (Fowler 1982) and
developing countries (Miller 1980) and they have always posed a
severe threat to antiquities. The notable increase in archaeological
activity in Greece which followed the post-war years (Petrakos
1982: 98) was in part a result of the pressure for the preservation
of a threatened cultural heritage.

Prehistoric archaeology, and with it Theocharis as a professional
archaeologist, were forced to face a number of new problems.
First was the absolute need for the collection of data, for chronology, for some sort of systematics. As the principal effort before
the war was directed towards the Bronze Age civilisations of the
Aegean, very little was actually known about the Stone Age itself
(Weinberg 1970: 557). Second came the problems of interpretation
which were also rapidly accumulating and demanding attention.
The major incentive was the work done in the Fertile Crescent
of south-western Asia by the Chicago expedition (Braidwood and
Howe 1960), which offered an interpretative framework of some
potential but, even more importantly, led the way towards an

elaboration of the concept of the neolithic in its application to Greece. It is in this context that one must conceptualise the introduction in Greece of the literature concerning the 'neolithic revolution', mainly that of Childe (1951, 1952).

Much work had been done in the field in the meantime, especially in Thessaly, and the pragmatic aspect of the argument was adequately described (Theocharis 1957, 1958, 1962). Backed by the German archaeological project of Thessaly which was producing similar results (Milojčić 1960), factual archaeological knowledge of the period was quickly moving towards standardisation, which at the time seemed necessary (Theocharis 1967: 127) although it later received much criticism (Chourmouziadis 1971: 187). In terms of methodology this effort was greatly influenced by the practice of V. Milojčić, who was applying what he termed a 'comparative-typological' method (Milojčić 1949). Obviously the method echoes distantly F. Ratzel's and G. Kossinna's ideas (Trigger 1978: 54–95), but also Childe's approach and the culture group concept, although a statement of paradigmatic preferences of some sort was tacitly avoided. In fact, the German version, as applied in Thessaly, is far more positivistic and pragmatic than the Childean historical explanations (Renfrew 1982: 5–23; Kotsakis 1983: 6), we we will see below.

It is not therefore at all strange that the outcome of this dual effort was on the one hand to systematise the available evidence for the beginning of the neolithic, and on the other to interpret the evidence in terms of cultural history (Theocharis 1967). The theoretical framework of this interpretative approach is strictly Childean (Theocharis 1967: 4, note 2). The title of the principal work is also very characteristic: *I Augi tis Thessalikis Proistorias* ('The dawn of Thessalian prehistory'), an obvious homage to Childe, but also containing the scarcely unnoticeable change of 'Civilisation' in the original, to 'prehistory'. This is no accident of course. It is implicitly explained by Theocharis himself in his introduction:

> adding new material . . . seems now more necessary and more important than any theoretical conjecture. . . . Our aim is to start from real facts *and not from an interpretative theory of culture* and add to the knowledge of the beginning of the neolithic in Thessaly.
>
> (Theocharis 1967: 5; my italics)

I believe that this statement of pragmatic faith is an accurate picture of Greek archaeology at the time. The theoretical paradigm of Childe's culture history is accepted, but not without a certain reluctance to assume the full responsibility of this commitment. The concept of history itself is fundamentally different: it is immediately reducible from the facts, no 'theoretical conjecture' is necessary. As Price has mentioned in his discussion of cultural materialism and American archaeology, 'History per se constitutes an *explanans*' (1982: 736). The *explanandum*, which in Childe's case might be 'social evolution', was thought to lie beyond archaeology. Materialist prospects on the other hand (Kohl 1981) and most of all the Marxist aspects of Childe's sociology (Spriggs 1977; Trigger 1980) were tacitly rejected or simply ignored. This is not an altogether unfamiliar stance for a considerable part of the European archaeology of the time (Kristiansen 1984: 74). However, in Greece of the post-war years, in so far as the dominant feature was an extremely unstable political scene, an archaeology of Marxist origins was not always simply a question of academic choice. Within this context explanation of the beginning of the neolithic in Greece was bound to be what a Binfordian would call 'idiographic'.

In many ways the introduction of the cultural-history paradigm in Greek archaeology, even though the limitations as described above were serious, was a predictable development. It was the closest possible to what archaeology in Greece has always thought itself to be about: establishing the continuity of Greek history. Placing the culture model in this framework seemed to fit very well indeed. Theocharis himself was reluctant to tackle this problem directly in the *Augi* volume, although he specifically discusses the point in a brief paper in 1969 (Theocharis 1969). Six years later, however, in a synthesis of the neolithic in Greece intended for a more general audience (Theocharis 1973), he stated:

> Greece is the land where the most ancient cultural tradition of the world is continuously active! . . . We are not of course referring to a racial continuity . . . We are simply stressing the fact that long-lasting and unbreakable ties are still active from the prehistoric times up to the present between the people, bearer and creator of this tradition, and the *place*.
>
> (Theocharis 1973: 20; author's italics)

This time the argument is not about something to be proven, as it used to be in the nineteenth or early twentieth centuries. It is rather a premise, an axiomatic statement, or even a part of the dominant ideology. But one should not fail to notice here the explicit diversion from the traditional ethnic model. Now, the centre of gravity shifts from an abstract ethnic identity to the much more versatile concept of place, the field of cultural activity. It is again not devoid of political meaning but it is opening the way for a new paradigm resting on the basic functionalist idea of a cultural entity functioning in many dimensions. It is clearly stated further on: 'culture . . . is an organic whole of material and intellectual achievements' (Theocharis 1973: 21). Functionalism of this kind is not alien to Childe's thinking (Kohl 1981: 91), nor even to former Greek ethnological studies (Kyriakidis 1939), but it seems more probable that it was introduced in Aegean archaeology as part of an explanatory scheme put forth by Renfrew in his influential book, *The Emergence of Civilization* (1972). The system and its subsystems model (pp. 19–23) was the pivotal point of this work (Gilman 1981: 2–3) which was specifically cited in 'Neolithic Greece' (Theocharis 1973). Theocharis describes the cultural entity in space not in terms of the systems theory *per se*, but nevertheless as the closely interrelated aspects of a single culture, the neolithic culture. In the same volume, the treatment of ideological behaviour such as mortuary practices (Chourmouziadis 1973: 201–12), of economic structures such as agriculture (J. Renfrew 1973: 147–64), animal husbandry (Bökönyi 1973: 179–200), together with hints on social structure (Theocharis 1973: 68–77), echoes very distantly the technomic, sociotechnic and ideotechnic subsystems of the Binfordian arsenal. The subsistence, technological, social, symbolic and trade subsystems of Renfrew's *Emergence* (1972: 21–3) are perhaps less vaguely implied, although no specific reference to the relevant literature is given, nor are the relevant terms used.

However, what is different in Theocharis's reconstruction of the neolithic and more generally in the Greek prehistory of the time, in comparison with contemporary developments in Anglo-Saxon archaeology, is not solely a question of terms. Rather, it is the reluctance to accept fully a rigid theoretical framework based foremost on a functionalist trend, the definite synchronic characteristics of which have had minimal hold on Greek intellectual tradition (Skouteri 1979). Historical reconstructions, on the contrary, not necessarily understood in all cases – as argued above –

in strict Childean terms (Childe 1958), offered considerably more time depth, which in the archaeology of the early 1970s was still regarded as the essential element for the study of Greek prehistory. Therefore, the anthropology vs. history debate current at the time in the Americas (Binford 1972) and Europe (Clarke 1968, 1972; Hawkes 1968; Renfrew 1973c) was once again decided in favour of history, not because a thorough discussion had taken place, but because the stakes of abandoning hastily a long tradition of historical reconstruction of continuity were deemed dangerously high.

The new paradigms: rejection and diversification

This conservative inertia in the use of the past and the specific role of traditionalism in Greek society had been nevertheless at times very strongly discredited on the basis of its often conspicuous – occasionally even blatant – political affiliations (Moshou 1983: 13–16). It took, however, a considerable span of time for these more general sociological remarks to reach archaeological discourse. It was only in 1978 – five years after 'Neolithic Greece' – that a paper challenging the theoretical background of normal archaeology appeared (Chourmouziadis 1978). In this paper Chourmouziadis chose to counter the arguments of traditional wisdom directly, by discussing a crucial problem hitherto completely invisible – save for various trivial assertions – in Greek prehistory. This is nothing less than the problem of ideology, a focal point in recent archaeological theory (Rowlands 1982; Shanks and Tilley 1982; Miller and Tilley 1984; Hodder 1986; Shennan 1986), but undoubtedly one underexploited at the time, or rather almost banished from the vocabulary of the New Archaeology under the charge of psychologism (e.g. Athens 1978: 354; Fritz 1978; but see also Friedman and Rowlands 1977).

It goes without saying that this choice was not unrelated to the political connotations that over the long history of Greek intellectual development had become gradually and inextricably tied to archaeological commonplaces. A radical critique of this collection of epistemological dead-ends would inevitably mean a reaction against its political alibis:

> these [social] relations within which . . . these objects are subjectified (i.e. acquire a historical character) are potential

relations which are established only through ideology. . . .
This forces me to believe that the archaeological material
which every systematic excavation brings to light and to our
disposal should not simply be evaluated in terms of typological or chronological classifications. . . . A restriction of this
kind does not advance research towards explaining or even
simply stating the problems related to a prehistoric settlement
(a prehistoric social formation) *in its totality.*

(Chourmouziadis 1978: 30–1; my italics)

It is not difficult to recognise in this early emphasis on material
culture as ideology definite Marxist (or neo-Marxist) tones. The
idea of social formation, the social relations of production, but
most of all the concept of totality of explanation, that is of explaining the deeper economic and ideological structures of prehistoric
society, are all familiar Marxist analytical categories. They are
here introduced as a direct rejection of a pragmatic, segmented
archaeology, which has often been accused of being reducible to
simple descriptive statements of dubious value. But at the same
time they are clearly aiming at a radically different conception of
the past, one that would treat it not simply as a token of an ethnic
or historic continuity, but as a living reality, paradigmatically
relevant to the present.

The concept of ideology itself is largely based on the Althusserian idea of the materiality of ideology, as described in *Positions*
(Althusser 1976). This materiality is sought by Chourmouziadis
in three distinct social practices (1978: 31). In spite of the use here
of some jargon from systems theory, such as 'negative feedback' or
'homeostasis', very little of classical systems theory (Clarke 1968;
Hill 1977) is in fact incorporated. The 'systems' in this context
are not conceived as holistic functionalist devices that maintain a
predefined stability and equilibrium (Hodder 1982: 3; Shanks and
Tilley 1987: 52–3) but as entities that embody the driving force
of the productive process. In this capacity, within the given social
formation, they are able to transform themselves as well as to
reproduce themselves with the intervention of ideology and they
have a definite historical content (Chourmouziadis 1979: 24–7).
No doubt much can be said also on the Althusserian conceptualisation of ideology, not least on his academic epistemological distinction between science and ideology, as Shanks and Tilley have
pointed out (1982: 121; see also Benton 1977: 182–92). The under-

estimation of the role of contradiction and conflict (Shanks and Tilley 1982: 131; Miller and Tilley 1984: 13) as a factor contributing to the formation of ideology is a characteristic that is also noticeable in the reconstructions of Greek prehistory under discussion. But whatever the minor reservations might be (see also Lianeris 1982), the fact remains that this paper marks a genuine split with a tradition that for decades dominated Greek archaeology.

The trend becomes even more pronounced with the increased influence of the French Marxist anthropologists who take up the approach to Marx's work formulated by Althusser which can be observed in later papers by Chourmouziadis (1980; 1981) on the 'neolithic mode of production'. The title itself indicates concern with the theoretical construction of non-capitalist primitive modes of production which is the main theme of the work of anthropologists such as Terray (1969, 1975), Godelier (1977, 1978, 1979) and Meillassoux (1964), who now appear for the first time in the archaeological literature in Greece. The neolithic mode of production is treated accordingly in close relation to ideological structures active within the social network (Chourmouziadis 1980: 121–2), although themes from the so-called Marxist orthodoxy such as the precedence in the last instance of material productive forces over productive relations are nevertheless not conclusively rejected (Chourmouziadis 1980: 120; 1979; 1983: 113–14).

Marxism was clearly the most powerful tool to face the content of the historical reconstructions which has haunted Greek archaeology ever since the nineteenth century. It showed if nothing else that there was in fact 'another way of telling' (Spriggs 1984) which had great explanatory potential. But the split I have just mentioned badly needed a methodological framework to become operational. This was sought in the materialism of the New Archaeology.

To neolithiko Dimini (Chourmouziadis 1979) is a major work that attempts precisely this difficult task. Just as *Emergence* (Renfrew 1972) before it had introduced systems theory into Aegean archaeology, this is in turn an introduction of New Archaeology into Greek literature, profuse with references to the work of Renfrew, Binford and Flannery, but at the same time offering a subtle critique of neo-positivistic empiricism. For Chourmouziadis, the basic premise is that the failure of past approaches to Greek prehistory is mainly a result of theoretical inadequacy. This is a famous Binfordism of course, but Chourmouziadis departs quickly from the neo-positivistic pragmatism (Kolakowski 1972: 10) by seeking explanations not in quantified (Binford 1962; Clarke 1968) or statistical (Salmon 1982) causal relationships, but in the parameters that are set by the mode of production (Chourmouziadis 1979: 17–19). This is essentially a historical approach not in the sense of continuity or cultural identity of some sort, but in the sense of the transformations of the mode of production which are thought to relate to the changes deducible from the archaeological record. Cultural change, a perennial archaeological problem, especially for Greece as Renfrew has aptly demonstrated (1972; 1979; Renfrew and Wagstaff 1982), is thus treated not as an adaptive process (Binford 1968) but as a result of concrete human actions, socially determined (Chourmouziadis 1979: 26).

At first glance there seems to be an unsurpassable contradiction between the acceptance of an essentially Marxist perspective and the empiricist neo-positivism of the New Archaeology programme. I have already argued how very remote is the relation between systems as understood by Chourmouziadis and as applied in the New Archaeology. Besides, in this broader sense, the 'systemic' character of many neo-Marxist approaches is well known and needs hardly any further comment. As Shennan remarks (1986: 329), even Friedman and Rowland's model (1977), one of the most influential Marxist syntheses of the last decade, has a definite systemic character, referring to the systems ideas in biology. Chourmouziadis himself discusses only in passing the theoretical affinities between the neo-Marxist positions and those of the New Archaeology (1979: n. 6). In outlining briefly this relationship one can point out that the affinities are based essentially not so much on an abstract interest in socio-economic process but rather on a more specific materialist approach (Kohl 1981). It derives from cultural materialism in anthropology (Price 1982) and shares with it the same rejection of Boas's historical particularism and the same inclination for the reconstruction of lawful human action. Broadly speaking, this is a common point between the two traditions of materialism, Marxist and non-Marxist – or should one say dialectical and non-dialectical (Harris 1968, 1978)? And so is the evolutionary perspective an inheritance from L. White's materialism (Binford 1972)?

This last matter requires greater elaboration than I am able to give here, and furthermore, in the case of Greek archaeology, it is somewhat beside the point. No explanation, however, of the relation between Marxist and New Archaeological paradigms in Greek archaeology is complete unless it is plainly understood that the motive behind the adoption of theoretical and methodological paradigms of this kind was the radical critique of current archaeological practices in Greece in their totality. That was a critique therefore which would aim at extending its range in many levels, political, ideological and epistemological, and was bound to be, at least at the beginning, selective in order to be effective.

There was a limited but active response to this bold critical venture by just a small number of archaeologists of the younger generation who tended to group around the journal *Anthropologika* published at Thessaloniki. A similar dissatisfaction with traditional paradigms is discernible in their work as well. Most of them are working within a Marxist framework (Efstratiou 1982: Moshou 1983; Kotsakis 1983; Andreou 1987), others are proceeding with in what Renfrew (1984) would call social archaeology (Pilali-Papasteriou 1989). In the meantime much sound and interesting work on different paradigms and novel objectives was underway, partly as a result of developments in Greece and other countries, partly under the influence of foreign archaeologists working in Greece. I will only briefly mention work on archaeometry summarised by Jones (1986) and ethno-archaeology (Efstratiou 1985), as well as palaeoethnobotany (Sarpaki 1987) and tool analysis (Christopoulou 1979; Moundrea-Agrafioti 1981). Better late than never, Greek archaeology was losing its innocence.

Spatial archaeology on the regional level has had a long history in Greece since the early travellers of the nineteenth century. In recent years, however, a new impetus has come from the systematic regional work carried out in different parts of Greece (Renfrew and Wagstaff 1982; Cherry 1983) and Greek archaeologists were not left much behind (Grammenos 1975, 1980; Sampson 1981; Matsas 1984; Fotiades 1985). Intrasite analysis was also applied to prehistoric settlements, with an emphasis on formal statistical analysis (Konsola 1984; Kotsakis 1987). Several important contributions finally appeared during this period studying aspects of prehistoric ideology, usually through mortuary remains (Gallis 1982; Koukouli-Chrysanthaki 1985) with an occasional pronounced materialistic approach (Doumas 1973, 1977).

Conclusions

There are some general characteristics about Greek archaeology one could now point out by way of conclusion. The most obvious is its relative reluctance to adopt the theoretical innovations coming from the metropolises of archaeology. Although Greece – as in many similar cases in the past – found itself in recent years in the privileged position of having Renfrew, one of the principal theoretical innovators, actually working on Greek prehistory, a related adoption of theoretical issues was, with the exceptions referred to above, very slow; sometimes the impression of stagnation is even given. This is not of course only a question of language barriers, or simply a symptom of the opposition between centre and periphery or the provinciality of Greek archaeology. After all, as discussed in the introduction to this chapter, exchanges to and from Greek archaeologists were always active one way or another. There are a number of possible academic reasons for this phenomenon which could give a tentative explanation. The academic system for instance was until recently very isolated and had difficulty in renewing itself or accepting innovations of any kind. It is typical that the first university textbook that referred to the modern archaeological literature appeared as late as 1982, and still made no specific mention of the work of Binford (Zois 1982). Furthermore, the professional employment of archaeologists in the Antiquities Service is still so desperately slow that the infusion of new ideas into the profession is literally minuscule. But it will rightly be pointed out that these explanations are so epiphenomenal as to beg the question.

What was described in the introduction to this chapter, following Trigger's classification, as the 'nationalistic' character of the discipline offers perhaps a much more plausible explanation of the asymptotical development of Greek theoretical archaeology. As argued throughout this chapter, selecting between changing paradigms was only too seldom a question of academic choice. Not only did popularised archaeological notions come to be deeply embedded in modern Greek state ideology, but they at times even became – and still are – part of actual and powerful programmes of political and social integration. The restoration of the monuments of the Acropolis is a good example of an archaeological work considered so exceptionally important nationally that politicians take an active interest in it. Archaeologists from their circumscribed social position had a limited potential to affect this historically formed ideological structure. On the contrary, as we have seen, there were efforts to bring prehistory into this ideological universe. This was the question of the prehistoric substratum of the Classical Greek civilisation, either ethnic, as was common before the war, or cultural, as claimed by Theocharis.

I am not suggesting that the quest for historical unity was necessarily a negative trait in itself, or that archaeology should become an apolitical pastime. All I am arguing is that the mystification of the Greek past, identified occasionally with powers of political oppression, deprived archaeology as a discipline of its real explanatory potential and hence of its ability to make a genuine contribution to social developments, and forced its theoretical apparatus into a relatively single-minded dead-end. It is in this social context that one should, I feel, see the reaction against the traditional paradigms which was expressed with the introduction of Marxist approaches. One should assess the relatively lesser influence of the New Archaeology in the same light. To accept a pure neo-positivist epistemological paradigm would seem to discontented archaeologists a poor antidote for the prevalent political commonplaces concerning the reconstruction of the past. Interestingly enough, however, the attack on cultural history, so ardently advocated by Binford, found fertile ground as it was identified, perhaps too enthusiastically, with a critique of the historical continuity concept, so very well known to all Greek archaeologists.

The Marxist critique of ethnocentrism with all its consequences for the ideological content of our reconstructions, as discussed earlier in this chapter, actually constitutes a versatile tool for opposing this essentially – from a Marxist point of view – ahistorical, i.e. not related to a specific economy and a specific society, 'historic' reconstruction. On the other hand a generalising approach which sees archaeological phenomena not as the manifestation of general laws with universal value but as instances of a regularity which helps the observer to understand the particular historic occurrence, certainly makes the distinction between New Archaeology and Marxist approaches much clearer; and as it essentially undermines the history–anthropology dichotomy, it is one that, it is to be hoped, will appear more often in the future.

There has recently been a revival of interest in historical reconstruction in archaeology (Hodder 1986; 1987a). Modern Greek prehistoric archaeology, as described on p. 77, will obviously proceed further along this path, which one way or another was never completely lost. The long-term history and the works of Braudel (Hodder 1987a: 2–4) had quite an early impact on Greek intellectuals (e.g. Moskof 1972), although this influence did not apparently reach disciplinary discourse in archaeology. None the less, a plea for the study of the specificity of Greek civilisation, just as Childe allegedly made for Europe (Hodder 1986: 86; 1987a: 4), can very easily be interpreted by Greek archaeologists struggling to define a new paradigm as a call to return to concepts from which they have only just been freed.

Notes

1. Numerous colleagues and friends have helped me clarify my ideas on the adventures of Greek archaeological theory. In particular I would like to thank Professor G. H. Chourmouziadis and Dr S. Andreou. Much of what is here presented is the result of the long discussions on archaeological theory we have had on different occasions. I would also like to thank Dr I. Alexandropoulos and Dr A. Moustaka. Thanks are due to Ms Alexandra Alexandri for commenting constructively on my text. Any faults are unfortunately my own.

2. All the Greek quotations in this paper are presented in my translation. For the 'History of the Greek Nation' in particular I chose to use my own translation instead of the publishers' 'History of the Greek World' as it obviously alters the focus of its content.

References

Althusser, L. (1976) *Positions*, Paris: Editions sociales.

Andreou, S. (1987) 'Metavoles stin katanomi kai tin hrisi metallikon antikimenon stis proimes Minoikes kinotites' ('Changes in the distribution and use of metal artefacts in the Early Minoan settlements'), *Anthropologika* 9.

Athens, J. S. (1978) 'Theory building and the study of evolutionary process in complex societies', in L. R. Binford (ed.) *For Theory Building in Archaeology*, New York: Academic Press.

Benton, T. (1977) *Philosophical Foundations of the Three Sociologies*, London: Routledge & Kegan Paul.

Binford, L. R. (1962) 'Archaeology as anthropology', *American Antiquity* 28: 217–25.

—— (1968) 'Post-pleistocene adaptations', in S. R. Binford and L. R. Binford (eds) *New Perspectives in Archaeology*, Chicago: Aldine.

—— (1972) *An Archaeological Perspective*, New York: Seminar Press.

Bökönyi, S. (1973) 'Ktinotrofia' ('Animal Husbandry'), in D. R. Theocharis (ed.) *Neolithiki Ellas*, Athens: Ethniki Trapeza tis Ellados.

Braidwood, R. J., Howe, R. and Howe, B (1960) *Prehistoric Investigations in Iraqi Kurdistan*, Chicago: The University of Chicago Press.

Cartledge, P. (1986) 'A new Classical archaeology?', *Times Literary Supplement* 1011, 12 September 1986.

Cherry, J. (1983) 'Frogs round the pond: perspectives on current archaeological survey in the Mediterranean area', in D. R. Keller and D. W. Rupp (eds) *Archaeological Survey in the Mediterranean Area*, British Archaeological Report, 155, Oxford.

Childe, V. G. (1951) *Social Evolution*, London: Watts & Co.

—— (1952) *New Light on the Most Ancient East*, London: Routledge & Kegan Paul.

—— (1958) 'Valediction', *Bulletin of the Institute of Archaeology* 1: 1–8.

Chourmouziadis, G. H. (1971) 'I diakekosmimeni keramiki tis archaioteras neolithikis periodou eis tin Thessalian' ('The painted pottery of the early neolithic period in Thessaly'), *Archaiologiki Ephimeris*: 165–87.

—— (1973) 'Tafika ethima' ('Burial customs'), in D. R. Theocharis (ed.) *Neolithiki Ellas*, Athens: Ethniki Trapeza tis Ellados.

—— (1978) 'Isagogi stis ideologies tis ellinikis proistorias' ('An introduction to the ideologies of Greek prehistory'), *Politis* 17: 30–51.

—— (1979) *To neolithiko Dimini* ('Neolithic Dimini'), Volos: Etairia Thessalikon Erevnon.

—— (1980) 'Isagogi sto neolithiko tropo paragogis, Meros A' ('An introduction to the neolithic mode of production, Part A'), *Anthropologika* 1: 118–29.

—— (1981) 'Isagogi sto neolithiko tropo paragogis, Meros B', *Anthropologika* 2: 39–49.

—— (1983) 'O perivolaris kai o diavatis' ('The gardener and the passer-by'), *Archaiologia* 9: 8–15.

—— (1986) 'Greek archaeology between the one-way street of its past and the labyrinth of its future', *Future Directions in Greek Archaeology Conference*, Cambridge (privately circulated).

Christopoulos, G., Bastias, I., Simopoulos, K. and Daskalopoulou, C. (1970) *Istoria tou Ellinikou Ethnous* ('History of the Greek Nation'), Athens: Ekdotiki Athinon.

Christopoulou, A. (1979) *Microwear Analysis of the Chipped and Ground Stone Tools from Sesklo A*, London: Institute of Archaeology.

Clarke, D., (1968) *Analytical Archaeology* London: Methuen.

—— (1972) 'Models and paradigms in contemporary archaeology', in D. Clarke (ed.) *Models in Archaeology*, London: Methuen.

Crawford, O. G. S. (1912) 'The distribution of Early Bronze Age settlements in Britain', *Geographical Journal:* 184–217.

Crossland, R. A. and Birchall, A. (eds) (1973) *Bronze Age Migrations in the Aegean, Proceedings of the First International Colloquium on Aegean Prehistory, Sheffield*, London: Duckworth.

Daniel, G. (1963) *The Idea of Prehistory*, Harmondsworth: Penguin.

Davis, R. S. (1983) 'Theoretical issues in contemporary Soviet paleolithic archaeology', *Annual Review of Anthropology* 12: 403–28.

Dimaras, K. Th. (1985) *Neoellinikos diafotismos* ('Greek enlightenment'), Athens: Ermis.

Doumas, Ch. (1973) 'Grave types and related burial practices during the Cycladic early bronze age', in C. Renfrew (ed.) *The Explanation of Culture Change: Models in Prehistory*, London: Duckworth.

—— (1977) *Early Bronze Age Burial Habits in the Cyclades*, Studies in Mediterranean Archaeology vol. XLVIII, Goterborg: Paul Astroms Forlag.

Earle, T. K. and Preucel, R. W., (1987) 'Processual archaeology and the radical critique', *Current Anthropology* 28 (4): 501–38.

Efstratiou, N. (1982) 'Archaiologika antikeimena: ekfraseis mias dynamikis diadikasias' ('Artefacts: expressions of a dynamic process'), *Anthropologika* 3: 79–86.

—— (1985) 'Ethnoarchaiologikes erevnes sti Thraki' ('Ethnoarchaeological research in Thrace'), *Archaiologia* 13: 20–6.

Fotiades, M. (1985) *Economy, Ecology and Settlement among Subsistence Farmers in the Serres Basin, Northeastern Greece, 5000–1000 B.C.*, Ann Arbor, Mich.

Fowler, D. D. (1982) 'Cultural resource management', in M. B. Schiffer (ed.) *Advances in Archaeological Method and Theory* vol. 5, New York: Academic Press.

Fox, Cyril (1922) *The Archaeology of the Cambridge Region*, Cambridge: Cambridge University Press.

Friedman, J. and Rowlands, M. J. (1977) 'Notes towards an epigenetic model of the evolution of "civilisation" ' in J. Friedman and M. J. Rowlands (eds) *The Evolution of Social Systems*, London: Duckworth.

Fritz, J. (1978) 'Palaeopsychology today: ideational systems and human adaptation in prehistory', in C. Redman (ed.) *Social Archaeology: Beyond Subsistence and Dating*, New York: Academic Press.

Gallis, K. (1982) *Kafseis nekron apo ti neolithiki epokhi sti Thessalia* ('Cremation burials from the neolithic period in Thessaly'), Athens: Ministry of Culture.

Gilman, A. (1981) 'The development of social stratification in bronze age Europe', *Current Anthropology* 22(1): 1–23.

Godelier, M. (1977) *Perspectives in Marxist Anthropology*, Cambridge: Cambridge University Press.

—— (1978) 'Infrastructures, societies and history', *Current Anthropology* 19 (4): 763–71.

—— (1979) 'Epistemological comments on the problems of comparing modes of production and societies', in S. Diamond (ed.) *Toward a Marxist Anthropology*, The Hague: Mouton.

Goldman, L. (1969) *The Human Sciences and Philosophy*, London: Cape Editions.

Grammenos, D. (1975) 'Apo tous proistorikous oikismous tis Anatolikis Makedonias' ('From the prehistoric settlements of Eastern Macedonia'), *Archaiologikon Deltion* 30: 193–234.

—— (1980) 'Symperasmata apo ti meleti ton proistorikon oikismon tis Anatolikis Makedonias' ('Conclusions on the study of the prehistoric settlements of Eastern Macedonia'), *Kavala and its Region, First Collo-quium*, Thessalonika: Institute of Balkan Studies.

Haley, J. B. and Blegen, C. W. (1928) 'The coming of the Greeks', *American Journal of Archaeology* 32: 141–54.

Harris, M. (1968) *The Rise of Anthropological Theory*, New York: Cromwell.

—— (1978) 'Comment on: *Ecology, Evolution and the Search for Cultural Origins*, P. Diener and E. Robkin', *Current Anthropology* 19 (3): 515–17.

Hawkes, J. (1968) 'The proper study of mankind', *Antiquity* 42: 255–62.

Hill, J. N. (1977) 'Systems theory and the explanation of change', in J. N. Hill (ed.) *Explanation of Prehistoric Change*', Albuquerque: University of New Mexico Press.

Hodder, I. (1982) 'Theoretical archaeology: a reactionary view', in I. Hodder (ed.) *Symbolic and Structural Archaeology*, Cambridge: Cambridge University Press.

—— (1984) 'Archaeology in 1984', *Antiquity* LVIII: 25–32.

—— (1986) *Reading the Past. Current Approaches to Interpretation in Archaeology*, Cambridge: Cambridge University Press.

—— (1987a) 'The contribution of the long term', in I. Hodder (ed.) *Archaeology as Long-term History*, Cambridge: Cambridge University Press.

—— (1987b) 'Comment on: *Processual Archaeology and the Radical Critique* by T. K. Earle and R. W. Preucel', *Current Anthropology* 28 (4): 516–17.

Jones, R. E. (1986) *Greek and Cypriot Pottery: a Review of Scientific Studies*, Athens: The British School at Athens.

Karouzos Ch. (1961) *Aristodikos*, Athens: Deutsches Archaologisches Institut.

—— (1967) *Archaia tehni* ('Ancient art'), Athens: Ermis.

Keramopoullos, A. (1932) 'Anaskafai kai erevnai en ti ano Makedonia' ('Excavations and explorations in Upper Macedonia'), *Archaiologiki Ephimeris*.

—— (1933) 'Anaskafai en ti ano Makedonia, Meros B' ('Excavations in Upper Macedonia'), *Archaiologiki Ephimeris*: 25–67.

Klejn, L. S. (1981) 'A panorama of theoretical archaeology', *Current Anthropology* 18 (1): 1–42.

Kohl, P. L. (1981) 'Materialistic approaches in prehistory', *Annual Review of Anthropology* 10: 89–118.

Kokkou, A. (1977) *I merimna gia tis archaiotites stin Ellada kai ta prota mouseia* ('The care for antiquities in Greece and the first museums'), Athens: Ermis.

Kolakowski, L. (1972) *Positivist Philosophy. From Hume to the Vienna Circle*, Harmondsworth: Penguin.

Konsola, D. (1984) *I proimi astikopoiisi stous protoelladikous oikismous* ('The early urbanization in Early helladic settlements'), Athens.

Kotsakis, K. (1983) *Kerameiki Tehnologia kai Kerameiki Diaforopoiisi. Provlimata tis graptis kerameikis tis Mesis Neolithikis epohis tou Sesklou* ('Ceramic technology and ceramic differentiation. Problems of the middle neolithic pottery of Sesklo'), Thessaloniki: University of Thessaloniki.

—— (1987) 'Apokatastasi katopseon passalopikton ikimaton me ti voithia ilektronikou ipologisti stin anaskafi tou Mandalou, D. Makedonias' ('Reconstruction of plans of post-houses with the aid of computer in the excavations of Mandalo, W. Macedonia'), *Eilapini, Papers Presented to Professor N. Platon*, Irakleion.

Koukouli-Chrysanthaki, C. (1985) *Protoistoriki Thassos I* ('Proto-historic Thassos, I'), Thessaloniki.

Kristiansen, K. (1984) 'Ideology and material culture: an archaeological perspective', in M. Spriggs (ed.) *Marxist Perspectives in Archaeology*, Cambridge: Cambridge University Press.

Kuhn, T. S. (1970) *The Structure of Scientific Revolutions*, Chicago: The University of Chicago Press.

Kyriakidis, S. (1939) *I ikogenia*, Thessalonika: University of Thessalonika.

Kyriakidou-Nestoroos, A. (1978) *I Theoria tis Ellinikis Laografias* (:The theory of Greek folklore studies'), Athens: Etairia Spoudon Neoellinikou Politismou kai Genikis Paidias.

Leone, M. P. (1982a) 'Childe's offspring', in I. Hodder (ed.) *Symbolic and Structural Archaeology*, Cambridge: Cambridge University Press.

—— (1982b) 'Some opinions about recovering mind', *American Antiquity* 47 (4): 742–60.

Leone, M. P., Potter, P. B. and Shackel, P. A. (1987) 'Toward a critical archaeology' *Current Anthropology* 28 (3): 283–302.

Lianeris, N. (1982) 'Logicosimeiotiki analysi tis meletis tou Giorgou Chourmouziadi' ('Logico-semiotic analysis of a paper by G. Hourmouziadis'), *Politis* 52: 36–47.

Mango, C. (1965) Byzantium and romantic Hellenism', *Journal of the Warburg and Courtauld Institutes* 28: 29.43.

—— (1984) 'Discontinuity with the classical past in Byzantium', in C. Mango, *Byzantium and its Image*, London: Variorum Reprints.

Marinatos, S. (1971) 'Kaineus: a further link between the Mycenaean and the Greek world', in John Boardman, M. A. Brown and T. G. E. Powell (eds) *The European Community in Later Prehistory, Studies in Honour of* D. S. Hawkes, London: Routledge & Kegan Paul.

—— (1973a) 'The first "Mycenaeans" in Greece', in R. A. Crossland and A. Birchall (eds) *Bronze Age Migrations in the Aegean*, London: Duckworth.

—— (1973b) 'Ethnic problems raised by recent discoveries on Thera', in R. A. Crossland and A. Birchall (eds) *Bronze Age Migrations in the Aegean*, London: Duckworth

Marx, K. (1976) *The German Ideology*, K. Marx and F. Engels, *Collected Works* Vol. 5, London: Lawrence & Wishart.

Matsas, D. (1984) 'Mikro Vouni Samothrakis: mia proistoriki koinotita s' ena nisiotiko systima toy BA Aigaiou' ('Mikro Vouni Samothrakis: a prehistoric community in an island system of the NE Aegean'), *Anthropologika* 6: 73–94.

Meillassoux, C. (1964) *Anthropologie économique des Gourd de Côte d'Ivoire*, Paris: Mouton.

Miller, D. (1980) 'Archaeology and development', *Current Anthropology* 21 (6): 709–26.

Miller, D. and Tilley, C. (1984) 'Ideology, power and prehistory: an introduction', in D. Miller and C. Tilley (eds) *Ideology, Power and Prehistory*, Cambridge: Cambridge University Press.

Milojčić, Vl. (1949) *Chronologie der jüngeren Steinzeit Mittel- und Südosteuropas*, Berlin.

—— (1960) *Hauptergebnisse der Deutschen Ausgrabungen in Thessalien 1953–1958*, Bonn: Rudolf Habelt Verlag.

Moshou, L. (1983) 'Ikismenos horos, paradosiologia kai istorika phenomena' ('Settled space, traditionalism and historical phenomena'), *Anthropologika* 4: 13–36.

Moskof, K. (1972) *I ethniki kai kinoniki sinidisi stin Ellada 1830–1909* ('National and social consciousness in Greece 1830–1909') Thessalonika.

Moundrea-Agrafioti, A. (1981) 'La Thessalie du sud-est au Néolithique: outillage lithique et osseux', Thèse de 3ème cycle, Départment d' ethnologie et préhistoire, Université Paris X.

Mylonas, G. (1928) *I neolithiki epochi en Elladi* ('The neolithic age in Greece'), Athens: Archaiologiki Etaireia.

—— (1929) *Excavations at Olynthos, I: The Neolithic Settlement*, Baltimore.

Nilsson, M. (1932) *The Mycenaean Origins of Greek Mythology*, Cambridge: Cambridge University Press.

Petrakos, V. (1982) 'Dokimio gia tin Archaiologiki Nomothesia' ('An essay on archaeological legislation'). Ipourgio Politismou kai Epistimon, Dimosieumata tou Archaiologikou Deltiou, Ar. 29, Ministry of Culture, Athens.

Pilali-Papasteriou, A. (1989) 'Social evidence from the interpretation of Middle Minoan figurines', in I. Hodder (ed.) *The Meanings of Things: Material Culture and Symbolic Expression*, London: Unwin Hyman.

Platon, N. (1965) *Crete*, Geneva: Archaeologia Mundi, Nagel.

Politis, A. (1984) *I anakalipsi ton ellinikon dimotikon tragoudion* ('The discovery of Greek folk songs'), Athens: Kentro Neoellinikon Erevnon.

Price, B. J. (1982) 'Cultural materialism: a theoretical review', *American Antiquity* 47 (4): 709–41.

Renfrew, C. (1972) *The Emergence of Civilisation. The Cyclades and the Aegean in the Third Millennium*, London: Methuen.

—— (1973a) 'Emporio kai tehniki exeidikefsi' ('Trade and craft specialisation'), in D. R. Theocharis (ed.) *Neolithiki Ellas*, Athens: Ethniki Trapeza tis Ellados.

—— (1973b) 'Problems in the general correlation of archaeological and linguistic strata in prehistoric Greece: the model of autochthonous origin', in R. A. Crossland and A. Birchall (eds) *Bronze Age Migrations in the Aegean*, London: Duckworth.

—— (1973c) *The Explanation of Culture Change: Models in Prehistory*, London: Duckworth.

—— (1979) 'Transformations', in C. Renfrew and K. Cooke (eds) *Transformations. Mathematical Approaches to Culture Change*, New York: Academic Press.

—— (1982) 'Explanation revisited', in C. Renfrew, M. J. Rowlands and B. A. Seagraves (eds) *Theory and Explanation in Archaeology*, New York: Academic Press.

—— (1984) *Social Archaeology*, Edinburgh: Edinburgh University Press.

Renfrew, C. and Wagstaff, M. (1982) *An Island Polity: the Archaeology of Exploitation in Melos*, Cambridge: Cambridge University Press.

Renfrew, J. (1973) 'Georgia' ('Agriculture'), in D. R. Theocharis (ed.) *Neolithiki Ellas*, Athens: Ethniki Trapeza tis Ellados.

Romaios, K. A. (1955) *Mikra meletimata* ('Small studies'), Thessaloniki: Etaireia Makedonikon Spoudon.

Rowlands, M. (1982) 'Processual archaeology as historical social science', in C. Renfrew, M. J. Rowlands and B. A. Segraves (eds) *Theory and Explanation in Archaeology*, New York: Academic Press.

—— (1984) 'Objectivity and subjectivity in archaeology', in M. Spriggs (ed.) *Marxist Perspectives in Archaeology*, Cambridge: Cambridge University Press.

Salmon, W. (1982) 'Causality in archaeological explanation', in C. Renfrew, M. J. Rowlands and B. A. Segraves (eds) *Theory and Explanation in Archaeology*, New York: Academic Press.

Sampson, A. (1981) *I neolithiki kai i protoelladiki I stin Euboia* ('The neolithic and the early Helladic I in Euboia'), Athens: Etaireia Euboikon Spoudon.

Sarpaki, A. A. (1987) 'The palaeoethnobotany of the West House, Akrotiri, Thera', Ph.D. thesis, Sheffield.

Shanks, M. and Tilley, C. (1982) 'Ideology, symbolic power and ritual communication: a reinterpretation of neolithic mortuary practices', in I. Hodder (ed.) *Symbolic and Structural Archaeology*, Cambridge: Cambridge University Press.

—— (1987) *Re-constructing Archaeology*, Cambridge: Cambridge University Press.

Shennan, S. (1986) 'Towards a critical archaeology?', *Proceedings of the Prehistoric Society* 52: 327–56.

Sherrat, A. (1980) *The Cambridge Encyclopedia of Archaeology*, Cambridge: Cambridge University Press.

Skopetea, E. (1984) *To protypo vasileio kai i megali idea* ('The model kingdom and "The Great Idea" '), Thessaloniki: University of Thessaloniki.

Skouteri, E. (1979) 'I anthropologia se krisi' ('Anthropology in crisis'), *Politis* 30: 20–35.

Snodgrass, A. M. (1987) *An Archaeology of Greece*, Berkeley and Los Angeles: University of California Press.

Spriggs, M. (1977) 'Where the hell are we?' in M. Spriggs (ed.) *Archaeology and Anthropology*, British Archaeological Report Supplementary Series 19, Oxford.

—— (1984) 'Another way of telling: Marxist perspectives in archaeology', in M. Spriggs (ed.) *Marxist Perspectives in Archaeology*, Cambridge: Cambridge University Press.

Svoronos, N. G. (1981) *Episkopisi tis neoellinikis istorias* ('A survey of modern Greek history'), Athens: Themelio.

—— (1987) *Analekta neoellinikis istorias kai istoriografias* ('Annals of modern Greek history and historiography'), Athens: Themelio.

Terray, E. (1969) *Le Marxisme devant les sociétés primitives*, Paris: Maspero.

—— (1975) 'Classes and class consciousness in the Abron kingdom of Gyaman', in M. Bloch (ed.) *Marxist Analyses and Social Anthropology*, London: Malaby.

Theocharis, D. R. (1957) 'Ai archai tou politismou en Sesklo' ('The beginnings of civilization at Sesklo'). *Praktika tis Akadimias Athinon* 32: 151–9.

—— (1958) 'Ek tis prokerameikis Thessalias' ('On preceramic Thessaly'), *Thessalika* A: 3–15.

—— (1962) 'Apo ti neolithiki Thessalia I' ('On neolithic Thessaly'), *Thessalika* D: 63–83.

—— (1967) *I Augi tis Thessalikis proistorias* ('The dawn of prehistoric Thessaly'), Volos: Etaireia Thessalikon Erevnon.

—— (1969) 'Proistorika themelia tou ellinikou politismou' ('Prehistoric foundations of Greek civilisation'), *Archaiologika Analekta ex Athinon* 2: 131–41.

—— (1970) 'I epochi tou lithou stin Ellada' ('The Stone Age in Greece') in G. Christopoulos *et al.* (eds) *Istoria tou Ellinikou ethnous*, Athens: Ekdotiki Athinon.

—— (ed.) (1973) *Neolithiki Ellas* ('Neolithic Greece'), Athens: Ethniki Trapeza tis Ellados.

Trigger, B. (1978) *Time and Traditions*, Edinburgh: Edinburgh University Press.

—— (1980) *Gordon Childe, Revolutions in Archaeology*, London: Thames & Hudson.

—— (1981) 'Anglo-American archaeology', *World Archaeology*, 13: 138–55.

—— (1984) 'Alternative archaeologies: nationalist, colonialist, imperialist', *Man* (NS) 19 (3): 355–70.

Tsountas, C. (1909) *Ai proistorikai akropoleis Diminiou kai Sesklou*, Athens: Archaiologiki Etaireia.

—— (1928) *Istoria tis archaias Ellinikis tehnis* ('The history of ancient Greek art'), Athens.

Weinberg, S. (1970) 'The stone age in the Aegean', *Cambridge Ancient History* vol. 1, Cambridge.

Whitley, J. (1987) 'Art history, archaeology and idealism: the German tradition', in I. Hodder (ed.) *Archaeology as Long-term History*, Cambridge: Cambridge University Press.

Zois, A. (1982) *Proistoriki kai protoistoriki archaiologia* ('Prehistoric and proto-historic archaeology'), Ioannina: University of Ioannina.

5

THE USE OF THEORY IN FRENCH ARCHAEOLOGY

Serge Cleuziou, Anick Coudart, Jean-Paul Demoule and Alain Schnapp[1]

Our point of departure is the pressing question put to us by Ian Hodder and Chris Tilley in a Cambridgeshire pub one evening in March 1986 over an excellent beer: why do French archaeologists, who are fortunate enough to speak the same language and breathe the same air as Althusser, Bourdieu, Foucault, Lévi-Strauss and some others – among them a psychoanalyst whom we have never heard of and who publishes only in very Parisian journals – why do these archaeologists use so little theory? We will try and answer that question in somewhat more detail than was possible that evening, but with two reservations. The first is that we do not necessarily feel a bond of solidarity with the entire community of French archaeologists simply because we live in France and are part of the same nation. We will only try to describe that community. The second is that we do not approve – and we will return to this – of the uncritical use of the work of these French intellectuals by some British and North American archaeologists. Indeed, it does not seem to us that applying the label 'Bourdieu' without further elaboration to a statement as obvious and full of common sense as 'a house is the product of ideas conceived and implemented as a result of past experience' lifts it to the heights of theoretical conceptualisation. Furthermore, it seems to us that the history of ideas and of the sciences is not autonomous, and that the history of theories used in archaeology cannot be separated from the concrete conditions of practical research or from the social function of archaeology in a particular country. That is why we will time and again return to these different themes.

To describe the position of theoretical archaeology in France seems indeed equivalent to posing the question: 'Why is there no theoretical archaeology in France?' In one of the two issues of

World Archaeology devoted to regional traditions of archaeological research, Audouze and Leroi-Gourhan (1981) titled their contribution 'France, a continental insularity'. In this manner they emphasised the autonomy of French research with respect to the two cultural traditions which have divided the archaeological world: the area of the culture-historical typology ('normative-distributional' in Binford's jargon) from the Rhine to the Moskow River, and the area of positivist anthropology from the eastern shores of the Channel to those of the Pacific. But this autonomy has not produced a rich crop of original work. The particular attention which is paid to excavation techniques, of which French archaeologists are sometimes unjustifiably proud, is after all the result of a late introduction of methods, British as far as stratigraphy is concerned, German and Russian as far as structures in position are concerned. The only original French contribution appears to be the very bad economic crisis in which its metropolitan archaeology found itself at the end of the 1970s, when the available resources were only one-tenth of those in comparable European countries. It seems useful to us in a volume like this to retrace briefly the history of French archaeological research in order to show how such a situation could ever have come about.

The missed paradigm

Without the slightest doubt, we may attribute the strong sense of autonomy of French archaeology to the hidden conviction that it is to a certain degree superior. If the nineteenth century is, from the perspective of philology and Classical archaeology, dominated by German science (Bollack and Wismann 1983), the idea of a French superiority finds its roots in the Enlightenment. The fifteen volumes of Montfaucon's *L'antiquité expliquée* published from 1716 to 1724, as well as the collection of *Antiquités égyptiennes, étrusques et grecques* of Caylus (1752–67), attest to the birth and expansion of an archaeological knowledge which held its own in what one might call 'the concert of the human sciences' (Schnapp 1982). Certainly, Montfaucon and Caylus were antiquarians, representatives of an archaeology which emphasised a direct approach to objects, the analysis of monuments outside their context. For both of them, *the monument is more important than the document.* Caylus did not limit himself to using antiquities in an illustrative manner. He wished to make the study of monuments into a specific means of acquiring knowledge about the past and to establish stylistic rules which would permit each object to be attributed to a period and to a place. However, because of his failure to place objects in a historical perspective, Caylus was unable to emulate Winckelmann and write a history which was based on more than simply the aesthetic interpretation of works of antiquity. But the care taken in collecting the objects, in describing them and publishing them, forms the basis of a technical knowledge which, through people like Millin (1826), and later Reinach, was to be the driving force of French Classical archaeology.

Why then, notwithstanding this prestigious tradition, did French archaeology in the first part of the nineteenth century fall behind German archaeology? This is due to the fact that in Germany the revolution of *Altertumwissenschaft* had begun, giving the philologists a decisive influence in the development of historical knowledge, and in the critical exploitation of what was acquired in the Renaissance. Philology, the queen of disciplines, secured its independence from theology, and affirmed itself as the bright light of the German universities, contributing to the construction of a scientific field dominated by German models. In its wake trailed Classical archaeology which found a place in German universities long before such a position was accorded to it in France, Great Britain or Italy.

Such a schematic picture needs elaboration, first because it tends to confuse Classical archaeology with archaeology. Certainly, the discoveries and the enormous prestige of Champollion and later Botta made far from negligible contributions to the birth of Egyptology and Assyriology (Daniel 1981: 64–81), but orientalism at that point in Europe developed more as a cultural area of study than as a subfield of archaeology. Certainly, archaeology contributed to the discovery of sites, monuments and inscriptions, but above all it was the interpretation of new languages and the annexation by history of new cultural provinces which was pre-eminent. The philological works of a Champollion or a Rawlinson were much more influential at that point than the exploratory work of a Botta or a Layard.

Our analysis suffers from an even graver lack. It does not take into account the appearance of the science of prehistory in the two pivotal decades between 1830 and 1850 (Laming-Emperaire 1964). This is a paradox which has troubled archaeology and in particular French archaeology. As far as his background, his literary interests and his culture are connected, Boucher de Perthes can in a certain way be connected with the Enlightenment. But the prehistoric archaeology which he established, like that of his forgotten predecessor Schmerling (De Laet 1981), owed only very little to the antiquarians of the eighteenth century. It sprang from physical anthropology which had completely different philosophical roots. The 'natural history of mankind', as it developed in the second part of the nineteenth century, was a natural science entirely, which forged its methods in the field by the positive analysis of remains. It demanded of experimentation and ethnological comparison what Classical archaeology demanded of aesthetics. This was a divergence rather than a convergence which even today characterises the field of archaeology, but it was also a break which explains the radically different objectives of prehistory and Classical or oriental archaeology in France. Men such as Boucher de Perthes, Lartet or de Mortillet did not have a place in the French academic system. Even if Lartet was belatedly appointed at the Musée d'Histoire naturelle just before his death, or if de Mortillet eventually found a post as the curator of the Musée des Antiquités Nationales in Saint-Germain-en-Laye, French prehistorians suffered until the 1950s under a double academic exclusion, both from the faculties of arts and from the faculties of science. At the very moment when French prehistory attracted attention by the richness of its sites and the qualities of de Mortillet as an organiser and theoretician, it was completely without any institutional support.

Nevertheless, the nomenclature of de Mortillet and his typological definitions of lithic industries imposed themselves as the frame of reference in the science of prehistory. His materialism, which even went as far as rejecting the idea of rock art (because of the assumed absence of religion among primitive people), was certainly not shared by all his colleagues and even less by his successors, but his enormous achievement in organising the data became the inevitable standard of prehistoric archaeology. Fragile but creative, this French prehistoric archaeology around the beginning of the twentieth century was preoccupied by the question of the natural history of human beings, to which Broca's school of anthropologists contributed very heavily (Schiller 1979). But if it was well, even superbly, equipped to study the palaeolithic period, it had yet to receive from Scandinavia, Great Britain, Germany and Central Europe the elements necessary for the development of proto-history, which at that point was still in an embryonic state. Notwithstanding the work of Déchelette – which was interrupted much too early as he was killed in the First World War – French prehistory did not reach the level of Scandinavian and Central European archaeology. Excavations were rare and depended entirely on private funding, and if the methods of Montelius were acknowledged and accepted, they did not in any way develop in an original manner (Grenier 1931).

The years of recession, 1920–60

It is tempting to see a turning-point just after the First World War, because the victory of 1918 brought less debate and less innovation to French science than the defeat of 1871. The war had weakened science, but that does not explain everything. Whereas the Durkheimian school under the leadership of Mauss continued on a course which had been temporarily interrupted, opening itself to linguistics, to comparative studies, and to orientalism, archaeology does not seem to have been affected by the same renaissance. Indeed, Hubert, the curator of the Musée des Antiquités Nationales in Saint-Germain-en-Laye, supported Mauss when he launched an extremely interesting research programme on the expansion of the Celts (Dumézil 1981: 18–19), while Classical archaeology (supported by the French Schools in Rome and Athens) pursued its slow development. However, notwithstanding the work of the Abbé Breuil, French prehistory no longer occupied the position it had in previous decades. Undoubtedly there were not enough qualified people, but there were even fewer academic positions and no legislation. After the war, young researchers revitalising the humanities flocked to the seminars of the sociologist Mauss, the sinologist Granet, the anthropologist Rivet and the linguist Meillet. By contrast, young archaeologists, and more particularly prehistorians, only found lectures at the Institut de Paléontologie Humaine, or those of people like Vauffray and Valois, who merely maintained a tradition rather than contributing to the creation of a framework for an expanding discipline. It was in this context that Leroi-Gourhan laid the basis for a comparative ethnography nourished by anthropology and orientalism. After de Mortillet, Leroi-Gourhan is without the slightest doubt the man who has contributed most to the current state of French prehistory and, like him, was an autodidact who brought as much passion to the understanding of 'systèmes techniques' as de Mortillet had to defining the laws of evolution. Leroi-Gourhan's originality shows most clearly in the way in which he broke with the tradition within which Bordes worked to develop and transform the typological heritage of Breuil. In doing so, he founded a prehistory in its own right. In this case – as in that of Lévi-Strauss for anthropology – the history of a discipline merges in part with the intellectual history of an exceptional personality, and this even more so because, up to the end of the 1950s, the landscape of French prehistory hardly changed. Moberg wrote twenty years later: 'Si on cherche à trouver une approche paléosociologique dans les trois lourds volumes presqu'officiels consacrés à la préhistoire de la France publiés en 1976, on a tendance à être déçu' (Moberg 1980: 313).[2]

In the absence of the necessary data, the neo-evolutionist arguments of Varagnac hardly extended beyond the readership of his journal *Archéocivilisation*, and are now completely forgotten. Whether he was concerned with human labour as a technical process, with hominisation, with the interpretation of rock art, or with excavation, the work of Leroi-Gourhan established a frame of reference, a field of questions which was as vital for prehistoric archaeology as was the work of Childe for proto-history. Clearly located on the interface of, on the one hand, traditional prehistory (which consisted of layers, profiles and lists of types) and, on the other hand, the human sciences (the tradition of Mauss and Granet, which Leroi-Gourhan knew but to which he did not belong), his work was received with disappointment rather than enthusiasm.

Let us be clear. The problems raised by Leroi-Gourhan have been debated, and rejected or accepted, but the consequences of his questions have not been fully drawn. Details have been retained but his approach as a whole has been rejected. The excavation techniques have been adopted when the strategy should have been. His criticism of simplistic analogies, rather than leading to a more sophisticated use of analogical reasoning, was understood as a complete rejection of all analogies. Several contributions to the colloquium devoted to Leroi-Gourhan (Actes du colloque du CNRS 1988) are very representative of this attitude.

The paradox of archaeology in France is due to repeated time-lags. At the same moment as a triumphant French prehistory was first being established, positivist history – such as the work of Monod, Seignobos, Perrot – was already creating its own academic network (Carbonnel 1976). In this manner a university framework was created for history as a discipline, a framework which was not available to the prehistorians of the generation of de Mortillet and Bertrand. When, in the 1920s, the humanities began their expansion around the journal *Année sociologique*, when Febvre of Bloch launched the *Annales*, prehistorians and archaeologists were not there to meet them (Schnapp 1981). From that point on, there was only the choice between an orthodoxy (represented by Breuil and Bordes for prehistory, and many others for Classical and oriental archaeology) and a heterodoxy which was represented by the work of Leroi-Gourhan. Practical, synthetic, anthropological and semiological, Leroi-Gourhan's prehistoric ethnology was the answer to a vision of archaeology which saw things only in terms of archaeological cultures and typologies. Any observer of the French archaeological scene at the beginning of the 1960s would have predicted the coming of a different archaeology. The approach of Leroi-Gourhan, which was to some degree echoed in oriental archaeology by the work of Gardin and Deshayes, seemed in a position to win. But that was not to be.

The 1960s and 1970s: some turbulence in an almost peaceful retro-archaeology

A student in the 1980s would find it difficult to imagine the degree to which French archaeology, in the field as well as in the university, apeared an intellectual desert at the beginning of the 1960s. This was exactly the moment when, in the humanities, French thought was in one of its most fertile and most exciting periods, with people like Sartre, Merleau-Ponty, Ricoeur, Lacan, Goldman, Lefebvre, Lévi-Strauss, Vernant, Braudel, Barthes, Althusser, Piaget and so many others. In this context, the collective work *Etudes archéologiques* edited by Courbin (1963) pales into insignificance and it had no intellectual influence outside the professional milieu in the strictest sense. But some of its contributions – such as Courbin's own on stratigraphic methods – scandalised many French archaeologists working overseas, notably those who had, for well over a century, been used to excavating the most prestigious sites of the Mediterranean basin in the most cursory way. In contrast, other contributions – such as those of

Leroi-Gourhan and Gardin – modestly announced the programme of the years to come. That is why for our generation these two authors are numbered among the very few touchstones available in French archaeology. In April 1969, when Gardin organised the symposium *Archéologie et calculateurs* in Marseille (Gardin 1970) – at which the majority of participants were foreigners – the young French archaeologists felt that they were part of a great event. It was in this messianic atmosphere that Soudsky, who had not yet left Bylany for Paris, prophesied, several months after the Prague and Paris Springs:

> La voie est longue, mais l'archéologie est enfin jeune. Les jeunes qui font des barricades sauront défaire celles qui entourent les sciences et les langues nationales, les domaines impénétrables de disciplines trop séparées, les terminologies et typologies 'paroissiales' . . . ; mais alors, qu'on change le système d'éducation et de formation des archéologues. Qu'on change les universités, les académies, les périodiques, les monographies, les musées, les archives, et les fouilles surtout. Tout est à faire.
>
> (Soudsky 1970: 53)[3]

In the two decades which followed, the young in question devoted every effort to the realisation of Soudsky's programme. Priority was given not to theoretical debates, but initially to the transformation of the structures and institutions in which research had to take place, to progress in techniques of excavation and documentation. These priorities were particularly important in France, where the lack of material support for archaeology, evidently a consequence of the absence of intellectual dimensions in the discipline, had had disastrous effects.

This strategy was also followed by Gardin and Leroi-Gourhan, each in his own way. After the syntheses published by Leroi-Gourhan in the middle of the 1960s on the structuralist interpretation of palaeolithic rock art and on the evolution of humanity in general (1964a, 1964b, 1965), he devoted himself exclusively to the painstaking excavation of a single Magdalenian site, Pincevent near Paris. Gardin applied himself essentially to the creation of computerised and non-computerised tools for documentation, to his CNRS laboratory, the Centre d'analyse documentaire pour l'archéologie, and to the institutional problems of scientific information in general (Gardin 1971b, 1972). Moreover, he was the main driving force behind what might have become a general restructuring of the organisation of archaeology in France around a national archaeological institute, the Centre de recherches archéologiques, located at Valbonne near Nice, which followed a deliberately selective policy of encouraging particular topics. The generation which followed and which listened to these people tried, through a systematic review of the funding and infrastructure of French archaeology (which had never been undertaken before), to make the real decision-makers aware of the extremely serious lack of funds for our discipline (Normand and Richard 1974; Chapelot et al. 1979). At the same time, they strove to redesign university teaching and to perfect excavation techniques.

In these circumstances, most energy was spent on activities related to these reforms. But the almost exclusive attention given to techniques of observation and documentation quickly became a negative element, indeed they became ends in themselves. Thus, in Classical archaeology, stratigraphic excavation became a goal in itself, and it is significant that Courbin, who was an agitator in the 1950s and 1960s, no longer exercised any intellectual influence. At the same time, in prehistoric archaeology, very refined techniques of excavation with a dentist's spatula and a fine brush – essential for the study of palaeolithic floors in situ – were applied thoughtlessly and without subtlety to any kind of situation. Developed initially, at the beginning of the 1960s, as a reaction against the rather crude excavation methods of non-professional archaeology – the only kind of archaeology existing at that time – this technique soon came to have a paralysing effect. Moreover, when Soudsky in 1971, almost twenty years after having elaborated methods of mechanical stripping in Bohemia, applied them to the neolithic sites in the Aisne valley, this innovation, which was accepted everywhere else in Europe, unleashed in France passions beyond measure. And in 1973, when the first report reviewing all the sites menaced by destruction in this same Aisne valley suggested that 'selection' of sites would be based on the priorities of available financing and scientific interest, the same passions erupted. There was no acceptable middle ground between an extremely detailed excavation of the palaeolithic type, and wilfully ignored total destruction.

In the area of data collection, archaeometry, which appeared at this time, added to the intellectual deadlock. The sense that it was possible to acquire data and to produce results which could be characterised as 'scientific', unlike the results of normal archaeological observation, made people feel they could dispense with thinking. Even though the physicists were just as unfamiliar with this kind of collaboration, this renunciation gave them a false sense of absolute power. At the beginning of the 1980s, when the balance of collaboration between physicists and archaeologists became more even (Berthoud and Cleuziou 1985b), the disappointments were great.

Documentation and information-processing had the same stagnating effect on interpretation. The interpretations which Leroi-Gourhan proposed for palaeolithic art in France and Cantabria were the result of the structural analysis of associations and non-associations among the animals and symbols painted on the walls of the caves. As such, it is equivalent to any other structuralist analysis – on mythology for example, a domain where analysis was normally followed by often very complex interpretative constructions. But the same Leroi-Gourhan, who had not hesitated a few years earlier to sketch a picture of the history of humanity and to prophesy its destiny (1965: 257–70), now rejected all generalisation, whether on art or on Pincevent, the site which he excavated. His seminar at the Collège de France (to which he was belatedly elected, as he also was, even later and almost *in extremis*, to the Académie des Inscriptions et Belles Lettres) was merely devoted to establishing a temporary vocabulary for archaeological excavations which was not only simply descriptive but in every way provisional.

The promotion of archaeological databases, the work of Gardin (see Borillo and Gardin 1974, for example), drifted in the same direction which was a paradox inasmuch as its intentions were both universalist and self-limiting. This also led to stagnation. The advent of archaeological databases was presented by Gardin (1971a, 1971b, 1975) as a salvation both for research institutions and for theoretical archaeology. The development of networks of interconnected databases which he prophesied required establishing uniform documentation, because in order to receive one has to give. This should have meant the end of the 'hoarding' of information which, especially in archaeology, has often been sufficient to assure social power to whoever holds the data. The prophecy postulated that databases would become effectively public, on the one hand because the financial cost of information technology was too high for a single individual or a single laboratory, and on the other hand because interconnectivity was essential to the functioning of the discipline. But with the emergence of micro-computers, the financial obstacle has been lifted, and connectivity is at present no more essential than before. On the contrary, individual ownership of micro-computers has made the sequestering of particular pieces of information even easier. It does not seem therefore as if technical innovation would in itself be sufficient to change the organisation of knowledge and power in a given society, but rather, would tend to reinforce it. This banal observation applies moreover to the social function of information technology in general (Nora and Minc 1978).

Another advantage of the databases might have been in the development of the universal descriptive languages which are indispensable to computerisation. This would have allowed us to move smoothly towards the establishment of an entirely formalised discipline, much as Mendeleev's table of the elements was a necessary stage on the road to universal laws in western physics; or, to express it in terms of structural linguistics, as if we were to pass progressively from –etic descriptive units to –emic interpretative units (Gardin 1967). Nothing of the kind happened. On the contrary, two kinds of enterprises developed which grew further and further apart. On the one hand, there evolved general interest documentation in museums, libraries and documentation centres with descriptive systems which were simplified to the extreme, as in any enterprise which has to manage its stock of spare parts. On the other hand there were specific projects set up by an individual or a laboratory which dealt with very specialised research and used descriptive languages which were sometimes not only very complex but could not be made compatible or interconnective. Thus we saw nothing but the reproduction, by means of electrons and silicon, of what had been happening for well over a century and a half by means of pieces of paper of different formats: the continued divergence of the same two institutional biases.

The descriptive *codes* elaborated by Gardin and his group remained without users or, if one accepts the idea they were prototypes, without descendants. Potential users of the best known among them, the *index de l'outillage* (Christophe and Deshayes 1964), admitted that they preferred sticking to the traditional method, that is to leaf through the 400 pages of the thesis (the 'construction' in the sense of Gardin) which Deshayes produced while he was working on it (Deshayes 1960), rather than to move to the rigorous but fastidious operations of description and comparison permitted by the 'peek-a-boo' card index (cards with 5,000 central perforations), which came with the work and which were still sited in their grey boxes on the top shelves of libraries. Skilfully constructed as it was, the machine which produced these cards should be in a museum of documentation techniques.

In prehistory, the analytical typology of Laplace, which had no direct social links to Gardin and Deshayes (who discovered it in 1972 when they attended a colloquium on databases), never managed to establish itself. It suffered from the handicap that it was very formal, too clumsy compared to the synthetic lists proposed by Bordes to actually be used, while its criteria seemed useless from the perspectives opened up by research on the technological anlysis of *débitage*. Doubtless, it would have allowed us to apply to flint tools the same classification studies and the same automatic seriation which were at the time being applied to objects as diverse as Roman amphorae (Fariñas del Cerro *et al.* 1977), archaic Greek *kuroi* (Borillo 1970) or *menhir* statues (Landau and de la Vega 1970). Failure, as far as a progressive transformation from the -*etic* to the -*emic* is concerned, has finally been admitted by Gardin himself (1979a, 1979b).

In the meantime, a certain number of enthusiastic archaeologists had invested considerable energy in the creation of the promised databases. Eight years after the colloquium on archaeological databases organised by Gardin in 1972 (Borillo and Gardin 1974), a review of the state of the known networks showed that not one of these projects had been completed, although some were close to it (Cleuziou and Demoule 1980a).

But that has not hindered anybody, least of all the discipline, which has continued to develop. In actual fact, with the demographic increases of the 1960s, greater financial support and the development of the Sous-direction de l'Archéologie, meetings, colloquia, seminars and conferences multiplied within the subdisciplines, at least as far as national archaeology is concerned. Through these means, traditional exchange networks which are much more empirical and not nearly as exhaustive or as objective as the ones information technology had made us dream of, function today in a relatively satisfactory manner.

However, the stagnating effect we mentioned earlier was not

accidental. It accompanies the trajectory of the human sciences as a whole. The interdependent emergence of information science, cybernetics and structuralism in the 1950s led by the mid 1960s to a generalised belief in the growing formalisation of these disciplines, of which Chomskian linguistics seemed to be the most established form. What was by then already called artificial intelligence seemed to be the ineluctable future. It was remarkable that France, with its strong Marxist tradition, and more general philosophical tradition, remained somewhat outside this current which was marked essentially by Anglo-American positivism. When it emerged in the French humanities, notably in the work of the mathematician B. Jaulin (B. Jaulin 1968), the ethnologist R. Jaulin (Richard and Jaulin 1971) and Gardin, it was in open hostility to the methods of the French humanities, which were cast down into the underworld of metaphysics and uncertainty. This rejection can also be seen in the work of Lévi-Strauss (Régnier 1971) as well as in the semiology of Barthes and Greimas (Gardin 1974, 1979a). But if the debunking aspect of these studies was perfectly clear and healthy, things tended to get more complicated when something new actually had to be created. The only issue then, and we will return to this point, was to formalise work which was traditional but in which, one 'had reason to think', the 'intuitive results' were interesting.

While this approach to research gradually came apart in the course of the first half of the 1970s, Chomsky and his school of linguistics ceased to enlighten the humanities. Hesitation replaced both. Certain people rushed headlong into the less austere charms of socio-biology which, again of Anglo-American origin, was almost immediately imported into France by the sociologist Morin and others. The far from innocent character of its presuppositions, notably as far as their political implications are concerned, finally destroyed this movement (Sahlins 1976; Thuillier 1976; Chapeville et al. 1979; Gould 1977; Jacquard 1982; Ruffié 1979, 1982). What happened to the formalisation of archaeology in France was just about the same as was happening at the same moment to the formalisation of the humanities in the rest of the world.

But which echoes of the intense debate which shook Anglo-American archaeology from the mid 1960s, more precisely from the 1965 meeting of the Society for American Archaeology in Denver, Colorado, eventually reached the continental isolation of France? And why did the almost exclusive concentration on the methods of archaeological reasoning and documentation in the limited number of French theoretical writings raise so little interest on the other side of the Atlantic? This is not the place to discuss which aspects of the New Archaeology were due to the history of ideas, and which were due to the particular sociological milieu of American university circles. As is clearly shown by Klejn (1977), it was already evident from the beginning of the 1960s that something was going to happen. But that 'something' was as dependent on an infusion of new data from the hard sciences as it was to the fact that the classical models of explanation had run out of steam. The latter was due to the growing dissatisfaction of a number of archaeologists with the weakness of their ways of reasoning and validation, to the emergence of quantitative methods, to the considerable development of fieldwork during the 1950s, and eventually to the renewal which came with new generations of scientists and researchers. If this phenomenon was more pronounced in America, so that developments there received more attention, it was in part due to the amplifying effect of the particular sociological milieu of American universities which we have already mentioned. In Europe, men as different as Moberg, Soudsky, Tabaczinsky and Klejn, but also Clarke and Renfrew, followed the same road without any particular connection with the plains of the Midwest. It is no coincidence that the year of the explosion, which will remain known in the annals of the historiography of archaeological research as the 'Binclarke' year, was precisely 1968. Nor is it mere chance that today we see the deconstructionist paradigm promulgated by Derrida applied to archaeology in England, which in the western world was the least affected by the social and intellectual upheavals of 1968, and applied most notably in the bosom of one of its most prestigious and conservative universities, that of Cambridge. In those earlier years, Derrida's paradigm was specifically proposed as an act of destruction necessary to permit intellectual rejuvenation.

In France, we estimate that many of these elements, but others as well, were present at the beginning of the 1970s in the teachings of Leroi-Gourhan and Soudsky. However, the latter's sojourn in France was too short (1971–6), and the former increasingly refused to take a broad sweep of focus. Intellectual, institutional and financial misery for the majority, theoretical stagnation and a focus on institutionalisation and fieldwork for others were the result. Contacts with American archaeology were mainly fleeting and individual, such as participation by researchers of one country in the conferences of the other. The authors of the present chapter first introduced the American discussions into France in 1973, in the *Annales* (Cleuziou *et al.* 1973). Even then we were expressing the reservations which would later be found in other comparable papers (Cleuziou and Demoule 1980a, 1980b). We can also point to the comments on articles in the journal *Current Anthropology* which were periodically sought from French archaeologists. A notable exception was the debate between Bordes and Binford on the significance of different Mousterian *facies*, interpreted by the former in terms of different cultures, and by the latter in terms of different functions (Bordes 1973; Binford 1973). To support his arguments, Binford depended on Bordes's type-lists, a tribute paid to the important position still occupied by traditional French prehistory, but also a weakness in the eyes of those in France who considered the work on descriptive criteria an absolute priority. The irony is that in actual fact the most conservative position is no doubt the most promising. We shall see in this respect that the interest of American scientists in the Périgord (Jelinek 1986) rapidly made Bordes and his work popular in the United States, whereas at the same time Leroi-Gourhan, whose work ought to have aroused much interest on the other side of the Atlantic but was not translated into English – and still is not and will not be translated into that language – remains entirely unknown there.

General books on archaeology are rare in France and ignore such debates entirely. This first book to deal with them was Moberg's *Introduction à l'archéologie*, a translation and revision of the original Swedish text by Moberg himself in collaboration with two of the authors of this chapter (Moberg 1976). Welcomed as quite innovative, it remained for a long time the only available reference for graduate students. As befitted the preoccupations of that period, it ended with a chapter on the structural transformations of the teaching and practice of archaeology needed in France. One still wonders why this book, which expressed an original and somewhat non-conformist position, was translated from French into several Romance languages (Italian, Portuguese), but has never been translated into English. Problems of communication are bilateral indeed.

The same debates were still absent in Camps's *La préhistoire*, although he cites Binford in passing as one of a number of authors of controversial theories on the Mousterian and the appearance of agriculture (Camps 1982: 168, 277). Pelletier's (1985) manual *L'Archéologie et ses méthodes* does not devote a single line to theoretical questions. We may also mention a book by Courbin (1981) with the slightly misleading title, *Qu'est ce que l'archéologie?* which is entirely devoted to a critique of the New Archaeology as a phenomenon. The approach chosen for this critique is a detailed explication of the text of about ten American articles. The exaggerated claims of these articles are easily demonstrated – they obviously do exist (Courbin also draws attention to mistakes in the English which does not prevent his book from having several mistakes in French). As if assuming a thorough knowledge of the sociology of French archaeology on the part of the reader, Courbin also makes a general attack without naming names on French archaeologists of the younger generation who are 'guilty' of innovations such as calculating percentages or using archaeo-magnetic prospection, methods he equates with the New Archaeology! Unfortunately for the reputation of French archaeology, an English translation of this book has recently appeared (1989). To give his crusade more force, Courbin translated Flannery's 'Gold Marshalltown' paper in the popular review *Archeologia* under the title 'La truelle d'or, parabole pour l'archéologie des années 1980'. We agree with him that this article 'paraît marquer une étape dans l'itinéraire spirituel d'un grand archéologue américain' (Courbin 1983).[4]

The annoying thing is that the journal in question had never informed its readers about developments in American archaeology, and has not even done so since. We may therefore wonder what its French readers have understood from this strange attack on people whom they had never heard of before. It is only with the *Nouvelles de l'archéologie*, a journal dealing with administrative information, research policy and the scientific aspects of archaeology, established in 1979 by Braudel's Maison des sciences de l'homme, that contacts with the Anglo-American world and discussions on theory and concepts become a consistent feature of French archaeology. As part of thematic dossiers on theoretical archaeology, ethno-archaeology and American prehistory, it has presented previously unpublished papers by Binford, Hodder, Sackett, Whallon and White, as well as regular reviews of the Anglophone literature. But by now we have reached the early 1980s.

The 1980s: debates, non-debates and perspectives

The 1980s saw one of the most remarkable turning-points in the history of French archaeology. This decade witnessed the same explosion of field research that Great Britain and the United States had seen about fifteen years before. The dramatic situation of rescue archaeology in France, emphasised by several reports mentioned above (Normand and Richard 1974; Chapelot *et al.* 1979; Querrien and Schnapp 1984), finally became apparent to the decision-makers concerned. It is significant that from then on major political figures expressed a personal interest in archaeology, an interest further accentuated by the economic crisis, which was also experienced as a cultural crisis. Just like Napoleon III and Field Marshal Pétain before him, President Mitterrand referred to our Gallic ancestors in his appeal for national unity. In September 1985, he gave a long speech on this theme from the heights of the Mont Beuvray (Mitterand 1985), the site where Vercingetorix was proclaimed chief of the general uprising against Julius Caesar. At the same time, he gave unprecedented funding for the excavation and preservation of the site, which had been partially excavated in the nineteenth century by Déchelette. The complete reorganisation of the Louvre Museum and the erection of a glass pyramid at the centre of the main court, is one of the major cultural works of his presidency. Rescue funds almost reached the levels current in neighbouring countries. A complete rescue archaeology on a contract basis (in 1989 employing 1,000 young archaeologists) and an embryonic privately funded archaeology appeared. At the present time, the effects of these upheavals are not really known in France although they have been well analysed in the Anglo-American countries.

These material and political facts should not distract us from the problems of theoretical archaeology. The American example, or to a lesser degree the British example, has on two occasions shown the impact of such an explosion of field data. The first time was with the New Deal and the large-scale works of the Tennessee Valley Authority. As Moberg had remarked (1976:29), these investigations quite naturally led to the development of quantitative methods because of the massive amount of material that had to be treated. The second time was in the 1970s and 1980s when the enormous development of contract archaeology as part of Cultural Resource Management caused the emergence of two kinds of research: contract archaeology, rich but dominated by a commercial logic and without much in the way of scientific problem-orientation; and academic archaeology, poor and therefore more and more orientated towards short-term projects with considerable theoretical pretensions. It would be good if French archaeology could learn from this American example and avoid making the same errors, the first effects of which can already be felt.

The growth of the quantity of data, the appearance of a new generation of archaeologists and the doubling of funding for professional archaeology also have positive aspects, if only in that they break existing habits. The notion of excavation strategy becomes indispensable in the context of large-scale rescue excavations, and as such leads to the development of a methodology of survey, sampling and quantitative techniques. Regional programmes, whether or not they include rescue excavations, provide a framework for focusing on the whole range of available methods, as has happened in the Aisne valley (*Revue archéologique de Picardie* 1982) or on the lakes of the Jura (P. Pétrequin 1986; Pétrequin and Pétrequin 1988a). We will therefore continue our survey of the different points which serve as a focus for arachaeological discussions in France and elsewhere, showing either how French archaeology is present in each of these debates or why it is absent, and why there are still grounds for optimism.

The logic of archaeological reasoning

From the beginning, Gardin's work has focused on the problems involved in the logic of archaeological reasoning. Apart from an attempt to move progressively from the *-etic* to the *-emic*, to which reference has already been made, Gardin drew attention very early on to the interesting potential of simulated archaeological reasoning. Except in a few cases, this point has not really raised very much interest in Anglo-American archaeology (Whallon 1982; Viera 1082; Richards and Ryan 1985). The very weak response to the English version of Gardin's main work (1979b) is significant in this respect. As one of the main intellectual proponents of American archaeology – and one who had at least read the book – said: 'Gardin ends there where I begin.'

Nevertheless, the apparent modesty of the French title of this book, *Une archéologie théorique*, is as misleading as the similar modesty of Binford's autohagiographic collection, *An Archaeological Perspective* (1972).

But the work of Gardin and his colleagues on the simulation of archaeological reasoning by a 'logicist' approach has recently been extended by a growth of interest in expert systems (Gardin *et al.* 1987) shortly after their practical and successful application elsewhere, most notably in the medical sciences. Another factor was the revival in the mid 1980s of interest in the metaphysic of 'artificial intelligence'. The latter, either under this name or under that of 'cognitive psychology' or some other title, is at present extremely popular among the Parisian intelligentsia. The same causes which produced the failures and disenchantments with this approach at the end of the 1960s may have the same effect now. Even if the human brain is by definition a material thing, nothing indicates that an electronic network is the most accurate reproduction of it. Thus, without denying the technical interest of this research, we can nevertheless foresee a new disenchantment in the medium term.

The main problem of these French studies which attempt to simulate archaeological reasoning is one which they openly acknowledge, an obvious lack of interest in the content of the subject which they discuss: 'logicism does not concern . . . the archaeological remains themselves, but what archaeologists say about them' (Gallay 1989: 28).

The attempt to reformulate the teachings of Leroi-Gourhan through the rules of archaeological reasoning set out by Gardin was to come from Geneva (Gallay 1986). The title of the book had to be prospective: *L'Archéologie demain*, since an *Archéologie aujourd'hui* had already been published (Schnapp 1980). Gallay makes wide use of ethno-archaeology, which he himself practised in the field in Africa, but tries to avoid the criticisms of reasoning by analogy expressed by Leroi-Gourhan. Analogy can be used effectively to discover regularities in human cultures, which should then be tested against archaeological facts, but only through a strict use of the logicist rules of archaeological reasoning. The importance of artificial intelligence and expert systems in that respect is highly proclaimed. The results of such an approach will clearly be much more limited than in anthropology or history, which are founded on a wider and richer range of facts, but the processes involved can nevertheless be judged to be scientific because logicist rigour has produced the results. Gallay proposes what he calls a 'craftsman's way of thought' – should this be linked in some way with the 'bricolage intellectuel' of Lévi-Strauss (1962: 26–47)? – which he feels is 'closer to science than philosophy is' (1986: 278). Philosophically speaking, the general tone of the book is strongly positivist, and rather closer to approaches in physical anthropology and biology. As the author is not entirely familiar with the historical or the ethnological perspective, this is not a bad thing. However that may be, its impact in France so far seems to have been rather limited.

Cultural models and cultural change

The major weakness of French archaeology in this respect is that the scepticism expressed – by Leroi-Gourhan, for example – concerning the construction of cultural models or the notion of culture itself, leads to the use of notions which are even more dangerous because they are implicit. As a result, for instance, the arsenal of natural sciences now used in any excavation of any size will eventually lead to environmentalist and determinist models (Coppens 1983, for example) which are simplistic, supposedly commonsense and therefore not criticised. Nevertheless, mainstream palaeolithic research influenced by Bordes is firmly located in the cultural-historical tradition, as is research on the neolithic and the Bronze and Iron Ages. The increasing importance of this tradition is due in part to the fact that recently scientific ties with Germany and Central Europe, which were for long almost non-existent, have tended to become more important. The pioneering efforts of Soudsky (1973) towards a formalisation of the notion of culture so far have not been been followed up. Similarly, the visits which Anglo-American researchers make to France from time to time (such as Scarre 1983 or Geddes 1986) tend to favour the development of evolutionary approaches, instead of diffusionist ones. Although these are fashionable, they do not always seem to relate to the facts, notably concerning the process of neolithisation in France. This bias in favour of evolutionism is evident in the tendency, in Anglophone countries, towards an immoderate use of radiocarbon datings. Although they are thought to be more exact than typological analysis, their error of measurement engenders false effects of contemporaneity, and thereby allows anti-diffusionist theories a platform.

On the other hand, in a completely different domain and despite criticism by Billig (1979) and Demoule (1980), diffusionism has been used massively in France by a group of intellectuals of the extreme Right, the *Nouvelle droite*, in order to explain the Indo-European phenomenon and to try and demonstrate the superiority of European civilisation. It is very clear that, in spite of some recent restatements (Renfrew 1987; Mallory 1989), the solution to this intriguing question is certainly not to be found in archaeology pure and simple but will require intense collaboration between archaeologists, linguists, ethnologists and mythologists to develop new theoretical models.

Some young researchers are interested in these problems and are increasingly participating in international colloquia presenting the modern debates on the great breaks in human history. Nevertheless, French archaeologists remain almost completely absent from the discussions on these topics, whether they are on hominisation, the appearance of modern man, the neolithic 'revolution' (Demoule 1982) or the emergence of state societies, even though French researchers handle highly accurate data. To take a striking example, the key studies on urbanisation in Iranian Khuzestan, which are of paramount importance to our understanding of the emergence of state societies, are all the work of American authors (Wright and Johnson 1975, among others) who relied heavily on the material gathered at Susa by French archaeologists during some ninety years of almost uninterrupted excavations. The exchange of data and visits by researchers across the Atlantic has been very active, but not a single paper on the theoretical results of this co-operation written by a French archaeologist can be cited. It is only for neolithisation that one may note on the one hand the work of the ethnologist Testart (1982), and on the other the very original positions taken by Cauvin (1978 and 1987) following his excavations in the Near East. Testart's book, and notably his comments on the importance of storage and accumulation techniques in the appearance of social differentiation, has been warmly welcomed by archaeologists – much more in fact than by ethnographers – but we are still waiting for a comprehensive archaeological work founded on the same considerations. Rather than using an environmentalist model, Cauvin sees the appearance of agriculture and stockraising as the answer to the social stress caused by sedentarisation of the Natufian hunter-gatherers in ever larger villages. Going a step further, he abandons all determinism to propose that the neolithic revolution itself must have been caused by a symbolic revolution which he discerns in the appearance of feminine figurines and a bull cult. This position, which converges with those of Hahn at the beginning of the century and of the French philosopher and mythologist Girard (1978), tends to ignore the fact that not a single fundamental innovation can actually be accepted, that is can transform the structure of the society concerned, unless it has become necessary and is forcing changes on the structure of society and society itself. Forgetting this is to forget that when a society transforms itself, it must be able to accept the principles underlying the change. In order to do so, these principles must already be part of the way in which the group conceptualises its world. We meet here the idea of the *milieu intérieur* as already proposed by Leroi-Gourhan in his attempt to explain technical innovation (1945: 354–55, 404–8). It is therefore normal that among societies which are on the way to neolithisation, the principle of fertility is already a part of their ritual practices (e.g. female figurines). Thus the principle exists at a secondary level (Godelier 1988), behind the dominant economic level, which is not yet that of agriculture. If misunderstood, this dialectical process may lead one to think that it is the 'realm of ideas' which rules the world. Hence Cauvin's erroneous return to symbolism carries within itself the danger of a return to idealism.

Symbolism is also manifest in the study of palaeolithic art. Due to the understandable attraction of Franco-Cantabrian rock art, symbolism is an area in which both American and French archaeologists have worked, as is shown by various kinds of approaches such as that of Conkey (1980, 1984) and Vialou (1987). This new symbolist theme, which has also appeared in Cambridge in other domains (Hodder 1982a, 1982b, 1987), is in fact for the study of a rock art a rethinking of the work of Leroi-Gourhan who always refused to move in this direction. The poet Bataille (1955) opened up this approach in his own way, but he was explicitly concerned with the field of literature. It is still too early to predict where the road followed by symbolist archaeology will lead.

The archaeology of death

Recent works attest to the emergence in France of an *archéologie funéraire* explicitly under the influence of either Anglo-American archaeology (e.g. Forest 1983 who refers to Binford and Saxe) or Germanic trends (Demoule 1988; Perrin and Ferrer 1987). Here again, French archaeologists were entirely unprepared for the critical explosion of data due to the development of rescue excavation. Only a handful of physical anthropologists were available for work on post-Pleistocene human remains and they had little more than a semblance of an institutional structure. The name Leroi-Gourhan is linked with an original, but for a long time very marginal, approach to the study of multiple burials. At a small excavation on a Chalcolithic hypogeum at Les Mournouards, Leroi-Gourhan and his team tried to put into practice the methods which should be used in a situation where, previously, masses of bones had been dug out in the crudest way because their interrelationships were assumed to be uninformative, due to supposedly mass deposition and post-depositional disturbances. These methods were later developed by Masset and Leclerc at La Chaussée-Tirancourt and now represent the standard for this type of excavation in France (Duday and Masset 1987). Highly developed technical skills are certainly of paramount importance in this school, but interpretation is not avoided, although probably no one would debate the issues raised by Shanks and Tilley (1982), for instance.

Archaeology and economy

For some time, there has existed in France in the work of Will, Vidal-Naquet and, more recently, Andreau, an approach which is well known to economic historians of the ancient world. However, this approach has had little effect on archaeology except in the very specific domain of studies concerning the production and trade of amphorae. There, it has given rise to systematic fieldwork, underwater as well as on land, which depends heavily on physico-chemical analyses and the quantitative treatment of data to achieve historical interpretations (Laubenheimer 1985; Tchernia 1986).

There is also a small school of Marxists in ancient history, notably grouped around Lévêque, and they have made some inroads into Iron Age archaeology (Daubigny 1984). This school is entirely independent of the research in social anthropology conducted by Godelier, Meillassoux, Terray and very recently, Testart (1985) which has led to results some of which have been used by certain Anglo-American archaeologists but have hardly been used in the Francophone world, except for Forest (1983), Gallay (1986) and Coudart (1991). As the tradition of French research in the area of Marxism and economic anthropology is so developed, this lack of communication between French social anthropologists and archaeologists is probably due more to the low level of the problems generally investigated in French archaeology than to any specific methodological inadequacy. Examples of detailed socio-economic models therefore remain rare (Holl 1986; Coudart 1987) and they use some concepts, such as information theory in particular, which have been worked out and developed by American archaeologists (Johnson 1982). It is also interesting to note how little work there is on trade and exchange which traces the origins of items through archaeometric data. Exceptions are the work on amphorae already mentioned and, in a different cultural area, a project on the circulation of copper in the third millennium in West Asia which, as far as its theoretical basis is concerned, depends entirely on the classical Anglo-American literature on this subject (Berthoud and Cleuziou 1985a, 1985b).

Archaeology and history

Collaboration between archaeology and ancient history in France has already been mentioned with respect to economy. The school of Vernant and Vidal-Naquet which integrates history, history of religion and anthropology has contributed to a focus on problems of social and economic history (Finley 1973), and to investigating the role of images in ancient Greece (Snodgrass 1987; Vernant and Bérard 1984; Durand 1986). This collaboration between investigations arising from a structuralist approach to the Greek tradition and an iconographic analysis plays, just as it does in prehistory, a heuristic role and emphasises the necessity of an archaeological hermeneutic.

It is well known that history is notably absent from the American New Archaeology. Conversely, it is striking to see how limited a role archaeology has played in the *Annales*, despite Febvre and Bloch's efforts and Braudel's interest in material culture (Revel 1978; Schnapp 1981). A glance at the bibliography in Braudel's last work (1986) shows the gap between the French historical school and archaeological research undertaken in the last twenty years concerning pre- and proto-historic societies. It is only in exceptional cases (Brun 1987) and, in general, through material culture studies (Coudart and Pion 1986) that prehistory and *histoire nouvelle* meet. Finally, the research undertaken by the Centre de recherches historiques of the VIth section of the Ecole pratique des hautes études (now the Ecole des hautes études en sciences sociales) has contributed to the development of a history of medieval deserted villages (Archéologie du village déserté 1970) and a social analysis of the medieval rural world. The most comprehensive synthesis in Europe on medieval villages is a collaborative work between a medieval historian and an archaeologist who was then teaching at the Ecole des hautes études en sciences sociales (Chapelot and Fossier 1980). It is true that the *Annales* have been the victim of their own success. Swept along by the expansion of publishing and the mass media, affected by a European crisis in economic and Marxist models, the journal has shifted its interest towards the *histoire des mentalités*, political history and the history of other cultural areas (Islam, the Orient, America) rather than towards synchronic history or the history of the *longue durée*. Is this a resurgence of the ideas of the 1950s? Is it a return to the culture history of events, evident in recently published works focusing on the history of urban France, of rural France, of the French family, and indeed even in the entire history of France itself?

Nevertheless, this somewhat diffused historical school, which seems in its peripheral studies to have lost its direction and in its centre to feed upon itself, could find new stimuli in the urban archaeology which has belatedly flourished in France in the 1980s. These large excavations, the most famous of which is that of the Louvre (Trombetta 1987), are in fact only beginning to realise their potential. They have already completely revolutionised our knowledge of daily life in medieval and modern cities. Other areas could also turn out to be very fertile. The work of Brunaux in Gournay-sur-Aronde (Brunaux 1986; Brunaux *et al.* 1985) throws totally new light on the cultic practices of the Celtic populations. Whether it is concerned with the Celtic expansion or the 'great invasions', archaeology in Western Europe is confronted with immense ethno-historical problems which it has hardly addressed as yet (Klejn 1977).

Cultural technology, ethno-archaeology and experimental archaeology

It is in the very specific field of cultural technology that the French have contributed something fairly original. This contribution is due to the confluence of three currents of thought. The first of these is ethnology in the strict sense, with the pioneering works of Haudricourt (whose complete works have been reissued: Haudricourt 1987; Haudricourt and Hédin 1987; Haudricourt and Dibie 1987), those of Leroi-Gourhan (1943, 1945, 1957) and those of Parain (1975, 1979), Gille (1978, 1980), Cresswell (1975), Sigaut (1985) and, very recently, Lemonnier (1986, 1987a, 1987b, 1989). The second is the ethnological approach applied to prehistory by Leroi-Gourhan (1985). The third current is the experimental research done on lithic technology by Tixier and his school (Tixier *et al.* 1980, 1984).

The ethnological approach to the study of technology and technological systems is well illustrated by the dynamic group who publish the journal *Techniques et cultures*. At present, this approach is of more immediate interest to archaeologists, who expect it to produce theories on the relationships between material culture and society, than it is to the wider circle of French ethnologists. Within experimental archaeology itself, it is only in the area of lithic technology that the subdiscipline in France has acquired for itself a reliable set of tools of observation and control. In other areas (bone tools, ceramics, metallurgy, agriculture), the work is generally rather embryonic or is essentially directed towards museum display (architecture in particular).

In archaeology, the development of studies of technology has therefore mainly contributed to our knowledge of the sourcing and distribution of lithic materials and of the operational sequences for the production of tools, particularly for the upper palaeolithic (Perlès 1989; Audouze 1987; Audouze, Karlin *et al.* 1988). In addition, developing from the work of Leroi-Gourhan, such studies have contributed to our knowledge of the technological and cognitive capacities which developed in the course of the lower and middle palaeolithic (Boëda 1986). This is certainly the only real innovation – since the fundamental work of Bordes and Leroi-Gourhan – in French palaeolithic research which, otherwise, seems to have languished in the last few years. It is reasonable to expect fertile results from these studies, not only for the palaeolithic but also for later periods.

Another area of research, closer to cultural anthropology, deals with the relationship between technological style and function. Recent work on this has been done in the archaeology of the architecture of the neolithic (Coudart 1987).

It is therefore towards technology that what in France is conventionally called the ethno-archaeological strategy has been directed (see Pétrequin and Pétrequin 1984; P. Pétrequin 1984 in particular). But before this could happen, French prehistoric archaeology had to liberate itself, at the beginning of the 1970s, from ethnological analogy. The development towards ethno-archaeology has consequently been rather belated. Going far beyond what Leroi-Gourhan had in mind when he condemned the simplistic use of analogy, prehistorians saved themselves the trouble of doing any social anthropology at all. It is therefore only very recently that ethno-archaeological research has been done in France and in Francophone countries. But this return to ethnology has been both cautious and profoundly empirical. This can be seen not only with regard to cultural technology (e.g. the studies of the lacustrine dwellings of Benin and of the lithic tools of New Guinea done by A.-M. and P. Pétrequin 1984, 1988b) but also with respect to analogy, reprieved by the use of the direct historical approach of assumed continuity (e.g. the study of the vernacular architecture of the Near East (Aurenche 1981, 1984)), or even through the formalisation of archaeological reasoning (Gallay 1981; Roux 1988).

Given their insufficient grounding in social anthropology, it is still risky for French and Francophone archaeologists to abandon this cautious empiricism and extrapolate beyond a level where the data can be checked and quantified. This is evident in several imprudent generalisations or analogies on social organisation (Gallay 1986; Roux 1985). However, most importantly, the entirety of these works, like ethno-archaeology in general, has produced a considerable harvest of data and new hypotheses. Two levels of questions are relevant here, and must be considered in the correct sequence. The first level concerns the data themselves: materials, objects, techniques, natural phenomena, etc., and the second concerns the reconstructions based on these data: demography, symbolic interpretation, cultural tradition, social organisation, etc. In addition, these data and questions must be evaluated against experiments and archaeometric analyses, as is at present being done by Pétrequin's group at Lake Chalain in the Jura. Thus, ethnographic observation generates hypotheses, and experiments and physico-chemical analyses evaluate interpretations. Thus, instead of borrowing models of behaviour directly from social anthropology and verifying their applicability to the archaeological or the ethnographic data for 'goodness of fit', French archaeologists predominantly choose to elaborate their models first on the fundamental level of direct data. This is done by a continuing confrontation between archaeological data, ethnographic observation, experiment and analyses, so that the socio-economic models are introduced only in the second instance, after each of the data has been checked. This process, which ignores the inductivism/deductivism debate so important in American New Archaeology, and the discussion of archaeological reasoning in *Logique de Port Royal* (Borillo 1971), was recently and sarcastically encapsulated by Haudricourt: 'Je n'ai jamais pu les distinguer [induction et déduction] et me contente de raisonner comme je peux' (Haudricourt and Dibie 1987: 15).[5]

We anticipate that the much more conceptual approach of Anglo-American archaeologists and the much more empirical approach of the French researchers will lead in a few years to rather similar models, probably at about the same time.

Conclusion

'L'archéologie est enfin jeune' (Soudsky 1970: 53): Soudsky's statement of 1969 probably applies better to the French archaeology of the late 1980s than to that of the late 1960s. Although not always controlled, the accelerating growth of the last few years has at least been accompanied by some necessary re-evaluation, even if the situation remains very confused. The exponential growth of the database led the way to intepretative studies which were simply inconceivable ten years ago, when France was a blank on some archaeological maps of Europe. After a stage – which obviously has to continue – in which priority has been given to techniques of data recovery, and to the organisation of the discipline, the idea of a unity of archaeology, or at least of some community of methods, is slightly more popular, and this encourages theoretical debate. The renewed interest in the most generalising parts of Leroi-Gourhan's work, and the hopes raised by new approaches to problems concerned with cultural technology, are encouraging signs. The road is long, however, and those who teach or work in rescue archaeology know how close to a nightmare the dream can be! Theoretical research in French archaeology still involves only a minority, but this minority is becoming larger, more active, and with a wider range of research interests. As a result of yet another time-lag in its history, this fruition comes paradoxically at a moment when the humanities, and even history, so brilliant when archaeology was at its lowest ebb, are facing an acute crisis, which is often referred to in journalistic terms as 'the death of the ideologies'.

Whatever the actual influence of debates which have taken place outside archaeology in France and outside France in archaeology, we have underlined some aspects of what could be specific French contributions. We do believe that the most promising is the emphasis on cultural technology, grounded in a long tradition which, after all, can be traced back to the Enlightenment and to the importance given to the social role of technology in the *Encyclopédie* of Diderot and d'Alembert. The eighteenth-century *encyclopédistes* accorded some political significance to their interest in technology. Similarly, it is our position that the status of archaeology cannot be separated from its role in society, and therefore that the political implications of interpretation about the past will some time have to be examined, a point largely ignored in the Anglo-American literature. The best current French examples suggest that interpretative work will remain very empirically grounded in an interaction between the data on the one hand and analogy, experimentation and analytical techniques on the other. This must avoid the obvious pitfalls of merely sterile description and low-level inferences which have impeded much of such research until now.

So are the arrogant 'Froggies' back? Certainly not! But the future richness of archaeological theory will of course depend on the interaction of different intellectual traditions, rather than on the adoption of a single 'correct' way of reasoning. At a moment when European universities are being compelled to merge in ambitious networks, French archaeology must face the challenge to bring its own modest contribution to a collaboration from which it has been absent for too long.

Notes

1. This contribution would not have been possible without Sander E. van der Leeuw, who translated it into English, or Stuart C. Brown, who spent countless hours with one of us deciphering the nuances and the logic of our French way of thinking in order to transpose them into the nuance and logic of the English language. To both of them, we express our friendship and gratitude.

2. 'If we try to find a palaeo-sociological approach in the three fat, almost official, volumes devoted to the prehistory of France published in 1976, we will be disappointed.'
3. 'The road is long but after all archaeology is young. The young people on the barricades will be able to destroy those other barricades surrounding the sciences and national languages, the impenetrable domains of disciplines which are too far separated, the "parochial" terminologies and typologies . . . , but at the same time we must change the education and training of archaeologists. Universities must be changed as well as the academies, the journals, the monographs, the museums, the archives and, above all, the excavations. There is much to do.'
4. '[This text] seems to mark an epoch in the spiritual journey of a great American archaeologist.'
5. 'I have never been able to distinguish between them [induction and deduction] and I am content to reason as best I can.'

References

Actes du colloque du CNRS (mars 1987) (1988) *André Leroi-Gourhan ou les voies de l'homme*, Paris: Albin Michel.
Archéologie du village déserté (1970) Cahiers des Annales 27, Paris: Ecole pratique des hautes études and Académie Polonaise des sciences.
Audouze, F. (1987) 'The Paris Basin in Magdalenian times', in O. Soffer (ed.) *The Pleistocene Old World, Regional Perspectives*, New York and London: Plenum Press.
Audouze, F., Karlin, C. *et al.* (1988) 'Taille du silex et finalité du débitage dans le Magdalénien du Bassin parisien', in M. Otte (ed.) *La Civilisation du Paléolithique supérieur de la Loire à l'Oder*, Oxford: British Archaeological Report International Series.
Audouze, F. and Leroi-Gourhan, And. (1981) 'France: a continental insularity', *World Archaeology* 13(2): 170–89.
Aurenche, O. (1981) *La Maison orientale, l'architecture du Proche Orient ancien des origines au milieu du quatrième millénaire*, Paris: Geuthner.
—— (ed.) (1984) *Nomades et sédentaires, perspectives ethnoarchéologiques*, Paris: E.R.C.
Bataille, G. (1955) *Lascaux ou la naissance de l'art*, Geneva: Skirra.
Berthoud, T. and Cleuziou, S. (1985a) 'Farming communities of the Oman Peninsula and the copper of Makkan', *Journal of Oman Studies* (2): 239–46.
—— (1985b) 'Archéométrie et archéologie, les leçons d'une expérience', in J.-L. Huot, M. Yon and Y. Calvet (eds) *De l'Indus aux Balkans, recueil à la mémoire de Jean Deshayes*, Paris: E.R.C.
Billig, M. I. (1979) *Psychology, Racism and Fascism*, Birmingham: Searchlight. French translation: Billig, M. (1981) *L'Internationale raciste, de la psychologie à la 'science' des races*, Paris: Maspéro.
Binford, L. R. (1972) *An Archaeological Perspective*, Chicago: Seminar Press.

—— (1973) 'Interassemblage variability: the Mousterian and the "functional" argument', in C. Renfrew (ed.) *The Explanation of Culture Change, Models in Prehistory*, London: Duckworth.

Boëda, E. (1986) *Approches technologiques du concept Levallois et évaluation de son champs d'application*, Thèse de l'Université de Paris X, Lille: Université de Lille, Atelier national de reproduction des thèses.

Bollack, M. and Wismann, B. (1983) *Philologie und Hermeneutik im 19 Jahrhundert (11)* Göttingen: Vandenhoeck und Ruprecht.

Bordes, F. (1973) 'On the chronology and the contemporaneity of different Paleolithic cultures in France', in C. Renfrew (ed.) *The Explanation of Culture Change, Models in Prehistory*, London: Duckworth.

Borillo, M. (1970) 'La vérification des hypothèses en archéologie: deux pas vers une méthode', in J.-C. Gardin (ed.) *Archéologie et calculateurs*, Paris: CNRS.

—— (1971) 'Formal procedures and the use of computers in archaeology', *Norwegian Archaeological Review* 4: 2–27.

Borillo, M. and Gardin, J.-C. (1974) *Les Banques de données archéologiques*, Paris: C.N.R.S.

Braudel, F. (1986) *L'Identité de la France*, Paris: Arthaud-Flammarion.

Brun, P. (1987) *Prince et princesse de la Celtique*, Paris: Errance.

Brunaux, J.-L. (1986) *Les Gaulois, sanctuaires et rites*, Paris: Errance.

Brunaux, J.-L., Méniel, P. and Poplin, F. (1985) 'Gournay 1: les fouilles sur la sanctuaire et l'*oppidum* (1974–1984)', *Revue Archéologique de Picardie*, special number.

Camps, G. (1982) *La Préhistoire, à la recherche du paradis perdu*, Paris: Librairie académique Perrin.

Carbonnel, C. O. (1976) *Histoire et historiens*, Toulouse: Presses universitaires de France.

Cauvin, J. (1978) *Les Premiers villages de Syrie-Palestine du IXème au VIIème millénaire avant J. C.*, Lyon: Collection de la Maison de l'Orient méditerranéen ancien 4.

—— (1987) 'L'apparition des premières divinités', *La Recherche* 194: 1472–80.

Chapelot, J. and Fossier, J. (1980) *Le Village et la maison au Moyen Age*, Paris: Hachette. English translation: Chapelot, J. and Fossier, J. (1985) *Village and House in the Middle Ages*, London: Batsford.

Chapelot, J., Querrien, A. and Schnapp, Al. (1979) 'L'archéologie en France, les facteurs d'une crise', *Le Progrès scientifique* 202: 57–110.

Chapeville, F., Grassé, P. P., Jacob, F., Jacquard, A., Ninio, J., Piveteau, J., de Ricqlès, A., Roger, J. and Thuillier, P. intérrogés par Noël, E. (1979) *Le Darwinisme aujourd'hui*, Paris: Le Seuil.

Christophe, J. and Deshayes, J. (1964) *Index de l'outillage, outils en métal de l'Age du Bronze, des Balkans à l'Indus*, Paris: CNRS.

Cleuziou, S. and Demoule, J.-P. (1980a) 'Situation de l'archéologie théorique', *Nouvelles de l'Archéologie* 3: 7–15.

—— J.-P. (1980b) 'Enregistrer, gérer, traiter les données archéologiques', in Al. Schnapp (ed.) *L'Archéologie aujourd'hui*, Paris: Hachette.

Cleuziou, S., Demoule, J.P., Schnapp, Al. and Schnapp, An. (1973) 'Renouveau des méthodes et théorie de l'archéologie,' *Annales, Econo-*

mie, Société, Civilisation 1: 35–51; reprinted in M. Borillo (ed.) (1978) *Archéologie et Calcul*, Paris: Union Générale d'Editions.

Conkey, M. (1980) 'Context, structure and efficacy in Paleolithic art and design', in M. L. Foster and S. Brandes (eds) *Symbol as Sense*, New York: Academic Press.

—— (1984) 'To find ourselves: art and social geography of prehistoric hunter-gatherers', in C. Schrire (ed.) *Past and Present in Hunter-Gatherer Studies*, New York: Academic Press.

Coppens, Y. (1983) *Le Singe, l'Afrique et l'homme*, Paris: Fayard.

Coudart, A. (1989) *Architecture et société néolithique: uniformité et variabilité, fonction et style de l'architecture dans l'approche des communautés du Néolithique danubien*, Thèse de l'Université de Paris I, Lille: Université de Lille, Atelier national de reproduction de thèse.

—— (1991) 'Social structure and relationships in prehistoric small-scale sedentary societies: the Bandkeramik neolithic groups', in S. Gregg (ed.) *'Between bands and states: sedentism, subsistence, and interaction in small-scale societies'*, Center for Archaeological Investigations (Occasional paper no. 9). Carbondale: Southern Illinois University.

Coudart, A. and Pion, P. (1986) *L'Archéologie de la France rurale, de la préhistoire aux temps modernes*, Paris: Belin.

Courbin, P. (1981) *Qu'est-ce-que l'archéologie?*, Paris: Payot. English translation: Courbin, P. (1989) *What is Archaeology? An Essay on the Nature of Archaeological Research*, Chicago and London: Chicago University Press.

—— (1983) 'La truelle d'or, parabole pour l'archéologie des années 1980', *Archeologia*, 178: 43–53.

—— (ed.) (1963) *Etudes archéologiques*, Paris: S.E.V.P.E.N.

Cresswell, R. (ed.) (1975) *Elément d'ethnologie*, Paris: Armand Colin.

Daniel, G. (1981) *A Short History of Archaeology*, London: Thames & Hudson.

Daubigny, A. (ed.) (1984) *Archéologie et rapports sociaux en Gaule*, Paris: Annales littéraires de l'Université de Besançon 290, Les Belles lettres.

De Laet, S. J. (1981) 'Philippe-Charles Schmerling (1791–1836)', in G. Daniel (ed.) *Towards a History of Archaeology*, London: Thames 8 Hudson.

Demoule, J.-P. (1980) 'Les Indo-européens ont-ils existé?' *L'Histoire* 28: 108–20.

—— (1982) 'Le Néolithique, une révolution?', *Le Débat* 20: 54–75.

—— (1988) 'The archaeology of death: formal analysis and anthropological models', in J. Brown, R. Chapman and L. Goldstein (eds) *Understanding the Dead: Theory, Context, and Time in Archaeology*, New York.

Deshayes, J. (1960) *Les Outils de bronze, de l'Indus au Danube, IV°-II° millénaire*, Paris: Geuthner.

Duday H. and Masset, C. (eds) (1987) *Anthropologie physique et archéologie. Méthodes d'étude des sépultures*, Paris: CNRS.

Dumézil, G. (1981) 'Entretien [avec J. Bonnet et D. Pralon]', in *Georges Dumézil, Cahiers pour un temps*, Paris.

Durand, J.-L. (1986) *Sacrifice et tabou en Grèce ancienne. Essai d'anthropologie religieuse*, Paris: La Découverte.
Fariñas del Cerro, L., Fernandez de la Vega, W and Hesnard, A. (1977) 'Contribution à l'établissement d'une typologie des amphores dites "Dressel 2–4" ', in *Méthodes classiques et méthodes formelles dans l'étude des amphores*, Paris and Rome: Ecole française de Rome.
Finley, M. I. (ed.) (1973) *Problèmes de la terre en Grèce ancienne*, Paris and The Hague.
Forest, J.-D. (1983) *Les Pratiques funéraires en Mésopotamie, du 5ème millénaire au début du 3ème, étude de cas*, Paris: E.R.C.
Gallay, A. (1981) *Le Sarnyéré Dogon, archéologie d'un isolat (Mali)*, Paris: E.R.C.
—— (1986) *L'Archéologie demain*, Paris: Belfond.
—— (1989) 'Logicism: a French view of archaeological theory founded in computational perspective', *Antiquity* 63: 27–39.
Gardin, J.-C. (1967) 'Methods for the descriptive analysis of archaeological material', *American Antiquity* 32(1): 13–30.
—— (1970) *Archéologie et calculateurs: problèmes mathématiques et sémiologiques*, Paris: CNRS.
—— (1971a) 'Archéologie et calculateurs: nouvelles perspectives', *Revue internationale des Sciences Sociales* XXIII (2): 204–18.
—— (1971b) *UNISIST. Etudes sur la réalisation d'un système mondial d'information scientifique*, Paris: UNESCO.
—— (1972) *L'Informatique et l'inventaire général*, Paris: Ministère des affaires culturelles.
—— (1974) *Les Analyses du discours*, Neuchatel: Delachaux & Nieslé.
—— (1975) 'Effets logiques des bases de données sur les disciplines d'érudition', *Revue Internationale des Sciences Sociales* XXVII: 815–30.
—— (1979a) *Une archéologie théorique*, Paris: Hachette.
—— (1979b) *Archaeological Constructs: an Aspect of Theoretical Archaeology*, Cambridge: Cambridge University Press.
—— (1981) 'Vers une épistémologie pratique en sciences humaines', in J.-C. Gardin, M.-S. Lagrange, J. M. Martin, J. Molino and J. Natali (eds) *La Logique du plausible*, Paris: Editions de la Maison des Sciences de l'Homme.
Gardin, J.-C., Guillaume, O., Herman, P.-Q., Hesnard, A., Lagrange, M.-S., Renaud, M. and Zadora-Rio, E. (1987) *Systèmes experts et sciences humaines: le cas de l'archéologie*, Paris: Eyrolles.
Geddes, D. (1986) *De la chasse au troupeau en Méditerrannée occidentale. Les débuts de l'élevage dans le bassin de l'Aude*, Toulouse: Editions de l'Ecole des hautes études en sciences sociales.
Gille, B. (1980) *Les Mécaniciens grecs. La naissance de la technologie*, Paris: Le Seuil.
—— (1978) *Histoire des techniques*, Paris: Gallimard, Encyclopédie de la Pléiade.
Girard, R. (1978) *Des choses cachées depuis le début du monde*, Paris: Grasset.
Gnoli, G. and Vernant, J.-P. (1982) *La Mort, les morts dans les sociétés*

anciennes, Paris and Cambridge: Editions de la Maison des Sciences de l'Homme.

Godelier, M. (1988) *Séminaire de l'Ecole des hautes études en sciences sociales*, Paris: Ecole des Hautes Etudes.

Gould, S. J. (1977) *Ever since Darwin. Reflections in Natural History*, New York: Norton & Company. French translation: Gould, S. J. (1979) *Darwin et les grandes énigmes de la vie*, Paris: Le Seuil.

Grenier, A. (1931) 'Archéologie gallo-romaine, première partie: généralités, travaux militaires', in J. Dechelette (ed.) *Manuel d'archéologie préhistorique, celtique et gallo-romaine*, vol. V, Paris: Picard.

Haudricourt, A.-G. (1987) *La Technologie, science humaine. Recherches d'histoire et d'ethnologie des techniques*, Paris: Editions de la Maison des Sciences de l'Homme.

Haudricourt, A.-G. and Dibie, P. (1987) *Les Pieds sur terre*, Paris: A. M. Métailié.

Haudricourt, A.-G. and Hédin, L. (1987) *L'Homme et les plantes cultivées*, Paris: A. M. Métailié.

Hodder, I. (1982a) *Symbols in Action. Ethnoarchaeological Studies of Material Culture*, Cambridge: Cambridge University Press.

—— (ed.) (1982b) *Symbolic and Structural Archaeology*, Cambridge: Cambridge University Press.

—— (ed.) (1987) *The Archaeology of Contextual Meanings*, Cambridge: Cambridge University Press.

Holl, A. (1986) *Economie et société néolithique du Dhar Tichitt (Mauritanie)*, Paris: E.R.C.

Jacquard, A. (1982) *Au péril de la sciences? Interrogations d'un généticien*, Paris: Le Seuil.

Jaulin, B. (ed.) (1968) *Calcul et formalisation dans les sciences de l'Homme*, Paris: CNRS.

Jaulin, R. (1968) 'Analyse formelle de la géomancie', in B. Jaulin (ed.) *Calcul et formalisation dans les sciences de l'Homme*, Paris: CNRS.

Jelinek, A. J. (1986) 'La coopération américano-française en archéologie préhistorique', Nouvelles de l'archéologie 22: 64–7.

Johnson, G. A. (1982) 'Organisational structure and scalar stress', in C. A. Renfrew, M. J. Rowlands and B Segraves (eds) *Theory and Explanation in Archaeology*, New York: Academic Press.

Klejn, L. S. (1977) 'A panorama of theoretical archaeology', *Current Anthropology* 18 (1): 1–42. French translation: Klejn, L. S. (1980) 'Panorama de l'archéologie théorique', in A. Schnapp (ed.) *L'Archéologie aujourd'hui*, Paris: Hachette.

Laming-Emperaire, A. (1964) *Origines de l'archéologie préhistorique en France, des superstitions médiévales à la découverte de l'homme fossile*, Paris: Picard.

Landau, J. and Fernandez de la Vega, W. (1971) 'A new seriation algorithm applied to European anthropomorphic statuary', in F. R. Hodson, D. G. Kendall and P. Tautu (eds) *Mathematics in the Archaeological and Historical Sciences*, Edinburgh: Edinburgh University Press.

Laubenheimer, F. (1985) *La Production des amphores en Gaule Narbonnaise*, Paris: Les Belles Lettres.

Lemonnier, P. (1986) 'The study of material culture today: towards an anthropology of technical systems', *Journal of Anthropological Archaeology* 5: 147–86.

—— (1987a) 'Le sens des flèches: culture matérielle et identité chez les Anga de Nouvelle Guinée', in *De la voûte céleste au terroir, du jardin au foyer*, Paris: Editions de l'Ecole des hautes études en sciences sociales.

—— (1987b) 'La technologie culturelle', *Le Courrier du CNRS*, supplement of 67: 26–30.

—— (1989) 'Bark capes, arrowheads and Concorde: on social representation of material culture', in I. Hodder (ed.) *The Meanings of Things, Material Culture and Symbolic Expression*, London: Unwin Hyman.

Leroi-Gourhan, And. (1943) *Evolution et techniques: L'homme et la matière*, Paris: Albin Michel.

—— (1945) *Evolution et techniques: Milieu et techniques*, Paris: Albin Michel.

—— (1957) 'Technique et société chez l'animal et chez l'homme', *Originalité biologique de l'homme, recherches et débats*, Paris: Fayard, Cahiers du CCIF.

—— (1964a) *Les Religions de la préhistoire*, Paris: Presses universitaires de France.

—— (1964b) *Le Geste et la Parole I. Technique et langage*, Paris: Albin Michel.

—— (1965) *Le Geste et la Parole II. La mémoire et les rythmes*, Paris: Albin Michel.

—— (1985) *Le Fils du temps: ethnologie et préhistoire (1935–1970)*, Paris: Fayard.

Lévi-Strauss, C. (1962) *La Pensée sauvage*, Paris: Plon.

Mallory, J. P. (1989) *Indo-Europeans. Language, Archaeology and Myth*, London: Thames & Hudson.

Millin, A. L. (1826) *Introduction à l'étude de l'archéologie*, Paris: chez Girard.

Mitterrand, F. (1985) 'Allocution prononcée par M. François Mitterrand, Président de la République, au Mont Beuvray, mardi 17 septembre 1985', *Nouvelles de l'Archéologie* 21: 51–5.

Moberg, C. A. (1976) *Introduction à l'archéologie*, Paris: Maspéro.

—— (1980) 'Vers une analyse sociologique en archéologie', in Al. Schnapp (ed.) *L'Archéologie aujourd'hui*, Paris: Hachette.

Nora, S. and Minc, A. (1978) *L'Informatisation de la société*, Paris: La documentation française/Le Seuil.

Normand, F. and Richard, A. (1974) 'L'archéologie française en crise', *La Recherche*: 754–62.

Parain, C. (1979) *Outils, ethnies et développement historique*, Paris: Editions sociales.

—— (ed.) (1975) *Ethnologie et histoire, Forces productives et problèmes de transition*, Paris: Editions sociales.

Pelletier, A. (ed.) (1985) *L'Archéologie et ses méthodes*, Rennes: Horvath.

Perlès, C. (in press) *Les Industries lithiques taillées de Franchthi, Grèce. Tome I: présentation générale et industries paléolithiques*, tome 2 *Le*

Mésolithique et le Néolithique initial, Indianapolis/Bloomington: Indiana University Press.

Perrin, P. and Ferrer, L.-C. (1987) *Les Francs. 1. A la conquête de la Gaule; 2. A l'origine de la France,* Paris: Armand Colin.

Pétrequin, A.-M. and Pétrequin, P. (1984) *Habitat lacustre du Bénin, une approche ethnoarchéologique,* Paris: E.R.C.

—— (1988a) *Les Néolithiques des lacs. Préhistoire des lacs de Chalain et de Clairvaux (4000–2000 av. JC),* Paris: Errance.

—— (1988b) 'Ethnoarchéologie de l'habitat en grotte de Nouvelle Guinée: une transposition de l'espace social et économique', *Bulletin du Centre genevois d'anthropologie* 1: 61–82.

Pétrequin, P. (1984) *Gens de l'eau, gens de la terre. Ethno-archéologie des communautés lacustres,* Paris: Hachette.

—— (ed.) (1986) *Les Sites littoraux néolithiques de Clairvaux-les-Lacs (Jura), I,* Paris: Editions de la Maison des Sciences de l'Homme.

Querrien, A. and Schnapp, A. (1984) 'Second rapport sur la politique de la recherche archéologique en France', *Nouvelles de l'Archéologie* 16:7–61.

Régnier, A. (1971) 'De la théorie des groupes à la pensée sauvage', in P. Richard and R. Jaulin (eds) *Anthropologie et calcul,* Paris: Union générale d'éditions.

Renfrew, C. (1987) *Archaeology and Language. The Puzzle of Indo-European Origins,* London: Jonathan Cape Ltd.

Revel, J. (1978) 'The *Annales,* continuities and discontinuities', *The Review* 1 (3/4): 9–18.

Revue archéologique de Picardie (1982) *Cinq années de fouilles dans la vallée de l'Aisne,* special number.

Richard, P. and Jaulin R. (eds) (1971) *Anthropologie et calcul,* Paris: Union générale d'éditions.

Richards, J. D. and Ryan, N. S. (1985) *Data Processing in Archaeology,* Cambridge: Cambridge University Press.

Roux, V. (1985) *Le Matériel de broyage. Etude ethnoarchéologique à Tichitt (Mauritanie),* Paris: E.R.C.

—— (1988) 'Etude ethnoarchéologique de quelques évaluations de productions céramiques protohistoriques', in Mission archéologique française en Asie centrale (ed.) *L'Asie centrale et ses rapports avec les civilisations orientales des origines à l'Age du fer,* Actes du colloque franco-soviétique de Paris (1985), Paris: Diffusion de Boccard.

Ruffié, J. (1979) 'Sociobiologie et génétique', *Le Monde,* 11 and 12 September.

—— (1982) *Traité du vivant,* Paris: Fayard.

Sackett, J. R. (1981) 'From de Mortillet to Bordes: a century of French Paleolithic research', in G. Daniel (ed.) *Towards a History of Archaeology,* Cambridge: Cambridge University Press.

Sahlins, M. (1976) *The Use and Abuse of Biology: an Anthropological Critic of Sociobiology,* Detroit and Ann Arbor: The University of Michigan Press. French translation: Sahlins, M. (1980) *Critique de la sociobiologie,* Paris: Gallimard.

Scarre, Ch. (ed.) (1983) *Ancient France, Neolithic Societies and their Landscapes*, Edinburgh: Edinburgh University Press.

Shanks, M. and Tilley, C. (1982) 'Ideology, symbolic power and ritual communication: a reinterpretation of neolithic mortuary practices', in I. Hodder (ed.) *Symbolic and Structural Archaeology*, Cambridge: Cambridge University Press.

Schiller, F. (1979) *Paul Broca*, Berkeley: University of California Press.

Schnapp, Al. (1981) 'Les Annales et l'archéologie: une rencontre difficile', *Mélanges de l'Ecole française de Rome – Antiquités* 93: 469–78.

—— (1982) 'Archéologie et tradition académique en Europe aux XVIII° et XIX° siècles', *Les Annales ESC* 5–6: 760–77.

—— (ed.) (1980) *L'Archéologie aujourd'hui*, Paris: Hachette.

Sigaut, F. (1985) 'More (and enough) on technology 1', *History and Technology* 2 (2): 115–32.

Snodgrass, A. (1987) 'The first figure scenes in Greek art', in *An Archaeology of Greece*, Berkeley: University of California Press.

Soudsky, B. (1970) 'Le problème des propriétés dans les ensembles archéologiques', in J.-C. Gardin (ed.) *Archéologie et calculateurs, problèmes mathématiques et sémiologiques*, Paris.

—— (1973) 'Higher level archaeological entities: models and reality', in C. Renfrew (ed.) *The Explanation of Culture Change. Models in Prehistory*, London: Duckworth.

Tchernia, A. (1986) *Le Vin dans l'Italie romaine. Essai d'histoire économique d'après les amphores*, Rome: Ecole française.

Testart, A. (1982) *Les Chasseurs-cueilleurs ou l'origine des inégalités*, Paris: Mémoires de la Société d'ethnologie.

—— (1985) *Le Communisme primitif. 1 Economie et idéologie*, Paris: Editions de la Maison des Sciences de l'Homme.

Thuillier, P. (1976) *Les Biologistes vont-ils prendre le pouvoir?*, Paris: Le Seuil.

Tixier, J., Inizan, M.-L. and Roche, H. (1980) *Préhistoire de la pierre taillée 1. Terminologie et technologie*, Paris: CNRS.

—— (1984) *Préhistoire de la pierre taillée 2. Economie du débitage laminaire*, Paris: CNRS.

Trombetta, P.-J. (1987) *Sous la pyramide du Louvre. Vingt siècles retrouvés*, Monaco: Le Rocher.

Vernant, J.-P. and Bérard, P. (1984) *La Cité des images*, Paris and Lausanne: LEP-Nathan. English translation: Vernant, J.-P. and Bérard, P. (in press) Princeton University Press.

Vialou, D. (1987) *L'Art des grottes en Ariège magdalénienne*, Paris: CNRS.

Viera, R. (1982) 'Typology, classification and theory building', in R. Whallon and J. A. Brown (eds) *Essays in Archaeological Typology*, Evanston: Illinois Centre for American Archaeology Press.

Whallon, R. (1982) 'Variables and dimensions: the critical step in quantitative typology', in R. Whallon and J. A. Brown (eds) *Essays in Archaeological Typology*, Evanston: Illinois Centre for American archaeology Press.

Wright, H. T. and Johnson, G. A. (1975) 'Population, exchange, and early state formation in southwestern Iran', *American Anthropologist* 77: 267–89.

6

THEORETICAL ARCHAEOLOGY IN BRITAIN

Timothy Champion

For academic archaeologists who began their careers in the period after the late 1960s, it may sometimes be difficult to imagine a time when archaeology in Britain did not seem to be in a state of theoretical ferment. Though it would be incorrect to describe British archaeology in the period before the mid 1960s as static, the rate of change since then has been substantially greater than before, and perhaps greater than in any period since the middle of the nineteenth century. It would, however, be easy to overestimate the extent to which this theoretical debate has attracted the interest or sympathetic understanding of archaeologists and has affected the day-to-day practice of many of them. In this chapter I shall look at some of the main ideas introduced into the subject, first from America and more recently from Europe, and at British reaction to them, and try to see what can be said about the reasons for these developments, and the extent of their acceptance.

Perhaps because of the great heterogeneity of the ideas and the sheer complexity of some of the concepts involved, there has been no general guide written to the intellectual history of British archaeology in the post-war period, though Trigger's survey (1990) includes a review of the broader Anglo-American tradition, but it should be noted that a similar complexity has not acted as a deterrent in related disciplines such as geography (Johnston 1986, 1987). Apart from reviews of some of the themes of recent debate (e.g. Hodder 1985, 1986a; Shennan 1986, 1987), it is curious that the only two assessments of the state of archaeology specifically in Britain have been published in German by German archaeologists who have worked in Britain (Härke 1983; Wolfram 1986).

Towards the New Archaeology

One of the first signs of the things to come was a review by David Clarke of Chang's *Rethinking Archaeology*, which began with one of his characteristically vivid images:

> From time to time, as the primitive Old World archaeologist squats on the shore of the primordial Atlantic, a passing current will wash up at his feet the ideograms of a distant civilisation – the baneful signs of distant archaeologists. With curiosity and persistence the aboriginal may laboriously run his finger along familiar signs in unfamiliar and difficult constructions. At such times an American book on archaeological theory presents the English-reading native with all the problems of relating Linear A to Linear B.
>
> (Clarke 1967: 237)

In these few words Clarke caught both the excitement and the difficulty of new ideas. The image remains strikingly apt, though I think many would now see the aboriginal archaeologist as no longer the passive recipient of waves of new ideas, but the active seeker after, and modifier of, appropriate ideas, in the creation of a new independent discipline, neither art nor science, neither history nor anthropology, but archaeology.

Clarke had himself been working towards a reformation of archaeology, which he saw as chaotically unsystematic, undisciplined, intuitive and empirical. His *Analytical Archaeology* (1968) was a bombshell. Drawing heavily on mathematical, statistical, scientific and geographical techniques, frequently before they were adequately synthesised within their own disciplines, it was a staggering work of intellectual eclecticism. It was simply not the sort of archaeology that British archaeologists were used to.

The reaction in Britain has been described by Chapman (1979). It varied from ignoring it, to ridiculing it, criticising its jargon (and overlooking its message), belittling it as having nothing new to say ('we have been doing this all the time'), and calling it un-British. Daniel has argued (1975: 371), in a passage that dismisses all post-1960s theoretical archaeology along with the lunatic fringe and forgeries, that it was only because of 'the bareness of the pre-Columbian record of archaeology' in which 'nothing happened of general interest to the student of world history' that 'American archaeologists, dismayed by their archaeological record, have sought refuge in theory and methodology'. Such views, though most cogently articulated by Daniel, may not have been atypical of many British archaeologists, amateur and professional.

Daniel did, however, organise a debate on the future of archaeology, which rumbled on in the pages of *Antiquity* until Clarke's famous 1973 article on the loss of innocence in archaeology, a polemic defence of the New Archaeology and a programme of work that he was never going to be able to carry out. This was perhaps the one time when important theoretical issues were openly debated in a journal with a comparatively wide and popular readership, though the antipathy of the editorial viewpoint was evident. It may be doubted how much was achieved by this, since the reactions to Clarke's article were very much the same as those to the original book – objections to the verbal medium and an unwillingness to confront the message it contained.

I doubt if many would now share such extreme reactions as those, but equally I doubt if many now read *Analytical Archaeology*. It was, as Chapman has argued, a book of the 1960s. It was prophetic; many of the methods and concepts of later archaeology were first suggested there. Of the four main 'paradigms' or modes of archaeological investigation which Clarke identified (1972), the ecological, geographical and anthropological have all flourished (Wolfram 1986: 38–105); only the study of cultural morphology and the definition of cultural entities now seems less important. As Shennan (1989) has emphasised, however, Clarke's concern for the analysis of culture, which may have seemed like the final days of the old Childean tradition, did at least show an interest in culture for its own sake, something which was largely missing from much of the processual archaeology that was to come, and which had to be rediscovered subsequently.

Clarke's *Analytical Archaeology* has left its legacy: an emphasis on methodology, and the refinement of procedures and concepts, the beginnings of a debate on the nature of knowledge and explanation in archaeology, perhaps above all a lively intellectual curiosity and a willingness to look beyond the subject itself to find new ideas. But it probably also signified a parting of the ways; from the early 1970s onwards, explicitly theoretical concerns have become progressively further removed, in language, audience and vehicle of publication, as well as in subject matter, from a traditional, empirical non-theoreticised archaeology.

Processual archaeology

At the same time as Clarke was preparing his attack on traditional archaeology, the various developments known collectively, but not very helpfully, as the 'New Archaeology' were taking place in the United States. Though they could be regarded in part as a sociological phenomenon, and a response to the expansion and changing nature of the archaeological profession in the 1960s and the new people coming into it at that time, there was also a very important theoretical element, inextricably linked in British eyes with the name of Lewis Binford. This movement contained many separate but interlocking elements. Some were negative, such as the rejection of traditional archaeology's emphasis on a culture-historical approach; some were more positive, such as a belief in past societies and social processes as the prime object of archaeology's endeavours, and the possibility of reconstructing them, the adoption of systems theory as a means of explaining social organisation, and a view of culture as an adaptive response. There was also an emphasis on explanation, in particular the adoption of a specific mode of scientific explanation which subsumed individual cases under general laws, and on scientific methodology. New aims required new techniques, and there was special emphasis on quantitative methods and mathematical models, in particular those derived from geography.

The leading advocate of the New Archaeology in Britain, though by no means an uncritical one, has been Colin Renfrew. Though sceptical of the search for general laws, he has maintained the emphasis on generalisation and explanation (Renfrew 1982a). Systems theory received its first and perhaps clearest exposition as an explanatory method in his analysis of the growth of Aegean civilisation (Renfrew 1972). The ideas of American neo-evolutionist anthropologists such as Fried and especially Service, with his schematic typology of band, tribe, chiefdom and state, were introduced and applied to European case studies (e.g. Renfrew 1973).

In this way there emerged a new mode of archaeological research and writing, which stressed the processes of social and economic change within a systems theory framework, with a particular interest in exchange, in ceremonial monuments (Renfrew 1973), cemeteries (e.g. Chapman *et al.* 1981), and settlement patterns and central places (e.g. Renfrew 1982b) as the evidence for those processes in the archaeological record. The methodology relied greatly on new scientific techniques, on quantification, and on geographical (Hodder and Orton 1976; Hodges 1987) and mathematical (Renfrew and Cooke 1979; Renfrew et al. 1982: 287–421) models. More recently, partly in response to the criticism that systems theory relies on external stimulus to account for long-term change, there has been an interest in the possibilities of explaining change through internal factors. Hence the interest in mathematical models such as catastrophe theory to explain sudden change (Renfrew 1978, 1979), and in self-organising systems (Allen 1982); hence also the analysis of the relationships between clusters of societies, the so-called 'peer polity interaction' (Renfrew and Cherry 1986), to explain patterns of shared development through endogenous factors.

Renfrew's work seems never to have attracted the same hostile reception as did Clarke's. In part this may have been due to the comparative lack of jargon, and the relative accessibility of his writing. More importantly, his approach has more often been the explanation of specific data than methodological exposition for its own sake. His own researches have been largely rooted in the problems of European prehistory, and he inevitably became involved there in arguments against the prevailing typological and culture-historical approach, with its emphasis on diffusion through migration or vague 'influence', as the explanation of culture change. But, as he put it himself:

> Usually . . . my starting point has been a specific problem arising within the geographical area and the time range of my work at that time. In many cases the problem has proved, at least in part, to be simply a variant of one very general question which recurs again and again in different parts of the world over the past century of archaeological research. . . . The solutions which emerge are, however, emphatically not specific to the single instance in relation to which they were originally conceived.
>
> (Renfrew 1984: 5)

On the contrary, the kind of archaeology advocated by Renfrew from the late 1960s onwards has become, in one form or another, and whether explicitly recognised or not, one of the prevailing modes of contemporary work in the discipline. This is the so-called 'processual archaeology' with its emphasis on social and economic processes, its systemic view of culture and its acceptance of neo-evolutionary social typologies, and employing a method-ology embracing all the new scientific, mathematical, statistical and geographical techniques. This general orientation towards a socio-economic archaeology, though by no means the only mode of pursuing research and enquiry, has come to represent one characteristic form of recent British archaeology (e.g. Renfrew and Shennan 1982; Champion *et al.* 1984; Collis 1984).

Reaction to the new processual archaeology

From the mid 1970s a series of alternative viewpoints to that of processual archaeology have been tried, adopted, rejected or modified. There is, as yet, no single stance that has achieved even general support; the picture is one of intellectual fragmentation and ferment, in which virtually the only common theme is reaction to the tenets of the New Archaeology, and which can only be described as post-processual archaeology (Hodder 1985).

In part this was because of the emergence of other, potentially more informative and illuminating approaches, in part it was the result of dissatisfaction with specific elements of the New Archae-ology (Hodder 1982c). Some of the objections to its tenets and the sort of explanations of the past it offered revolved around its functionalist account of human culture and social organisation, reducing a rich variety of human experience to mere adaptive strategies against a non-human environment; material culture is more than just tools for survival or an information system for efficiency of adaptation. The adoption of a systems theory approach to explanation also led to the denial of an active role to the individual, who was very largely obscured in the discussion of systems and subsystems as the key explanatory units. Further-more, it made it difficult to locate the causes of social change within the society itself; in a systems theory which assumes homeostatic equilibrium, positive-feedback deviation-amplifying mechanisms require an external stimulus; hence the interest in environmental change or population growth, frequently regarded as an external or independent variable, not subject to social con-trol.

A further criticism was the alleged failure of the processual approach to produce any valid and informative generalisations; the quest for general laws may have been vain, but the status of the generalisable propositions about the past that had been produced was still somewhat uncertain. At the same time, the cost to be paid for seeking generalisation, in the form of the loss of attention paid to the uniqueness of the context of individual past societies and their historical development, was felt by some to be too high.

Production and reproduction

From the mid 1970s there has been a series of new influences on British archaeology, though now the waves bringing the baleful signs of other intellectual cultures have come from across the English Channel rather than the Atlantic. One of the first of these has been the French school of so-called neo-Marxist anthropology; the revitalisation during the 1960s of Marx's treatment of precapitalist societies, under the influence of philosophers such as Althusser, produced a distinctive school of anthropologists of whom Godelier, Terray and Meillassoux have had the greatest effect (Kahn and Llobera 1981; Bloch 1983). The aim of this school was to develop means of analysing precapitalist societies in terms of the same ideas of contradiction and conflict that Marx had used for capitalism itself, and it did so with its concepts of mode of production, social formation, social reproduction and structural causality. The sources of power and conflict in society were not limited to control of subsistence production, but also included control of biological reproduction, status, knowledge and prestige items, and in particular control over their circulation, dissemination and exchange. Ethnographic and ethnohistoric research provided specific models linking land, material culture, men and women, and concentrating on alliance structures, the ancestors and exchange; the work of Meillassoux (1972) and Friedman (1975, 1979) has been particularly influential. Another very important element in this approach is the emphasis on ideology, not in the sense of a shared general view of the world, but of beliefs whose function is to naturalise or legitimate the asymmetrical relationships within a society, or to mask them or deny their existence. The projection of such ideologies through the manipulation of material culture and ritual activity makes this a well-known field of anthropological study, and a potentially very fruitful one for archaeologists.

The ideas of this school of anthropology, first advertised by Friedman and Rowlands (1977), have inspired a number of studies by British archaeologists, such as that by Frankenstein and Rowlands (1978) of south-western Germany in the early Iron Age, by Parker Pearson (1984) of Iron Age Jutland, by Tilley (1984) of middle neolithic Sweden, or the more extensive interpretations of British prehistory by Bradley (1984) and by Clarke, Cowie and Foxon (1985). There are a number of features which seem to have made it particularly attractive, not least the way in which some of the evidence produced by the traditional concerns of European and British archaeology could be utilised in this new approach. Studies of subsistence agriculture through field systems and storage facilities, aided by recent advances in the recovery and identification of plant and bone remains, and of exchange systems, particularly in the light of the scientific analyses now increasingly available, have provided important evidence for this sort of approach, while much of the material of European prehistory has been recovered from ritual monuments, funerary contexts and hoards, where a consideration of the ritual and ideological context is inescapable; archaeology has not yet, however, found a way of dealing with two of the other elements that are important in these models, patrilineal descent groups and the movement of women in marriage alliances.

Another attraction of this approach is that it places the explanation of social change firmly within the society itself. Although it shares with the systems theory approach a belief in the connections between different facets of society, such as subsistence, exchange and social organisation, each society is conceived of as having within it the seeds of change, contradictions which can only be resolved by change and which constrain, but do not determine, the precise pattern that change will take. The kind of explanation offered, therefore, is very different, not the subsumption of a specific case to a generalisation, but rather the understanding or interpretation of a specific case in its unique historical context.

There has, therefore, been considerable interest in the study of prestige items and their circulation and consumption, both in the context of prestige goods economies and as symbols of social status. Discussions of ideology have been particularly concerned with the role of tombs and other monuments in rituals associated with the celebration of the ancestors, in contrast to the emergence of practices which explicitly acknowledge the power of individuals or are designed to deny it.

136

A further development of this approach is the recognition that the networks of exchange and interaction to which societies belong, and the structures of dominance which they symbolise, are very extensive. Wallerstein's (1974) study of the rise of European capitalism used concepts of regional economy and world-system to analyse these relationships, but, as Ekholm (1981) argued, such structures were not confined to the relatively recent historical period of capitalist economies, but extended back at least to the rise of the earliest civilisations and the consequent emergence of major differences in social and economic organisation between societies in a regional network. The recognition of the regional scale necessary for the appropriate analysis of such developments lies behind the attempts to adapt Wallerstein's core-and-periphery concepts to the context of precapitalist societies, and the study of long-distance exchange links, especially in prestige goods, through which they were articulated (Frankenstein and Rowlands 1978; Gledhill 1978; Rowlands 1980; Rowlands *et al.* 1987; Champion 1989).

Material culture

The neo-Marxist approach raised many questions, but it placed the emphasis of discussion firmly on questions of conflict within society, the different and conflicting strategies pursued by individuals within society, the interaction of individual action and social structure, and of ideology, its effectiveness and its relationship to social reality. It shared with processual archaeology not only the concept of linkages between the various subdivisions of human culture, but also a perception of the past as somehow objectively knowable through the medium of the archaeological record. This process was seldom described or discussed, let alone seen as particularly problematic. The evidence was believed to consist primarily of material culture items as the passive residues of past behaviour and to form a 'record' or 'reflection' of that behaviour; the business of the archaeologist was to find the correct method of reconverting those present residues into past behaviour. Despite many insights into the social and physical processes relating the present evidence to the past (Schiffer 1976, 1987), the basic role of material culture as the passive, albeit transformed, residue of the past was not seen as a critical problem.

This approach to the role of material culture, the nature of the archaeological record and the appropriate procedures for using it to illuminate the past have now all been called into question. The initial thrust to this challenge came from ethnographic fieldwork by Hodder (1982a), who argued that material culture was not merely the passive residue of functional needs, but on the contrary, should be seen as having symbolic meaning and as active, creating social relationships, with an internal logic which is part of the way that society organises itself and its relations with the world; clothing, for instance, is not just a functional response to the need to provide protection against the environment, but also a medium for symbolic meanings and an active social strategy. The emphasis should be on the meaning, not the function, of material culture, but that meaning will be specific to the social and historical context of usage.

The archaeological record, in so far as it is comprised of items of material culture, therefore, is not a passive reflection of past behaviour, but a meaningfully constituted part of past social action. In order to understand it, it is necessary not so much to find the correct procedures for working back from the record through the various transformational processes to make inferences about the past, but to find ways of interpreting the meaning of past culture.

One of the first attempts to address this problem adopted a structuralist approach (e.g. Hodder 1982b). The patterns identifiable in material culture were seen as structured sets of oppositions, and ultimately as specific embodiments of the underlying structure of principles with which society categorised its human and physical environment and ordered its social relationships. These principles might be embodied in different ways in different areas of material culture (burials, houses, ceramic decoration), but it was they that constituted the ultimate explanation for past cultures and it was the task of archaeology to elucidate these principles and the ways in which material culture embodied them.

Herein lay some of the problems for this approach. The underlying, structuring principles of past societies were for the most part incapable of verification independently of the material evidence on the basis of which they were being suggested (though the more recent historical periods might offer other sources of information). Clearly an interpretation could be more persuasive if it could be credibly worked out in a variety of fields of material culture, but the question was how, if at all, it was possible to distinguish between alternative suggestions, and how it was possible to give credence to any particular one. Furthermore, as archaeology tended more and more to be a science of material culture, the role of the more remote prehistoric past, where certainty was impossible, became correspondingly diminished.

Another approach, which also lays great emphasis on the symbolic meaning of material culture, turns again to the concept of ideology, though in a rather wider sense than the illusory false consciousness of Marxist analysis. Ideology is not just a mask of social reality, but a part of that reality and a part of the principles in terms of which individuals organised their lives and their action, and therefore an integral part of the past which archaeology seeks to investigate (e.g. Miller and Tilley 1984). Through this concept of ideology, it is theoretically possible to link the interpretation of the symbolic meanings of material culture with the explanation of social organisation and longer-term social change. The wider range of evidence used in such an account of a past society offers the possibility of assessing the interpretation in different areas of culture, to give a means of judging its appropriateness.

Yet another approach is what Hodder (1986a) has called contextual archaeology. As well as the functions and symbolic meaning of material culture, he distinguishes a contextual meaning: the relationship between material culture and its meaning may ultimately be arbitrary, but it derives at least part of its meaning from its context and from preceding contexts. The emphasis is now upon the context of culture and the historical sequence of culture; the importance of culture history is reasserted, as is also the affinity of archaeology to history. To illustrate the kind of historical explanation to be derived from this approach, the philosophy of Collingwood is invoked with its idea of rethinking past thoughts. The archaeological record forms not an evidential basis for inferences, but a 'text' which has to be read.

The problems of this approach are of two sorts. The first are practical, to show how it is possible to develop an archaeology of contextual meaning, particularly for prehistoric societies with no independent sources of evidence. In two recent volumes Hodder has tried to demonstrate the potential of this approach, with detailed studies of contextual meanings (1987a) and long-term historical sequences (1987b) of both modern and more remote societies. The success of these case studies varies considerably; the most persuasive are those derived from the most recent periods, where other non-material forms of evidence are available as sources of meaning, and the possibility of reading such meanings into the more remote past remains doubtful. On the contrary, Barrett (1987, 1988) has argued that it is impossible; we may be able to see how types of material culture were used in active strategies of negotiating social relationships, and see something of the specific areas of culture in which such discourse operated, but we can never gain access to the actual meaning which past societies would have attached to their material objects. His study (1989) of the transition from the Late Bronze Age to the Iron Age shows how it is possible to interpret the material record in this light, in terms of changing social relationships.

The other problems are of a more theoretical nature, concerning the concepts of 'reading the text' and of 'meaning'. In place of an archaeological 'record' which contains some sort of objective account of the past if we have the correct means of deciding it, it is now suggested that we should think of the evidence of the past as a 'text' to which archaeologists as readers give meaning (Hodder 1988, 1989a; Tilley 1990). At the heart of this debate are matters of fundamental importance concerning the nature of the relationship between the archaeologists and the evidence, and how to characterise it; the metaphor of neither a record nor a text seems perfectly to describe the way in which the evidence constrains but does not determine the possibility of interpretation. These, however, are questions that have not yet been fully addressed, let alone resolved.

A critical archaeology

A third major response to the positivism of the new processual archaeology has been the growth of a critical self-awareness of the context in which archaeology as an academic discipline operates, and the historical specificity of the concepts it applies to its analysis of the past. This has drawn attention particularly to questions about the role of archaeology and a vision of the past in the development of modern European societies and in current political discourse, and also about the problems of extending to other societies the categories of discussion derived from our own uniquely European perceptions.

These questions, though already beginning to surface, were brought very much to the fore in the context of the World Archaeological Congress in 1986 (Ucko 1987). The programme, announced three years before and developed in the intervening period, included sessions on such topics as archaeological objectivity, the politics of the past and the reburial of human remains. These were questions which had seldom, if ever, been discussed in such depth or so explicitly in an archaeological forum, but it was the decision of the organising committee to exclude South African and Namibian participants that focused public debate on the traditional image of archaeology as an objective and apolitical academic discipline which should be free of such overtly political stances. As some archaeologists argued, however, the issues are not simple (e.g. Hodder 1986b); quite apart from the very convoluted concept of academic freedom, the idea of a neutral, apolitical scientific sphere of activity is itself a political construct of post-Renaissance European thought. It is one that has played a considerable part in the scientific and technological enterprise that underlay European capitalist expansion and domination; ideas of progress and social evolution likewise provided part of the philosophical background and justification for such expansion. Archaeology can now be seen to have a role in political strategies of domination and resistance or exclusion (Gathercole and Lowenthal 1990; Stone and Mackenzie 1990).

On the whole, however, archaeologists have been reluctant to grasp the consequences of such arguments that archaeology is not a neutral pursuit, but part of the wider public and political practice of contemporary society, influenced by it and in turn influencing it. It may well be that for the moment the contribution of the archaeological past to contemporary debate is low; as Shennan (1986: 337) has suggested, the irony of one of the most overtly Marxist analyses of British prehistory being published by Her Majesty's Stationery Office is comprehensible if archaeology is thought to be minimally relevant. The political context of our perception of the past has been highlighted in other ways, however. Girouard (1981), for instance, has made clear the importance of the reworking of medieval chivalry and the cult of the English gentleman for Victorian imperial expansion, while the growth of a new heritage industry has raised questions about the rose-tinted vision of the past it portrays (Wright 1985; Hewison 1987). At the present time, discussion of the proposed national core curriculum has made clear the extent of government control of the teaching of the historic past in schools.

The role of the more distant prehistoric past may be slight, but it is not negligible. Archaeology plays a significant part in the concepts of Celtic nationalism which are a continuing and unresolved problem for the United Kingdom (e.g. Sheehy 1980; Delaney 1986). The annual rituals associated with the celebration of the summer solstice at Stonehenge have become a symbol of the struggle between law, order and convention on the one hand and, on the other, a life-style that rejects many of the accepted values of contemporary Britain; they are also a focus for the opposition between the established appropriation of the site as a monument to be visited, admired and interpreted under closely controlled access, but remote from current concerns, and an alternative vision of it as central to a whole way of life.

These are, however, questions that archaeologists have been reluctant to see as germane to their own subject, though there has been more attention paid to the influence of contemporary political and social ideas on the study and presentation of the past (e.g. Trigger 1981, 1984, 1990). Much of this has been at the general level of the Anglo-American tradition of archaeology, and we still lack any detailed discussion of the development of British archaeology within contemporary British society comparable to that of Patterson (1986) for the United States. Some specific points have been made, however. Museums have been recognised for some time as having a great capacity for moulding the public's historical and political perception of the past (Horne 1984; Lumley 1988), but Shanks and Tilley (1987a: 68–99) have been more concerned with the aesthetics of museum display and the way presentation establishes a relationship between the visitor and the past, divorcing the objects from their past context and from any present meaning, as part of the culture industry of capitalist society.

Again, Rowlands (1984: 154) has argued that the concept of a European prehistory only makes sense as an area of archaeological enterprise in the context of a modern perception of an entity of Europe, with its own problems of unity and distinctiveness and its own appeal to the past. More specifically, it has been argued (Champion 1987: 99; 1990) that the programme of studies within the fields of European prehistory and medieval archaeology has, at least in part, been determined by perceptions of the past moulded by the interests of modern nation states. In more general terms, it has been suggested that the emphasis in contemporary archaeology on the trajectory from simple to complex societies represents the imposition on the past of a modernising ethos and the primacy of European experience (Rowlands 1986).

In a rather different vein, there has been an increasing interest in the nature of the contemporary practice of archaeology. Tilley (1989) has discussed the nature of the public reaction to excavation, while various authors (Hodder 1989b; several papers in *Archaeological Review from Cambridge* 8(2) (1989)) have analysed the experience of writing in archaeology and its relationship to other forms of literary output. Feminist critiques have also been brought to bear on the discipline, not only for the lack of women in our representation of the past but also for their minor and predominantly lowly role in the contemporary profession (Sorensen 1988).

Recognition of the political and social context of the practice of archaeology, and the consequent necessity of abandoning notions of an objective, scientific and value-free subject, is one thing; assessing the implications of such a recognition is another. One of the most sustained discussions of such questions and one of the most specific answers is that of Shanks and Tilley (1987a, 1987b). For them the solution is to follow the German Frankfurt School of social philosophy, which claims a privileged position for its Critical Theory, regarding knowledge (in our case archaeological knowledge) as an instrument of power, and the true role of the subject as the exposing of ideology and the freeing of individuals from ideological subjugation. Contemporary archaeology, with its separation of theory and practice, its claims to scientific generalisation and objectivity, its emphasis on economic behaviour and social evolution, its divorcing of the past from the present, its isolated professionalisation and institutionalisation, is an element in the structures of power and knowledge by which the capitalist economies of Europe have come to dominance. In contrast, archaeology should be a means of exposing these ideologies, of reasserting the role of the past in the discourse of the present, and engaging in a critique of modern society: 'archaeology is nothing if it is not critique' (Shanks and Tilley 1987b: 213). Such a prescription, radically at variance with traditional perceptions of the nature and role of archaeology, is not without its own problems concerning the nature of the domination in society expressed through the manipulation of knowledge of the past, the kinds of questions about the past that it would be most concerned with, or the sort of practice of archaeology that it would generate. It has not yet been subjected to detailed criticism or implementation, so it remains to be seen what effect it will have.

Underlying all these considerations are some of the most important problems for archaeology at the present time. Its practitioners have been reawakened to the social context of their subject, but have yet to find a way of coming to terms with the closely related questions of objectivity versus subjectivity, of relativism versus generalisation (Rowlands 1984). At the extremes are views which would now find few supporters; an archaeology so aware of the social context of the subjective construction of the past in the interests of dominant groups in society that it is doubtful whether there is any way of discriminating between competing visions of the past or any really informative role for archaeology in illuminating the past for our better understanding, versus an archaeology that is wedded to an objective analysis and explanation of the past through universal concepts, which runs the risk of dehumanising the human past and denying the variety of human experience in the past and the social context of its study in the present. Though in recent years with the first flush of new awareness of the social context of archaeology, there has been a tendency to lurch towards the subjectivist view, there can equally be no denying the fact that many archaeologists would feel that we have made significant progress in understanding the human past in a way which presupposes the possibility of some form of generalisable discussion. It is precisely in the identification of how we can avoid the crude choice between dehumanising science or an anything-goes relativism that one of the major problems of contemporary archaeology lies.

The impact of theoretical debates

Knowledge does not exist in a social vacuum, nor is an academic discipline free of social and political ties, as the growth of a critical self-awareness in British archaeology has made abundantly clear. An academic discipline such as archaeology also has its own internal system of institutional organisation, which itself has an effect on the organisation of knowledge and debate, and is frequently characterised by a variety of modes of working or 'disciplinary matrices' (Kuhn 1970: 152). It remains, therefore, to consider the extent to which these theoretical developments have affected British archaeology as a whole, and the reasons why they have occurred, and why to that particular extent.

It must be immediately apparent to anyone having a perceptive acquaintance with the British archaeological scene that a concern with theoretical archaeology has not been universally shared throughout the discipline or the profession. It would certainly not form part of the popular perception of contemporary archaeology, as witnessed by the subject's exposure in the press and on television. Despite an increasing volume of media coverage, the dominant theme is still that of the archaeologist as the seeker after treasure, the discoverer of new and spectacular facts and the historian of the rise of great civilisations, an image only reinforced by such mythical, but influential, stereotypes of the archaeologist as Indiana Jones. Similarly in magazines designed to present archaeology to a wider popular audience, such as *Current Archaeology* and *Archaeology Today*, most of the theoretical ferment of the last twenty years has gone unnoticed. In the latter it has for the most part been totally ignored, while in the former it has either been ignored or has suffered from a critical antipathy in editorial comments or in book reviews: Clarke's *Analytical Archaeology* (1968) was described as 'one of the most dangerous' books in archaeology, while Hodder's *Reading the Past* (1986a) was dismissed as 'the ultimate egghead's guide to all the latest in archaeological jargon' and, 'considering its inherently incomprehensible subject, surprisingly well written'.

Nor indeed would the theoretical debate be regarded as of more than peripheral interest by many professional archaeologists. Many parts of the field of archaeology remain virtually untouched. It is undoubtedly true that the theoretical discussions in archaeology have been very largely carried on by those whose primary interest in chronological terms lies in the prehistoric period. To the extent that much of the early theoretical debate focused on questions about the nature of explanation and the explanation of the processes of social change, it may be that those who operated predominantly in the Classical, Roman and medieval fields felt such concerns to be irrelevant to those periods with an established framework of historically documented narrative. Renfrew (1980) distinguished what he called the 'great tradition' of archaeology in the Mediterranean lands and the Near East, a tradition which regarded the principles and theory of archaeology as simple and self-evident, and archaeology itself as one element in a mature

academic approach to the appreciation of Europe's cultural ancestry in the Classical past. His paper called for an effort to bridge
the 'great divide' which separated this tradition from modern
anthropological archaeology, for the benefit of both sides. Snodgrass (1984, 1985) has echoed that call, and has also demonstrated
something of the achievements of Classical archaeology and the
potential of its enormously rich and detailed database. In recent
years there have been a number of attempts to realise that potential
(e.g. Morris 1987).

Similarly in the medieval period, the prevailing tradition of
research has been within frameworks of historical explanation,
with archaeology seen as subsidiary to history and providing it
with illustrative detail, and with little interest in the kind of
approach adopted in American historical archaeology (South
1977a, 1977b). Indeed, the contrast between the British, and
indeed European, approach to medieval archaeology and that
adopted to the archaeology of the historically documented periods
in other parts of the world, especially former colonial territories,
is particularly revealing of the broader political sphere within
which archaeology operates; medieval archaeology has very largely
been constrained by the prevailing European mode of historical
consciousness, with its implicit acceptance of European superiority, and its ideologically laden emphasis on descent from the
Classical world and on the literary record as the primary means
of establishing and transmitting our knowledge of it (Champion
1990). Within such a tradition, archaeology has mostly followed
the programme established by history, and has failed to see Europe
as part of the wider study of the history of agrarian civilisations
(e.g. Hall 1985; Baechler et al. 1988; Crone 1989).

There are, of course, exceptions; Rahtz (1981, 1983) and Hodges
(1983) have explored some of the implications of the New Archaeology for the study of the medieval period, but they are for the
most part setting out programmatic statements of possibilities
rather than reviewing completed work. The more recent reactions
to the New Archaeology described earlier seem not yet to have
affected medieval archaeology, despite its obvious potential, for
instance for the study of the meaning of variation in material
culture in a historically known context. Those studies that have
recently appeared, whether in the form of a general review (Austin
1990) or a specific case study (Austin and Thomas 1990), only
serve to show the wealth of the potential. Nevertheless, despite

Clarke's recognition long ago (1972: 18) that the historical periods would offer an important testing ground for theories of interpretation since archaeological data could be set alongside independent sources of information, little has been done to capitalise on this possibility, either to test theories originating in the prehistoric field or to enrich our understanding of the archaeology of later times.

Though it might at first sight seem odd that such an obvious and ideal opportunity has been missed, it must be remembered that medieval archaeology as it is practised in Britain developed in very different circumstances from the historical archaeology of the United States, and was in fact something of a reaction to the excessively architectural and art-historical approach to the physically surviving material of the medieval period, to the exclusion of other parts of the archaeological record. There has, in fact, been work of this sort of considerable archaeological interest in the medieval and post-medieval periods, but it has been done as much by historians as by archaeologists; to cite a few examples, studies of artefact decoration (Richards 1987), funerary ritual (Giesey 1960; Pader 1982; Gittings 1984), the landscape of power (Williamson and Bellamy 1987), and the iconography of power (Strong 1984) deal with topics well known to prehistoric archaeologists, while Cannadine's (1983) study of British royal ritual and monument-building explores a much more sophisticated means of analysing the meaning and context of such activity than has been developed in comparable prehistoric studies.

It is very difficult to form any reliable estimate of the degree to which theoretical issues are part of current archaeological concerns, but to the extent that publications are an accurate reflection of those concerns, then their role is a minor one. The Council for British Archaeology's *British Archaeological Abstracts* gives a good impression of the annual published output of the subject, and the items abstracted under the heading 'Theory and principles', in use since 1983, may serve as an approximate measure of theoretical concerns. In the seven years from 1983 to 1989, out of 14,236 abstracted items, only 227 have been listed in that classification. It is true that some publications classified under other headings may have a strong theoretical orientation, for instance in the fields of education and presentation, and that other headings may reflect important developments of recent years such as quantitative methodology or environmental studies, but even so the proportion is not high. It is even lower when the authorship of those 227 items is considered, since less than half of them are by British authors or in British publications, the majority originating in North America.

There has been little impact on traditional modes of publication such as journals, though in the natural sciences the establishment of new subdisciplines or new theoretical orientations is regularly signalled by the appearance of new journals. There is no major British journal, newly founded or of longer standing, that is wholly or mainly devoted to theoretical debate in archaeology; only the *Journal of Archaeological Science* has signalled the emergence of a new specialism. The major journals retain their annual schedule (not one suited to lively discussion) and their role as authoritarian providers of timeless facts; how far this is the result of deliberate editorial policy, and how far the perceived image of the journals has served to deter submission of theoretical articles, is not easy to answer, but I suspect that on the whole the major journals are not regarded by authors as appropriate places to publish such material. The periodicals with more frequent appearances, in particular *Current Archaeology* and *Antiquity*, have had editorial stances notably hostile to such developments in archaeology, though the contents and editorial attitude of the latter have been substantially revised since the late 1980s.

In fact, it is two of the 'lesser' journals that have come nearest to being specialist journals of theoretical archaeology, *Archaeological Review from Cambridge* and *Scottish Archaeological Review*; apart from these, we might cite the anthropological journal *Man* as a regular vehicle for contributions to theoretical archaeology. It is interesting that, each in its own way, these three journals are somehow peripheral to the mainstream of established British archaeology: one produced by students, one published in Scotland independently of an institution, and one focused on a related discipline. Otherwise, many of the 'new' 'theoretical' contributions have appeared in books, especially of collected papers or conference proceedings; we should note in particular some of the British Archaeological Reports volumes and the New Directions in Archaeology series published by Cambridge Univeristy Press. The nature of these publication outlets has perhaps made it easier to ignore theoretical publications, or dismiss them with complaints about the high price being asked for something with no new facts in it.

There has been little impact on the universities. In most departments the syllabus remains doggedly devoted to regional and chronological approaches to archaeology, with little emphasis on thematic or generalised approaches, or on the teaching of the methodology, epistemology and philosophy of archaeology. Some departments have responded to recent advances by introducing courses in such fields as environmental archaeology, computing or quantitative methods, but in some places, I suspect, the teaching of courses on the history, methods and principles of archaeology carries a low priority and a low status, is regarded as a bore, and is inflicted on the junior members of staff; in any case, it seldom ranges far beyond an uncritical narrative of some of the major advances in archaeological knowledge or methods, or a consideration of excavation techniques and some basic operational concepts such as typology or stratigraphy. There are of course exceptions, but the teaching and discussion of the sort of topic outlined above has not been practised by more than a handful of our departments. It is, however, in the university sector, or at least in some of the university departments, rather than in any other branch of the archaeological profession, that the theoretical debate has been carried on to the extent that it has in Britain.

There has been little impact on other institutions of archaeological organisation. Among the period societies and other national bodies, the Prehistoric Society has reflected some of these trends in its conferences, but otherwise there has been little sign that these institutions have recognised such developments, let alone been actively engaged in promoting them. While other changes in the nature of modern British archaeology have been marked by the formation of such groups as the Standing Conference of Archaeological Unit Managers, the Institute of Field Archaeologists, the Association for Environmental Archaeologists or the Lithics Study Group, the main institutional response academically has been the emergence of the Theoretical Archaeology Group (TAG), though the sense in which it is a formal or even informal study group rather than an *ad hoc* committee structure for arranging a conference is questionable (Fleming and Johnson 1990). It sprang initially from a joint meeting of staff and students of the Southampton and Sheffield departments organised by Colin Renfrew in 1977, to provide precisely this sort of forum for theoretical discussion. It went open in 1979 and has since then organised a series of annual open meetings.

The large numbers of people attending recent TAG conferences is a testimony to its popularity as a forum, but is it a testimony to the popularity of theoretical archaeology? The intellectual scope of the papers has certainly widened in the last few years, to the point where the organisers of one recent meeting felt it necessary to remind us in their call for papers that they should have a substantial theoretical content. It is true that there is a very high level of participation, and a wide range of theoretical topics have been discussed at TAG, many receiving their first public airing there, but perhaps we are seeing not only an interest in theoretical archaeology, but also a sign of the changing social composition of the research community of professional archaeologists, who have come to regard existing institutions as irrelevant and now feel the need to have a forum appropriate to their interests. There is, after all, an enormous difference between the meetings arranged by the Theoretical Archaeology Group and those of the Society of Antiquaries of London, not only in the subject matter but also in the physical surroundings, the structure of the event, the age, professional status and aspirations of those attending, and the nature of the social gatherings with which the academic business is surrounded. The new series of annual conferences initiated by the Institute of Field Archaeologists in 1987 will offer another meeting place for the members of a growing profession; to judge from its first few years, it too has proved a considerable success, with some overlap with TAG in both membership and debate, and it remains to be seen whether a specifically theoretical forum emerges in the future, with a distinct content and clientele.

There has been some impact on the practice of archaeology in the field, and some of the innovations ushered in during the 1960s, if not exactly central to the theoretical concerns of the New Archaeology, have become widely diffused. In particular there has been a ready acceptance of the rapidly developing new techniques for data recovery and the confrontation of the problems they pose. The recovery of environmental and economic evidence, for instance, is now a regular part of most, though not all, archaeological research. Computerised systems for data recording and analysis are becoming more widespread. There has also been a greater recognition of the need to understand and control the mechanisms through which this flood of data is produced, and to monitor the effect of site formation processes and our own sampling strategies on the creation of the archaeological record as we perceive it. Though explicitly probabilistic sampling strategies are still rare, there is a greater recognition of the questions raised by the nature of the sample recovered, whether it is determined by contingent factors of access, availability and imminent destruction, or by the judgement of the investigator. There is also a greater awareness of the variety of past cultural and taphonomic processes that underlie the archaeological record, and have to be considered in its interpretation.

It would be perverse to deny the considerable advances made in British archaeology in these directions in recent years, but they are all at a comparatively low methodological and technical level, and there has been less effect on other levels, for example the overall design of research programmes, the investigation of generalised socio-economic themes or the exploration of the meaning of variability in material culture. In some regions of Britain and for some periods of the past, it must be admitted, the available data are simply not good enough for this sort of enquiry to begin, since despite often considerable archaeological effort, the right kind of information is frequently not available, or collected in a systematic enough way to be used with any confidence in its reliability. These are serious problems, and there undoubtedly remains a major task of basic data collection if many of the questions about the past raised by recent theoretical debates are to be successfully tackled. Only rarely, however, have the implications for the recovery, recording and presentation of data through excavation or other fieldwork been realised. Most importantly, I know of no general attempt to assess the relevance of recent theoretical debates to the practice of field archaeology; all too often they seem to be regarded as irrelevant, while work in the field continues in a determinedly empirical and unselfcritical way.

The social context

Is it possible to say why these theoretical issues have concerned British archaeology so much, in contrast to some other European countries, and why on the other hand their effect has not been greater? The answers to such questions lie more in a consideration of the recent social and economic history of Britain than specifically in archaeology itself – or even in its political history, for it may be no coincidence that an explicitly critical archaeology has developed during the lifetime of one of the most dogmatic right-wing governments in recent times, when many areas of public and intellectual life have become more highly politicised than ever before. It is, however, part of the responsibility of a mature discipline to be prepared to engage in such discussion of its growth.

Part of the answer is to be found in the development of education in recent decades. The decline of Classics is both cause and effect of an eclipse of the role of the Classical world in modern perceptions of the roots of European culture; it has resulted not only in the loss of the traditionally dominant approach to the past and of history as the means of elucidating it, but also in the education of many more school children and students (among them David Clarke and Colin Renfrew) in other modes of thought, such as those of the natural sciences. These attitudes were themselves merely part of the changing social and intellectual climate of the period after the Second World War, a time of optimism about the potential of science and technology to explain the world and to improve it. The status of science was high, and the attraction to other disciplines of adopting the trappings and terminology of science was correspondingly great. Equally, the reaction to scientific, processual archaeology should be seen in the context of a growing pessimism about the ability of science to solve the problems of the world, an interest in alternative technologies, the growth of the various conservation and ecological movements, and a marked decline in the popular estimation of science which is reflected, among other things, by the rapid decline in numbers of applicants to universities for science courses.

The post-war expansion of secondary and then tertiary education facilities has also been of major importance, in particular the growth of the universities in the 1960s and 1970s. Many new departments of archaeology were founded at that time, including some of those which have played the largest part of the theoretical debates discussed above. Within a period of about ten years a whole new generation of archaeologists had been recruited to the universities, and among this peer group were many who had been heavily influenced by the theoretical debates of the late 1960s or taught by some of its leading exponents. Thus this injection of new blood into the university system brought with it an interest in new theoretical ideas.

Part of the answer is also to be found in the nature of the British university system, which is not as conservative, authoritarian or professorially dominated as in some other European countries, or as politically constrained as in others. The intellectual climate is one which accepts the concept of academic progress through change. By and large, and especially in the humanities, individual members of staff are allowed considerable freedom to choose the particular orientation of their teaching, research and publication within the broadest limits of their discipline. At the postgraduate level, too, this has meant that a higher value is placed on contradicting or refining received ideas than on slavishly elaborating the ideas of one's professor or supervisor. British universities have therefore provided a forum which permits or even encourages the discussion of new theoretical ideas.

More generally, the growth of archaeology within the expanding university system should be seen as one aspect of the economic prosperity of the 1960s. Another aspect was the massive programme of urban redevelopment and other engineering projects such as motorway construction, as well as changes in the agriculture and forestry industries, which led to the growth of the rescue archaeology movement (Jones 1984). One of the great achievements of the last twenty years has been the success of pressure groups such as Rescue in raising the profile of archaeology publicly and politically, and heightening public awareness of the threats to the survival of the evidence. Government funding for rescue archaeology rose rapidly in the 1970s, and has been very largely maintained in subsequent years; more recently, indirect government support through the Manpower Services Commission and now an increasing willingness on the part of developers to fund rescue work have meant a steady growth in this field. This expansion of archaeological activity, coupled with the British practice of using so-called 'volunteer' workers, frequently graduates, rather than manual labourers, has in turn led to the unprecedented expansion of the archaeological profession in the areas of excavation and fieldwork. There has been analogous growth of professional employment in related fields concerned primarily with the preservation of the archaeological evidence, especially in museums and planning offices.

Within a short space of time, archaeology has changed almost out of all recognition. From being the rather small and esoteric concern of a few universities and museums, it has grown greatly in numbers, and in the heterogeneity of its institutional structures, and of their practical or academic involvement. Each of these branches of the profession, however, is operating within its own particular constraints. Rescue archaeology has grown up very largely divorced from universities and their academic debates, but subject to its own obligations to developers and funding authorities, which have seldom allowed it to go far beyond the basic recovery of evidence. As this side of the profession has grown, so has its dominance within archaeology, at least in quantitative terms of personnel. The expansion of the universities ceased in the early 1970s, and the next few years seem likely to bring a contraction in that area (Austin 1987). The long-term consequences of proposals in the late 1980s for the restructuring of higher education in Britain, which are designed to make the nature and scope of courses offered more responsive to student demand, are very difficult to assess; one possibility is that archaeology courses will become more strictly vocational, with more emphasis on methodology and practice, and even less on theory. Some universities, on the other hand, have already introduced courses in the general field of heritage management, which ought in principle to offer the opportunity to consider such theoretical matters as the presentation of the past and the construction of meaning.

Predictions of this sort are hazardous in the extreme, but it seems likely that, despite any growth in the volume of archaeological activity in the coming years, the increased separation of the various branches of the profession and the increasingly differentiated and demarcated disciplinary matrices within which they will be working may well mean that the ever more abstruse theoretical debate will be progressively confined to a small section of the archaeological community.

References

Allen, P. M. (1982) 'The genesis of structure in social systems: the paradigm of self-organisation', in C. Renfrew, M. J. Rowlands and B. A. Segraves (eds) *Theory and Explanation in Archaeology: the Southampton Conference*, London: Academic Press.

Austin, D. (1987) 'The future of archaeology in British universities', *Antiquity* 61: 227–38.

—— (1990) 'The "proper study" of medieval archaeology', in D. Austin and L. Alcock (eds) *From the Baltic to the Black Sea: Studies in Medieval Archaeology*, London: Unwin Hyman.

Austin, D. and Thomas, J. (1990) 'The "proper study" of medieval archaeology: a case study', in D. Austin and L. Alcock (eds) *From the Baltic* to the Black Sea: Studies in Medieval Archaeology, London, Unwin Hyman.

Baechler, J., Hall, J. A. and Mann, M. (1988) Europe and the Rise of Capitalism, Oxford: Basil Blackwell.

Barrett, J. C. (1987) 'Contextual archaeology', Antiquity 61: 468–73.

—— (1988) 'Fields of discourse: reconstructing a social archaeology', Critique of Anthropology 7(3): 5–16.

—— (1989) 'Food, gender and metal: questions of social reproduction', in M. L. Sorensen and R. Thomas (eds) The Bronze Age–Iron Age Transition in Europe, British Archaeological Reports International Series 483, Oxford.

Bloch, M. (1983) Marxism and Anthropology, Oxford: Oxford University Press.

Bradley, R. J. (1984) The Social Foundations of Prehistoric Britain, London: Longmans.

Cannadine, D. (1983) 'The context, performance and meaning of ritual: the British monarchy and the "invention of tradition", c. 1820–1977', in E. Hobsbawm and T. Ranger (eds) The Invention of Tradition, Cambridge: Cambridge University Press.

Champion, T. C. (1987) 'The European Iron Age: assessing the state of the art', Scottish Archaeological Review 4: 98–107.

—— (ed.) (1989) Centre and Periphery: Comparative Studies in Archaeology, London: Unwin Hyman.

—— (1990) 'Medieval archaeology and the tyranny of the historical record', in D. Austin and L. Alcock (eds) From the Baltic Sea: Studies in Medieval Archaeology, London: Unwin Hyman.

Champion, T. C., Gamble, C. S., Shennan, S. J. and Whittle, A. W. R. (1984) Prehistoric Europe, London: Academic Press.

Chapman, R., Kinnes, I. and Randsborg, K. (eds) (1981) The Archaeology of Death, Cambridge: Cambridge University Press.

Chapman, R. W. (1979) ' "Analytical archaeology" and after – introduction', in N. Hammond (ed.) Analytical Archaeologist: Collected Papers of David L. Clarke, London: Academic Press.

Clarke, D. L. (1967) 'Review of K. C. Chang, Rethinking Archaeology', Antiquity 41: 237–8.

—— (1968) Analytical Archaeology, London: Methuen.

—— (1972) 'Models and paradigms in contemporary archaeology', in D. L. Clarke (ed.) Models in Archaeology, London: Methuen.

—— (1973) 'Archaeology: the loss of innocence', Antiquity 47: 6–18.

Clarke, D. V., Cowie, T. G. and Foxon, A. (1985) Symbols of Power at the Time of Stonehenge, Edinburgh: Her Majesty's Stationery Office.

Collis, J. R. (1984) The European Iron Age, London: Batsford.

Crone, P. (1989) Pre-industrial Societies, Oxford: Basil Blackwell.

Daniel, G. E. (1975) 150 Years of Archaeology, London: Duckworth.

Delaney, F. (1986) The Celts, London: Hodder & Stoughton.

Ekholm, K. (1981) 'On the structure and dynamics of global systems', in J. S. Kahn and J. R. Llobera (eds) The Anthropology of Pre-capitalist Societies, London: Macmillan.

Fleming, A. and Johnson, M. (1990) 'The Theoretical Archaeology Group (TAG): origins, retrospect, prospect', *Antiquity* 64: 303–6.

Frankenstein, S. and Rowlands, M. J. (1978) 'The internal structure and regional context of early Iron Age society in south-west Germany', *Bulletin of the University of London Institute of Archaeology* 15: 73–112.

Friedman, J. (1975) 'Tribes, states and transformations', in M. Bloch (ed.) *Marxist Analyses and Social Anthropology*, London: Malaby.

—— (1979) *System, Structure and Contradiction: the Evolution of 'Asiatic' Social Formations*, Copenhagen: National Museum of Denmark.

Friedman, J. and Rowlands, M. J. (eds) (1977) *The Evolution of Social Systems*, London: Duckworth.

Gathercole, P. and Lowenthal, D. (eds) (1990) *The Politics of the Past*, London: Unwin Hyman.

Giesey, R. E. (1960) *The Royal Funeral Ceremony in Renaissance France*, Geneva: Droz.

Girouard, M. (1981) *The Return to Camelot: Chivalry and the English Gentleman*, New Haven and London: Yale University Press.

Gittings, C. (1984) *Death, Burial and the Individual in Early Modern England*, London: Croom Helm.

Gledhill, J. (1978) 'Formative development in the north American Southwest', in D. Green, C. Haselgrove and M. Spriggs (eds) *Social Organisation and Settlement*, British Archaeological Reports International Series 47, Oxford.

Hall, J. A. (1985) *Powers and Liberties: the Causes and Consequences of the Rise of the West*, Oxford: Basil Blackwell.

Härke, H. (1983) 'Archäologie in Grossbritannien', in H. Härke (ed.) *Archäologie und Kulturgeschichte: Symposium zu Zielvorstellung in der deutschen Archäologie*, privately published.

Hewison, R. (1987) *The Heritage Industry*, London: Methuen.

Hodder, I. R. (1982a) *Symbols in Action: Ethnoarchaeological Studies in Material Culture*, Cambridge: Cambridge University Press.

—— (ed.) (1982b) *Symbolic and Structural Archaeology*, Cambridge: Cambridge University Press.

—— (1982c) 'Theoretical archaeology: a reactionary view', in I. R. Hodder (ed.) *Symbolic and Structural Archaeology*, Cambridge: Cambridge University Press.

—— (1985) 'Post-processual archaeology', *Advances in Archaeological Method and Theory* 8: 1–26.

—— (1986a) *Reading the Past*, Cambridge: Cambridge University Press.

—— (1986b) 'Politics and archaeology in the World Archaeological Congress 1986', *Archaeological Review from Cambridge* 5: 113–18.

—— (ed.) (1987a) *The Archaeology of Contextual Meanings*, Cambridge: Cambridge University Press.

—— (ed.) (1987b) *Archaeology as Long-term History*, Cambridge: Cambridge University Press.

—— (1988) 'Material culture texts and social change: a contextual discussion and some archaeological examples', *Proceedings of the Prehistoric Society* 44: 67–75.

—— (1989a) 'This is not an article about material culture as a text', *Journal of Anthropological Archaeology* 8: 250–69.

—— (1989b) 'Writing archaeology: site reports in context', *Antiquity* 63: 268–74.

Hodder, I. R. and Orton, C. (1976) *Spatial Analysis in Archaeology*, Cambridge: Cambridge University Press.

Hodges, R. A. (1983) 'New approaches to medieval archaeology, part 2', in D. A. Hinton (ed.) *25 Years of Medieval Archaeology*, Sheffield: Department of Prehistory and Archaeology, University of Sheffield.

—— (1987) 'Spatial models, anthropology and archaeology', in J. M. Wagstaff (ed.) *Landscape and Culture: Geographical and Archaeological Perspectives*, Oxford: Blackwell.

Horne, D. (1984) *The Great Museum: the Re-presentation of History*, London: Pluto Press.

Johnston, R. J. (1986) *Philosophy and Human Geography: an Introduction to Contemporary Approaches*, 2nd edn London: Edward Arnold.

—— (1987) *Geography and Geographers: Anglo-American Human Geography since 1945*, 3rd edn London: Edward Arnold.

Jones, G. D. B. (1984) *Past Imperfect: the Story of Rescue Archaeology*, London: Heinemann.

Kahn, J. S. and Llobera, J. R. (eds) (1981) *The Anthropology of Pre-capitalist Societies*, London: Macmillan.

Kuhn, T. S. (1970) 'Reflections on my critics', in I. Lakatos and A. Musgrove (eds) *Criticism and the Growth of Knowledge*, Cambridge: Cambridge University Press.

Lumley, R. (ed.) (1988) *The Museum Time-machine: Putting Cultures on Display*, London: Comedia.

Meillassoux, C. (1972) 'From reproduction to production', *Economy and Society* 1: 93–105.

Miller, D. and Tilley, C. J. (eds) (1984) *Ideology, Power and Prehistory*, Cambridge: Cambridge University Press.

Morris, I. (1987) *Burial and Ancient Society*, Cambridge: Cambridge University Press.

Pader, E. J. (1982) *Symbolism, Social Relations and the Interpretation of Mortuary Remains*, British Archaeological Reports British Series 130, Oxford.

Parker Pearson, M. (1984) 'Economic and ideological change: cyclical growth in the pre-state societies of Jutland', in D. Miller and C. J. Tilley (eds) *Ideology, Power and Prehistory*, Cambridge: Cambridge University Press.

Patterson, T. (1986) 'The last sixty years: towards a social history of Americanist archaeology in the United States', *American Anthropologist* 88: 7–26.

Rahtz, P. A. (1981) *The New Medieval Archaeology*, York: University of York.

—— (1983) 'New approaches to medieval archaeology, part 1', in D. A. Hinton (ed.) *25 Years of Medieval Archaeology*, Sheffield: Department of Prehistory and Archaeology, University of Sheffield.

Renfrew, C. (1972) *The Emergence of Civilisation: the Cyclades and the Aegean in the Third Millennium* B.C., London: Methuen.

—— (1973) 'Monuments, mobilization and social organization in neolithic Wessex', in C. Renfrew (ed.) *The Explanation of Culture Change*, London: Duckworth.

—— (1978) 'Trajectory, discontinuity and morphogenesis: the implications of catastrophe theory for archaeology', *American Antiquity* 43: 202–22.

—— (1979) 'Systems collapse as social transformation: catastrophe and anastrophe in early state societies', in C. Renfrew and K. Cooke (eds) *Transformations: Mathematical Approaches to Culture Change*, London: Academic Press.

—— (1980) 'The great tradition versus the great divide: archaeology as anthropology?', *American Journal of Archaeology* 84: 287–98.

—— (1982a) 'Explanation revisited', in C. Renfrew, M. J. Rowlands and B. A. Segraves (eds) *Theory and Explanation in Archaeology: the Southampton Conference*, London: Academic Press.

—— (1982b) 'Socio-economic change in ranked societies', in C. Renfrew and S. J. Shennan (eds) *Ranking, Resource and Exchange: Aspects of the Archaeology of Early European Society*, Cambridge: Cambridge University Press.

—— (1984) 'Social archaeology, societal change and generalisation', in C. Renfrew, *Approaches to Social Archaeology*, Edinburgh: Edinburgh University Press.

Renfrew, C. and Cherry, J. (eds) (1986) *Peer Polity Interaction and Sociopolitical Change*, Cambridge: Cambridge University Press.

Renfrew, C. and Cooke, K. (eds) (1979) *Transformations: Mathematical Approaches to Culture Change*, London: Academic Press.

Renfrew, C. and Shennan, S. J. (eds) (1982) *Ranking, Resource and Exchange: Aspects of the Archaeology of Early European Society*, Cambridge: Cambridge University Press.

Renfrew, C., Rowlands, M. J. and Segraves, B. A. (eds) (1982) *Theory and Explanation in Archaeology: the Southampton Conference*, London: Academic Press.

Richards, J. D. (1987) *The Significance of Form and Decoration of Anglo-Saxon Cremation Urns*, British Archaeological Reports British Series 166, Oxford.

Rowlands, M. J. (1980) 'Kinship, alliance and exchange in the European Bronze Age', in J. Barrett and R. Bradley (eds) *Settlement and Society in the British Later Bronze Age*, British Archaeological Reports British Series 83, Oxford.

—— (1984) 'Conceptualizing the European Bronze and Early Iron Ages', in J. Bintliff (ed.) *European Social Evolution*, Bradford: University of Bradford.

—— (1986) 'From simple to complex: a modernist fantasy in prehistory', in T. C. Champion and M. J. Rowlands (eds) *Comparative Studies in the Development of Complex Societies*, vol. 1, duplicated typescript, Southampton: World Archaeological Congress.

Rowlands, M. J., Kristiansen, K. and Larsen, M. T. (eds) (1987) *Centre and Periphery in the Ancient World*, Cambridge: Cambridge University Press.

Schiffer, M. B. (1976) *Behavioural Archaeology*, New York: Academic Press.

—— (1987) *Formation Processes of the Archaeology Record*, Albuquerque: University of New Mexico Press.

Shanks, M. and Tilley, C. J. (1987a) *Re-constructing Archaeology: Theory and Practice*, Cambridge: Cambridge University Press.

—— (1987b) *Social Theory and Archaeology*, London: Polity Press.

Sheehy, J. (1980) *The Rediscovery of Ireland's Past: the Celtic Revival 1830–1930*, London, Thames & Hudson.

Shennan, S. J. (1986) 'Towards a critical archaeology?', *Proceedings of the Prehistoric Society* 52: 327–38.

—— (1987) 'Trends in the study of later European prehistory', *Annual Review of Anthropology* 16: 365–82.

—— (1989) 'Archaeology as archaeology or as anthropology? Clarke's *Analytical Archaeology* and the Binfords' *New Perspectives in Archaeology* 21 years on', *Antiquity* 63: 831–5.

Snodgrass, A. M. (1984) 'The ancient Greek world', in J. Bintliff (ed.) *European Social Evolution*, Bradford: University of Bradford.

—— (1985) 'The new archaeology and the classical archaeologist', *American Journal of Archaeology* 89: 31–7.

Sorensen, M.-L. (1988) 'Is there a feminist contribution to archaeology?', *Archaeological Review from Cambridge* 7: 9–20.

South, S. (1977a) *Method and Theory in Historical Archaeology*, New York: Academic Press.

—— (ed.) (1977b) *Research Strategies in Historical Archaeology*, New York: Academic Press.

Stone, P. and Mackenzie, R. (eds) (1990) *The Excluded Past: Archaeology in Education*, London: Unwin Hyman.

Strong, R. (1984) *Art and Power: Renaissance Festivals 1450–1650*, Woodbridge: Boydell Press.

Tilley, C. (1984) 'Ideology and the legitimation of power in the middle neolithic of southern Sweden', in D. Miller and C. J. Tilley (eds) *Ideology, Power and Prehistory*, Cambridge: Cambridge University Press.

—— (1989) 'Excavation as theatre', *Antiquity* 63: 275–80.

—— (ed.) (1990) *Reading Material Culture: Structuralism, Hermeneutics and Post-structuralism*, Oxford: Basil Blackwell.

Trigger, B. (1981) 'Anglo-American archaeology', *World Archaeology* 13: 138–55.

—— (1984) 'Alternative archaeologies: nationalist, colonialist, imperialist', *Man* 19: 355–70.

—— (1990) *A History of Archaeological Thought*, Cambridge: Cambridge University Press.

Ucko, P. J. (1987) *Academic Freedom and Apartheid*, London: Duckworth.

Wallerstein, I. (1974) *The Capitalist World-system*, vol. 1, New York: Academic Press.

Williamson, T. and Bellamy, L. (1987) *Property and Landscape: a Social History of Land Ownership and the English Countryside*, London: George Philip.

Wolfram, S. (1986) *Zur Theoriediskussion in der prähistorischen Archäologie Grossbritanniens*, British Archaeological Reports International Series 306, Oxford.

Wright, P. (1985) *On Living in an Old Country: the National Past in Contemporary Britain*, London: Verso.

7

THEORY IN SCANDINAVIAN ARCHAEOLOGY SINCE 1960: A VIEW FROM NORWAY

Bjørn Myhre[1]

Introduction

We are living in the post-modern period; everything seems to be post- at the moment. It has become a general trend to look back to the past for ideas and traits and to incorporate them into modern constructions. Different directions and approaches can thrive side by side, without hard discussion on what is right or wrong, without a clear view that there is only one way to follow. The philosophy of post-modernism is to be found within architecture, art and literature, but also within philosophy, science, art and the humanities. Some say it has become a way of living (Baudrillard 1981; Lyotard 1979; Hviid Nielsen 1986), an attitude which has left its imprint on archaeology as well.

The twenty-five years of inspiring discussion between followers of traditional and New Archaeology, and between different approaches within the New Archaeology, seem to have ended, and we may ask if the discipline is on the way to a sort of theoretical relativism. There is not one archaeology or one prehistory any more, but many, depending on the philosophical or political theory of the archaeologist. Even the much reviled years of the 1950s seem to be of interest; we hear slogans like 'Back to the 50s', meaning back to pre-processual archaeology to investigate what we lost during the 1960s and 1970s 'to rebuild the bridges which were so harshly broken by processual archaeology, reevaluate what has been termed the "long sleep of archaeological theory" ' (Hodder 1986: 176).

I would like to present my personal views on how Scandinavian archaeology developed during these twenty-five years. On the one hand I would like to comment on the influence of British and American archaeology. It is, however, my impression that the theoretical discussion in Scandinavia also followed an independent direction under influences from other disciplines in the humanities and social sciences and from the philosophy of science.

It is necessary to distinguish between the concepts of method, models and theory. 'Theory is what decides our choice of data and the interpretation of our analysis' (Larsson 1986: 5), and 'theory constitutes our data by preceding them, forming the frame of reference within which questions are formulated. Its function is first to generate hypotheses, then to predict solutions' (Dommasnes 1987: 6). We construct models to clarify our theory and research process, and we use methods to handle our data, as a form of argument to translate data into knowledge (Dommasnes 1987; Hill 1972: 73). Theory may then be defined as: a) a general conception of humanity and society that can be found in all the human disciplines; and b) a more specific view that guides the archaeologist's choice of data and special methods. Or, to follow David Clarke, a comprehensive archaeological general theory with the following subtheories: pre-depositional theory, depositional theory, post-depositional theory, retrieval theory, analytical theory and interpretative theory (1973: 16).

Scandinavian theoretical archaeology, 1960–1975

David Clarke saw four competing paradigms or approaches in the archaeological scene of 1972: the morphological, the anthropological, the ecological and the geographical paradigms, that were cross-cut by a number of new methodologies. He compared the situation at that time with T. S. Kuhn's description of a pre-paradigmatic phase, and he found himself in an intermediate period between, on the one side, the paradigmatic phase of the traditional post-war archaeology characterised by 'an artefact-based, particularised, qualitative, culture-historical paradigm' (Clarke 1972: 43) and, on the other side, a new more uniform paradigmatic phase that was to come. He found that contemporary archaeology exhibited the diverse and rapid change described by Kuhn as characteristic of the pre-paradigmatic phase.

Generally speaking, such a broad description of the discipline's development from the 1950s to the 1970s may be applied to

Scandinavian archaeology too (Selinge 1979a, Hyenstrand 1979, 1981). But it is difficult to accept that the post-war situation was so uniform. At least three of Clarke's four competing approaches also existed in the late 1940s and the 1950s; and there was strong competition between the followers of the morphological (or typological) paradigm and the ecological and geographical paradigms (Kristiansen 1978a; Becker 1979; Jensen 1979a). Clarke clearly also exaggerated the situation for British archaeology in the 1950s (compare works by Graham Clark, Gordon Childe and E. C. Curwen).

The late 1940s and early 1950s seem in fact to have been an optimistic and creative period for archaeology in Scandinavia. A historical and economic approach was emphasised, with the aim of reconstructing culture history, settlement development and past lifeways. Intensive mapping and inventorisation of ancient monuments progressed, and large-scale excavations with participants from all the Nordic countries triggered the development of new excavation techniques independent of similar developments in England. Interdisciplinary research projects with botanists and zoologists as participants were started. Such projects were mostly led by archaeologists outside the morphological/typological research direction. These archaeologists were not so easily trapped in the archaeological culture concept, but gave priority to a direct historical approach, using analogies from early historic time (Hagen 1953; Hougen 1947; Hatt 1949, 1957; Troels-Smith 1953; Klindt-Jensen 1957; Stenberger 1955).

Such approaches and a basically positivist attitude had created a scientific background that made it easy to incorporate some of the new ideas and methods of the 1960s, especially in Norway and Sweden which have different research traditions from Denmark (Jensen 1966; Kristiansen 1984a; Hyenstrand 1985; Myhre 1985; Christophersen 1989). Consequently, it is difficult to agree with Kristian Kristiansen (1984a: 206) following Colin Renfrew (1982), that Scandinavian archaeology during the 1960s was sound asleep. But it was turning a bit senile and needed new inspiration or, to quote Gutorm Gjessing (1975) it was suffering from the eye disease glaucoma and needed an operation to get a wider view, with the philosophy of science as its instrument.

In the early 1960s we can already detect new developments within the so-called four paradigms of David Clarke, seeds of new theories that are still active and being debated. Instead of *paradigms* I will, in the following, call these directions *approaches*, and use the concept *paradigm* for the main theories that direct the discipline.

The anthropological approach

The 1950s had been a formative period for the social sciences in Scandinavia. During the years around 1960 new teaching departments in social anthropology, ethnology and sociology were established at the universities of Oslo and Bergen, for example. At an early phase they were much influenced by American anthropology and sociology, and especially by the active milieu at the University of Chicago, where Fredrik Barth and Gutorm Gjessing had studied both archaeology and anthropology around 1950 (Barth 1947; Gjessing 1951; Klausen 1981: 108–11). Fredrik Barth, the founder of Norwegian social anthropology, took his Ph.D. in Cambridge in 1956, and he introduced the British school of social anthropology to Scandinavia.

During the early 1960s social anthropology, ethnography and ethnology became popular secondary subjects for students of archaeology, and gradually the new anthropological theory found its way into archaeological circles, though not yet into the literature. But archaeologists like Walter Taylor, Gordon Willey, Albert Spaulding and anthropologists like Julian Steward, Leslie White, Raymond Firth and Edmond Leach became familiar names as authors of educational literature for students of archaeology (Moberg 1961; Myhre 1964).

Fredrik Barth and his teaching, however, soon began to influence archaeological theory. Knut Odner's ecological study 'Ullshelleren in Valldalen' (published 1969, but written in 1966–7) used a model that was inspired by Barth's processual interaction model combining game theory, human ecology theory and systems analysis. It is a model which describes people's choice of different economies; not only ecology and technology, but also social organisation and cultural and psychological factors, are taken into consideration (Odner 1969). The same model and approach was used by Else Johansen Kleppe in her study of an Iron Age society in Finnmark (1973, 1975). Here for the first time we can recognise concepts and theories of processual archaeology and systems analysis in Scandinavia, introduced via anthropology from Chicago and Cambridge, Binford's (1972: 1) and Clarke's (1968) universities, respectively.

Knut Odner also made an important study of Norwegian Iron Age society, introducing neo-evolutionary anthropological theory and the substantivist economic theory of Karl Polanyi, and using anthropological and historical models and analogies. His works published in 1972 and 1973 were mainly written in the late 1960s (1973: 1). They set a trend for Scandinavian archaeology during the 1970s.

The anthropological definition of culture as mainly constituted by an integrated complex of ideas, norms, skills and knowledge (Taylor 1948: 101-1) was confronted with the traditional archaeological definition of culture as an assemblage of artefacts and traits that repeatedly occur together. Fredrik Barth's definition as 'the sum of knowledge and skill that characterise a local population', and his opinion that archaeology can only reconstruct very limited parts of prehistoric cultures (1961: 35, 42), was a great challenge. While most archaeologists disregarded the problem, some desperately sought help in international archaeology (for a review see Østmo 1989).

One solution was to follow Phillips and Willey's procedure of studying archaeological units that were primarily 'defined segments of the total continuum in time and space' (1958: 15), through the concepts of phase, horizon and tradition (Myhre 1964; Hagen 1970: 128). Others found an acceptable formula in Binford's definition of culture as primarily an 'extrasomatic system that is employed in the integration of a society with its environment and with other sociocultural systems' (1965: 205), thereby setting strict limits to what parts of the human past could be studied by archaeologists (Hagen 1980: 6; Kokkonen 1984: 162). David Clarke's *Analytical Archaeology* was first considered as a new Bible that should provide the solution of how to combine archaeological culture and living peoples, but his recipe also had its weaknesses (Moberg 1970).

The discussion about the usefulness of the archaeological concept of culture also raised the question of archaeology's ability to study two of the main mechanisms that were thought to change a culture; migration and diffusion (Magnus and Myhre 1972). Internal developments within regional segments of archaeological cultures became a safe path of research that many Scandinavian archaeologists followed (Hagen 1970: 128).

The typological approach

One of the most exciting developments in the 1960s was to be found within the typological approach. The numerous new excavations brought a large amount of new material to the museums, and it had to be studied with modern tools. Statistics, mathematics, electronic data processing and other quantitative methods found their way into Scandinavian archaeology. Again we can see an influence from the University of Chicago: Professor Carl Axel Moberg from Gothenburg was a visiting professor there in 1963, working with Binford and Braidwood among others, and he introduced the American quantitative archaeology and the discussion of the nature of types and attributes (Malmer 1988).

Already in 1957 Mats P. Malmer had presented quantitative and cartographic methods inspired by the Swedish human geographer T. Hägerstrand (1952, 1953). Later came the influence of J. C. Gardin (1967) and his Centre d'Analyse Documentaire pour l'Archéologie in Marseille, also transmitted by Moberg, and the numerical taxonomy of Sokal and Sneath (1963). Active research centres with data processing facilities developed in Aarhus, Gothenburg and Bergen (Voss 1967, 1970; Cullberg 1968, 1970; Moberg 1969; Herteig 1965, 1966). The journal *Norwegian Archaeological Review* was started in Bergen in 1967, and the first volumes concentrated mainly on quantitative and taxonomic methods and the interpretation of archaeological data.

Central to this discussion was Professor Mats P. Malmer from Stockholm who, in 1962 and 1963, published two books primarily focused on methodological and theoretical problems in archaeology, which had a formative influence on Scandinavian archaeology. He introduced what he called a rationalistic way of reasoning (a hypothetico-deductive method) as opposed to an empirical approach (an inductive approach). Malmer argued for logically correct verbal definitions as basic to the method and theory of archaeology, as well as for the use of models and the testing of well-formulated hypotheses to achieve results through verification or falsification.

As archaeologists, we have to build our study on material remains, and primarily on similarities and dissimilarities between objects. Malmer's main thesis is that 'physical similarity entails a probability of every other form of similarity, i.e. similarity in respect of time, use, name and environment. A correctly defined type corresponds to a concrete historic situation' (1963a: 264). He hoped to overcome the subjective element in scientific reasoning through a rationalistic approach (1968: 37). Mats P. Malmer made few references to the sources of his approach in 1962–3, but it seems clear that his argumentation is influenced by the continental, positivist tradition of the Vienna school, by Ludwig Wittgenstein and the Finnish philosopher G. H. von Wright (Malmer 1963b: 11, 222), while C. G. Hempel and Karl R. Popper were not known to him at that time (personal letter, 7 August 1987). In an article on archaeological positivism in 1984 Malmer explains his views in a broader context. He refers especially to Hempel's philosophy and equates the concept of rationalism with the positivist approach of Binford and the New Archaeology. 'I have always shared the neo-archaeological conviction about the archaeological material's potential for knowledge: the information is there' (1984: 265).

Malmer's approach could actually have constituted a very strong bridge between the artefact/culture-based archaeology and the environmental/ecological school, and could have had a similar effect in Scandinavia in the early 1960s to that of the New Archaeology in the USA in the 1970s. But Scandinavian archaeologists did not grasp the full potential of his work at that time, and discussions mostly concentrated on his rationalistic/deductive approach, opposing the traditional empirical/inductive line that dominated Scandinavian archaeology at that time. The discussion between him and Egil Bakka in the *Norwegian Archaeological Review* 1968–9 presents many of the same arguments as a recent discussion between Binford and Gould in *American Antiquity* (1985: 580–90, 638–44).

Most of the quantitative methods of Scandinavian archaeology in the 1960s and early 1970s were in fact inductive in approach, and the belief that computers would detect operative types turned out to be ill-founded. It was the next generation of archaeologists who were to take seriously Binford's warning in the *Norwegian Archaeology Review*: 'It is essential for gaining a more reliable understanding of the past, that we do not waste our technical skills trying to answer bad questions, arising from bad methodology and a naïve understanding of the character of the archaeological record' (1971: 16).

The geographical approach

Settlement history based on the geographical study of farmsteads, house sites, field systems and barrows has a long tradition in Scandinavia (Hatt 1949, 1957; Ambrosiani 1964; Myhre 1972; Becker 1980b). During the 1960s the Swedish human geographers took a strong interest in the study of prehistoric agrarian landscapes and introduced new methods 'aiming at explaining the spatial development of society' (Widgren 1985: 156).

The inspiration came from the New British Geography with its quantitative and locational methods (Haggett 1965). But Swedish geographers had themselves played an important part in this development within the subject (Hägerstrand 1952, 1953; Hannerberg 1970). Through the study by Sven-Olof Lindquist of the prehistoric culture landscape of Östergötland in 1968, the modern geographical approach was introduced into Scandinavian archaeology, and immediately a fierce debate started. But as described in connection with the typological approach, it was not the field evidence, the field techniques or the results that aroused discussion. It was once again the empirically orientated methods of archaeology versus the hypothetico-deductive method and model-building of geography that were at stake (Widgren 1985: 156; Ambrosiani 1968: 306; Baudou 1973; Sporrong 1974).

But soon the human geography of Sweden came to influence Scandinavian archaeology tremendously, exactly as the New Geography had in England in the 1960s and 1970s. When the archaeologist Åke Hyenstrand wrote in 1982 that the two subjects with their different starting points now worked within a common research trend (1982: 59), the geographers did not disagree (Widgren 1985: 157).

The ecological/economic approach

The general interest in environmental problems underwent a great expansion in Scandinavia during the 1960s and early 1970s, and the study of ecology within the natural sciences was established at the universities. Human ecology, or cultural ecology, and the evolution of ancient environments were given more attention (Welinder 1984). Because of industrial development, rescue archaeology came to take most of the time and resources of Scandinavian archaeology. Large interdisciplinary projects within the framework of rescue archaeology co-operated with institutes of botany, geology and zoology at the universities (Johansen 1973; Baudou 1972; Stjernquist 1981; Andersen *et al.* 1983).

As a result of this development rescue archaeology and major archaeological institutions in Denmark and Norway were organised under the Ministry of Environment. Consequently the whole attitude of the subject changed dramatically during these years. From being a history- and humanities-based subject, it became primarily environmental, and the study of man and his natural environment was given highest priority, in practical fieldwork, in teaching and in the theoretical approach (Kristiansen 1972, 1978a; Moberg 1978a, 1978b; Hagen 1980; Kyhlberg 1982; Furingsten 1983; Myhre 1989).

Scandinavian archaeology around 1975

Scandinavian archaeology developed tremendously during the 1960s and early 1970s. From being a minor part of museum studies, it became a discipline with large field institutes and medium-sized teaching departments at the universities. But did its fundamental theory change? Not specifically; I agree with Axel Christophersen that it was more a matter of scale and change in methods and techniques (Christophersen 1989:41). The subject was becoming more international, and it was turning most of its antennae from the European continent towards England and North America. Through influences from other subjects within Scandinavia, such as social anthropology, human geography and ecology, a new platform had been built that made it easier to accumulate and use the new ideas of Anglo-American archaeology. Carl-Axel Moberg at the University of Gothenburg was probably the Scandinavian archaeologist who was best informed about the different international trends within the subject, and he played an important role as an intermediary between Scandinavia and other countries in this transition period when old traditions were challenged by the New Archaeology (1969, 1978b).

One of the most important developments, in my opinion, was the introduction and gradual acceptance of the deductive way of reasoning, first introduced by Mats Malmer under the name of rationalism, and later also through co-operation with human geography. Quantitative methods and computers were also important, in spite of numerous failures and discouragement in the first instance because the traditional inductive way of reasoning could not easily be applied to the new methods. Hypothesis testing, model-building and the need for strict definitions brought a dramatic change in traditional archaeology. Even if this way of reasoning already existed, it now became more conscious, and procedures were made more explicit. But inductive or deductive, the dominant theory was still positivist, believing that objective information and knowledge could be buried in archaeological material (Christophersen 1989). The question of objective knowledge in archaeology had, however, already been raised by Arne B. Johansen in 1969 (see p. 172).

Another important development was that social anthropology overtly confronted Scandinavian archaeology with the problem of constructing living societies from material remains. The traditional concepts of type and culture in particular were shaken. Many tried to overlook this basic problem of archaeology, and took an optimistic attitude towards social anthropology, looking for the possibility of studying economic, social and political structures and processes inspired by for example Renfrew's and Binford's works. The seeds of a social archaeology had been sown (Stjernquist 1971; Randsborg 1974, 1975).

Towards a new paradigm?

In about 1975 Scandinavian archaeology reached a theoretical platform similar to British archaeology's, though partly by different paths and strongly coloured by Scandinavian research traditions. Scandinavian archaeology in general was probably more conservative. More archaeologists were working in traditional ways, but the new ideas were of a similar kind.

What then was the answer to David Clarke's prediction of, or hope for, a new uniform paradigm in archaeology?

The answer, in Scandinavia as in Britain, was a research design where the different approaches of the 1960s were incorporated within a common systemic strategy. It seems to me that the years around 1975 were an important turning point in Scandinavia. The basis for a more direct acceptance of Anglo-American archaeology was built, and books by Clarke (1972), Renfrew (1973a, 1973b) and Binford (1972) had a great influence. At the same time the ideas of Esther Boserup on agricultural growth and demography

(1965), of Elman Service on primitive social organisation (1962, 1975) and Higgs on palaeoeconomy (1972) were incorporated.

Characteristic in these years was the dominant position of ecological, economical and geographical traditions in the systemic approach. The neo-evolutionary theory of Sahlins (1972), Service (1962) and Fried (1967) was adapted rather uncritically, resulting in an ecological-systemic-neo-evolutionary approach – or should we call it a paradigm, following Kuhn's definition of a paradigm as an exemplary way of solving scientific problems within a specific subject (Johannesen 1986: 145) Within this paradigm a reductionist systems theory based on ecological, economic and social subsystems came to dominate Scandinavian archaeology for nearly a decade (see also Larsson 1986: 8). This approach was dominated by a series of works by Stig Welinder (1975, 1977, 1979, 1983), but most Scandinavian archaeologists patterned their research within this paradigm (e.g. Selinge 1979a; Hyenstrand 1979, 1981; Myhre 1978; Mikkelsen 1978; Kristiansen 1978a; Håland 1981) which also came to dominate more popular review books (Burenhult 1982; Jensen 1979b, Magnus and Myhre 1976) and museum exhibitions, especially in Denmark. Was such a development in Clarke's mind when he predicted a single uniform paradigm in the future? The development of Scandinavian archaeology came very close to it during the late 1970s.

Recent directions in Scandinavian archaeology

Archaeology is not a subject within the natural sciences, despite what many of us nearly came to believe, and as a human science it has to be multi-paradigmatic (Johannesen 1984: 66). Within Scandinavia arguments for new approaches were heard as early as the beginning of the 1970s, especially within the paradigms of Marxism and structuralism. These views were mostly expressed in the newly established journal *Kontaktstensil*, which is a forum for Scandinavian students of archaeology (e.g. Bang 1974; Jespersen 1972; Kristiansen 1972; Lejon 1974; Moberg 1978b). The strongest arguments against the systemic approach were, however, aimed at its positivist philosophy.

Non-positivist theory

A fierce debate about positivism in science and the humanities developed in Scandinavian universities around 1968. The so-called neutral non-political research of archaeology was also questioned (Gjessing 1969, 1974). The solution suggested by most critics was a Marxist approach, but it never gained a strong foothold before the end of the 1970s.

The clearest anti-positivist view in Scandinavian archaeology was expressed by Arne Johansen when he took up the important question of the nature of archaeological data in 1969 and 1974. He was concerned about the question of objectivity and subjectivity in archaeological research, and like Mats Malmer and the New Archaeology he advocated the deductive approach, but at the same time completely rejected inductive reasoning (see also Johansen 1984). Johansen also questioned the basis of archaeological research, namely the relation between theory and empirical data. In his opinion, archaeological data have no existence of their own, but are created through the hypotheses of researchers and the problems they pose.

> The central and unifying mechanism in culture-historic research is that data must be defined before they can be discovered . . . This leads to the paradox and circular reasoning that while a theory of man and culture must exist before data come into existence, the same batch of data later on is used in building up such theories.
>
> (Johansen 1969: 100–1)

Consequently, according to Johansen, it is impossible to do objective research in the way Mats Malmer and the New Archaeology suggest, testing a hypothesis and thereby creating new knowledge.

> The only way to overcome the tendency to gather an increasing amount of support for theories already established, is to consciously create new models of man, and different models from what is generally accepted. Then we can hope to discover fundamentally new types of data and to see the world in a different way.
>
> (1969: 26–7).

Johansen was therefore rejecting the logical-positivist approach of Hempel and the New Archaeology in the sense that the approach

172

cannot produce more answers than are already present in the questions. He was inspired by Karl Popper's searchlight theory (Dommasnes 1987: 2), but because of the inductive and positivist elements in that philosophy, Johansen was more interested in the school of philosophy of science following the traditions of Wittgenstein, especially the works of Feyerabend (Johansen 1974: 100–4). During the 1950s this school had already strongly opposed the logical empiricists (Johannesen 1986: 121).

The archaeological approach of Johansen was not taken seriously by Scandinavian archaeologists for many years, and the debate still runs on. As he also rejected inductive reasoning completely, he annoyed both empiricists and rationalists. But his view that archaeology can never become an objective science has gradually been accepted by most theorists (for a different view, see Malmer 1984). The question of inductive or deductive reasoning is, however, still discussed, even if most archaeologists agree that both approaches are necessary in empirical science (Christophersen 1982a; Herschend 1982; Dommasnes 1987).

Johansen's great achievement is that Scandinavian archaeology began to debate its own subjectivity or objectivity at a rather early stage. It was no longer a question of the actual knowledge, but what kind of knowledge we want, and what kind of problems we want to find a solution to. He has, however, in my opinion rightly been criticised for not discussing the most important question of all: what kind of social theory shall we then base our analysis on (Christophersen 1982b: 147)?

Already in 1978 Christian Keller had published a book with the aim of demonstrating how the archaeological past influences present-day society, and how present ideologies form our construction of the past. He follows the same line of reasoning as Shanks and Tilley (1987) and Ian Hodder in many of his publications from the 1980s. Keller's conclusion is that archaeologists must be more aware of their political and ideological influence in modern society, and must explicitly analyse and express the fundamentals of their scientific goals and research (1978: 91–8). His book opened the eyes of many Scandinavian archaeologists, and resulted in the loss of ideological innocence, to quote Clarke (1973).

Kristian Kristiansen has published several important studies on the influence of present Danish society on archaeological research and attitudes (1981, 1984a). During 1980s many controversial

political aspects of Scandinavian societies were reflected in archaeological research, as in feminist archaeology, the prehistory of
children, the archaeology of power, death, war and aggression,
and not least the study of ethnicity (Næss 1984; Lillehammer
1986; Andreassen 1986; Lindman 1986; Welinder 1988).

In Norway especially the strong Saami/Lappish political movement of the 1980s has made it necessary for archaeologists to take
a stand on the question of a Saami or Norwegian prehistory. The
problems of having an archaeology based primarily on political
ideologies are often discussed (Keller 1978: 93; Mahler *et al.* 1983;
Hagen 1986; Olsen 1986). It seems to me that the critical/political
aspect of archaeological theory has come further in Scandinavia
than in most other western countries, at least until the World
Archaeological Congress of Southampton in 1986.

Structuralism and Marxism

As in England, the paradigms of structuralism and Marxism have
recently been given priority by many Scandinavian archaeologists.
There is a strong influence from the works of Ian Hodder (1982a,
1982b), Michael Rowlands (1980, 1984) and Christopher Tilley
(1984) on the one hand, and the French Marxist anthropologists
on the other. I would like to call attention to the special impact
structural–Marxism has had on both social anthropology and
archaeology, mainly through the influence of Jonathan Friedman
(1975a, 1975b, 1978), who since the mid 1970s has lived in Copenhagen and Lund. The first archaeological articles designed according to his approach were already being published in the later 1970s
(Spång 1977; Christophersen 1982a). Through social anthropologists like Knut Odner (1979), Kaisa Ekholm (1979) and Kirsten
Hastrup *et al.* (1975) the message was spread. The neo-evolutionist
and basically materialist traditions in Scandinavian archaeology
were transmitted rather easily into this form of structural-Marx-
ism. A leading archaeologist working along these lines is Kristian
Kristiansen (1978b, 1982).

Already in 1974 the structuralism of Claude Lévi-Strauss was
recommended to Scandinavian archaeologists as a theory that
could give meaning to the concept of material culture. Culture
should be seen as a means of communication and structuring of
symbols (Bang 1975). Problems of semiotics and archaeology were
discussed in connection with Scandinavian petroglyphs (Nord-

bladh 1978), and concrete examples of this approach were published in 1979 in a special volume of the Danish journal *Hikuin* (Hodder 1979; Lévi-Strauss 1979; Højlund 1979). It had little effect on Scandinavian archaeology at that time, but in recent years several of the young archaeologists have followed Ian Hodder's approach in *Symbols in Action* (1982a) and *Symbolic and Structural Archaeology* (1982b), seeing the artefacts as symbols of values, norms and positions in early societies (Jennbert 1984; Olsen 1985b, Mikkelsen *et al.* 1986; Bostwick Bjerck 1988).

A certain development within the symbolic approach, which can be related to Fredrik Barth and the book *Ethnic Groups and Boundaries* (1969), is also of importance in this connection. Material traits are here seen as idioms signalling ethnic identity, and ethnicity is defined as a kind of social organisation. Already in 1977 Randi Haaland and Else Johansen Kleppe tried to apply this theory to the study of ethnic groups in prehistoric society. Inspired by Hodder (1982a) and as a consequence of the Saami/Lappish political movement since 1979, a number of works on archaeology and ethnicity have appeared (Olsen 1985a; *Norwegian Archaeological Review* 1985; Næss 1985). Once again Knut Odner came to play a central role through his book *Finner og Terfinner* where he discusses the question not only of early Saami ethnicity but also of early Saami language, drawing on results from his own ethno-archaeological research (1983, 1985).

An interest in archaeology and the history of religion (Steinsland 1986), as well as archaeology and the history of language (Haaland and Haaland 1982; Haaland 1987; Odner 1987), can also be seen.

Several attempts have been made lately to incorporate structural Marxism, symbolism and the ideological aspects of material culture into a general theory, following for example Shanks and Tilley (1982) and also drawing on articles on ideology and material remains by Michael Parker Pearson (1984a, 1984b). In this approach the primary interest is not with the economic and social systems but with the superstructure of the society. Followers of this theory argue mainly within a Marxist framework (Hermerén 1984; Kristiansen 1984b; Larsson 1986; Olsen 1984).

Future directions

Scandinavian archaeology is on the way towards freeing itself from positivist philosophy, and heading towards a more subjective attitude which is conscious and goal-directed. This opens up new approaches and exciting new problems to investigate. Themes connected with migrations, early languages, religion, ethnicity and political organisation have come back on the archaeological agenda. An optimistic mood is in the air.

But pessimistic voices are also heard, warning that we are cutting loose from old truths and safe ground. In Scandinavia many archaeologists are still searching for *the* right direction. Structuralism and Marxism are such directions, based on well-established theories. Another direction is to base the subject on a hermeneutic philosophy, which seeks not explanation but understanding and interpretation, which is holistic but also particular, which is both inductive and deductive, and is historical in its approach (Johansson and Liedman 1983: 87, 180). Hermeneutics has for many years been accepted in other culture-historical disciplines (Johannesen 1984, 1986), and Norwegian social anthropology has for example been said to be based on a solid hermeneutic tradition (Klausen 1981: 162). Several Scandinavian archaeologists have also expressed hermeneutic views (Keller 1978: 81; Dommasnes 1987), and the concept *understanding* instead of *explanation* has become fashionable. Archaeology in Scandinavia has actually always been strongly influenced by hermeneutics in its research, but it has seldom been expressed so explicitly as in recent years.

At the bottom of the theoretical discussion always lies the interpretation of the basic archaeological concepts: type and culture (Hodder 1982a: 1). Perhaps non-verbal communication theory and semiotics will help us to give the concepts a new content, seeing the artefacts as a symbolic code expressing norms, values and meaning. Contextual source criticism is, however, badly needed (Hodder 1986: 118; Mikkelsen *et al.* 1986).

Returning to David Clarke's statement of 1972, we can now see that some aspects of his 1950s paradigm again appear acceptable. Archaeology is again particularistic, historical, qualitative and artefact-based (as it actually always has been). But post-New Archaeology, or post-processual archaeology, is not only that. It is also subjective and anti-positivist, multi-paradigmatic and pluralistic, more politically and ideologically conscious, both a humanistic and a social science (Hodder 1985; Shanks and Tilley 1987; Olsen 1987). This subjective, pluralistic attitude is not specific to archaeology but is a reflection of post-modern philosophy. According to Hodder (1986: 1), the New Archaeology of the 1960s and early 1970s was flawed, but in my opinion it was a necessary transformation period for a young discipline on its way to a humanistic scientific basis.

Notes

This chapter presents a selected part of the theoretical discussion on archaeology in Scandinavia, representing my personal views on the subject in early 1987, with minor, later revision. I am especially grateful to Axel Christophersen, Kristian Kristiansen, Mats P. Malmer and Stig Welinder for their comments on the manuscript. All translations of quotes are mine.

References

Ambrosiani, B. (1964) *Fornlämningar och bebyggelse*, Uppsala.
—— (1968) 'Review of S. O. Lindquist: Det förhistoriska kulturlandskapet i Östra Östergötland', *Fornvännen* 67: 302–9.
Andersen, S.Th., Aabye, B. and Odgaard, B. V. (1983) 'Environment and man', *Journal of Danish Archaeology* 2.
Andreassen, R. L. (1986) 'Kjønnsrolleperspektivet i arkeologien', *Kvinner i arkeologi i Norge* 2: 22–44.
Bakka, E. (1968) 'Methodological problems in the study of gold bracteates', *Norwegian Archaeological Review* 1: 5–56.
Bang, C. (1974) ' "Archaeology as anthropology" eller Neoarkæologiens velsignelser', *Kontakstensil* 6: 43–67.
—— (1975) 'Etnografi i arkeologien", *Kontaktstensil* 9: 49–70.
Barth, F. (1947) 'Nye muligheter for aldersbestemmelser av arkeologiske funn', *Viking* XI: 267–9.
—— (1961) 'Diffusjon – et tema i studiet av kulturelle prosesser', in A. M. Klausen, *Kultur og Diffusjon*, Oslo: Universitetets Etnografiske Museum.
—— (ed.) (1969) *Ethnic Groups and Boundaries*, Oslo: Universitetsforlaget.
Baudou, E. (1972) 'A programme for archaeological and ecological research of prehistoric and historical material from Northern Sweden', in G. Berg (ed.) *Circumpolar Problems, Habitat, Economy and Social Relations in the Arctic*, Umeå.
—— (1973) 'Arkeologiska undersökningar på Halleby. Del 1', *Studies in North-European Archaeology* 3.
Baudrillard, J. (1981) 'Sur le nihilisme', *Simulacres et Simulation*, Paris.
Becker, C. J. (1979) 'Arkæologien i Danmark – i går, i dag og i morgen', *Fortid og nutid* XXVIII: 3–11.
—— (1980a) 'Hva sker der i dansk arkæologi? Kendsgerninger og teorier omkring vor opfattelse af Danmarks forhistorie', *Grundvidenskaben i dag* 22.

—— (1980b). 'Viking-age settlements in western and central Jutland. Introductory remarks', *Acta Archaeologica* 50: 89–94.

Binford, L. R. (1962) 'Archaeology as anthropology', *American Antiquity* 28: 217–55.

—— (1965) 'Archaeological systematics and the study of cultural process', *American Antiquity* 31: 203–10.

—— (1971) 'Comments on formal procedures and the use of computers in archaeology', *Norwegian Archaeological Review* 4: 16.

—— (1972) 'Introduction', *An Archaeological Perspective*, New York/ London: Seminar Press.

—— (1985) 'Brand X versus the recommended product', *American Antiquity* 50(3): 580–90.

Boserup, E. (1965) *The Conditions of Agricultural Growth*, London: Allen & Unwin.

Bostwick Bjerck, L. (1988) 'Remodelling the neolithic in southern Norway: another attack on a traditional problem', *Norwegian Archaeological Review* 21: (1): 21–33.

Burenhult, G. (1982) *Arkeologi i Sverige 1. Fångstfolk och herdar*, Höganäs.

Christophersen, A. (1982a) 'Dreng, thegn, landmen and kings. Some aspects of the forms of social relations in Viking society during the transition to historical times', *MLUHM 1981–82*: 115–34.

—— (1982b) 'Arkeologi, ideologi og objektivitet – et stridsspørsmål', *Fornvännen* 77: 141–8.

—— (1989) 'Teorigrunnlaget og metodeutvikling i nordisk arkeologi på 1970- og 1980-tallet. Noen kritiske refleksjoner over temaet "archaeology is archaeology is archaeology" ', *Universitets Oldsaksamlings Årbok 1986–1988*: 39–48.

Clarke, D. L. (1968) *Analytical Archaeology*, London: Methuen.

—— (1970) 'Analytical archaeology – epilogue. Reply to the comments on analytical archaeology', *Norwegian Archaeological Review* 3: 25–34.

—— (ed.) (1972) *Models in Archaeology*, London: Methuen.

—— (1973) 'Archaeology: the loss of innocence', *Antiquity* 47: 6–18.

Cullberg, C. (1968) 'On artifact analysis', *Acta Archeologica Lundensia* 4: (7).

—— (1970) 'A contribution to the discussion of typological concepts in archaeology. Reply to comments on artifact analysis', *Norwegian Archaeological Review* 3: 50–72.

Dommasnes, L. H. (1985) 'Analyse av faktorer som virker inn på fagets innhold', *Kvinner i arkeologi i Norge* 1: 25–37.

—— (1987) 'On hypothesis, inference and man in Norwegian archaeology', *Norwegian Archaeological Review* 20 (1): 1–10.

Dunnell, R. C. (1986) 'Methodological issues in Americanist artifact classification', *Advances in Archaeological Method and Theory* 9: 149–207.

Ekholm, K. (1979) 'Arkeologi som samhällsvetenskap', *Kontaktstensil* 16: 8–24.

Friedman, J. (1975a) 'Tribes, states and transformations', in M. Bloch (ed.) *Marxist Analysis and Social Anthropology*, London: Malaby Press.

—— (1975b) 'Evolutionary models in anthropology', unpublished, Institute of Ethnology and Anthropology, University of Copenhagen.
Friedman, J. and Rowlands M. (1978) (eds) *The Evolution of Social Systems*, London: Duckworth.
Furingsten, A. (1983) 'Nordisk arkeologi – tradisjonell eller nytänkande?', *Arkeologi i Sverige RAA rapport 1980* 1983 (3): 107–28.
—— (1985) 'Samhällsförändringar i ett långtidsperspektiv', *GOTARC*, Series B, 1.
Gardin, J. C. (1967) 'Methods for the descriptive analysis of archaeological material', *American Antiquity* 32: 13.
—— (1980) *Archaeological Constructs: an Aspect of Theoretical Archaeology*, Cambridge: Cambridge University Press.
Gebauer, A. B. (1978) 'The meaning of Material Culture', *Kontaktstensil* 26/27: 53–86.
Gjessing, G. (1951) 'Arkeologi og etnografi', *Viking* XV: 115–36.
—— (1969) 'Archaeology, nationalism and society', *The Teaching of Archaeological Anthropology*, Chicago.
—— (1974) 'Arkeologi, nasjonalisme og politikk', *Kontaktstensil* 6: 19–29.
—— (1975) 'Nye signaler i arkeologien', *Arkeologiske Skrifter fra Historisk museum i Bergen* 2: 49–72.
—— (1977) 'Idéer omkring førhistoriske samfunn', *Univ. Oldsaksamlings Skrifter* 2.
Gould, R. A. (1985) 'The empiricist strikes back: reply to Binford', *American Antiquity* 50 (3): 638–44.
Haaland, R. (1977) 'Archaeological classification and ethnic groups', *Norwegian Archaeological Review* 10: 1–17.
—— (1981) 'Migratory herdsmen and cultivating women. The structure of Neolithic seasonal adaptation in the Khartoum Nile environment', Doctoral thesis, University of Bergen.
—— (1987) 'Indo-europeerne i Europa. Det indo-europeiske problem' in K. Kristiansen (ed.) *Nordisk TAG. Rapport fra den første TAG-conference i Helsingør 15–17.11.1985*, Copenhagen.
Haaland, R. and Håland, G. (1982) *Verdenshistorien I. I begynnelsen*, Oslo: Aschehoug.
Hagen, A. (1953) 'Sostelid. Studier i jernalderens gårdssamfunn', *Univ. Oldsaksamlings Skrifter* 4.
—— (1970) 'Refleksjoner over noen arkeologiske problemstillinger og tolkningsmuligheter', *Viking* XXXIV: 111–62.
—— (1980) 'Trends in Scandinavian archaeology at the transition to the 1980s', *Norwegian Archaeological Review* 13 (1): 1–8.
—— (1986) 'Arkeologi og politikk', *Viking* XLIX: 269–78.
Hägerstrand, T. (1952) 'The propagation of innovation waves', *Lund Studies in Geography*, Series B, 4, Lund.
—— (1953) *Innovationsförloppet ur korologisk synpunkt*, Lund.
Haggett, P. (1965) *Locational Analysis in Human Geography*, London: Arnold.
Hannerberg, D. (1970) *Korologiska populationsmodeller*, Stockholm.
Hastrup, K. *et al.* (1975) *Den ny antropologi*, Copenhagen.

179

Hatt, G. (1949) 'Oldtidsagre', *Videnskabernes Selskab, Arkæologiskkunsthistoriske Skrifter* II (1). Kbh.
—— (1957) *Nørre Fjand. An Early Iron-Age Village Site in West-Jutland,* Kbh.
Hermerén, G. (1984) 'Positivistic and Marxist ideals of science and their consequences for research', in B. Stjernquist (ed.) *Perspectives on Archaeological Theory and Method,* Report series 20, Lund.
Herschend, F. (1982) 'Ett grundläggande teoretiskt problem', *Fornvännen* 77: 148–51.
Herteig, A. (1965) 'Moderne databehandling i gjenstandsforskningen', *Museumsnytt* 14: 27–32.
—— (1966) 'Bør arkeologiens uttrykksmidler i støpeskjeen?', *Naturen* 1966: 293–303.
Higgs, E. (ed.) (1972) *Papers in Economic Prehistory,* Cambridge.
—— (1975) *Paleoeconomy,* Cambridge.
Hill, J. N. (1972) 'The methodological debate in contemporary archaeology: a model', in D. L. Clarke (ed.) *Models in Archaeology,* London.
Hodder, I. (1979) 'The maintenance of group identities in the Baringo District, W. Kenya', *Hikuin* 5: 79–96.
—— (1982a) *Symbols in Action,* Cambridge: Cambridge University Press.
—— (1982b) 'Theoretical archaeology: a reactionary view', in I. Hodder (ed.) *Symbolic and Structural Archaeology,* Cambridge: Cambridge University Press.
—— (1984) 'Archaeology in 1984', *Antiquity* 58: 25–32.
—— (1985) 'Postprocessual archaeology', *Advances in Archaeological Method and Theory* 8: 1–26.
—— (1986) *Reading the Past. Current Approaches to Interpretation in Archaeology,* Cambridge: Cambridge University Press.
Højlund, F. (1979) 'Stenøkser i Ny Guineas Høyland', *Hikuin* 5: 31–48.
Hougen, B. (1947) *Fra seter til gård,* Oslo.
Hviid Nielsen, T. (1986) 'Narrebildet, Rasjonalisten og prosumenten', *Samtiden* 4: 8–13.
—— (1953) *Innovationsförloppet ur korologisk synpunkt,* Lund.
Hyenstrand, Å. (ed.) (1979) *Aktuell arkeologi,* Stockholm: Riksantikvarieämbetet.
—— (1981) 'Paradigm, system, program – aspekter på arkeologi', in Å. Hyenstrand (ed.) *Dokumentation-forskning,* Stockholm: Riksantikvarieämbetet.
—— (1982) *Forntida samhällsformer och arkeologiska forskningsprogram.* Riksantikvarieämbetet, Sth.
—— (1985) 'Swedish archaeology in the 1980s', *Journal of Danish Archaeology* 4: 185–7.
Jennbert, K. (1984) 'Den produktiva gåvan. Tradition och innovation i Sydskandinavien för omkring 5300 år sedan', *Acta Arch. Lundensia 4* 65–90.
Jensen, J. (1966) 'Arkæologi og kulturforskning', *Historisk tidsskrift* 1966: 1–30.

—— (1979a) 'Oldtidens samfund. Tiden indtil år 800', *Dansk Social Historie* 1: 1–270.

—— (1979b) 'En kommentar til debatten om dansk arkeologi – fortid og fremtid', *Fortid og Nutid* XXVIII: 64–9.

Jespersen, K. (1972) 'Arkæologi og den historiske materialisme', *Kontaktstensil* 4: 65–90.

Johannesen, K. S. (1984) 'Vitenskapsfilosofi og fagkonsepsjon', in *Objektivitetsproblemet i vitenskapane*, Bergen: University of Bergen.

—— (1986) *Tradisjoner og skoler i moderne vitenskapsfilosofi*, Bergen: Sigma Forlag.

Johansen, A. B. (1969) 'Høyfjellsfunn ved Lærdalsvassdraget. Den teoretiske bakgrunn og de første analyseforsøk', *Årbok for Universitetet i Bergen, 1968* 4: 1–159.

—— (1973) 'The Hardangervidda project for interdisciplinary cultural research', *Norwegian Archaeological Review* 6 (2): 60–119.

—— (1974) 'Forholdet mellom teori og data i arkeologi og andre erfaringsvitenskaper', *Arkeologiske Skrifter* 1.

—— (1982) 'Arkeologiens teori og data', *Fornvännen* 77: 212–25.

—— (1984) 'Aksiomer i arkeologi', *Rapport. Arkeologisk serie 1984* 1: 21–38.

Johansen, Ø. (1981) 'Metallfun i østnorsk bronsealder', *Univ. Oldsaksamlings Skrifter* 4.

Johansson, I. and Liedman, S. E. (1983) *Positivism och Marxism*, Norstedts, Sth.

Keller, Chr. (1975) 'Økonomiske teorier i arkeologien', *Kontaktstensil* 10: 8–21.

—— (1976) 'Nordisk vikingtid, forsøk på en økonomisk modell', *Univ. Oldsaksamlings Årbok 1972–74*:99–110.

—— (1978) *Arkeologi: virkelighetsflukt eller samfunnsforming*, Oslo: Universitetsforlaget.

Klausen, A. M. (1981) *Antropologiens historie*, Oslo: Gyldendals Fakkelbøker.

Kleppe, E. J. (1973) 'Human økologi og analyse av forhistoriske samfund', *Kontaktstensil* 5: 72–85.

—— (1975) 'Antropologisk arkæologi. Et teoretisk og metodisk indlæg', *Arkeologiske Skrifter* fra Historisk museum i Bergen 2: 107–12.

—— (1977) 'Archaeological material and ethnic identification', *Norwegian Archaeological Review* 10: 32–45.

—— (1986) 'Religion expressed through bead use: an ethno-archaeological study of Shilluk, S. Sudan', in Gro Steinsland (ed.) *Words and Objects. Towards a Dialogue between Archaeology and History of Religion*, Oslo: Universitetsforlaget.

Klindt-Jensen, O. (1957) Bornholm i folkevandringstiden og forutsætningerne i tidlig jernalder', *National Museum Skrifter* II.

Kokkonen, J. (1984) 'On the prospects of structural and semiotic approaches in archaeology', *Suomen Antropologia* 4: 159–64.

Kristiansen, K. (1972) 'Arkæologisk teori – et foreløpig oplæg', *Kontakstensil* 4: 31–64.

—— (1978a) 'Dansk arkæologi – fortid og fremtid', *Fortid og Nutid* XXVII: 279–319.

—— (1978b) 'The consumption of wealth in Bronze Age Denmark', in K. Kristiansen and C. Paludan-Müller (eds) *New Directions in Scandinavian Archaeology*, Copenhagen.

—— (1981) 'A social history of Danish archaeology (1805–1925)', in G. Daniel (ed.) *Towards a History of Archaeology*, London.

—— (1982) 'The formation of tribal systems in later European prehistory: Northern Europe 4000–500 BC', in C. Renfrew, M. Rowlands and B. Segraves (eds) *Theory and Explanation in Archaeology*, London: Academic Press.

—— (1984a) 'Danish archaeology in the 1980's', *Journal of Danish Archaeology* 3: 205–13.

—— (1984b) 'Ideology and material culture: an archaeological perspective', in M. Spriggs (ed.) *Marxist Perspectives in Archaeology*, Cambridge: Cambridge University Press.

—— (ed.) (1987) *Nordisk TAG. Rapport fra den første TAG-konference i Helsingør, 15–17/11.1985*, Copenhagen.

Kristiansen, K. and Paludan-Müller, C. (eds) (1978) *New Directions in Scandinavian Archaeology*, Copenhagen: National Museum of Denmark.

Kuhn, T. S. (1970) *The Structure of Scientific Revolutions*, Chicago.

Kyhlberg, O. (1982) 'Arkeologi i Norden under 1900-tallet. En bibliografisk analys av doktorsavhandlingarna från 1897', *Arkeologiska rapporter och medelanden från institutionen för arkeologi vid Stockholm Universitet* 12.

Larsson, T. (1986) 'The Bronze Age metalwork in southern Sweden', *Archaeology and Environment* 6.

Lejon, A. (1974) 'Positivisme og Marxisme', *Kontaktstensil* 6: 30–9.

Lévi-Strauss, C. (1979) 'A native community and its life-style', *Hikuin* 5: 97–110.

Lindman, G. (1986) 'Førhistoriska aggressionsstrukturer i det västsvenska landskapet', *GOTARC, Series B* 2.

Lillehammer, G. (1986) 'Barna i Nordens forhistorie. Metodegrunnlag og kilders bærekraft', *Kvinner i arkeologi i Norge* 2: 3–21.

Lindquist, S. O. (1968) 'Det förhistoriska kulturlandskapet i Östra Östergötland', *Acta Universitatis Stockholmiensis* 2.

Lyotard, J. F. (1979) *La Condition postmoderne*, Paris.

Magnus, B. and Myhre, B. (1972) 'The concept immigration in archaeological contexts', *Norwegian Archaeological Review* 5 (2): 45–61.

—— (1976) 'Norges Historie 1', *Fra jegergrupper til høvdingsamfunn*, Oslo: Cappelen.

Mahler, D. L., Paludan-Müller, C. and Hansen, S. S. (1983) *Om Arkæologi. Forskning, formidling, forvaltning – for hvem?* Copenhagen: Hans Reitzel.

Malmer, M. P. (1957) 'Pleionbegreppets betydelse för studiet av förhistoriska innovationsförlopp', *SMYA-FFT* 58: 160–84.

—— (1962) 'Jungneolitische studien', *Acta Arch. Lundensia* 8 (2).

—— (1963a) 'Metodproblem inom järnålderns konsthistoria. Methodological problems in the history of art during the Scandinavian Iron Age', *Acta Arch. Lundensia* 8 (3).

—— (1963b) 'Empirism och rationalism i arkeologisk forskning', *Fynd*, Gothenburg.

—— (1968) 'Comments on methodological problems in the study of gold bracteates', *Norwegian Archaeological Review* 1: 36–44.

—— (1980) 'Arkeologiens mål och material', *Fornvännen* 75: 260–5.

—— (1984) 'Arkeologisk positivism', *Fornvännen* 79: 260–8.

—— (1988) 'Carl-Axel Moberg', *Norwegian Archaeological Review* 21 (2): 61–4.

Mikkelsen, E. (1978) 'Seasonality and mesolithic adaption in Norway', in K. Kristiansen and C. Paludan-Müller (eds) *New Directions in Scandinavian Archaeology*, Copenhagen: National Museum of Denmark.

Mikkelsen, E., Stensdal Hjelvik, D. and Welinder, S. (eds) (1986) 'Det 4. Nordiske Bronsealder-Symposium på Isegran 1984', *Varia* 12, Oslo: Oldsaksamling.

Miller, D. and Tilley, C. (eds) (1984) *Ideology, Power and Prehistory*, Cambridge: Cambridge University Press.

Moberg, C.-A. (1961) 'Mängder av fornfynd', *Göteborg Univ. Årsskrift* LXVII, Gothenburg.

—— (1969) *Introduktion till Arkeologi. Natur och Kultur*, Stockholm.

—— (1970) 'Comments on analytical archaeology', *Norwegian Archaeological Review* 3: 21–5.

—— (1978a) 'Some developments in North European prehistory in the period 1969–76', *Norwegian Archaeological Review* 11: 6–17.

—— (1978b) 'Traditioner i arkeologi', in *Humaniora på undantag?*: 217–40, Stockholm.

Myhre, B. (1964) 'Metodeproblem i senere års arkeologisk forskning', *Stavanger Museums Årbok* 1964: 5–28.

—— (1972) 'Funn, fornminner og ødegårder', *Stavanger Museum Skrifter* 7, Stavanger.

—— (1978) 'Agrarian development, settlement history and social organiz-ation in SW Norway in the Iron Age', in K. Kristiansen and C. Paludan-Müller (eds) *New Directions in Scandinavian Archaeology*, Copenhagen.

—— (1985) 'Trends in Norwegian archaeology', *Journal of Danish Archaeology* 4: 179–85.

Myhre, B. (1989) 'Teori i praksis', *Univ. Oldsaksamlings Årbok 1986–88*: 59–72, Oslo.

Myrvoll, S. (1985) 'Forskningspolitiske implikasjoner – strategier og hand-lingsprogram', *Kvinner i arkeologi i Norge* 1: 52–8.

NAR, *Norwegian Archaeological Review*, Oslo/Bergen.

Nordbladh, J. (1978) 'Images as messages in society. Prolegomena to the study of Scandinavian petroglyphs and semiotics', in K. Kristiansen and C. Paludan-Müller (eds) *New Directions in Scandinavian Archaeology*, Copenhagen: National Museum of Denmark.

Næss, J.-R. (1984) 'Gravskikkforskningens skiftende skjebne. Om å være i tiden', *Rapport. Arkeologisk serie 1984* 1, Trondheim.

—— (ed.) (1985) 'Arkeologi og etnisitet', *AmS Varia* 15, Stavanger: Arkeologisk museum i Stavanger.

Odner, K. (1969) 'Ullshelleren i Valldalen, Røldal. En studie i økologiske tilpasninger', *Årbok for Universitetet i Bergen* 1969, Bergen.

—— (1972) 'Ethno-historic and ecological settings for economic and social models of an Iron Age society', in D. L. Clarke (ed.) *Models in Archaeology*, London.

Odner, K. (1973) 'Økonomiske strukturer på Vestlandet i eldre jernalder', unpublished, Historical Museum, Bergen.

—— (1979) 'Evolusjonistiske modeller belyst ved tidlige statsdannelser og imperier. Leslie White, Samuel Eisenstadt and Maurice Godelier' *Occasional Papers 1979*, 1, Oslo: Institute for Social Anthropology, University of Oslo.

—— (1983) 'Finner og Terfinner. Etniske prosesser i nordre Fenno-Skandinavia', *Occasional Papers in Social Anthropology* 9, Oslo.

—— (1985a) 'Modellbygging og etnisitet', in J. R. Næss (ed.) 'Arkeologi i etnisitet', *AmS Varia* 15, Stavanger.

—— (1985b) 'Saamis (Lapps), Finns and Scandinavians in history and prehistory. Ethnic origins and ethnic processes in Fenno-Scandinavia', *Norwegian Archaeological Review* 18 (1–2): 1–13.

—— (1987) 'Samisk språk og etnisitet. Arkeologiske og sosialantropologiske bidrag til eldste språkhistorie', in K. Kristiansen (ed.) *Nordisk TAG. Rapport fra den første TAG-Conference i Helsingør, 15–17.11.1985* Copenhagen.

Olsen, B. (1984) 'Stabilitet og endring. Produksjon og samfunn i Varanger 800 f.Kr.–1700 e.Kr', Unpublished magister thesis, University of Tromsø.

—— (1985a) 'Comments on Saamis, Finns and Scandinavians in history and prehistory', *Norwegian Archaeological Review* 18: 13–18.

—— (1985b) 'Arkeologi og etnisitet, et teoretisk og empirisk bidrag', in J. R. Naess (ed.) 'Arkeologi i etnisitet', *Ams Varia* 15, Stavanger.

—— (1986) 'Norwegian archaeology and the people without (pre) history, or how to create a myth of a uniform past', *Archaeological Review from Cambridge* 5 (1).

—— (1987) 'Arkeologi, tekst, samfunn. Fragmenter til en post-prosessuell arkeologi', Stensilserie B, Historie/arkeologi nr.24, University of Tromsø.

Parker Pearson, M. (1984a) 'Economic and ideological change', in D. Miller and C. Tilley (eds) *Ideology, Power and Prehistory*, Cambridge: Cambridge University Press.

—— (1984b) 'Social change, ideology and the archaeological record', in M. Spriggs (ed.) *Marxist Perspectives in Archaeology*, Cambridge: Cambridge University Press.

Phillips, P. H. and Willey, G. (1958) *Method and Theory in American Archaeology*, Chicago: University of Chicago Press.

Randsborg, K. (1974) 'Social stratification in Early Bronze Age Denmark', *Prähistorische Zeitschrift* 49: 38–61.

—— (1975) 'Social dimensions of early neolithic Denmark', *Proceedings of the Prehistoric Society* 41: 105–18.

Renfrew, C. (1973a) *Before Civilization. The Radiocarbon Revolution and Prehistoric Europe*, London: Jonathan Cape.
—— (ed.) (1973b) *The Explanation of Culture Change*, London: Duckworth.
—— (1982) 'Explanation revisited', in C. Renfrew, M. Rowlands and B. Segraves (eds) *Theory and Explanation in Archaeology*, New York: Academic Press.
—— (1984) *Approaches to Social Archaeology*, Cambridge, Mass.: Harvard University Press.
Rowlands, M. (1980) 'Kinship, alliance and exchange in the European Bronze Age', in J. Barrett and R. Bradley (eds) *Settlement and Society in the British Later Bronze Age*, BAR British Series 83, Oxford.
—— (1984) 'Conceptualizing the European Bronze and Early Iron Ages', in J. Bintliff (ed.) *European Social Evolution*, Bradford.
Rowlands, M. and Friedman, J. (1977) *The Evolution of Social Systems*, London: Duckworth.
Sahlins, M. (1972) *Stone Age Economics*, Chicago: Aldine.
Sahlins, M. and Service, E. (1960) *Evolution and Culture*, Ann Arbor.
Selinge, K.-G. (1979a) 'Några aspekter på arkeologisk debatt och metod', in Å. Hyenstrand (ed.) *Aktuell arkeologi*, Stockholm: Riksantikvarieämbeter.
Selinge, K.-G. (1979b) 'Agrarian settlements and hunting grounds', *Thesis and Papers in N. European Archaeology* 8, Stockholm.
Service, E. (1962) *Primitive Social Organization*, New York: Random House.
—— (1975) *Origins of the State and Civilization*, New York: Norton & Co.
Shanks, M. and Tilley, C. (1982) 'Ideology, symbolic power and ritual communication: a reinterpretation of neolithic mortuary practices', in I. Hodder, (ed.) *Symbolic and Structural Archaeology*, Cambridge: Cambridge University Press.
—— (1987) *Re-Constructing Archaeology*, Cambridge: Cambridge University Press.
Sokal, R. and Sneath, P. (1963) *Principles of Numerical Taxonomy*, San Francisco/London: Freeman & Co.
Sporrong, U. (1974) 'Comments on Iron Age farms in SW Norway', *Norwegian Archaeological Review* 7: 58–63.
Spång, L. G. (1977) 'Teorier om förhistorisk ekonomi', *Kontaktstensil* 14: 96–116.
Steinsland, G. (1986) *Words and Objects. Towards a Dialogue Between Archaeology and History of Religion*, Oslo: Universitetsforlaget.
Stenberger, M. (ed.) (1955) 'Vallhager', *A Migration Period Settlement on Gotland/Sweden* I-II, Copenhagen: Munksgaard:
Stjernquist, B. (1967) 'Models of commercial diffusion in prehistoric times', *Scripta Minora 1965–1966* (2), Lund.
—— (1971) 'Archaeological analysis of prehistoric society', *Scripta Minora 1971–1972* (1), Lund.
—— (1981) 'Gårdlösa, an Iron Age community in its natural and social setting', *Royal Society of Letters at Lund. Monographs LXXV*, Lund.

—— (ed.) (1984) 'Perspectives on archaeological theory and method', *Report Series 20*, Lund.

Straume, E. (1986) 'Norsk arkeologi de siste 20 år. Forholdet mellom hjemlig tradisjon og internasjonale strømninger i forskningen', *Viking* XLIX: 257–68.

Stummann Hansen, S. (1984) 'Gudmund Hatt. The individualist against his time', *Journal of Danish Archaeology* 3: 164–9.

Taylor, W. W. (1948) *A Study of Archeology*, Memoirs of the American Anthropological Association 69, New York.

Tilley C. (1984) 'Ideology and the legitimation of power in the Middle Neolithic of S. Sweden', in D. Miller and C. Tilley, (eds) *Ideology, Power and Prehistory*, Cambridge: Cambridge University Press.

Troels-Smith, J. (1953) 'Ertebøllekultur – Bondekultur. Resultater af de sidste 10 års undersøgelser i Aamosen', *Aarbøger for nordisk Oldkyndighed*: 5–62, Copenhagen.

Voss, O. (1967) 'Dokumentationsproblemer indenfor arkæologien', *KUML 1966*: 97–134, Århus.

Voss, O. (1970) 'Comments on Artifact Analysis', *Norwegian Archaeological Review* 3: 35–72.

Welinder, S. (1975) 'Prehistoric agriculture in eastern Middle Sweden', *Acta Arch Lundensia* 4.

—— (1977) 'Ekonomiska processar i förhistorisk expansion', *Acta Arch. Lundensia* 7.

—— (1979) 'Prehistoric demography', *Acta Archeologica Lundensia* 8.

—— (1983) 'The ecology of long-term change', *Acta Arch. Lundensia* 9.

—— (1984) 'Ekologisk arkeologi – hur en forskningsinriktning kommer och går', *Rapport. Arkeologisk serie 1984* (1), Trondheim.

—— (1989) 'Arkeologi med stort Q', *Univ. Oldsaksamlings Årbok 1986–88*, Oslo.

Wenke, R. J. (1981) 'Explaining the evolution of cultural complexity: a review', in M. B. Schiffer (ed.) *Advances in Archaeological Method and Theory* 4, New York.

Widgren, M. (1985) 'Archaeology and geography in Sweden. Common research themes and contrasting views in the last twenty years', *Archaeology and Environment* 4: 155–62.

Østmo, E. (1989) 'Begrepet arkeologisk kultur og dets anvendelighet ved studiet av bronsealder og keltertid', *Univ. Oldsaksamlings Årbok 1986–88*, Oslo.

8

ALL QUIET ON THE WESTERN FRONT? PARADIGMS, METHODS AND APPROACHES IN WEST GERMAN ARCHAEOLOGY

Heinrich Härke[1]

German archaeology deservedly enjoys a reputation for meticulous excavation, careful study of artefacts, and thorough publication of finds and findings. But it is not renowned for lively debate on theoretical and methodological issues. The reason is simple and straightforward: there has hardly been a debate on such matters in recent decades. And whatever debate there was had no significant effect on the outlook or approaches of archaeologists in German-speaking countries.

German archaeological theory and method before the 1960s

The almost complete absence of theoretical discussion in West German archaeology since 1945, and particularly in the last twenty years, is a curious phenomenon. It was not always like that. In the first quarter of this century, and to a certain degree throughout the first half, German archaeological thinking had a profound influence on European archaeology, in some areas (such as Scandinavia and the Netherlands) until as late as the 1960s. Today, the area dominated by the German tradition of 'pre- and proto-history' has shrunk to the German-speaking countries proper (Germany, Austria and Switzerland). But in many countries of Eastern Europe, a strong undercurrent of German archaeological tradition is still apparent, although it was half hidden, before 1989, under the thick coating of an officially imposed philosophy.

Just before, and around, the turn of the century, Scandinavian and German archaeologists laid the foundations of archaeology as a discipline by developing methods of chronology, artefact analysis and excavation. Paul Reinecke's studies established the chronological framework of later prehistory as it still stands today (Reinecke 1902a, 1902b, 1911, 1924, 1965). He advanced the study of chronology (as established by the Swedish scholar Oscar Montelius) by basing his identification of chronological horizons primarily on combinations of artefact types associated in archaeological contexts, rather than on the typological evolution of individual types. And Carl Schuchhardt was the first continental European excavator (after Pitt-Rivers in England) to identify post-holes during his investigations of fortifications in northern and central Germany (Schuchhardt 1909), thus giving excavators a tool for identifying timber constructions, and raising excavation methods above the level reached by Heinrich Schliemann's pioneering excavation of Troy in the 1870s.

Shortly before the First World War, Gustaf Kossinna (professor of German Archaeology at Berlin from 1902) gave prehistoric archaeology the first paradigm of its own: the ethnic paradigm. He called it the *siedlungsarchäologische Methode* (settlement-archaeological method (Kossinna 1911a)), but in spite of its name, it did not anticipate modern settlement archaeology in the field. His method combined typological and cartographic analysis and was based on several fundamental assumptions. First, distinctive artefact types may be used to identify 'cultures'. Second, the distributions of such artefact types reflect 'cultural provinces'. Third, clearly defined cultural provinces coincide with the settlement areas of tribal or ethnic groups. Fourth, the respective tribes or ethnic groups may be identified with historical peoples by projecting back from later, historical periods, provided there has been no major discontinuity or sudden change in the archaeological record. Kossinna interpreted these in terms of migrations. Otherwise, he firmly believed in autochthonous cultural development.

Kossinna's approach had a profound influence on the further development of European archaeology. Oswald Menghin, who extended the *Kulturkreis* theory of the Vienna school of ethnography into prehistoric archaeology, basically used Kossinna's method (Menghin 1936). Gordon Childe's well-known definition of archaeological cultures as 'certain types of remains ... constantly recurring together', and their identification as the material

8.1 Gustaf Kossinna (1858–1931) with friends and colleagues.

expression of 'peoples' (Childe 1929: v-vi), was directly based on Kossinna's assumptions. Childe's independent contribution was the emphasis on material assemblages (rather than individual artefact types), and the preference for a social, as against an ethnic or racial, interpretation of archaeological cultures (Veit 1984).

189

The debate in European archaeology about Kossinna's method continued into the middle of this century. Its eventual rejection by post-war German archaeologists was not just the consequence of their realising its inherent weaknesses (Wahle 1941), but also the consequence of its political exploitation during the Third Reich (see below, p. 205). One of Kossinna's foremost critics was Hans Jürgen Eggers who, with refined methods of archaeological source criticism, demonstrated that many of Kossinna's apparently straightforward interpretations were based on wrong assumptions about the nature of archaeological distributions.

Central to Eggers's source criticism was the distinction between 'living culture', 'dead culture' (i.e. those parts of a living culture which survive in the soil or above ground) and 'retrieved culture' (i.e. those parts of the dead culture found by the archaeologist (Eggers 1951: 23–4)). This distinction became a cornerstone of his 'comparative geographical–cartographic method' (Eggers 1950), also called 'archaeological-geographical method' (Eggers 1959: 295), which aimed at deriving historical conclusions from archaeological distributions by unravelling their inherent problems (conditions of survival and retrieval, sampling bias, etc.). It was, in a way, the systematised continuation of Kossinna's cartographic method without the ethnic interpretation.

The great attraction of this line of research in the early decades after the Second World War is reflected in the periodical *Archaeologia Geographica* which was founded by Eggers and promoted geographical, topographical and environmental approaches in archaeology in the 1950s and 1960s. Eggers also dealt with the question of inferring social status from burials, and his article on the Roman Iron Age 'princely burials' of the so-called Lübsow type (Eggers 1949/50) revived the post-war interest in this approach, the origins of which go back to the time between the wars (Veeck 1926).

Herbert Jankuhn expanded the geographical and social approaches into other fields. After his pre-war excavations in the Viking trading site of Haithabu (Hedeby; Jankuhn 1937, 1943), he was the first archaeologist to explore the social and economic implications of the emergence of such proto-urban *emporia* or ports of trade (Jankuhn 1956). During his survey work in northern Germany, Jankuhn developed an interdisciplinary approach to settlement studies (see numerous papers of the 1950s and 1960s, collected and reprinted in Jankuhn 1976; also the textbook Jankuhn 1977) which influenced archaeological projects in Germany, the Netherlands and Denmark.

Among the generation immediately following Eggers and Jankuhn, Günter Smolla and Karl Narr particularly have shown an active interest in theoretical issues. Smolla's article on the epistemological problems of archaeological interpretation (1964) raised questions which were only taken up again some twenty years later by Lewis Binford in his call for a critical examination of our 'uniformitarian assumptions', those assumptions which link our experience of the present to our interpretation of the past (Renfrew and Shennan 1982: 163). And in a contribution to a political encyclopedia, Narr (1966) made critical observations on the contemporary development of German archaeology, and on the link between this and the ideological misuse of archaeology in the past, thus touching on a problem which most other German archaeologists preferred to ignore.

The last twenty years

But from the late 1960s onwards, German archaeology as a whole failed to respond to the theoretical and methodological debate that started in America and had just reached Europe via Britain. The New Archaeology, which first became known in Germany through the publications of David Clarke (1968, 1972), was dismissed by most German-speaking archaeologists variously as unsound theorising, as models without supporting evidence, or as 'old wine in new barrels'. This kind of wholesale dismissal was, at the same time, the justification for not attempting to provide alternative ideas or paradigms.

Although West German university teachers and students showed some sporadic interest in American and British ideas in the early 1970s, this interest seems to have faded rather rapidly and was never really expressed in published theoretical studies or practical applications of new ideas and models. The first critical summaries of the American New Archaeology in German periodicals were published in 1978 (Bayard 1978; Eggert 1978a); and the first detailed account by a German author of the British debate since 1968 was published only a few years ago – in a British series (Wolfram 1986).

Behind this slow, and in some quarters non-existent, reaction lies a widespread distrust of theory and generalisation among the post-war generation of German prehistorians. In fact, this applies not just to prehistoric archaeology but, in varying degrees, to all branches of archaeology: pre- and protohistory (up to, and including, the early Middle Ages), Roman provincial archaeology, and medieval archaeology.

Near Eastern archaeology and Classical archaeology have always been a different story because of the types of evidence they have to deal with. Consequently, both subjects have close links with historical and linguistic subjects. Classical archaeology in Germany presents a fragmented picture which makes it difficult to speak of one Classical archaeology. It is still dominated by art-historical approaches, which sets it apart from all other branches of archaeology.[2] Near Eastern archaeology, on the other hand, has been influenced by American colleagues working in the same field, particularly by their models of agricultural and urban origins. But as this is an independent academic subject usually based in separate departments, little of this influence filtered through into the study of European pre- and protohistory, although some of it reached neolithic research.

Due to 'the atomic nature of German scholarship' (Sherratt 1984: 437), there are also some clear differences between the branches of German archaeology concerned with the material remains of Europe north of the Alps, and it is probably best to deal with them one by one and try to summarise in a few words their outlook and development over the past two decades.

In palaeolithic and mesolithic archaeology, most of the effort seems to have gone into description, although anthropological perspectives are not altogether absent from the work of the last decades (for reviews, see Bosinski 1975, 1983; Müller-Beck 1983). The foremost centres of research have been, and still are, Tübingen and Cologne. The Institute for the Archaeology of Hunter Societies (*Jägerische Archäologie*) at Tübingen University, apart from excavating palaeolithic sites in southern German caves, has done some wide-ranging work including fieldwork in Eskimo archaeology (e.g. Müller-Beck 1977). A department for African research (Forschungsstelle Afrika) has been established at the University of Cologne. The work being carried out there includes the improvement of analytical techniques in lithic studies and of intrasite spatial analysis (e.g. Cziesla 1988). There is an increasing emphasis on natural sciences, and the use of computers is becoming commonplace in all major projects. A lot of recent interest has focused on the 'refitting' of stone artefacts (Cziesla 1986; Cziesla et al. 1990). In all of this, mesolithic archaeology has been the poor relation of palaeolithic research (Cziesla 1987).

If there is one branch in German pre- and protohistory which may be perceived as 'progressive' and open to new ideas and developments, it is neolithic archaeology. In the early 1970s, Sielmann adopted an environmental approach to the analysis of the south-west German neolithic (Sielmann 1971a, 1971b), possibly stimulated by Anglo-American ideas, but continuing an older German tradition in the analysis of neolithic settlement patterns (Schwarz 1948). Also in the 1970s, the larger-scale excavations on the Aldenhovener Platte near Cologne uncovered an entire neolithic landscape, making it a splendid example of interdisciplinary settlement research.[3] Some experiments were undertaken to supplement the excavations of earthworks (Lüning 1971), at a time when German colleagues had hardly begun to accept the notion of experimental archaeology (for changed attitudes in this respect, see Fansa 1990).

But although German students of the neolithic are often well aware of the work done abroad, their own stimulating projects have been carried out with a bare minimum of theory, or more often no theory at all (Lüning 1973, 1975). A discussion on the concept of archaeological cultures started with two papers on neolithic topics (Lüning 1972; Hachmann 1973; cf. p. 199), but it did not really affect the research and interpretations by German neolithic scholars (cf. Veit 1989). In this field, their main achievement remains identifying numerous local and regional groups and cultures, and placing them in chronological sequences (e.g. Raetzel-Fabian 1986).

As far as approaches and attitudes are concerned, the study of later prehistory occupies the other end of the spectrum (cf. the surveys by Schauer 1975; Schaaff 1975). It is in the archaeology of the Bronze and Iron Ages that the influence of the antiquarian school of Gero von Merhart (professor of prehistory at Marburg 1928–49, the first chair of prehistoric archaeology established in Germany) is most obvious. Some of the consequences are the pursuit of typology and chronology as an end in itself, and an overemphasis on hoards and burials (particularly rich burials, or Fürstengräber). The virtually isolated cases of extensive and long-lasting excavations in the Heuneburg Early Iron Age hill-fort (Gersbach 1978; Kimmig 1975) and the Manching Late Iron Age

8.2 Gero von Merhart (1866–1959) working on the teaching collection of his Marburg department. Reproduced by permission of the University of Marburg.

oppidum (Krämer 1975, 1985; Krämer and Schubert 1970) only serve to highlight the relative neglect of settlement research and the almost complete absence of models in this field (Härke 1979: *passim*). Much of the recent criticism by British archaeologists of the German archaeological tradition was, in actual fact, aimed at Bronze and Iron Age archaeology (e.g. Champion and Megaw 1985: 3; Collis 1980: 151; 1984: 283; Renfrew and Shennan 1982: 9–10, 65 note 6, 68–9, 74).

There have been attempts to break out of the constraints of the antiquarian approach. In the 1950s and 1960s, Sangmeister masterminded a wide-ranging research project involving some 40,000 spectrographic analyses of bronze and gold artefacts from all over Europe, and leading to the cultural-historical interpretation of the chronological and spatial patterns of metal types emerging from the statistical analysis (Junghans et al. 1960, 1968; Hartmann 1970; Sangmeister 1969, 1975). Unfortunately, this ambitious project was allowed to lapse without reaching its aims as envisaged by Sangmeister, although more recently efforts in this field have been resumed by a new research committee.[4]

From a theoretical point of view, Bergmann's ethnic and socio-political interpretations of Bronze Age distributions in northern Germany (Bergmann 1968, 1970, 1972, 1987) were even more important because he tried to use historical and anthropological concepts to overcome the limitations of the traditional definition of an archaeological 'culture'. This attempt was dismissed without generating a wider debate, ostensibly because it went beyond the limitations of the archaeological evidence, but probably also because it was uncomfortably close to Kossinna's method (see above, p. 188).

One of the few attempts at developing a model for later prehistoric settlement patterns was Kimmig's topographical analysis of the locations of rich burials around Early Iron Age *Fürstensitze* ('princes' seats', i.e. hill-forts with imported Greek pottery in their occupation layers). His intepretation of the patterns in terms of areas of political control used a model that was derived from the pattern of small German states in the seventeenth and eighteenth centuries (Kimmig 1969). The simplistic interpretation of all Mediterranean 'imported goods' in Early Iron Age burials as trade items was challenged by Fischer (1973), who used ancient textual sources (but not anthropological models) to demonstrate that many such finds are likely to have been gifts to native magnates. Some of the most imaginative work in German Iron Age archaeology has been carried out by Pauli. He suggested interpretations for unusual or deviant burial practices and developed a social model for the marked cultural change in the transition from the Hallstatt to the LaTène period (Pauli 1975, 1978).

Proto-historic archaeology (dealing with the Roman Iron Age and the early Middle Ages) has its share of traditional, antiquarian approaches, but on the whole it presents a more lively and varied picture. Much of this is due to the influence of Herbert Jankuhn (professor of pre- and protohistory at Göttingen, 1956–74) who taught his own brand of socio-economic archaeology, encouraging

8.3 Herbert Jankuhn (1905–90) contemplating excavation findings in northern Germany. Reproduced by permission of Mrs Ilse Jankuhn.

interdisciplinary approaches and diachronic studies. His pupils have continued the debate on the social interpretation of burials (Capelle 1971; Gebühr 1974, 1975, 1976; Köhler 1975; Rolle 1979; Schlüter 1970; Steuer 1968, 1982, 1984; Steuer and Last 1969). This debate has drawn in protohistorians from outside the 'Göttingen school' (e.g. Christlein 1973; Müller-Wille 1978; Vierck 1980; Werner 1968), and also from outside Germany (e.g. Hedeager 1980; Martin 1976), but it has completely ignored the contemporaneous Anglo-American debate on the question (Härke 1989a). However, this disregard has been entirely mutual.

The 'Göttingen school' has also put its stamp on northern German settlement archaeology, particularly along the North Sea coast where waterlogged sites offer rich potential for interdisciplinary approaches. An entire institute at Wilhelmshaven, the Niedersächsisches Institut für historische Küstenforschung (better known under its old name of Institut für Marschen- und Wurtenforschung), has since 1947 been devoted to the application of archaeological, geographical and environmental approaches to coastal research. Their best-known projects are the excavation of a complete Roman Iron Age village on an artificial mound (*Wurt* or *terp*) in the coastal marsh, the Feddersen Wierde (Haarnagel 1979; Hayen *et al.* 1981; Körber-Grohne 1967), and the archaeological exploration of an entire settlement cell around Flögeln, a Roman Iron Age village near the coast (Schmid 1978; Zimmermann 1974, 1978). Also along the North Sea littoral, Müller-Wille's study of field systems (Müller-Wille 1965) continued the tradition of Jankuhn's seminal work (Jankuhn 1956/57). In western and southern Germany, the problem of continuity from the Roman to the post-Roman period has been the object of much research (for a survey, see Böhner 1975). One of the most successful approaches applied to this question is the archaeological-topographical analysis of small areas which was pioneered by Böhner (1958: 285–326) and taken up by others (e.g. Weidemann 1968, 1970, 1972).

But burial analysis and settlement research cannot conceal the fact that chronological and typological artefact studies continue to dominate wide areas of proto-historic archaeology. The ghosts of the Nazi past still haunt German archaeologists studying those periods in which the ethnic label 'Germanic' can properly be applied to archaeologically defined groups. There is, therefore, still some way to go towards a cultural and social history of early Germanic societies, in spite of some encouraging beginnings (Mildenberger 1977; von Uslar 1980). Another problem of proto-historic studies is the sometimes uncritical use of historical, written sources for the interpretation of archaeological evidence, more often than not preventing an independent explanation which is not distorted by fragmentary, and incompletely understood, sources.

Roman provincial archaeology and medieval archaeology are both concerned with the material remains of fully historical periods, but neither has yet developed a theory or methodology to cope with the unique combination of the different types of evidence involved.

In Roman provincial archaeology this question has not even been discussed in past decades. The approaches to analysis and interpretation of the archaeological evidence in this field are virtually the same as fifty years ago. The publication by Spitzing (1988) of a villa, with an explicitly problem-orientated evaluation of the data and using scientific evidence to elucidate the economic structure around the site, is an exception that only serves to highlight the rule. Also, Roman provincial archaeology in Germany has focused too much on the Romans and neglected the natives – unlike in the Netherlands where archaeologists in recent years have made significant progress towards a better understanding of the interrelation between these two very different types of societies (Brandt and Slofstra 1983; Willems 1986). In Germany, Gechter and Kunow have recently started to explore this promising field of cultural and economic contact between Romans and natives in the frontier zone of the Roman Empire (Gechter 1979; Gechter and Kunow 1983; Kunow 1987). Kunow (1988, 1989) has now also introduced applications of geographical theory into this old and very conservative branch of German archaeology.

Medieval archaeology, by way of contrast, is a young discipline which has become recognised as a subject of its own in the past twenty years and is still somewhat uncertain about its aims, its methods (particularly concerning the use of written sources) and even its definition. It has been seen as an ancillary discipline to medieval history (Jankuhn 1973), the archaeological branch of medieval studies (Fehring 1987) or an independent discipline with aims different from that of history (Schlesinger 1974). This uncertainty has given rise not to a fundamental debate on theories and models but to a wide variety of approaches in a theoretical vacuum. Some of the most significant achievements have been made in the study of deserted medieval villages (*Wüstungsforschung*; e.g. Janssen 1965, 1975) and in urban archaeology (*Stadtkernforschung*; for a comprehensive survey of medieval archaeology, see Fehring 1987).

The present character of West German archaeology

The above survey, superficial as it necessarily is, does show that there has been virtually no wider debate on aims, methods and theory in West German archaeology in the past two or three decades. There have been occasional publications on these matters:

Narr (1974) made some observations on trends in prehistoric archaeology which were followed up by Behrens (1984) ten years later; Narr (1982) also discussed in an article the concepts of 'structure' and 'event'; Eggert (1976) argued against a methodological link between prehistoric archaeology and cultural anthropology, and he reviewed, and dismissed, the American New Archaeology (Eggert 1978a); Ziegert (1980) made critical comments on the preponderance of data-orientated approaches in German archaeology, and demanded more problem-orientated research; and a number of Ziegert's students dealt with theoretical and methodological issues in their theses (Dotzler 1984; Frerichs 1981; Ghonheim-Graf 1978; Nestler 1982).

But these publications do not add up to a theoretical debate because they are isolated instances spread over a couple of decades, and because there have been no clear themes. The exceptions were a discussion by Goldmann, Eggert and Ziegert on chronological methods (seriation, statistics of artefact associations, and radiocarbon dating; see below, pp. 201, 211), and an extensive debate on the concept of archaeological cultures (Bergmann 1968, 1970, 1972, 1987; Lüning 1972; Hachmann 1973: 79–88; 1987; Eggert 1978b, Veit 1989), the overall effect of which on approaches and practical work seems to have been negligible. Another problem has been that several of the few articles on theoretical questions were published in little-known, or non-archaeological and non-historical, periodicals (e.g. Narr 1974, 1982). This unimpressive record is occasionally defended by German archaeologists pointing out that a good deal of the German debate is carried out in book reviews. While there is an element of truth in this argument, it cannot stand up because 'debate' in reviews is, by definition, a one-sided affair. And there is no German archaeological periodical publishing articles with comments and replies in the way that *Current Anthropology* and *Norwegian Archaeological Review* do.

German attitudes towards the Anglo-American debate and towards the New Archaeology are largely negative and even dismissive. More often than not, this rejection is accompanied by uncertainty about the aims and contents of the debate in American, British and more recently Scandinavian archaeology. One of the most frequent objections by German traditionalists to the New Archaeology is that its models ignore the influence of the individual on the course of (pre-)history. For the medieval archaeologist Fehring (1987: 236), the 'anti-historical' outlook of the

New Archaeology and anthropology is reason enough to judge both irrelevant to his field. The emergence of what has been termed 'post-processual archaeology' is virtually unknown among German-speaking archaeologists. And feminist perspectives have not yet found their way into mainstream archaeological research and publications in Germany.

The absence of a theoretical debate has meant that there is now general uncertainty about what models are admissible in the interpretation of European archaeological evidence. Anthropological models and ethnographic parallels are usually rejected out of hand by German archaeologists dealing with later prehistory and protohistory. Yet this rejection arises not from reasoned theoretical argument, but from vague feelings about differences between 'cultural spheres'. Incidentally, such feelings had already been vented by Kossinna and led him to warn against the use of ethnographic parallels (Kossinna 1911b: 128). The last systematic discussion of the relation between archaeological and ethnographic evidence dates back to the late 1960s (Vossen 1969). On the other hand, historical parallels with the Middle Ages are all too often accepted uncritically by prehistorians. The unconsidered use of the feudal model for Early Iron Age social structures is a case in point (Frankenstein and Rowlands 1978: 73–5).

The rejection of processual archaeology and of anthropological models has produced marked weaknesses in the explanation of culture change, e.g. the transitions from the mesolithic to the neolithic (for a review, see Lüning et al. 1989), from the Bronze Age to the Iron Age (Härke 1989b), and from the Iron Age to the Roman and post-Roman periods (Härke 1989c). The lack of convincing explanations in spite of persistent efforts has been acknowledged, in one case (the end of the Bronze Age) by one of the most eminent German prehistorians (Kimmig 1982: 42–3). But this realisation has not led to an abandonment of the largely descriptive approaches and historicising interpretations.

Another effect of the particularist attitude can be seen in the lack (if not complete absence) of synthesis in virtually all branches and fields of German archaeology. The standard argument against synthesis runs something like this: 'We need more data before we can write history'. But no attempt is ever made to determine how much data are needed, and what exactly they are needed for. This has led to what Collis recently lamented as 'the sad fate of parts of the German school of archaeology': merely describing the material 'without questioning whether this has any value whatsoever' (1984: 283). The founding in the early 1980s of an institute for general and comparative archaeology at Bonn (Kommission für Allgemeine und Vergleichende Archäologie) is unlikely to broaden the perspectives of German archaeology as it seems so far to be little more than the extension of data collection in the German tradition on a world-wide scale.

The general absence of a theoretical and methodological debate has been mirrored in the relative decline of student activities. In the late 1960s and early 1970s, there was a lively student scene: archaeology students had set up their own organisation, the Schleswiger Kreis, and students were prominently involved in founding the Deutsche Gesellschaft für Ur- und Frühgeschichte (DGUF) which was intended to become a forum for discussion. But the latter has made virtually no impact on German archaeology as a whole; and while in the 1970s, the Schleswiger Kreis published a series of booklets on science and interdisciplinary studies in archaeology, the main publishing venture by students today is a series of typological handbooks.[5]

It is particularly at the student level, though, and among young colleagues that the arrival of the computer may influence and change not just techniques but also attitudes and approaches. Characteristically, however, one of the first uses computers were put to in German archaeology was seriation for chronological analysis (Goldmann 1972, 1974, 1979). Scientific foundations have put substantial funds into the acquisition of mainframe computers for use in archaeology, but the splendid isolation of the mainframe specialists has ensured that the impact of these investments on archaeology as a whole has been negligible. The microcomputer may lead to greater changes, although its presence is making itself felt only very slowly as German universities have not channelled as much money into the creation of a microcomputer base as have most British and American universities. Gebühr's contributions, in particular, demonstrate that this innovation is forcing some German archaeologists to reflect on the nature of their data and critically assess the value of their approaches (Gebühr 1983; Gebühr and Kampffmeyer 1980/81).

Overall, then, the outside critics of the 'German tradition of archaeology' appear to be right: German archaeology as a whole is out of touch with the theoretical debate in Anglo-American archaeology, with recent developments in British, Dutch and

Scandinavian archaeology, and with new ideas in general. This apparent isolation has been increased by a marked language shift towards English: German is no longer the *lingua franca* of central and northern European archaeology; in this function, it has been largely replaced by English in the post-war decades.

But it must be emphasised that this linguistic divide works both ways, and the other way round it almost becomes a language barrier: while most German archaeologists are able to communicate in English, few native English-speaking colleagues read or understand German equally well. This has, no doubt, contributed towards the recognisable trend among British and American archaeologists to avoid the effort required to find out what has been going on in German archaeology. A classic example of the possible consequences may be found in environmental archaeology. When British palaeobotanists and archaeologists got their environmental bandwagon rolling in the early 1970s, they virtually reinvented the wheel, because they were not aware of the relevant research that had been done in German-speaking countries in the preceding decade. This caused justifiable indignation, and some wider scepticism about supposedly 'new' trends, among German colleagues (Willerding 1977). Burial analysis is another example of this lack of communication (see above, p. 196).

It is therefore important that the positive aspects of the German archaeological tradition are not entirely forgotten in this discussion, even though few of them have a direct bearing on the question of theory. One aspect that has already been mentioned above (p. 193) is the interdisciplinary approach in settlement archaeology. This is, in principle, well established and supported, and German palaeobotanists such as Behre, Hopf, Knörzer, Körber-Grohne and Willerding have made outstanding contributions to environmental, economic and settlement studies. The multidisciplinary research institute in Wilhelmshaven, on the North Sea coast, has already been referred to (p. 197). And in south-west Germany, a new wetlands research project with an interdisciplinary approach was launched only a few years ago with generous funding, under the old-fashioned name of *Pfahlbauforschung*, 'Lake Villages Research' (Strahm 1987; Schlichtherle and Wahlster 1986). The technical excellence displayed here and at other excavations (e.g. the spectacular Hochdorf barrow of Early Iron Age date; Biel 1985) makes the absence of archaeological theory in Germany appear even more peculiar.

Other features which outsiders would readily associate with German archaeology are an awareness of the history of research, a disciplined approach to dealing with material evidence and dating, and systematic documentation and data presentation. The detailed discussion of the relevant *Forschungsgeschichte* (history of research) constitutes a compulsory introductory chapter of every thesis, monograph and major article. German archaeologists, therefore, treat with scepticism publications which fail to include older, and foreign, literature – a frequent sin in many recent British and American publications (Härke 1984: 419; Pauli 1988: 296).

The systematic and meticulous treatment of material evidence is an acknowledged part of the German tradition. Artefact typology and dating sequences are an integral (often the main) part of university courses in archaeology. Every publication is expected to show that the authors 'know their material' and understand its problems and limitations. There is an uneasiness, and sometimes deep suspicion, among German archaeologists about what they see as a lack of discipline and care on the part of many New Archaeologists when dealing with material evidence. This uneasiness is not limited to traditionalists, it is also widespread among more open-minded young colleagues (e.g. Veit 1984: 352, note 132).

Comprehensive documentation and data presentation are part and parcel of the same German attitude. But beyond that, there is a recognisable desire to collect evidence in catalogues, and to describe and codify knowledge in 'manuals' and encyclopediae. Müller-Karpe's (1966–80) handbook of prehistory and the new edition of the Hoops encyclopedia (in progress) continue the tradition of the first, four-volume edition (Hoops 1911–19), the fifteen-volume Ebert (1924–32) encyclopedia of prehistory, and the twenty-four-volume Pauly–Wissowa encyclopedia of Classical antiquity and archaeology (von Pauly 1893–1963). Monograph series on artefact types and sites such as the present *Prähistorische Bronzefunde* series and the old series on the *Oberrätisch-Germanische Limes* are another expression of this desire for complete collection and presentation of the evidence.

There is, thus, some silver lining on what otherwise looks like a rather dark cloud. But disciplined approaches to research history and material evidence cannot detract from the fact that in present-day German archaeology there is no body of theory, and there is no public discussion on aims and methods. Approaches to the evidence are determined by a positivist attitude variously described by German critics as 'sherd-counting' (Pauli 1984a: 11) and 'stamp-collecting' (Jankuhn, personal communication). The interpretation of the evidence is dominated by a particularist outlook which prevents generalisation. Sherratt (1984: 437) has aptly and concisely characterised this situation: 'Prehistoric archaeology in Germany remains very close to its raw material, frowning alike on synthesis and generalisation.' The overall effect is that archaeology is pursued largely as an end in itself, it is art for art's sake.

How could it happen?

The reasons for this state of affairs are complex, and most of them are to be found in recent history. In order to understand this, it is necessary to go back to Kossinna and to the turn of the century.

German prehistoric archaeology has two roots: the eighteenth-century romantic movement, and nineteenth-century anthropology. But due to the heavy emphasis on Classical education in Humboldt's reform of the Prussian university system in the early nineteenth century, the archaeology of Classical and oriental antiquity was the first to become established as an academic discipline. The establishment of native Celtic and particularly Germanic archaeology took longer, and Kossinna became its foremost exponent. He founded a Gesellschaft für Deutsche Vorgeschichte (Society for German Prehistory), and in 1911 he gave a lecture to this society on 'German prehistory, an eminently national discipline' (Kossinna 1912a). In this lecture, he argued the outstanding cultural achievements of the prehistoric Germani, citing as proof the metalwork of the Nordic Bronze Age; and he called on the honour and the patriotic feelings of the members of the Berlin Academy of Sciences, asking them to give the same support (financial and institutional) to prehistoric archaeology as already given to Roman, Greek, Egyptian and oriental archaeology.

This sounds innocuous enough: calling the Nordic Bronze Age 'Germanic' seemed justified in terms of Kossinna's settlement-archaeological method (see p. 188); and the nationalist undertones of the lecture were entirely in keeping with the general attitudes of the times. After all, Kaiser Wilhelm II himself had said in 1890 that 'we should educate young Germans, not young Greeks and Romans' (quoted after Smolla 1984/85: 12). But there is a more sinister, ethnocentric side to Kossinna's views. His publications show an underlying belief in a Nordic, Aryan race, descended from the Indo-Germans (i.e. Indo-Europeans), with physical and intellectual qualities superior to those of other races (e.g. Kossinna 1912b; 1928: 126–8; 1932: 7–8). For Kossinna, the key to European, and thus world, history lay in the dynamic of the repeated movements southwards of this Nordic race. Incidentally, Kossinna's contemporary opponent Schuchhardt held very similar views (Schuchhardt 1935: *passim*).

It is obvious that such a belief, coupled with the ethnic interpretation of archaeological cultures, would lend itself readily to political exploitation. The first clear hint of this came in 1919 when Kossinna used archaeological finds to suggest the Germanic ancestry of the 'Polish Corridor' (parts of Posen and West Prussia ceded to Poland in the Versailles Treaty) since the Iron Age, and Polish archaeologists responded by claiming a Slav ancestry for this area since the Bronze Age, using Kossinna's own method (see Eggers 1959: 236–7).

But the most blatant and even oppressive misuse of Kossinna's ethnic and racial views took place after his death (1931), in the Third Reich, 1933–45. To the Nazis, the political relevance of Kossinna's approach must have been immediately obvious: his views on the racial origin and history of the Germans provided a pseudo-scientific underpinning of their 'master race' ideology; and his identification of former Germanic settlement areas provided the historical justification of their expansion against neighbouring territories.

The importance that the Nazis attached to archaeology was demonstrated by the speed with which they attempted to take control of archaeological institutions. As early as 1933, all archaeological societies came under pressure to affiliate to the society founded by Kossinna, now renamed Reichsbund für Deutsche Vorgeschichte (Imperial Association for German Prehistory). In 1934, the party official in charge of ideological education, Alfred Rosenberg, created in his office (Amt Rosenberg) a 'Prehistory Department' under the archaeology lecturer Hans Reinerth whose task was to achieve a reorientation of prehistoric archaeology towards a *völkische Vorgeschichte* (ethnic, i.e. Germanic, prehistory). A year later, the commander of the SS, Heinrich Himmler, founded his own science organisation Deutsches Ahnenerbe (German Forefathers' Heritage) which had sections for biology, medicine, folk studies and archaeological excavations, the latter from 1938 when it took over the Haithabu project (see Jankuhn 1943: 10). The declared purpose of this organisation was to 'explore the space, spirit, deed and heritage of the Indo-Germans of northern racial origin', but the creation of a scientific theory of German dominance is supposed to have been the ultimate aim of Ahnenerbe (Kater 1974). The rivalry between these two Nazi organisations split the German archaeologists, but it also created the space in which many of them could continue their work without too much direct interference from party officials (Bollmus 1970: 153–235).

However, the idea of independent and objective research was often ridiculed by Nazi officials who demanded politicised and ideologically useful research. And the ideological usefulness of prehistoric archaeology is reflected in its unprecedented expansion in the Third Reich: the number of archaeology chairs at German universities was increased from one to eight in the first three years (1933–5); by 1939, prehistory was being taught at more than twenty-five universities; and the number of academically qualified prehistorians had doubled by 1941. But the price for this support was collaboration or, at the very least, conformity. Prominent archaeologists who came under pressure to resign from their posts or offices included not only Jews (Gerhard Bersu and Paul Jacobsthal), but significantly also some colleagues such as Gero von Merhart who simply ignored the now obligatory Kossinna method, and Karl Herrmann Jacob-Friesen who, in the pre-Nazi era, had disputed the methodological basis of Kossinna's ethnic interpretation of archaeological cultures (Jacob-Friesen 1928). The blatant attempts to put ideological pressure on the method and direction of archaeological research were extended, during the war, into occupied countries (Kater 1974: 145–90, 269–73; Blindheim 1984; Hagen 1985/86).

It was inevitable, therefore, that the ethnic paradigm should be thoroughly discredited after the end of the Third Reich (although the ethnic question resurfaced, in a somewhat different form, after 1969 in Scandinavian archaeology; see the chapter by Myhre in this volume). Since 1945, German archaeologists have suffered from what Smolla (1980) has termed the 'Kossinna syndrome'. But as if to rub the message in, the political exploitation of, and pressure on, German archaeology did not end with the Third Reich: it continued, with a very different orientation, in East

Germany where archaeologists had to subscribe, or pay lip-service, to Marxist historical philosophy and where the evolutionary paradigm (as laid down by Engels 1884) was obligatory until the fall of the communist regime in 1989.

The effect on West German archaeologists has been described thus by Narr (1966: 382):

> Deterred by the ideological and political misuse [of archaeology], the majority of scholars have retreated into a merely cautiously ordering and registering positivism, which itself is intolerant at times and is prepared to reject all other orientations as not seriously scientific or even as fanciful.

Even mere speculation in the interpretation of archaeological evidence (as advocated by von Uslar 1955) has become a victim of this attitude.

The hasty and ill-planned expansion of the West German university system in the late 1960s and 1970s generated a further problem: it created a large number of additional teaching posts which had to be filled within a short time, often with less qualified candidates than would have been the case under ordinary circumstances. This problem has been recognised and frankly admitted by the most senior academic administrators.[6] It is tempting to suggest that it also created the conditions for the continued stagnation of German archaeological theory throughout the 1970s and 1980s. By way of contrast, the virtually contemporaneous expansion of archaeology at British universities had markedly different effects (see the chapter by Champion in this volume).

The German university system, and particularly its career structure for lecturers, may have made the difference. Before the recent changes in the system, junior lecturers (*Assistenten*) were expected to have a doctorate, would obtain their job through recommendation rather than by application, and would get a fixed-term contract during which they would have to write their *Habilitation* thesis. This is a major research project which has to be accepted by the professorial staff of the faculty and which, in addition to a trial lecture and a trial seminar, establishes the candidate's qualification for lecturing at a German university. The requirement of *Habilitation* has undoubtedly contributed to over-specialisation ('funnel-vision' in the words of A. Sherratt) among senior academics. Even more importantly, it is not hard to imagine how such a system can create an atmosphere in which the next generation of lecturers is unlikely to stray far from the path of accepted wisdom. A side-effect of this system of long apprenticeship is that German university teachers start formal lecturing rather later in their career than their American and British colleagues.

Of all the other archaeologists in West Germany, those in the major research institutions (mainly the Römisch-Germanische Kommission at Frankfurt and the Römisch-Germanisches Zentralmuseum at Mainz) should have been able to give a lead by responding to the theoretical challenges from abroad, but they failed to do so, probably because they have been subject to much the same constraints and pressures as their colleagues in the universities. Field archaeologists in regional and local units or in state inspectorates usually have practical concerns which they consider more pressing than the need for archaeological theory, and the German *Bodendenkmalpflege* is no exception to this international rule.

The problems of positivism and particularism may have been exacerbated by the lack of a thriving amateur scene and, ironically, by the comparatively generous funds for research and excavations. On the positive side, funding bodies such as the Deutsche Forschungsgemeinschaft and the Volkswagenstiftung have provided favourable conditions for the continuity of major projects over decades. But both generous funding and the relative unimportance of amateurs, have obviated the need for communication with a wider public, and this is clearly reflected in the fact that German popular books on archaeology are not normally written by professional archaeologists (although this is changing slowly). This has not only increased the isolation of the subject, it has also meant that there was no external incentive to produce syntheses.

Prospects and recent developments

Although there seems little prospect of a radical change in this overall situation in the near future, there have been some developments which reflect a critical reassessment of current methods and attitudes, and an increasing interest in theoretical issues.

After Kossinna had been anathema for decades, cited only to demonstrate the errors of the past, several recent publications (Smolla 1980, 1984/85; von Krosigk 1982; Veit 1984, 1989) have dealt with him in a more balanced way, trying to see his method in the context of the evolution of prehistoric archaeology – something which had been demanded several years before by the Soviet archaeologist Klejn (1974: 44). Such publications represent a very important attempt to overcome the 'Kossinna syndrome', to go beyond the simplistic condemnation of his political misuse, and to prepare the way for a reappraisal of his role in archaeological theory. This, in turn, could be the first step towards coming to terms with the unsavoury past of archaeology in the Third Reich. In terms of Kuhn's theory of scientific progress (1970: 10–21), such a step would have a significance beyond its political content. Having gone through a 'pre-paradigm' period, German archae-ology adopted its 'first paradigm' (i.e. Kossinna's ethnic paradigm) and then had it removed because it had been misused politically (see above, p. 205). As there has been no 'new paradigm' (the next step in Kuhn's scheme), West German archaeology has, in a sense, reverted to a 'non-paradigm' situation.

The unification of West and East Germany poses a similar problem. In the wake of the collapse of the communist regime in East Germany in 1989, there is now a danger that the public revulsion against anything Marxist and communist, and the politi-cal and administrative changes unification will inevitably bring, might sweep aside forty years of East German archaeology because of its historical-materialist paradigm (true or enforced). If that were done in haste, without further scrutiny and thorough dis-cussion, it would mean the imposition, again, of intellectual amnesia for political reasons, and it would add an 'Engels syn-drome' to the 'Kossinna syndrome'. The ghosts of the past, be they red or brown, must be laid, or there can be no future: this is a clear lesson that arises from the post-war history of German archaeology.

But this backward look must be complemented by an appreci-ation of the debate outside Germany in the past twenty years. Even in this respect, the reappraisal of Kossinna might prove helpful: Smolla (1984/85: 13–14) has suggested that it could pro-vide the starting point for a debate between the German and Anglo-American traditions because some of Kossinna's views (e.g. on the scientific nature of prehistoric archaeology) bridge the gap between the two. Some recent publications by senior German colleagues (e.g. Behrens 1984; Fischer 1987), although not present-ing anything new, may indicate a renewed interest in reflecting on, and restating, the aims of traditional German archaeology. By way of contrast, a recent thesis on the New Archaeology in Britain (Wolfram 1986) indicates a growing willingness among the younger generation to look across the fence surrounding the German tradition of archaeology in its 'self-inflicted isolation' (Narr 1974: 124–5). This change in attitude, slow though it may be, coincides with an increasing awareness among German historians and ethnographers of the need for theory in, and social and cultural anthropological approaches to, cultural history (Vierhaus 1989: 135; similarly Elwert 1989: 159).

It is exactly this awareness which, a few years ago, led to the emergence of an informal group of young colleagues whose aim was to start a debate on the state and future direction of German archaeology (Härke 1989c). Significantly, this Unkeler Kreis (Unkel Circle, named after the place of its first meeting near Bonn) comprises archaeologists from outside German universities, and Dutch and Danish colleagues have played an important role in it. There is no uniformity of ideas and concepts in this small group; the only common attitudes are dissatisfaction with the present constraints of German archaeology, and the conviction that archaeology must make a contribution to a wider cultural history or anthropology. While some members have looked to the Anglo-American New Archaeology for inspiration, others view it with considerable scepticism which is based not so much on theoretical objections to its paradigms and approaches as on a negative assessment of its results which all too often seem to lag far behind its loudly and arrogantly proclaimed objectives.

Several meetings of the Unkeler Kreis have been held so far, resulting in the publication of two booklets containing a review of the state of German archaeology (Härke 1983) and a discussion of approaches to the study of social structures and the interrelation between centre and periphery (Pauli 1984b). The circulation of these informal, *samizdat*-style proceedings has sparked a discussion which needs to be widened by larger seminars and more formal publications. A first attempt in this direction has been made with an invitational seminar on 'Continuity and Discontinuity' which is being prepared for publication (for a preliminary report, see Härke 1989c).

The student scene, dormant for a long time, has seen a new burst of activity in the very recent past. During the nationwide student strike in West Germany at the end of 1988, workshops on theory, New Archaeology, the state and aims of German archaeology, women and gender relations in prehistory, archaeology and the public, and archaeology in the Third Reich were set up or reinvigorated in a large number of archaeology depart-ments. A first meeting of archaeology students from West German universities was held in 1989 at Kiel. It resulted in the general conclusion that the subject is in need of reappraisal, and that the nationwide student meetings should be continued on an annual basis (Spitzner-von der Haar 1989).

Although seemingly not directly relevant to the question of theory, several recent articles on chronological issues (Eggert *et al.* 1980; Eggert and Lüth 1987; Eggert and Wotzka 1987; Eggert 1988; Ziegert 1983) may be seen as part of this general trend of reappraisal. They expose fundamental inconsistencies and weak-nesses in methods and even foundations of conventional chrono-logical analysis, and they coincide with significant advances of dendrochronology in Germany in the last few years. Together, these developments might lead to some rethinking of the favourite pursuit of German archaeologists who had been curiously unaffec-ted by the 'radiocarbon revolution'.

Something is stirring on the Western Front. Now we have to wait and see if the German archaeologists will actually come out of their trenches. The debate which has gone on in American, British and Scandinavian archaeology since the 1960s may be about to start in Germany. And the outcome may be rather different from the Anglo-American New Archaeology and the British post-processual archaeology. The future promises to be much more interesting than the recent past.

Notes

1. My sincere thanks are extended to all colleagues who attended the first four symposia of the Unkeler Kreis: J. H. F. Bloemers, J. Eckert, M. Gebühr, M. and M. Gechter, J. and U. Giesler, K. Kristiansen, J. Kunow, L. Pauli and W. J. H. Willems. The present chapter owes a great deal to the papers and discussions at these meetings. L. Pauli, A. Sherratt, R. Bradley, B. Myhre and V. Schimpff made valuable comments on various drafts. E. Cziesla and H. Döhl very kindly provided additional information on the situation of, respectively, palaeolithic research and Classical archaeology.
2. Whitley (1987) has dealt with this question in some detail. He stresses the idealistic and aesthetic perspectives of German Classical archae-ology which he sees rooted in the philosophies of Winckelmann, Kant and Hegel; and he interprets this emphasis as the answer of the German school of archaeology to the dangers of the Anglo-American empiricist approach (Whitley 1987: 15). While his basic observation

on the perspectives of Classical archaeology is undoubtedly correct, his interpretation is somewhat misleading. Winckelmann is the acknowledged father of Classical archaeology, but the influences of Kant and Hegel are much more diffuse, and neither clearly perceived nor explicitly acknowledged. And the art-historical orientation of Classical archaeology is most certainly not a conscious reaction by German archaeologists to Anglo-American empiricism, but simply the approach seen as most appropriate for dealing with the type of evidence Classical archaeologists are faced with. In this approach, German Classical archaeology is different not just from Anglo-American archaeology but also from all other branches of archaeology in Germany.

3. A dozen interim reports on the archaeological and environmental results of this project have been published in the *Bonner Jahrbücher* 171–82 (1971–82).

4. The Kommission für Metallurgie des Altertums was set up in the early 1980s by the Römisch-Germanisches Zentralmuseum at Mainz and the Max-Planck Institute of Nuclear Physics at Heidelberg. Its research reports have been published in the *Jahrbuch des Römisch-Germanischen Zentralmuseums* 31–3 (1984–6).

5. The older, scientific series was: *Informationsblätter zu Nachbarwissenschaften der Ur- und Frühgeschichte (Schriften des Schleswiger Kreises*, edited by V. Arnold, R. Busch *et al.*), vols 1–7, Göttingen 1970–6. The more recent typological series is: *Göttinger Typentafeln zur Ur- und Frühgeschichte Mitteleuropas*, vols 1–6, Göttingen, 1983–4.

6. In a speech at Hamburg in 1986, the President of the West German *Rektorenkonferenz* (Committee of University Vice-Chancellors), Prof. Dr Theodor Berchem, said: 'Whereas in times of rapid expansion, even some mediocre young colleagues had good, or even excellent, chances of obtaining a professorial post, nowadays even the best [scholars] in many disciplines have no chances at all' (*Forum*, the magazine of the Stifterverband für die deutsche Wissenschaft, 6 December 1986, p. 5).

References

Bayard, D. (1978) '15 Jahre "New Archaeology": eine kritische Übersicht', *Saeculum* 29: 69–106.

Behrens, H. (1984) 'Tendenzen in der Urgeschichtsforschung: Überlegungen zu K. J. Narrs gleichlautendem Beitrag', *Archäologisches Korrespondenzblatt* 14: 453–7.

Bergmann, J. (1968) 'Ethnosoziologische Untersuchungen an Grab- und Hortfundgruppen der älteren Bronzezeit in Nordwestdeutschland', *Germania* 46: 224–40.

—— (1970) *Die ältere Bronzezeit Nordwestdeutschlands: Neue Methoden zur ethnischen und historischen Interpretation urgeschichtlicher Quellen*, Kasseler Beiträge zur Vor- und Frühgeschichte, Marburg: Elwert.

—— (1972) 'Ethnos und Kulturkreis: zur Methodik der Urgeschichtswissenschaft', *Praehistorische Zeitschrift* 47: 105–10.

—— (1987) *Die metallzeitliche Revolution: Zur Entstehung von Herrschaft, Krieg und Umweltzerstörung*, Berlin: Reimer.

Biel, J. (1985) *Der Keltenfürst von Hochdorf*, Stuttgart: Theiss.

Blindheim, C. (1984) 'De fem lange år på Universitets Oldsaksamling', *Viking* 48: 27–43.

Böhner, K. (1958) *Die fränkischen Altertümer des Trierer Landes*, Germanische Denkmäler der Völkerwanderungszeit B1, Berlin: Mann.

—— (1975) 'Probleme der Kontinuität zwischen Römerzeit und Mittelalter in West- und Süddeutschland,' in *Ausgrabungen in Deutschland, gefördert von der Deutschen Forschungsgemeinschaft 1950–1975* Teil 2, Monographien des Römisch-Germanischen Zentralmuseums 1, 2, Mainz and Bonn: RGZM & Habelt.

Bollmus, R. (1970) *Das Amt Rosenberg und seine Gegner*, Studien zur Zeitgeschichte, Stuttgart: Deutsche Verlags-Anstalt.

Bosinski, G. (1975) 'Arbeiten zur älteren und mittleren Steinzeit in der Bundesrepublik Deutschland 1949–1974', in *Ausgrabungen in Deutschland, gefördert von der Deutschen Forschungsgemeinschaft 1950–1975* Teil 1, Monographien des Römisch-Germanischen Zentralmuseums 1, 1, Mainz and Bonn: RGZM & Habelt.

—— (1983) 'Die jägerische Geschichte des Rheinlandes: Einsichten und Lücken', *Jahrbuch des Römisch-Germanischen Zentralmuseums Mainz* 30: 81–112.

Brandt, R. and Slofstra, J. (1983) *Roman and Native in the Low Countries: Spheres of Interaction*, British Archaeological Report S184, Oxford.

Capelle, T. (1971) *Studien über elbgermanische Gräberfelder in der ausgehenden Latènezeit und der älteren römischen Kaiserzeit*, Münstersche Beiträge zur Vor- und Frühgeschichte 6, Hildesheim: Lax.

Champion, T. C. and Megaw, J. V. S. (eds) (1985) *Settlement and Society: Aspects of West European Prehistory in the First Millennium* B.C., Leicester: Leicester University Press.

Childe, V. G. (1929) *The Danube in Prehistory*, Oxford: Clarendon.

Christlein, R. (1973) 'Besitzabstufungen der Merowingerzeit im Spiegel reicher Grabfunde aus West- und Süddeutschland', *Jahrbuch des Römisch-Germanischen Zentralmuseums* 20: 147–80.

Clarke, D. L. (1968) *Analytical Archaeology*, London: Methuen.

—— (ed.) (1972) *Models in Archaeology*, London: Methuen.

Collis, J. (1980) 'Review of G. Mildenberger 1979, *Germanische Burgen*. Münster, Aschendorff', *Antiquity* 54: 150–1.

—— (1984) 'What do we want to know?' in A. Cahen-Delhaye, A. Duval, G. Leman-Delerive and P. Leman (eds), *Les Celtes en Belgique et dans le nord de la France: les fortifications de l'âge du fer*, Revue du nord, numéro spécial hors série: 283–5.

Cziesla, E. (1986) 'Über das Zusammenpassen geschlagener Steinartefakte', *Archäologisches Korrespondenzblatt* 16: 251–65.

—— (1987) 'Mesolithic research in Western Germany', *Mesolithic Miscellany* 8 (2): 6–8.

—— (1988) 'Über das Kartieren von Artefaktmengen in steinzeitlichen Grabungsflächen', *Bulletin de la Société Préhistorique Luxembourgeoise* 10: 5–53.

Cziesla, E., Eickhoff, S., Arts, N. and Winter, D. (eds) (1990) *The 'Big Puzzle': International Symposium on Refitting Stone Artefacts, Monrepos 1987*, Studies in Modern Archaeology 1, Bonn: Holos.

Dotzler, G. (1984) *Ornament als Zeichen. Methodologische Probleme der archäologischen Interpretation*, Arbeiten zur Urgeschichte des Menschen 8, Frankfurt, Bern, New York and Nancy: Lang.

Ebert, M. (1924–32) *Reallexikon der Vorgeschichte*, Berlin: de Gruyter.

Eggers, H. J. (1950) 'Die vergleichende geographisch-kartographische Methode in der Urgeschichtsforschung', *Archaeologia Geographica* 1: 1–3.

—— (1951) *Der römische Import im freien Germanien*, Atlas der Urgeschichte 1, Hamburg: Museum für Völkerkunde und Vorgeschichte.

—— (1949/50) 'Lübsow, ein germanischer Fürstensitz der älteren Kaiserzeit', *Praehistorische Zeitschrift* 34/35: 58–111.

—— (1959) *Einführung in die Vorgeschichte*, Sammlung Piper, Munich: Piper.

Eggert, M. K. H. (1976) 'On the interrelationship of prehistoric archaeology and cultural anthropology', *Praehistorische Zeitschrift* 51: 56–60.

—— (1978a) 'Prähistorische Archäologie und Ethnologie: Studien zur amerikanischen New Archaeology', *Praehistorische Zeitschrift* 53: 6–164.

—— (1978b) 'Zum Kulturkonzept in der prähistorischen Archäologie', *Bonner Jahrbücher* 178: 1–20.

—— (1988) 'Die fremdbestimmte Zeit: Überlegungen zu einigen Aspekten von Archäologie und Naturwissenschaft', *Hephaistos* 9: 43–59.

Eggert, M. K. H. and Lüth, F. (1987) 'Mersin und die absolute Chronologie des europäischen Neolithikums', *Germania* 65: 17–28.

Eggert, M. K. H. and Wotzka, H. -P. (1987) 'Kreta und die absolute Chronologie des europäischen Neolithikums', *Germania* 65: 379–422.

Eggert, M. K. H., Kurz, S. and Wotzka, H. -P. (1980) 'Historische Realität und archäologische Datierung: zur Aussagekraft der Kombinationsstatistik', *Praehistorische Zeitschrift* 55: 110–45.

Elwert, G. (1989) 'Ethnologische Artefakte und die theoretische Aufgabe der empirischen Sozialwissenschaften', *Saeculum* 40: 149–60.

Engels, F. (1884) *Der Ursprung der Familie, des Privateigentums und des Staates: im Anschluss an Lewis H. Morgans Forschungen*, Zürich: Hottingen.

Fansa, M. (ed.) (1990) *Experimentelle Archäologie in Deutschland*, Archäologische Mitteilungen aus Nordwestdeutschland, Beiheft 4, Oldenburg i.O.: Isensee.

Fehring, G. P. (1987) *Einführung in die Archäologie des Mittelalters*, Die Archäologie: Einführungen, Darmstadt: Wissenschaftliche Buchgesellschaft.

Fischer, F. (1973) 'ΚΕΙΜΗΛΙΑ. Bemerkungen zur kulturgeschichtlichen Interpretation des sogenannten Südimports in der späten Hallstatt- und frühen Latène-Kultur des westlichen Mitteleuropa', *Germania* 51: 436–59.

Fischer, U. (1987) 'Zur Ratio der prähistorischen Archäologie', *Germania* 65: 175–95.

Frankenstein, S. and Rowlands, M. J. (1978) 'The internal structure and regional context of Early Iron Age society in south-western Germany', *Bulletin of the Institute of Archaeology, University of London* 15: 73–112.

Frerichs, K. (1981) *Begriffsbildung und Begriffsanwendung in der Vor- und Frühgeschichte: Zur logischen Analyse archäologischer Aussagen*, Arbeiten zur Urgeschichte des Menschen 5, Frankfurt and Bern: Lang.

Gebühr, M. (1974) 'Zur Definition älterkaiserzeitlicher Fürstengräber vom Lübsow-Typ,' *Praehistorische Zeitschrift* 49: 82–128.

—— (1975) 'Versuch einer statistischen Auswertung von Grabfunden der römischen Kaiserzeit am Beispiel der Gräberfelder von Hamfelde und Kemnitz', *Zeitschrift für Ostforschung* 24: 433–56.

—— (1976) *Der Trachtschmuck der älteren römischen Kaiserzeit im Gebiet zwischen unterer Elbe und Oder und auf den westlichen dänischen Inseln*, Göttinger Schriften zur Vor- und Frühgeschichte 18, Neumünster: Wachholtz.

—— (1983), 'Erst die Methode, dann die Fragestellung? Veränderte Arbeitsweisen durch die elektronische Datenverarbeitung', *Archäologische Informationen* 5: 11–19.

Gebühr, M. and Kampffmeyer, U. (1980/81) 'Überlegungen zum Einsatz von Kleinrechnern in der Ur- und Frühgeschichtsforschung', *Acta Praehistorica et Archaeologica* 11/12: 3–20.

Gechter, M. (1979) 'Die Anfänge des Niedergermanischen Limes', *Bonner Jahrbücher* 179: 1–138.

Gechter, M. and Kunow, J. (1983) 'Der frühkaiserzeitliche Grabfund von Mehrum: ein Beitrag zur Frage von Germanen in römischen Diensten', *Bonner Jahrbücher* 183: 449–68.

Gersbach, E. (1978) 'Ergebnisse der letzten Grabungen auf der Heuneburg bei Hundersingen (Donau)', *Archäologisches Korrespondenzblatt* 8: 301–10.

Ghonheim-Graf, I. (1978) *Möglichkeiten und Grenzen archäologischer Interpretation: Eine aktual-archäologische Untersuchung an afrikanischen Gruppen*, Arbeiten zur Urgeschichte des Menschen 3, Frankfurt and Bern: Lang.

Goldmann, K. (1972) 'Zwei Methoden chronologischer Gruppierung', *Acta Praehistorica et Archaeologica* 3: 1–34.

—— (1974) 'Die zeitliche Ordnung prähistorischer Funde durch Seriation', *Archäologisches Korrespondenzblatt* 4: 89–94.

—— (1979) *Die Seriation chronologischer Leitfunde der Bronzezeit Europas*, Berliner Beiträge zur Vor- und Frühgeschichte, Neue Folge 1, Berlin: Spiess.

Haarnagel, W. (1979) *Die Grabung Feddersen Wierde. Methode, Hausbau, Siedlungs- und Wirtschaftsformen sowie Sozialstruktur*, Feddersen Wierde 2, Wiesbaden: Steiner.

Hachmann, R. (1973) 'Die östlichen Grenzen der Michelsberger Kultur', in *Symposium über die Entstehung und Chronologie der Badener Kultur*, Bratislava: Slovak Academy of Sciences.

—— (ed.) (1987) *Studien zum Kulturbegriff in der Vor- und Frühgeschichtsforschung*, Saarbrücker Beiträge zur Altertumskunde 48, Bonn: Habelt.

Härke, H. G. H. (1979) *Settlement Types and Settlement Patterns in the West Hallstatt Province*, British Archaeological Report S57, Oxford.

—— (ed.) (1983) *Archäologie und Kulturgeschichte. Symposium zu Zielvorstellungen in der deutschen Archäologie*, Unkel: Unkeler Kreis.

—— (1984) 'Review of C. Renfrew and S. Shennan (eds) *Ranking, Resource and Exchange*', *Proceedings of the Prehistoric Society* 50: 418–20.

—— (1989a) 'Die anglo-amerikanische Diskussion zur Gräberanalyse', *Archäologisches Korrespondenzblatt* 19: 185–94.

—— (1989b) 'Transformation or collapse? Bronze Age to Iron Age settlement in West Central Europe', in M. L. S. Sørensen and R. Thomas (eds), *The Bronze Age – Iron Age Transition in Europe*, British Archaeological Report S483, Oxford.

—— (1989c) 'The Unkel symposia: the beginnings of a debate in West German archaeology?', *Current Anthropology* 30: 406–10.

Hagen, A. (1985/86) 'Arkeologi og politikk', *Viking* 49: 269–78.

Hartmann, A. (1970) *Prähistorische Goldfunde aus Europa*, Studien zu den Anfängen der Metalurgie 3, Berlin: Mann.

Hayen, H., Ullemeyer, R., Tidow, K. and Ruttner, R. (1981) *Einzeluntersuchungen zur Feddersen Wierde. Wagen, Textil- und Lederfunde, Bienenkorb, Schlackenanalysen*, Feddersen Wierde 3, Wiesbaden: Steiner.

Hedeager, L. (1980) 'Besiedlung, soziale Struktur und politische Organisation in der älteren und jüngeren römischen Kaiserzeit Ostdänemarks', *Praehistorische Zeitschrift* 55: 38–109.

Hoops, J. (ed.) (1911–19) *Reallexicon der germanischen Altertumskunde*, Strassburg: Trübner.

Hoops Reallexikon der germanischen Altertumskunde (1968 seqq.) edited by H. Beck, H. Jankuhn, R. Ranke and R. Wenskus, 2nd edn, Berlin and New York: de Gruyter.

Jacob-Friesen, K. H. (1928) *Grundfragen der Urgeschichtsforschung. Stand und Kritik der Forschung über Rassen, Völker und Kulturen in urgeschichtlicher Zeit*, Festschrift zur Feier des 75jährigen Bestehens des Provinzial-Museums/Veröffentlichungen der urgeschichtlichen Abteilung des Provinzial-Museums zu Hannover 1, Hanover: Helwingsche Verlagsbuchhandlung.

Jankuhn, H. (1937) *Haithabu: Eine germanische Stadt der Frühzeit*, Neumünster: Wachholtz.

—— (1943) *Die Ausgrabungen in Haithabu (1937–1939): Vorläufiger Grabungsbericht*, Deutsches Ahnenerbe, Reihe B, 3, Berlin-Dahlem: Ahnenerbe.

—— (1956) *Haithabu: Ein Handelsplatz der Wikingerzeit*, 3rd edn, Neumünster: Wachholtz.

—— (1956/57) 'Ackerfluren der Eisenzeit und ihre Bedeutung für die frühe Wirtschaftsgeschichte', *Bericht der Römisch-Germanischen Kommission* 37/38: 148–214.

—— (1973) 'Umrisse einer Archäologie des Mittelalters', *Zeitschrift für Archäologie des Mittelalters* 1: 9–19.

—— (1976) *Archäologie und Geschichte: Vorträge und Aufsätze. I. Beiträge zur siedlungsarchäologischen Forschung*, Berlin and New York: de Gruyter.

—— (1977) *Einführung in die Siedlungsarchäologie*, Berlin and New York: de Gruyter.

Janssen, W. (1965) *Königshagen. Ein archäologisch-historischer Beitrag zur Siedlungsgeschichte des südwestlichen Harzvorlandes*, Quellen und Darstellungen zur Geschichte Niedersachsens 64, Hildesheim: Lax.

—— 1975. *Studien zur Wüstungsfrage im fränkischen Altsiedelland zwischen Rhein, Mosel und Eifelnordrand*, Beihefte der Bonner Jahrbücher 35, Cologne: Rheinland-Verlag.

Junghans, S., Sangmeister, E. and Schröder, M. (1960) *Metallanalysen kupferzeitlicher und frühbronzezeitlicher Bodenfunde aus Europa*, Studien zu den Anfängen der Metallurgie 1, Berlin: Mann.

—— (1968) *Kupfer und Bronze in der frühen Metallzeit Europas*, Studien zu den Anfängen der Metallurgie 2, Berlin: Mann.

Kater, H. (1974) *Das Ahnenerbe der SS 1935–1945: Ein Beitrag zur Kulturpolitik des Dritten Reiches*, Stuttgart: Deutsche Verlags-Anstalt.

Kimmig, W. (1969) 'Zum Problem späthallstättischer Adelssitze', in K.-H. Otto and J. Herrmann (eds) *Siedlung, Burg und Stadt. Studien zu ihren Anfängen*, Deutsche Akademie der Wissenschaften zu Berlin, Schriften der Sektion für Vor- und Frühgeschichte 25, Berlin: Akademie-Verlag.

—— (1975) 'Early Celts on the Upper Danube: the excavations at the Heuneburg', in R. Bruce-Mitford (ed.) *Recent Archaeological Excavations in Europe*, London: Routledge & Kegan Paul.

—— (1982) 'Bemerkungen zur Terminologie der Urnenfelderkultur im Raum nordwestlich der Alpen', *Archäologisches Korrespondenzblatt* 12: 33–45.

Klejn, L. S. (1974) 'Kossinna im Abstand von vierzig Jahren', *Jahresschrift für mitteldeutsche Vorgeschichte* 58: 7–55.

Köhler, R. (1975) *Untersuchungen zu Grabkomplexen der älteren römischen Kaiserzeit in Böhmen unter Aspekten der religiösen und sozialen Gliederung*, Neumünster: Wachholtz.

Körber-Grohne, U. (1967) *Geobotanische Untersuchungen auf der Feddersen Wierde*, Feddersen Wierde 1, Wiesbaden: Steiner.

Kossinna, G. (1911a) *Die Herkunft der Germanen. Zur Methode der Siedlungsarchäologie*, Mannus-Bibliothek 6, Würzburg.

—— (1911b) 'Anmerkungen zum heutigen Stand der Vorgeschichtsforschung', *Mannus* 3: 127–30.

—— (1912a) *Die deutsche Vorgeschichte, eine hervorragend nationale Wissenschaft*, Mannus-Bücherei 9, Würzburg.

—— (1912b) 'Erich Blume', *Mannus* 4: 451–6.

—— (1919) 'Die deutsche Ostmark, ein Heimatboden der Germanen', *Oberschlesien* 17 (12).

—— (1928) *Ursprung und Verbreitung der Germanen in vor- und frühge-schichtlicher Zeit*, Mannus-Bibliothek 6, Leipzig: Kabitzsch.
—— (1932) *Germanische Kultur im 1. Jahrtausend nach Christus*, Mannus-Bibliothek 50, Leipzig: Kabitzsch.
Krämer, W. (1975) 'Zwanzig Jahre Ausgrabungen in Manching, 1955 bis 1974', in *Ausgrabungen in Deutschland, gefördert von der Deutschen Forschungsgemeinschaft 1950–1975* Teil 1, Monographien des Römisch-Germanischen Zentralmuseums 1, 1, Mainz and Bonn: RGZM & Habelt.
—— (1985) *Die Grabfunde von Manching und die latènezeitlichen Flach-gräber in Südbayern*, Die Ausgrabungen in Manching 9, Wiesbaden: Steiner.
Krämer, W. and Schubert, F. (1970) *Die Ausgrabungen in Manching 1955–1961: Einführung und Fundstellenübersicht*, Die Ausgrabungen in Manching 1, Wiesbaden: Steiner.
Kuhn, T. S. (1970) *The Structure of Scientific Revolutions*, 2nd edn, Chicago: Chicago University Press.
Kunow, J. (1987) 'Das Limesvorland der südlichen Germania Inferior', *Bonner Jahrbücher* 187: 63–77.
—— (1988) 'Zentrale Orte in der Germania Inferior', *Archäologisches Korrespondenzblatt* 18: 55–67.
—— (1989) 'Strukturen im Raum: geographische Gesetzmässigkeiten und archäologisches Befunde aus Niedergermanien', *Archaeologisches Korre-spondenzblatt* 19: 377–90.
Lüning, J. (1971) 'Das Experiment im Michelsberger Erdwerk in Mayen', *Arhcäologisches Korrespondenzblatt* 1: 95–6.
—— (1972) 'Zum Kulturbegriff im Neolithikum', *Praehistorische Zeit-schrift* 47: 145–73.
—— (1973) 'Neolithic periods', *Eiszeitalter und Gegenwart* 23/24: 360–70.
—— (1975) 'Die Erforschung des Neolithikums in der Bundesrepublik Deutschland', in *Ausgrabungen in Deutschland, gefördert von der Deut-schen Forschungsgemeinschaft 1950–1975* Teil 1, Monographien des Römisch-Germanischen Zentralmuseums 1, 1, Mainz and Bonn: RGZM & Habelt.
Lüning, J., Kloos, U. and Albert, S. (1989) 'Westliche Nachbarn der bandkeramischen Kultur: La Hoguette und Limburg', *Germania* 67: 355–420.
Martin, M. (1976) *Das fränkische Gräberfeld von Basel-Bernerring*, Basler Beiträge zur Ur- und Frühgeschichte, Basle: Archäologischer Verlag.
Menghin, O. (1936) 'Grundlinien einer Methodik der urgeschichtlichen Stammeskunde', in H. Arntz (ed.) *Germanen und Indogermanen (Fest-schrift H. Hirt)*, Indogermanische Bibliothek III 15, vol. 1, Heidelberg: Winter.
Mildenberger, G. (1977) *Sozial- und Kulturgeschichte der Germanen*, Urban-Taschenbücher 149, 2nd edn, Stuttgart: Kohlhammer.
Müller-Beck, H. (ed.) (1977) *Excavations at Umingmak on Banks Island, N.W.T., 1970 and 1973: Preliminary Report*, Urgeschichtliche Material-hefte 1, Tübingen: Archaeologica Venatoria.

—— (ed.) (1983) *Urgeschichte in Baden-Württemberg*, Stuttgart: Theiss.

Müller-Karpe, H. (1966–80) *Handbuch der Vorgeschichte*, Munich: Beck.

Müller-Wille, M. (1965) *Eisenzeitliche Fluren in den festländischen Nordseegebieten*, Landeskundliche Karten und Hefte der Geographischen Kommission für Westfalen, Reihe 'Siedlung und Landschaft in Westfalen', 5, Münster: Geographische Kommission.

—— (1978) 'Frühmittelalterliche Prunkgräber im südlichen Skandinavien', *Bonner Jahrbücher* 178: 633–52.

Narr, K. J. (1966) 'Archäologie und Vorgeschichte', in C. D. Kernig (ed.) *Sowjetsystem und demokratische Gesellschaft: Eine vergleichende Enzyklopädie* vol. 1, Freiburg, Basle and Vienna: Herder.

—— (1974) 'Tendenzen in der Urgeschichtsforschung', *Grenzfragen* 4: 85–125.

—— (1982) 'Struktur und Ereignis: Einige urgeschichtliche Aspekte', *Grenzfragen* 11: 35–61.

—— (1985) 'Review of K. Frerichs, *Begriffsbildung und Begriffsanwendung in der Vor- und Frühgeschichte*', *Bonner Jahrbücher* 185: 544–6.

Nestler, A. (1982) *Reduktion und Rekonstruktion archäologischer Befunde*, Arbeiten zur Urgeschichte des Menschen 6, Frankfurt and Bern: Lang.

Pauli, L. (1975) *Keltischer Volksglaube. Amulette und Sonderbestattungen am Dürrnberg bei Hallein und im eisenzeitlichen Mitteleuropa*, Münchener Beiträge zur Vor- und Frühgeschichte 28, Munich: Beck.

—— (1978) 'Ungewöhnliche Grabfunde aus frühgeschichtlicher Zeit. Archäologische Analyse und anthropologischer Befund', *Homo* 29: 44–53.

—— (1984a) 'Neue Archäologie – ein alter Hut [Review of L. Binford (1984) *Die Vorzeit war ganz anders*, Munich: Harnack]', *Frankfurter Allgemeine Zeitung*, 7 September 1984, p. 11.

—— (ed.) (1984b) *Archäologie und Kulturgeschichte 2. Beiträge zur Erforschung von Sozialstrukturen und Randkulturen*, Saerbeck: Unkeler Kreis.

—— (1988) 'Review of J. Bintliff (ed.) *European Social Evolution*', *Germania* 66: 294–6.

Raetzel-Fabian, D. (1986) *Phasenkartierung des mitteleuropäischen Neolithikums: Chronologie und Chorologie*, British Archaeological Report S316, Oxford.

Reinecke, P. (1902a) 'Zur Kenntnis der La Tène-Denkmäler der Zone nordwärts der Alpen', in *Festschrift zur Feier des fünfzigjährigen Bestehens des Römisch-Germanischen Centralmuseums zu Mainz*, Mainz: von Zabern.

—— (1902b) 'Zur Chronologie der zweiten Hälfte des Bronzealters in Süd- und Norddeutschland', *Correpondenz-Blatt der Deutschen Gesellschaft für Anthropologie, Ethnologie und Urgeschichte* 33: 17–27.

—— (1911) [numerous individual contributions in] *Die Altertümer unserer heidnischen Vorzeit* 5, Mainz: von Zabern.

—— (1924) 'Zur chronologischen Gliederung der süddeutschen Bronzezeit', *Germania* 8: 43–4.

—— (1965) *Mainzer Aufsätze zur Chronologie der Bronze- und Eisenzeit*, Bonn: Habelt.

Renfrew, C. and Shennan, S. (eds) (1982) *Ranking, Resource and Exchange: Aspects of the Archaeology of Early European Society*, New Directions in Archaeology, Cambridge: Cambridge University Press.

Rolle, R. (1979) *Totenkult der Skythen*, Vorgeschichtliche Forschungen Neue Folge 18, Berlin: de Gruyter.

Sangmeister, E. (1969) 'Zur Ausbreitung der Metalltechnik in Europa', *Germania* 46: 4–10.

—— (1975) 'Die Anfänge der Metallurgie in Europa', in *Ausgrabungen in Deutschland, gefördert von der Deutschen Forschungsgemeinschaft 1950–1975* Teil 3, Monographien des Römisch-Germanischen Zentralmuseums 1, 3, Mainz and Bonn: RGZM & Habelt.

Schaaff, U. (1975) 'Ausgrabungen zur Eisenzeit in Deutschland', in *Ausgrabungen in Deutschland, gefördert von der Deutschen Forschungsgemeinschaft 1950–1975* Teil 1, Monographien des Römisch-Germanischen Zentralmuseums 1, 1, Mainz and Bonn: RGZM & Habelt.

Schauer, P. (1975) 'Forschungen zur Geschichte der Bronzezeit in Deutschland', in *Ausgrabungen in Deutschland, gefördert von der Deutschen Forschungsgemeinschaft 1950–1975* Teil 1, Monographien des Römisch-Germanischen Zentralmuseums 1, 1, Mainz and Bonn: RGZM & Habelt.

Schlesinger, W. (1974) 'Archäologie des Mittelalters aus der Sicht des Historikers', *Zeitschrift für Archäologie des Mittelalters* 2: 7–31.

Schlichtherle, H. and Wahlster, B. (1986) *Archäologie in Seen und Mooren*, Stuttgart: Theiss.

Schlüter, W. (1970) 'Versuch einer sozialen Differenzierung der jungkaiserzeitlichen Körpergräbergruppe von Hassleben-Leuna anhand einer Analyse der Grabfunde', *Neue Ausgrabungen und Forschungen in Niedersachsen* 6: 117–45.

Schmid, P. (1978) 'New archaeological results of settlement structures (Roman Iron Age) in the northwest German coastal area', in B. Cunliffe and T. Rowley (eds), *Lowland Iron Age Communities in Europe*, British Archaeological Report S48, Oxford.

Schuchhardt, C. (1909) 'Die Römerschanze bei Potsdam nach den Ausgrabungen von 1908 und 1909', *Praehistorische Zeitschrift* 1: 209–38.

—— (1935) *Alteuropa: die Entwicklung seiner Kulturen und Völker*, 3rd edn, Berlin: de Gruyter.

Schwarz, K. (1948) 'Lagen die Siedlungen der linearbandkeramischen Kultur Mitteldeutschlands in waldfreien oder bewaldeten Landschaften?' in K. Schwarz (ed.) *Strena Praehistorica (Jahn-Festschrift)*, Halle/Saale: Niemeyer.

Sherratt, A. G. (1984) 'From stone to iron', *Times Literary Supplement*, 20 April 1984, p. 437.

Sielmann, B. (1971a) 'Der Einfluss der Umwelt auf die neolithische Besiedlung Südwestdeutschlands unter besonderer Berücksichtigung der Verhältnisse am nördlichen Oberrhein', *Acta Praehistorica et Archaeologica* 2: 65–197.

—— (1971b) 'Zur Interpretationsmöglichkeit ökologischer Befunde im Neolithikum Mitteleuropas', *Germania* 49: 231–8.

Smolla, G. (1964) 'Analogien und Polaritäten', in R. von Uslar and K. J. Narr (eds) *Studien aus Alteuropa (Tackenberg-Festschrift)*, Beihefte der Bonner Jahrbücher 10/I, pt. I, Cologne: Böhlau.

—— (1980) 'Das Kossinna-Syndrom', *Fundberichte aus Hessen* 19/20: 1–9.

—— (1984/85) 'Kossinna nach 50 Jahren: Kein Nachruf', *Acta Praehistorica et Archaeologica* 16/17: 9–14.

Spitzing, T. (1988) *Die römische Villa von Lauffen a.N. (Kr. Heilbronn)*, Materialhefte zur Vor- und Frühgeschichte in Baden-Württemberg 12, Stuttgart: Theiss.

Spitzner-von der Haar, J. (1989) 'Was ist in unserem Fach an den Unis los? Bundesweites Treffen der UFG Studentinnen und Studenten 16.–18. Juni 1989 in Kiel', *Archäologische Informationen* 12: 86–91.

Steuer, H. (1968) 'Zur Bewaffnung und Sozialstruktur der Merowingerzeit', *Nachrichten aus Niedersachsens Urgeschichte* 37: 18–87.

—— (1982) *Frühgeschichtliche Sozialstrukturen in Mitteleuropa*, Abhandlungen der Akademie der Wissenschaften in Göttingen, Philologisch-Historische Klasse III 128, Göttingen: Vandenhoek & Ruprecht.

—— (1984) 'Die frühmittelalterliche Gesellschaftsstruktur im Spiegel der Grabfunde', in H. Roth and E. Wamers (eds) *Hessen im Frühmittelalter*, Sigmaringen: Thorbecke.

Steuer, H. and Last, M. (1969) 'Zur Interpretation der beigabenführenden Gräber des achten Jahrhunderts im Gebiet rechts des Rheins', *Nachrichten aus Niedersachsens Urgeschichte* 38: 25–88.

Strahm, C. (1987) 'Zur Einführung: Das Forschungsvorhaben "Siedlungsarchäologische Untersuchungen im Alpenvorland" ', *Archäologische Nachrichten aus Baden* 38/39: 4–10.

Veeck, W. (1926) 'Der Reihengräberfriedhof von Holzgerlingen', *Fundberichte aus Schwaben* Neue Folge 3: 154–201.

Veit, U. (1984) 'Gustaf Kossinna und V. Gordon Childe: Ansätze zu einer theoretischen Grundlegung der Vorgeschichte', *Saeculum* 35: 326–64.

—— (1989) 'Ethnic concepts in German prehistory: a case study on the relationship between cultural identity and archaeological objectivity', in S. Shennan (ed.) *Archaeological Approaches to Cultural Identity*, London, Unwin Hyman.

Vierck, H. (1980) 'Ein westfälisches "Adelsgrab" des 8. Jahrhunderts n.Chr.', *Studien zur Sachsenforschung* 2: 457–88.

Vierhaus, R. (1989) 'Traditionen vergleichender historischer Kulturwissenschaft in Deutschland: Bemerkungen und Fragen', *Saeculum* 40: 132–5.

von Krosigk, H. Gräfin Schwerin (1982) *Gustaf Kossinna. Der Nachlass – Versuch einer Analyse*, Offa-Ergänzungsreihe 6, Neumünster: Wachholtz.

von Pauly, A. F. (1893–1963) *Real-Encyclopädie der classischen Altertumswissenschaft*, ed G. Wissowa, Stuttgart: Metzler.

von Uslar, R. (1955) 'Über den Nutzen spekulativer Betrachtung vorgeschichtlicher Funde', *Jahrbuch des Römisch-Germanischen Zentralmuseums* 2: 1–20.

—— (1980) *Die Germanen vom 1.–4. Jahrhundert n.Chr.* Handbuch der europäischen Wirtschafts- und Sozialgeschichte, Stuttgart: Klett.

Vossen, R. (1969) *Archäologische Interpretation und ethnographischer Befund. Eine Analyse anhand rezenter Keramik des westlichen Amazonasbeckens*, Hamburger Reihe zur Kultur- und Sprachwissenschaft 1, Munich: Renner.

—— (1970) 'Klassifikationsprobleme und Klassifikationssysteme in der Amerikanischen Archäologie', *Acta Praehistorica et Archaeologica* 1: 29–79.

Wahle, E. (1941) *Zur ethnischen Deutung frühgeschichtlicher Kulturprovinzen. Grenzen der frühgeschichtlichen Erkenntnis I*, Sitzungsberichte der Heidelberger Akademie der Wissenschaften, Philosophisch-historische Klasse, Jahrgang 1940/41, 2, Heidelberg: Winter.

Weidemann, K. (1968) 'Die Topographie von Mainz in der Römerzeit und dem frühen Mittelalter', *Jahrbuch des Römisch-Germanischen Zentralmuseums* 15: 146–99.

—— (1970) 'Zur Topographie von Metz in der Römerzeit und im frühen Mittelalter', *Jahrbuch des Römisch-Germanischen Zentralmuseums* 17: 147–71.

—— (1972) 'Untersuchungen zur Siedlungsgeschichte des Landes zwischen Limes und Rhein vom Ende der Römerherrschaft bis zum Frühmittelalter', *Jahrbuch des Römisch-Germanischen Zentralmuseums* 19: 99–154.

Werner, J. (1968) 'Bewaffnung und Waffenbeigabe in der Merowingerzeit', in *Ordinamenti militari in occidente nell'alto medioevo*, Settimane di studio del centro italiano di studi sull'alto medioevo 15, Spoleto.

Whitley, J. (1987) 'Art history, archaeology and idealism: the German tradition' in I. Hodder (ed.) *Archaeology as Long-term History*, New Directions in Archaeology, Cambridge: Cambridge University Press.

Willems, W. J. H. (1986) *Romans and Batavians: a Regional Study in the Dutch Eastern River Area*, Amsterdam: University of Amsterdam.

Willerding, U. (1977) 'Review of E. S. Higgs (ed.) *Papers in Economic Prehistory*', *Praehistorische Zeitschrift* 51: 199–205.

Wolfram, S. (1986) *Zur Theoriediskussion in der prähistorischen Archäologie Grossbritanniens*, British Archaeological Report S306, Oxford.

Ziegert, H. (1980) 'Objektorientierte und problemorientierte Forschungsansätze in der Archäologie', *Hephaistos* 2: 53–65.

—— (1983) ' "Kombinationsstatistik" und "Seriation"; Zu Methode und Ergebnis der Bronzezeit-Chronologie K. Goldmanns', *Archäologische Informationen* 5: 21–52.

Zimmermann, W. H. (1974) 'A Roman Iron Age and Early Migration settlement at Flögeln, Kr. Wesermünde, Lower Saxony', in T. Rowley (ed.) *Anglo-Saxon Settlement and Landscape*, British Archaeological Report 6, Oxford.

—— (1978) 'Economy of the Roman Iron Age settlement at Flögeln, Kr. Cuxhaven, Lower Saxony: husbandry, cattle farming and manufacturing', in B. Cunliffe and T. Rowley (eds.) *Lowland Iron Age Communities in Europe*, British Archaeological Report S48, Oxford.

9

THEORY IN POLISH ARCHAEOLOGY 1960–90: SEARCHING FOR PARADIGMS

Zbigniew Kobyliński[1]

During the last forty years Polish post-war archaeology has passed through stages of fluctuating interest in theoretical problems. After a period of heated discussion in the 1950s and early 1960s, striving for a self-definition of the methodological position of the discipline on the basis of recently accepted ideological systems in the second half of the 1960s and in the 1970s we observed a long and deep crisis of cognitive consciousness in Polish archaeology. Some scholars pointed out during that time that the achievements in data collection during field research should be accompanied with equally intense attempts to make the theoretical foundations of archaeology more precise (Nadolski 1963: 583; Trudzik 1971: 5). But they received no serious response. The first attempts at surmounting this crisis could be observed no earlier than the late 1970s and early 1980s. The theoretical debate in Polish ethnography followed exactly the same course (cf. Piątkowski 1985: 37–8).

Restraints on the development of archaeological theory

One of the main factors responsible for this longstanding neglect of theoretical problems in both the related disciplines was – and still is – the isolation of the Polish scientific milieu from external, foreign influences. This isolation makes it extremely difficult to initiate and sustain contacts with foreign scientific institutions, and also limits access to foreign literature, in particular to new theoretical concepts (Frankowska 1973; Urbańczyk 1983) A temporary improvement in the inflow of English-language theoretical archaeological literature in the second half of the 1970s and the beginning of the 1980s was short and diminished dramatically in 1982.

A measure of Polish archaeology's growing isolation from the new tendencies in western countries is the fact that David Clarke's famous book *Analytical Archaeology*, published in 1968, waited for discussion in Polish literature until 1974 (Tabaczyński and Pleszczyńska 1974; see also Kmita 1973), but the first Polish papers referring directly to the questions and concepts raised by the American New Archaeology appeared no earlier than around 1980 (e.g. Kobylińska 1980a, 1980b; Urbańczyk 1980). It should be stressed, moreover, that this important theoretical movement has never been seriously and critically presented and discussed in Polish archaeological literature. In the broad circle of Polish archaeologists it still remains almost completely unknown. Recently published criticism of the New Archaeology, inspired above all by the works of Courbin (1982) and Hodder (1982), whose arguments are quoted in Polish literature without real investigation of problems, discourages Polish archaeologists from reading the works written by New Archaeologists and presents a negative image of this theoretical direction as 'the completely abortive attempt to build archaeological theory' (Tabaczyński 1984, 1985a) or even refusal to formulate theory (Stoczkowski 1988). The recent 'post-processual' trends in British theoretical debate are also almost completely unknown in the community of Polish archaeologists (the only exception is the brief presentation in Pałubicka and Tabaczyński 1986: 64–6).

The crisis of Polish archaeology's cognitive consciousness would not be so serious if its isolation did not go hand in hand with other, parochial problems. The impossibility of finding ready theoretical solutions abroad should encourage Polish archaeologists to reach out to the local philosophical background and construct original Polish theoretical concepts. Such a specific Polish trend of enquiry has always been the definition and aims of archaeology in relation to other historical disciplines.

Contrary to the American tradition of including archaeology in the group of anthropological sciences, in the opinion and consciousness of Polish archaeologists this discipline has always functioned in close relation to history. Discussions concerning the status of archaeology, its subject of study and its goals, initiated directly after the Second World War, are still alive (see e.g. Hensel 1973a, 1984a, 1986; Trudzik 1971; Żak 1966, 1968). In the 1950s, when, under the influence of the Soviet model for the organisation of science, the new discipline – the history of material culture, containing both archaeology and ethnography – was called into existence, its role and place were discussed (e.g. Hołubowicz 1955; Kulczycki 1955; Wielowiejski 1970). Unfortunately, institutional bonds between archaeology and ethnology as one subject in universities, and in the joint research institute of the Polish Academy of Sciences established in 1953, did not help to reveal an anthropological perspective to archaeologists. Just the opposite occurred. Ethnography came to be understood as a subdiscipline of history.

Much energy has been spent on discussing the definitions of the terms 'archaeology' and 'prehistory' and the question of whether archaeology is an independent scientific discipline or a discipline auxiliary to prehistory. According to a recent statement by Hensel (1986), archaeology has a twofold nature, independent and auxiliary at the same time. Archaeology is seen as an independent science for those stages of the historical process which history cannot embrace in a more exhaustive way and auxiliary for those periods in which there is not the slightest doubt about the primacy of history. Although this opinion seems to be generally accepted in Polish archaeology, there are still traces of different regional traditions in the understanding of the subject and its scientific status. At present, for example, in Warsaw and Cracow one can study archaeology in the university, but in Poznań prehistory is taught. Although these discussions had no effect on Polish archaeologists' empirical research practice, they are nevertheless evidence of a feverish search for identity, of a desire to define the subject matter and purpose of the discipline.

Another problem specific to Polish theoretical debates was the 'theory of archaeological sources', including the definition of the ontological characteristics of archaeological evidence, consideration of the role of the archaeologist in creating evidence, and problems of biases inherent in the archaeological record. The concept of a two-step reflection of historical reality in the archaeological record was one of those offered. The need to distinguish between potential archaeological sources and those which were observed was pointed out, and the ability of an archaeologist's socio-cultural milieu and individual predispositions to influence the evidence created in the form of an archaeological record was discussed (e.g. Antoniewicz and Wartołowska 1955; Gediga 1971;

Godłowski 1962; Hołubowicz 1961; Kowalczyk 1963; Trudzik 1965, 1971).

At the same time, however, many Polish archaeologists expressed their belief in the existence of 'pure' facts and inherently objective 'raw sources', which should be gathered in the greatest possible number without any interpretation (e.g. Jażdzewski 1981: 54–5). Such an approach has been criticised by Tabaczyński (1971), who argued that an 'archaeology without models is actually full of hidden models'. The necessity to create and verbalise models in archaeological reasoning was also discussed by Godłowski (1976).

All these deliberations on the characteristics of the source-creating process in archaeology have been connected with similar intellectual developments in Polish historiography. In particular discussion focused on the classification of historical sources proposed by Gerard Labuda (1957), who made distinctions between the ergotechnic, the sociotechnic and the psychotechnic sources (quite similar to those later defined by Lewis Binford) (e.g. Trudzik 1971; Maetzke et al. 1978; Maetzke 1986). A serious impact on these discussions was also made by the theory that selective mechanisms created the archaeological evidence (Eggers 1959; Tabaczyński 1964).

If these and other theories have never been formulated in a cohesive and mature manner, the main cause is organisational: the division of the Polish archaeological community into four separate branches – museums, universities, curators of archaeological monuments and the Polish Academy of Sciences – without any common platform for discussion and exchange of ideas. Other causes include an obsolete university education system which encourages intellectual passivity, and a hierarchy of scientific degrees in which a scholar does not achieve independent status until the age of 40.

A specific role was also played by the enlarging of the number of huge field expeditions excavating mainly early medieval sites in connection with the millennial anniversary of the Polish state. This project, proposed by W. Hensel just after the war (Hensel 1946) but with its apogee in the late 1960s, absorbed a majority of archaeologists, and the deluge of finds gathered within a short time overtook the analytical capabilities of Polish scholars. This enormous project has diverted the attention of Polish archaeologists to the problem of techniques of excavation and recording rather than to theoretical questions.

The 'external' reason for this campaign, and for all the research problems traditionally explored by Polish archaeology, should be clearly seeen. For many years after the war, Polish archaeology was designed to gather evidence for the Slavic ethnicity of prehistoric inhabitants of Polish lands. This was a consequence of a social demand to respond to the nationalistic, pan-Germanic theories of German archaeologists, put forward by Gustaf Kossinna before the First World War. Ethnic studies in Polish archaeology still have this political aspect, although recently the ideological character of this manner of doing archaeology has often been exposed and criticised (e.g. Minta-Tworzowska 1986; Żak 1977a, 1981). And Kossinna's 'settlement-archaeological method', with different ethnic qualifications given to the same archaeological units, was frequently used by Polish archaeologists even after the last war. The positive result of this situation was a focus on the theoretical problems of ethnicity and its archaeologically visible correlates (e.g. Bukowski 1984; Godłowski 1979; Hensel 1973b, 1978, 1984b; Jażdżewski 1969; Kobyliński 1988a; Malinowski 1980; Żak 1973, 1985), and of the archaeological visibility of discontinuities in socio-cultural processes (Kobyliński 1988h; Tabaczyński 1976, 1985b).

Another enormous field project is now being undertaken: the 'Archaeological Map of Poland' (Konopka 1984). Every spring and autumn, many younger archaeologists do systematic field-walking all over Poland. There is little concern with theoretical considerations, although the problems of archaeological visibility of sites, the techniques of their discovery and recording, and optimal sampling strategies in settlement studies are discussed by many field archaeologists (e.g. Brzeziński et al. 1985; Kobyliński 1984; Kruk 1970; Mazurowski 1980).

Finally, an important but not equally recognised influence was the role of historical materialism as the compulsory ideology, determining both the understanding of the developmental mechanisms and human societies and consequent research directions and procedures. Initially this ideology undoubtedly stimulated the development of theoretical reflection in Polish archaeology. The later crisis was, however, to a large degree connected with the growth of dogma within this ideology and with the fact that in spite of what was stated in syllabuses Marxism was not in fact incorporated in the research practice of archaeologists. The renewed wave of methodological and theoretical activity by Polish archaeologists is again closely related to a revival of discussions on the interpretation of Marxism in the Polish philosophical milieu. The influence of this ideology was therefore complex, and there is nothing strange in the fact that extremely different evaluations of its impact on theoretical questions in Polish archaeology have been expressed (Hensel 1974 and Kurnatowski 1971: 309 vs. Urbańczyk 1983: 214).

Anyway, one cannot overlook the fact that in the second half of the 1950s and early 1960s a large number of programmatic announcements were drawn up in the Polish literature presenting the paradigm for archaeology according to the materialistic ontological perspective of Marxist philosophy. The aim of archaeology, which was then understood as an independent scientific discipline, involved studying and formulating the laws of development of human societies (Antoniewicz and Wartołowska 1955; Hensel 1958; Hołubowicz 1961; Wartołowska 1964). From the principles of Marxian dialects, specific methodological postulates were derived, such as studying a phenomenon in terms of its internal completeness and its external sets of relationships, and the carrying out of problem-orientated research. Very similar ideas, though derived from quite different philosophical foundations, can be found in the much later works of the American New Archaeology. A peculiar paradox of Polish archaeology is that these innovative, seminally important theoretical statements, forgotten for some twenty years, were rediscovered in the late 1970s, under foreign influence, when faint echoes of the theoretical debate in western countries caused renewed interest on our own tradition (Maetzke, et al. 1978: 20).

Unfortunately, the general character of the Marxist theory of society makes it impossible to use as a direct guideline in empirical studies, and there have so far been no attempts to operationalise it. Only with reference to prehistoric economics have there been some attempts to build models derived from general Marxist theory (see the introductory remarks made by Tabaczyński 1966), but inspired by French Marxists' ideas rather than by 'classical' Marxism.

External and internal influences

In such a situation, the main theoretical efforts of Polish archaeologists in the 1960s and 1970s focused on defining theoretical

constructs, such as the notion of 'type' (Balcer 1970; Dymaczewski 1968; Kozłowski 1972). A notable factor which enlivened the
discussion was the response to David Clarke's *Analytical Archaeology*. In the years 1971 to 1980 several papers had been published
all devoted to the discussion of the notion of the 'archaeological
culture' and the methods for its empirical determination (e.g.
Baranowski 1974; Drozdek 1980; Godłowski 1976; Konopka
1978; Kozłowski 1975; Pałubicka 1974; Tabaczyńska and Tabaczyński 1973/Tabaczyński 1971, 1976). The positive response to
Clarke's book (despite many minor criticisms) resulted from the
fact that it dealt with problems which were important from the
point of view of the then prevailing culture-historical paradigm in
archaeology. In Polish archaeology the main areas of interest have
always been chronology, typology and cultural taxonomy, all serving the goal of a much higher ultimate order: the establishment
of the origins of ethnic groups, their culture and the detection of
the influences and contacts between them (cf. Schild 1980a). While
such considerations are theory-laden, the theory was mostly
unconscious. The most explicit theoretical discussion concerned
the meaning of variability in Stone Age lithic industries (e.g.
Kozłowski 1972; Schild 1965, summarised recently by Lech 1988;
see also Wyszomirska 1987). As a result of inspiration partly
from James Sackett's theory of style in archaeology (1977; also
Kobylińska 1980b), and partly from concepts in the theory of art,
the focus of research in Stone Age archaeology recently shifted
from typological and culture-historical variability towards stylistic
variability in stone artefacts (Tomaszewski 1988a).

In the late 1970s a few Polish archaeologists became to some
extent acquainted with the American New Archaeology. The
anthropological perspective proposed by Lewis Binford has been
effectively accepted by some younger scholars (e.g. Kobyliński
and Tomaszewski 1980), but the older ones have rejected it, stating
that it is alien to European tradition. Some scholars have claimed
both perspectives as equally important (Maetzke *et al.* 1978),
trying to show that there is no contradiction between the 'traditional' and the 'New' archaeology. The same criticism as previously addressed to Clarke, that he fails to notice that both
disciplines – history and anthropology – are in fact equally important cognitive prospects, complementary to each other (Tabaczyński and Pleszczyńska 1974), was then applied to American New
Archaeology. According to Tabaczyński (1985a: 172), the 'New'

Archaeology should be considered not as opposed to 'traditional' archaeology but rather as one of the most interesting manifestations of the multidirectional process of archaeology's theorisation, a process which began long before Binford's works appeared. In Tabaczyński's opinion (1985a: 175) the New Archaeology had not proposed any theory which would essentially enrich the historical narration. Tabaczyński made two mistakes in his critique of the New Archaeology: treating all the theoretical movements in modern West European and American archaeology as one consistent orientation, for which the most representative are still the early works by Hill (1970) and Watson, LeBlanc and Redman (1971); and (as has recently been pointed out by Ostoja-Zagórski 1988, in his apology for the New Archaeology) looking for a specifically archaeological theory and consequently taking the New Archaeology to task for adopting a model from the other scientific disciplines.

The New Archaeology reached Poland during the period of activity of the 'Poznań School' of Polish Marxist philosophers. Members of this school (of whom the most important are Jerzy Kmita and Leszek Nowak) made a formal interpretation of the principles of Marxian dialectics, which had until then remained an apparent enigma. They also formulated a model of research procedure in science, particularly in the humanities and social sciences. Finally, they drew attention to the external determinants of scientific cognition and developed a research orientation called 'historical epistemology' (e.g. Kmita 1976; Nowak 1977a; Pałubicka 1977). Polish historians entered the debate (Buksiński 1982; Piekarczyk 1970, 1976; Pomorski 1986; Topolski 1976, 1977, 1978) and, slightly later, so did archaeologists.

Two scholars, Stanisław Tabaczyński of the Institute of History of Material Culture in Warsaw, and Jan Żak of the University of Poznań, were both involved for a long time in theoretical discussion, to which small groups of students and younger scholars then gathered. The group of archaeologists from Poznań, more isolated from foreign influences and very critical in their attitude to the American New Archaeology, had stronger and more consistent ties with the local milieu of philosophers and theoreticians in the humanities. Their particular interest was the history of theoretical orientations in archaelogy, especially the question of the distinctive characteristics of positivist and neopositivist archaeology. In the recent opinion of Czerniak and Kośko (1987: 43), the New Archaeology 'is undoubtedly some progress, but not sufficient to eliminate errors of positivist thinking.'

The Warsaw group developed traditional theoretical interests in the source-creating process at the same time as being open to foreign ideas. At the beginning of the 1980s the seminar led by Tabaczyński became the main centre of theoretical discussion in Poland. Most of the Polish archaeological community, however, remained indifferent to these intellectual efforts. The negative result of this situation was a widening of the gap between practitioners and theoreticians with theoretical discussions being monopolised by a very small group.

Both the trends influencing Polish archaeologists searching for theoretical inspirations, namely the 'New Archaeology' and the local philosophical discussions, focused on methodological problems, particularly on the question of models of explanation. Under these influences, in the publications by the younger generation of Polish archaeologists, attempts were made to show that the model of explanation adequate for highly developed empirical sciences can also be applied to archaeology (e.g. Kobyliński 1981a). Examples of clearly hypothetico-deductive reasoning have also been presented (e.g. Henneberg *et al.* 1978; Rysiewska 1980). The most explicit example of controversy between the 'hypotheticists' and the 'empiricists' or 'inductionists' has been the lively debate over a model of rotational exploitation and shifting settlement in the neolithic period (e.g. Czerniak and Piontek 1980a, 1980b; Czerniak 1985; Bogucki and Grygiel 1980; Grygiel 1987).

It is not therefore true that, as Bogucki stated recently (1985), the debate 'as to what constituted the adequate determination of the causal relationships among prehistoric phenomena, has not really taken place in Europe'. This debate began later in Poland than in other countries, but it is alive (see the brief report in Milisauskas 1986). It has been expressed in the journal *Archeologia Polski* (e.g. Czerniak 1985; Kobylińska and Kobyliński 1985; Kobyliński 1981a; Piontek 1982, 1988; Żak 1975), and recently in two books written or edited by Tabaczyński: 'Theory and practice of archaeological research' (Pałubicka and Tabaczyński 1986) and 'Medieval archaeology' (Tabaczyński 1987). It seems that during this discussion some important questions have been answered in an original way thanks to the influence of the local philosophical background.

Theoretical issues in Polish archaeology

First of all, it has been shown that discussion of the logical correctness of explanation procedures should be preceded by discussion of the subject matter of archaeological studies, particularly of the characteristics of the historical process, its motor forces and regulatory mechanisms (see especially Żak 1975, 1977b, including the assertion that the role of the human individual in history should be appreciated). According to Tabaczyński, the fundamental issue is 'the relationship between the cultural divisions envisaged by an archaeologist investigating fossil materials and the real socio-cultural articulation of a historical process' (Pałubicka and Tabaczyński 1986). One of the main arguments against the New Archaeology has been its underestimation of this important question (e.g. Tabaczyński 1985a: 172).

The 'Poznań philosphical school' has also drawn archaeologists' attention to the problem of 'historical epistemology', i.e. the question of factors determining the development of science. It has been argued that every discipline passes through the same stages of theoretical consciousness – from 'mythology' to 'science' (Nowak 1977a; Kobyliński and Tomaszewski 1980; Ostoja-Zagórski 1988). The process of moving beyond a positivist theory of cognition has been described by Pałubicka and Tabaczyński (1986). The thresholds of these stages are determined by different understandings of the relation between the object of research and the object of perception. It has been stressed that the theoretisation of archaeology or any other discipline is a consequence of the refutation of the thesis of factuality, i.e. the assumption that it is possible to know the essence of studied phenomena through observation. Thus, post-positivist science breaks with commonsense images of the world (Pomorski 1986).

The idea of multi-level ontological structures of phenomena and of the existence of an underlying structure is derived from Marxian dialectics (Nowak 1977b). It is also assumed that essence is changeable and the aim of the theoretical sciences is not only to study all the factors determining this essence but also to know the rules of 'underlying movement', i.e. the rules governing changes in the essences of phenomena. Starting from this ontological vision of reality, the general principle of explanation through the building of idealised theories has been formulated. It has been assumed that the discovery of essential factors determining the course of events may be possible only on the basis of assumptions concerning the lack of interference from all the factors involved except one. Such a first stage is followed by a gradual consideration of all other factors and their influences, until a factual law is formulated concerning the specific situation and involving a unique configuration of all the determinant factors (Nowak 1975; Henneberg *et al.* 1978; Kobyliński 1981a). In this way every individual event is at the same time unique and typical, a manifestation of certain detectable regularities.

The problem of determinism vs. indeterminism in social reality has also been discussed (Kobyliński 1981b; Urbańczyk 1981a). It has been proposed that it is not necessary for scientific theories describing social phenomena to consist of deterministic laws, or of laws stating a probability close to 1. Such a theory can be built from selective-adaptational laws, as in contemporary interpretations of Marxian historical materialism (Klawiter 1974). The thesis of human activity (Topolski 1973a) or creativity (Sztompka 1981) is the fundamental paradigm for the contemporary Polish interpretation of Marxian theory in the social and historical sciences. The famous statement by Marx in the *Eighteenth Brumaire of Louis Bonaparte* is apposite here: 'People themselves make their own history, but they do not make it freely.' Russell made the similar statement: 'We can do as we please, but we cannot please as we please.' Human individuals are active subjects of history and objective reality does not impose on them directly, does not determine ready solutions, but selects these solutions indirectly. Human activity therefore has a dual nature. It involves subjective senses and objective results, determined by actual patterns of socio-economic relations (Żak 1975). Tracing human activity has been recognised as a principal guideline for the study of prehistory (e.g. Żak 1977b).

Moreover, the structure of the social world consists of several emergent levels: the level of individuals, the level of small social groups with face-to-face relationships, and the macro-structural level of great social systems (Szmatka 1980). Even if individual human behaviour is not externally determined, we cannot assume a macro-indeterminism of social processes, because the macro-social level is not only the simple aggregate of individual behaviours (Amsterdamski 1983). Human individuals participate in many small social groups at a time, and knowledge about possible patterns of behaviour is determined by this participation.

Some examples of the application of such a selective-adaptational version of Marxist theory of the origins of cultural phenomena (with special attention paid to the functional-genetic model of explanation proposed by J. Plechanov) have been presented in Polish archaeology. For example, there has been reference to the problem of the origins of a consistent style of artistic objects as a result of the assimilation of multi-directional influences (Kobylińska 1981), and to the phenomenon of the semantisation of an artefact which has a primary techno-utilitarian function (Kobyliński 1988d). In Plechanov's concept, if in a given socio-economic system U there appears a positively evaluated circumstance S constantly produced by phenomenon Z, then Z is considered as a natural symptom of S and is used in U to communicate or manifest S, its properties being held in common and aesthetically associated. His theory is a good example of the adaptational and statistical nature of the Marxist approach to the explanation of cultural phenomena. Another example is the adaptational reconstruction of Engels's conception of primitive societies as determined by life reproduction patterns rather than by economic production (Burbelka 1980), and the consequent attempt to formulate a separate historical materialistic theory of 'tribal formation'.

When discussing the 'hypothetistic' or 'naturalistic' concept of theorisation in archaelogy it has been argued (Tabaczyński 1984: 244; 1985a: 179) that theory should involve reflection on the 'context of discovery'. This means that theory has not yet described how the archaeologist formulates laws, what is the inspiration in modelling the factors describing the essence of studied phenomena (this question is clearly present in the works of Żak and his students). Like Lewis Binford, some Polish scholars accepted the thesis that the source of theoretical assumption is unimportant (Piontek 1982). Others have argued that the student of the past must not use the image of the world shaped in contemporary European culture to reconstruct conditions of past phenomena, because different axiologic and ontologic prospects prevailed (e.g. Kobylińska and Kobyliński 1985). It has been stressed that the construction of theory and models should be preceded by a phase of ethno-archaeological study of the phenomena in question. This idea has resulted in renewed interest in the problem of using ethnographic analogies in archaeological reasoning (Kobyliński 1981a; 1985; Kozłowski 1979; Posern-Zieliński and Ostoja-Zagórski 1977; Prinke 1973). In particular, the problem of the conditions and limits of adequacy of the ethnographically derived economic, ecological and demographic models of pottery production has been discussed (e.g. Kobylińska and Kobyliński 1981, 1982, 1990).

Increasing interest in the behavioural approach, mainly in Stone Age archaeology (e.g. Schild *et al.* 1975; Schild 1980b; Tomaszewski 1986) but also in pottery studies (e.g. Buko 1990) and in building ecological and demographical models (e.g. Czerniak and Piontek 1980a; Henneberg 1975; Henneberg and Ostoja-Zagórski 1977; Henneberg *et al.* 1978; Henneberg *et al.* 1975; Kozłowski and Kozłowski 1983; Ostoja-Zagórski 1974; Ostoja-Zagórski and Strzałko 1984; Piontek and Czerniak 1981; Piontek 1988) among Polish archaeologists can also be seen in the 1970s, to a large degree independent of American or British ideas. Settlement studies in Polish archaeology have always been influenced by the works of German archaeologists, particularly Herbert Jankuhn and the group gathered around the journal *Archaeologia Geographica*. This approach put particular emphasis on constructing settlement maps and relating them (with no discussion of the biases inherent in such maps) to the reconstruction of the natural environment in prehistory. This conception gave rise to enormous projects with the object of cataloguing all the archaeological sites in Poland. Extensive theoretical discussions (summarised by Kurnatowski 1978; cf. also Kruk 1980) connected with settlement archaeology dealt with the definition of the subject matter of this orientation (namely with the definition of such terms as 'settlement' or 'microregion'). In the early 1980s some new aspects were added to these discussions (such as the problem of simulation modelling, application of the methods of spatial analysis, sampling at the regional and intrasite level, site catchment analysis, etc.) under the influence of British and American publications (e.g. Dulinicz 1983; Kobyliński 1986, 1987; Kobyliński and Urbańczyk 1984), but they have not seriously touched the traditional model of settlement studies. Settlement archaeology is therefore still considered only an introductory stage of research, the ultimate goal of which is to define geographical ranges of socio-cultural systems. Analyses of maps are qualitative in nature and ignore the danger of identifying the constructed maps with a past socio-cultural reality (Dulinicz and Kobyliński 1990).

In the second half of the 1970s a renewed interest in the theory of archaeological sources became apparent. This subject, as has already been noted, was traditionally seen as one of the most important, and the main error of the New Archaeology was seen to be the lack of discussion of this question (Urbańczyk 1981b). The New Archaeology has been termed positivistic because of the lack of consideration it gives to the complex nature of processes creating the archaeological source. Some of the problems studied by Polish archaeologists were: what is the ontological status of an archaeological source; how objective is the archaeological record; what kind and amount of information on the socio-cultural past is lost during the source-creating processes, etc. (Maetzke et al. 1981; Maetzke 1986; Urbańczyk 1981b). During this discussion it has been stressed by many scholars that facts are co-created by the researcher, and even the archaeological techniques of excavation are theory-laden (e.g. Czerniak 1985). Again, these statements were in large measure stimulated by the opinions of theoreticians of history, such as Stanisław Piekarczyk, active in the Warsaw University milieu, who stressed that the model created by the historian is not only a model of studied reality, but is also a model of his or her own 'mental template' (Piekarczyk 1976; Topolski 1977). Within this framework some attempts were recently undertaken to present biases inherent in any classification of archaeological data (e.g. Kobyliński 1990; Tomaszewski 1988a).

This consciousness has led some archaeologists to an idealistic position advocating the humanism of archaeology against the tendency to formalise, quantify and computerise the archaeological record. Such a theoretical position is to a large degree a consequence of the recent 'discovery' of phenomenology and hermeneutics by some younger archaeologists in Poland (e.g. Lichy 1988; Makiewicz and Prinke 1981; Maryniak 1986; Posern-Zieliński 1982). However, Polish philosophers and historians had shown that some specifically humanist interpretation (i.e. one taking the premise that people's behaviour is rational and based on their knowledge, see Kmita 1971; Topolski 1973b) is not necessarily incompatible with the explanations used in the natural sciences, or calling it 'understanding', as opposed to 'explanation' (Nowak 1978; Topolski 1978: 8–34). The neurophysiological theory of two modes of thinking – analogic or preverbal, and categorical or abstract, hemispherically localised and with completely different characteristics (see Beck 1978) – has also been used as an argument against hermeneutical insight (Kobyliński 1989). According to this concept, all study of the meaning of past cultural phenomena should take account of the continuous transition away from a preponderantly analogical, and towards a preponderantly abstract, mode of thinking in humans, as a result of the evolution of the functional asymmetry of brain hemispheres due to social training. Consequently, although a modern person is still capable of symbolic thinking, the historical process of evolution of thought makes it impossible to 'understand' past symbols (Kobyliński 1988c). It is, rather, structural semiotics which gives archaeologists guidelines for interpreting the culturally meaningful remains of past societies (Augustynowicz 1988).

Polish ethnography and archaeology 'discovered' structuralism in the 1970s, following the translation of books by Claude Lévi-Strauss and members of the Soviet semiotic school from Tartu (e.g. Zalizniak et al. 1977). The discovery brought a real change to the way of doing ethnography in Poland (e.g. Wasilewski 1980; Stomma 1986). So far there have been few attempts to apply these methodologies to the studies of archaeological remains (e.g. Tomicki 1974; Kobyliński 1988d), although some research programmes have been published (e.g. Horbacz and Lechowicz 1981; Kobyliński 1988c). According to some authors, an archaeological source belongs generally if not exclusively among those sources which can be defined as direct, not addressed, and must not be included in the category of signs (Negroni Catacchio 1986). According to many others, even an artefact with primary techno-utilitarian functions bears semiotic information and may be open to cultural interpretation. Theory and methods for studying such cognitive prehistoric systems were discussed during a conference in Warsaw in 1982, organised by archaeologists of the youngest generation (Kobyliński et al. 1988). So far, the phenomenological approach, whose main influence is Eliade, prevails in Polish works in 'comparative symbology'. This approach has produced inventories of (essentially or only superficially) similar material symbols in various regions and various cultures in the search for universal archetypes (e.g. Krzak 1985), rather than studies attempting to understand the contextual meaning of particular symbolic systems.

A very important Polish contribution to studies of cognitive systems is the theory of polysemantisation of cultures, in which the Polish philosopher and writer Stanisław Lem (1965; see also Piekarczyk 1972) has shown that it is naïve to think that in a complex community only one semiotic system would have operated at one time. In previous archaeological literature this problem was often neglected, which produced socio-cultural models of past reality which were completely non-historical (Urbańczyk 1981b). The question of the initial moment of the process of cultural polysemantisation has been the subject of interest particularly for Tabaczyński (e.g. 1987: 73–9), who would tend to place it as early as the neolithic in Central Europe.

Quite a new area of theoretical research in Polish archaeology is what we could call 'sociology', or even 'psychology of knowledge'. The influence of the archaeologist's own value system on his or her statements and theories had already been indicated (e.g. Kloska 1977; Kobyliński and Połubińska 1982), but important developments stimulating reflection on the extra-archaeological – both philosophical and commonsensical – factors conditioning our archaeological theories have come only recently from the post-processual trends abroad. A paper on 'Neolithic chauvinism' in northern Norwegian archaeology (Olsen 1988) inspired studies on 'Mesolithic chauvinism' in Polish theories of neolithisation (Tomaszewski 1988b, 1991). Studies of the images of man in various archaeological theories and their commonsense basis were undertaken recently by Stoczkowski (1990) under the inspiration of J.-P. Gardin, his university tutor and adviser. I would expect more works of this type to appear soon, especially ones revealing the external ideological and political sources of images of the past created in East European archaeologies after the last war.

Conclusion

There are various theoretical orientations, more or less self-conscious, in the Polish archaeological milieu at present. Following the recent dramatic political changes in Poland and the whole of Eastern Europe one could predict that the importance of Marxist orientations, no longer supported by official ideology, would diminish significantly. However, I would rather suggest an opposite scenario. Free from the hated compulsory ideology which prevented any serious interest in Marxist philosophy, Polish archaeologists will now be able to explore Marxian theory dispassionately.

In any case, despite many differences, what unites structural semiotics and phenomenology with dialectical Marxism is an ontological perspective which, contrary to neopositivism, treats the superficial layer of reality which is accessible to direct archaeological observation, as a particular sign of a hidden structure, which should be the actual object of study.

Thus Polish archaeology, or rather its small, most conscious part, regardless of its Marxist or structuralist orientation, rejects the 'colloquial', commonsense understanding of the object of perception of the discipline. According to Polish philosophers, making this rejection is a sign that it has crossed the threshold which leads to a really theoretical science.

Note

1. I wish to thank Ian Hodder both for the inspiration for this chapter and for his helpful suggestions on an earlier draft.

References

Amsterdamski, S. (1983) *Nauka a porzadek swiata*, Warsaw: PWN.

Antoniewicz, W. and Wartołowska, Z. (1955) 'Archeologia, jej cele i zadania', *Dawna Kultura* 2: 97–103, 180–4.

Augustynowicz, G. (1988) 'Rzeczy i mity', in Z. Kobyliński., B. Lichy and P. Urbańczyk (eds) *Myśl przez pryzmat rzeczy*, Warsaw: ODZ.

Balcer. B. (1970) 'W sprawie klasyfikacji materiałów krzemiennych', *Wiadomości Archeologiczne* 35: 147–63.

Baranowski, T. (1974) 'Pojęcie kultury archeologicznej', *Kwartalnik Historii Kultury Materialnej* 22: 155–64.

Beck, B. (1978) 'The metaphor as a mediator between semantic and analogic modes of thought', *Current Anthropology* 19: 83–97.

Bogucki, P. (1985) 'Theoretical directions in European archaeology', *American Antiquity* 50: 780–8.

Bogucki, P. I and Grygiel, R. (1980) 'On the socioeconomic system of European Neolithic populations', *Current Anthropology* 21: 803–4.

Brzeziński, W., Dulinicz, M., Kobyliński, Z., Lichy, B. and Moszczyński, A. (1985) 'Rozpoznawanie stanowisk osadniczych metoda reprezentacyjna', *Sprawozdania Archeologiczne* 37: 251–70.

Buko, A. (1990) *Ceramika wczesnopolska*, Wroclaw: Ossolineum.

Bukowski, Z. (1984) 'Problematyka osadnicza dorzecza Odry, Wisły i Bugu w II i w I poł. I tysiąclecia p.n.e. jako jeden z elementów poznawczych dla badań nad topogenezą Słowian', *Archeologia Polski* 29: 291–315.

Burbelka, J. (1980) *Epoki i formacje. Proba rekonstrukcji adaptacyjnej*, Wroclaw: Ossolineum.

Buksiński, T. (1982) *Metodologiczne problemy uzasadniania wiedzy historycznej* Warsaw: PWN.

Clarke, D. L. (1968) *Analytical Archaeology*, London: Methuen.

Courbin, P. (1982) *Qu'est-ce que l'archéologie? Essai sur la nature de la recherche archéologique*, Paris: Gallimard.

Czerniak, L. (1985) 'Uwagi na temat statusu poznawczego "wiedzy źródłowej" w prahistorii', *Archeologia Polski* 30: 459–69.

Czerniak, L. and Kosko, A. (1987) 'Prehistory and the "theoretical turn" in science', *Folia Praehistorica Posnaniensia* 3: 43–63.

Czerniak, L. and Piontek, J. (1980a) 'Próba modelowego opisu form organizacji społecznej i gospodarczej ludnosci "kultur wstęgowych" na podstawie analizy zespołow osadniczych typu Brześć Kujawski', *Archeologia Polski* 24: 335–61.

Czerniak, L. and Piontek, J. (1980b) 'The socioeconomic system of European Neolithic populations', *Current Anthropology* 21: 97–100.

Drozdek, A. (1980) 'On determining the origin of archaeological culture', *Norwegian Archaeological Review* 13; 61–8.

Dulinicz, M. (1983) 'Niektóre aspekty zastosowania w archeologii geograficznych metod analizy przestrzennej osadnictwa', *Kwartalnik Historii Kultury Materialnej* 31: 299–315.

Dulinicz, M. and Kobylinski, Z. (1990) 'Archeologiczne mapy osadnicze i ich przydatność do koomputerowej analizy przestrzennej', *Archeologia Polski*, in press.

Dymaczewski, A. (1968) 'O systematyzacji typologicznej w archeologii', *Slavia Antiqua* 15: 263–74.

Eggers, H. J. (1959) *Einfuhrung in die Vorgeschichte*, Munich: Piper Verlag.

Frankowska, M. (1973) 'Etnografia polska po II wojnie swiatowej', in M. Terlecka (ed.) *Historia etnografii polskiej*, Wroclaw: Ossolineum.

Gediga, B. (1971) 'Z zagadnień obiektywności dokumentacji archeologicznej', *Acta Universitatis Wratislaviensis. Studia Archeologiczne* 4: 71–9.

Godłowski, K. (1962) 'Uwagi o niektórych zagadnieniach interpretacji źrodeł archeologicznych', *Prace i Materiały Muzeum Archeologicznego i Etnograficznego w łodzi. Seria Archeologiczna* 8: 79–99.

—— (1976) 'W sprawie modelu postępowania badawczego w archeologii', *Historyka* 6: 73–9.

—— (1979) *Z badań nad zagadnieniem rozprzestrzenienia Słowian*, Cracow: UJ.

Grygiel, R. (1987) 'Uwagi na marginesie polemiki Lecha Czerniaka i Janusza Piontka', *Archeologia Polski* 32: 394–9.

Henneberg, M. (1975) 'Notes on the reproduction possibilities of human prehistorical populations', *Przeglad Antropologiczny* 41: 75–89.

Henneberg, M. and Ostoja-Zagórski, J. (1977) 'Próba modelowej rekonstrukcji gospodarki mieszkańców halsztackich grodów typu biskupińskiego', *Kwartalnik Historii Kultury Materialnej* 25: 319–40.

Henneberg, M., Piontek, J. and Strzałko, J. (1978) 'Natural selection and morphological variability: the case of Europe from neolithic to modern times', *Current Anthropology* 19: 67–82.

Henneberg, M., Ostoja-Zagórski, J., Piontek, J. and Strzałko, J. (1975) 'Główne załozenia teoretyczno-metodyczne oraz mozliwości badań biologii populacji pradziejowych w Europie Srodkowej', *Przeglad Archeologiczny* 23: 187–231.

Hensel, W. (1946) *Potrzeba przygotowania wielkiej rocznicy*, Poznan.

—— (1958) 'W sprawach terminologicznych', *Wiadomości Archeologiczne* 25: 175–9.

—— (1973a) 'Zakres i zadania archeologii', *Slavia Antiqua* 20: 131–5.

—— (1973b) 'Etnogeneza Słowian – niektóre problemy', *Slavia Antiqua* 20: 1–14.

—— (1974) 'Pomniki kultury – źródłem świadomości narodu', *Archeologia Polski* 19: 279–82.

—— (1978) 'A method of ethnic qualification of archaeological sources', *Archaeologia Polona* 18(1977): 7–35.

—— (1984a) 'La sémantique logique dans l'archéologie', *Archaeologia Polona* 21/22(1983): 173–85.

⌐—— (1984b) *Skad przyszli Słowianie*, Warsaw.

—— (1986) 'Archeologia. Treść i zakres', in W. Hensel, G. Donato and S. Tabaczyński (eds) *Teoria i praktyka badań archeologicznych*, Wroclaw: Ossolineum.

Hodder, I. (1982) 'Theoretical archaeology: a reactionary view', in I. Hodder (ed.) *Symbolic and Structural Archaeology*, Cambridge: Cambridge University Press.

Hołubowicz, W. (1955) 'Uwagi o historii kultury materialnej jako nauce', *Kwartalnik Historii Kultury Materialnej* 3: 563–85.

—— (1961) *O metodzie publikacji żródeł archeologicznych*, Warsaw: Ossolineum.

Horbacz, T. and Lechowicz, Z. (1981) 'O wybranych aspektach poznania w archeologii', *Archeologia Polski* 26: 403–9.

Jazdzewski, K. (1969) 'O mozliwościach poznawczych archeologii w kwestiach etnicznych', *Prace i Materiały Muzeum Archeologicznego i Etnograficznego w zodzi. Seria Archeologiczna* 16: 7–21.

—— (1981) *Pradzieje Europy*, Warsaw: PWN.

Klawiter, A. (1974) 'On the status of historical materialism', in L. Nowak (ed.) 'Polish contributions to historical materialism', *Revolutionary World* 14 (special issue).

Kloska, G. (1977) 'Wartości w poznaniu historycznym' in J. Litwin (ed.) *Zagadnienia historiozoficzne*, Warsaw: PWN.

Kmita, J. (1971) *Z metodologicznych problemów interpretacji humanistycznej*, Warsaw: PWN.

—— (1973) 'Semiotyka humanistyczna wobec tzw. zasady "dostatecznej racji" w badaniach historycznych', in *Problemy nauk pomocniczych historii* vol. 2, Katowice.

—— (1976) *Szkice z teorii poznania naukowego*, Warsaw: PWN.

Kobylińska, U. (1980a) 'Problemy, metodyi implikacje amerykańskie; "socjologii ceramicznej" ', *Archeologia Polski* 25: 193–203.

—— (1980b) 'Jamesa Sacketta koncepcja stylu w archeologii', *Archeologia Polski* 24: 413–40.

—— (1981) 'Sambian style in the early Roman period: problem of the origin and development of aesthetic norms', *Archaeologia Polona* 20: 123–58.

Kobylińska, U. and Kobyliński, Z. (1981) 'Kierunki etnoarcheologicznego badania ceramiki', *Kwartalnik Historii Kultury Materialnej* 29: 43–53.

—— (1982) 'W kierunku systemowego badania ceramiki zabytkowej: koncepcje Sandera E. van der Leeuwa', *Archeologia Polski* 27: 449–57.

—— (1985) 'Symulacja, idealizacja i "indukcjonizm" w badaniach ceramiki zabytkowej', *Archeologia Polski* 30: 229–34.

—— (1990) 'Pottery types and modes of production', *Archeologia Polski*.

Kobyliński, Z. (1981a) 'Badania etnoarcheologiczne a nomotetyzacja archeologii', *Archeologia Polski* 26: 7–47.

—— (1981b) 'Archeologia jako nauka historyczna', *Archeologia Polski* 26: 219–25.

—— (1984) 'Problemy metody reprezentacyjnej w archeologicznych badaniach osadniczych', *Archeologia Polski* 29: 7–40.

—— (1985) 'Cognitive possibilities of ethnoarchaeology: some theoretical considerations', *Ethnologia Polona* 11: 273–80.

—— (1986) 'Koncepcja "terytorium eksploatowanego przez osade" w archeologii brytyjskiej i jej implikacje badawcze', *Archeologia Polski* 31: 7–30.

—— (1987) 'Podstawowe metody analizy punktowych układów przestrzennych', *Archeologia Polski* 32: 21–53.

—— (1988a) 'An ethnic change or a socio-economic one?: the fifth and sixth centuries AD in the Polish lands', in S. Shennan (ed.) *Archaeological Approaches to Culture Identity*, London: Allen & Unwin.

—— (1988b) 'The settlement structure and the settlement process: the identification of the continuity and change in a socio-cultural system in time', *Archaeologia Polona* 25/26: 121–55.

—— (1988c) 'Ethnoarchaeological cognition and cognitive ethnoarchaeology', in I. Hodder (ed.) *The Meanings of Things: Material Culture and Symbolic Expression*, London: Allen & Unwin.

—— (1988d) 'Things as symbols: the boat in the early medieval culture of northern Europe', *Archaeologia Polona* 27: 185–200.

—— (1989) 'Explanations or understanding: an attempt at critical analysis of antinaturalistic paradigms in archaeology', *Archaeologia Polona* 28.

—— (1990) 'Problemy klasyfikacji zjawisk kulturowych w archeologii', in J. Piontek (ed.) *Pojecie cechy w naukach o człowieku*, in press.

Kobyliński, Z. and Połubińska, K. (1982) 'Konflikt systemów wartości jako problem metodologiczny nauk antropologicznych', in J. Lipiec (ed.) *Człowiek i świat wartości*, Cracow: KAW.

Kobyliński, Z. and Tomaszewski, A. J. (1980) 'Rozwój nauk antropologicznych w perspektywie idealizacyjnej koncepcji nauki: przypadek archeologii', *Człowiek i Swiatopoglad* 5: 99–110.

Kobyliński, Z. and Urbańczyk, P. (1984) 'Modelowanie symulacyjne pradziejowych procesów osadniczych', *Kwartalnik Historii Kultury Materialnej* 32: 67–94.

Kobyliński, Z., Lichy, B. and Urbańczyk, P. (eds) (1988) *Myśl przez pryzmat rzeczy*, Warsaw: ODZ.

Konopka, M. (1978) 'Kultura archeologiczna – teoria i praktyka', *Archeologia Polski* 23: 183–91.

—— (1984) 'Carte des sites archéologiques en Pologne, methodes et organisation', *Archaeologia Polona* 21/22(1983): 187–216.

Kowalczyk, J. (1963) 'Terminologiczne konsekwencje', *Wiadomości Archeologiczne* 29: 1–5.

Kozłowski, J. K. (1972) 'On the typological classification of stone artifacts', *Sprawozdania Archeologiczne* 24: 455–66.

—— (1975) 'Model postępowania badawczego w archeologii', *Historyka* 5: 25–45.

—— (1979) 'Uwagi o analogowym modelu etnologicznym w archeologii', *Historyka* 10: 83–99.

Kozłowski, J. K. and Kozłowski, S. K. (eds) (1983) *Człowiek i środowisko w pradziejach*, Warsaw: PWN.

Kruk, J. (1970) 'Z zagadnień metodyki badań poszukiwawczych', *Sprawozdania Archaeologiczne* 22: 445–56.

—— (1980) 'Remarks on studies concerning the geography of settlement of prehistoric communities', in R. Schild (ed.) *Unconventional Archaeology*, Wroclaw: Ossolineum.

Krzak, Z. (1985) 'Symbolika i funkcja dawnych labiryntów', *Archeologia* 34(1983): 211–19.

Kulczycki, J. K. (1955) 'Założenia teoretyczne historii kultury materialnej', *Kwartalnik Historii Kultury Materialnej* 3: 519–62.

Kurnatowski, S. (1971) 'O konieczności klasyfikacji czynności badawczych archeologów', *Sprawozdania Archeologiczne* 23: 307–11.

—— (1978) 'Funkcje analizy osadniczej w procesach badawczych nauk geograficznych i historyczno-społecznych ze szczególnym uwzglednieniem archeologii i prahistorii', *Przegląd Archeologiczny* 26: 147–87.

Labuda, G. (1957) 'Próba nowej systematyki źródeł historycznych', *Studia Zródłoznawcze* 1: 3–48.

Lech, J. (1988) 'O rewolucji neolitycznej i krzemieniarstwie. I. Wokół metody', *Archeologia Polski* 33: 273–345.

Lem, S. (1965) *Filozofia przypadku*, Craków: Wydawnictwo Literackie.

Lichy, B. (1988) 'Psychospołeczne determinanty obrządku pogrzebowego', in Z. Kobyliński, B. Lichy and P. Urbańczyk (eds) *Myśl przez pryzmat rzeczy*, Warsaw: ODZ.

Maetzke, G. (1986) 'Zródła archeologiczne jako odwzorowanie procesu społeczno-kulturowego', in W. Hensel, G. Donato and S. Tabaczyński (eds) *Teoria i praktyka badań archeologicznych*, Wroclaw: Ossolineum.

Maetzke, G., Pleszczyńska, E. and Tabaczyński, S. (1981) 'Problems of inference based on stratigraphic sequences: a tentative model', *Archaeologia Polona* 20: 159–76.

Maetzke, G., Rysiewska, T., Tabaczyński, S. and Urbańczyk, P. (1978) 'Problemy analizy opisowej w badaniach wielowarstwowych obiektów archeologicznych', *Archeologia Polski* 23: 7–52.

Makiewicz, T. and Prinke, A. (1981) 'Teoretyczne mozliwości identyfikacji miejsc sakralnych', *Przegląd Archeologiczny* 28: 57–90.

Malinowski, T. (1980) 'Niektóre mozliwości określania zasięgów etnicznych w młodszych okresach pradziejów', *Słupskie Prace Humanistyczne* 1: 183–8.

Maryniak, B. (1986) 'Niektóre problemy metodologiczne zastosowania komputerów i informatyki w archeologii'. Paper presented at the conference on computer methods in archaeology, Warsaw.

Mazurowski, R. (1980) 'Metodyka archeologicznych badań powierzchniowych, Poznan: PWN.

Milisauskas, S. (1986) 'Selective survey of archaeological research in Eastern Europe', American Antiquity 51: 779–98.

Minta-Tworzowska, D. (1986) 'Model prahistorii inspirowany przez historiozofie', Archeologia Polski 31: 397–425.

Nadolski, A. (1963) 'Uwagi o metodzie publikacji źródeł archeologicznych', Kwartalnik Historii Kultury Materialnej 11: 83–9.

Negroni Catachio, N. (1986) 'Wytwarzanie wiedzy archeologicznej', in W. Hensel, G. Donato and S. Tabaczyński (eds) Teoria i praktyka badań archeologicznych, Wroclaw: Ossolineum.

Nowak, L. (1975) Idealization: a Reconstruction of Marx's Ideas, Amsterdam: Gruner.

—— (1977a) U podstaw dialektyki Marksowskiej, Warsaw: PWN.

—— (1977b) Wstęp do idealizacyjnej teorii nauki, Warsaw: PWN.

—— (1978) 'Humanistyka a przyrodoznawstwo: próba analizy programu antynaturalistycznego', Przegląd Antropologiczny 44: 119–26.

Olsen, B. (1988) 'Interaction between hunter-gatherers and farmers: ethnographical and archaeological perspectives', Archeologia Polski 33: 425–34.

Ostoja-Zagórski, J. (1974) 'From studies on the economic structure at the decline of the Bronze Age and the Halstatt Period in the North and West zone of the Odra and Vistula basins', Przegląd Archeologiczny 22: 123–50.

—— (1988) 'Empiria i teoria w badaniach archeologicznych', Archeologia Polski 33: 247–72.

Ostoja-Zagórski, J. and Strzałko, J. (1984) 'Biologic-cultural changes in the Halstatt period in the microregion of Sobiejuchy near Żnin, Bydgoszcz voivodship', Archaeologia Polona 23: 23–48.

Pałubicka, A. (1974) 'Pozytywistyczne oraz instrumentalistyczne ujęcia tzw. kultur archeologicznych', Studia Metodologiczne 12: 89–105.

—— (1977) Orientacje epistemologiczne a rozwój nauki, Warsaw: PWN.

Pałubicka, A. and Tabaczyński, S. (1986) 'Społeczeństwo i kultura jako przedmiot badań archeologicznych', in W. Hensel, G. Donato and S. Tabaczyński (eds) Teoria i praktyka badań archeologicznych, Wroclaw: Ossolineum.

Piątkowski, K. (1985) 'Problematyka teoretyczna w powojennej etnografii polskiej', Lud 69: 35–61.

Piekarczyk, S. (1970) 'Propozycje teorii', Przegląd Historyczny 61: 95–111.

—— (1972) 'Z problemów polisemantyzacji kultury', Studia Zródłoznawcze 16: 1–24.

—— (1976) 'Rozwazania o poznaniu historycznym', Studia Zródłoznawcze 20: 141–62.

Piontek, J. (1982) 'Wielkość grupy lokalnej a badania ilościowe ceramiki', Archeologia Polski 27: 461–4.

—— (ed.) (1988) Szkice z antropologii ogólnej, Poznan: UAM.

Piontek, J. and Czerniak, L. (1981) 'Uwagi o rekonstrukcji rozwoju biologiczno-kulturowego populacji pradziejowych', *Przegląd Antropologiczny* 46:(1980): 329–36.

Pomorski, J. (1986) 'Historia teoretyczna wobec historii klasycznej', in *Pamietnik XIII Powszechnego Zjazdu Historyków Polskich*, Wroclaw: Ossolineum.

Posern-Zieliński, A. (1982) 'Inspiracja fenomenologiczna w archeologicznych studiach nad religiami społeczeństw pradziejowych', *Przegląd Archeologiczny* 30: 187–200.

Posern-Zieliński, A. and Ostoja-Zagórski, J. (1977) 'Etnologiczne interpretacje i analogie etnograficzne w postepowaniu badawczym archeologii i prahistorii', *Slavia Antiqua* 24: 39–70.

Prinke, A. (1973) 'Mozliwości porównawczego stosowania danych etnograficznych w archeologii', *Etnografia Polska* 17: 41–65.

Rysiewska, T. (1980) 'La structure patriarcale des clans comme type hypothétique de la structure sociale des groupes humaines dans la culture lusacienne', *Archaeologia Polona* 19: 7–48.

Sackett, J. R. (1977) 'The meaning of style in archaeology: a general model', *American Antiquity* 42: 369–79.

Schild, R. (1965) 'Remarques sur les principes de la systématique culturelle du Paleólithique', *Archeologia Polona* 8: 67–81.

—— (1980a) 'Preface', in R. Schild (ed.) *Unconventional Archaeology* Warsaw: Ossolineum.

—— (1980b) 'Introduction to dynamic technological analysis of chipped stone assemblages', in R. Schild (ed.) *Unconventional Archaeology* Warsaw: Ossolineum.

Schild, R., Marczak, M. and Królik, H. (1975) *Pożny mezolit*, Warsaw: Ossolineum.

Stoczkowski, W. (1988) 'Kłopoty z "nowa archeologia", czyli o teorii i pozytywiźmie', *Archeologia Polski* 33: 461–71.

—— (1990) 'Miedzy archeologia metafizyka, czyli rozwazania o regułach spekulacji', *Archeologia Polski*, in press.

Stomma, L. (1986) *Antropologia kultury wsi polskiej XIX w.* , Warsaw: PAX.

Szmatka, J. (1980) *Jednostka i społeczeństwo*, Warsaw: PWN.

Sztompka, P. (1981) 'Marksowski model człowieka', *Poznańskie Studia z Filozofii Nauki* 6: 261–84.

Tabaczyńska, E. and Tabaczyński, S. (1973) 'Archeologiczne problemy etnogenezy i ekspansji ludów Bantu', *Archeologia Polski* 18: 201–13.

Tabaczyński, S. (1964) 'O aktualnych problemach warsztatu badawczego prahistoryka', *Archeologia Polski* 9:223–65.

—— (1966) 'Stuctures économiques des sociétés barbares en Europe centrale', *Archeologia Polona* 9:131–47.

—— (1971) 'Kultura. Znaczenie pojęcia i problemy interpretacyjne w badaniach archeologicznych', *Archeologia Polski* 16: 19–36.

—— (1976) 'Kultura i kultury w problematyce badań archeologicznych', *Archeologia Polski* 21: 365–74.

—— (1984) 'Archeologia-historia-antropologia kultury (na marginesie "Teorii wiedzy historycznej" Jerzego Topolskiego)', *Kwartalnik Historii Kultury Materialnej* 32: 223–45.

—— (1985a) 'Tradycja pozytywistyczna wobec "nowej archeologii" (na marginesie ksiazki Paula Courbina *Qu'est-ce que l'archéologie?*)', *Archeologia Polski* 34(1983): 171–80.

—— (1985b) 'Zjawisko nieciągłości jako przedmiot analizy archeologicznej', *Folia Praehistorica Posnaniensia* 1(1984): 7–22.

—— (1987) *Archeologia średniowieczna*, Wroclaw: Ossolineum.

Tabaczyński, S. and Pleszczyńska, E. (1974) 'O teoretycznych podstawach archeologii (prezentacja i próba analizy pogladów D. L. Clarke'a)', *Archeologia Polski* 19: 7–94.

Tomaszewski, A. J. (1986) 'Metoda składanek wytworów kamiennych i jej walory poznawcze', *Archeologia Polski* 31: 239–77.

—— (1988a) 'Wytwory kamienne i styl', *Archeologia Polski* 33: 7–66.

—— (1988b) 'Foragers, farmers and archaeologists', *Archeologia Polski* 33: 434–41.

—— (1991) 'Est-ce que l'archéologie sert seulement à manger?' *Nouvelles de l'Archéologie*, in press.

Tomicki, R. (1974) 'Żmij, Żmigrody, Wały Żmijowe. Z problematyki religii przedchrześcijańskich Słowian', *Archeologia Polski* 19: 483–508.

Topolski, J. (1973a) 'Aktywistyczna koncepcja procesu dziejowego', in J. Kmita (ed.) *Elementy marksistowskiej metodologii humanistyki*, Poznan: PWN.

—— (1973b) 'Dyrektywa racjonalizowania działań ludzkich' in J. Kmita (ed.) *Elementy marksistowskiej metodologii humanistyki*, Poznan: PWN.

—— (1976) *Methodology of History*, Warsaw: PWN.

—— (1977) 'Marksistowska epistemologia a konstytuujaca rola pytań w pojmowaniu źródła historycznego', in J. Kmita (ed.) *Założenia teoretyczne badań nad rozwojem historycznym*, Warsaw: PWN.

—— (1978)*Rozumienie historii*, Warsaw: PWN.

Trudzik, Z. (1965) 'Zródła archeologiczne na tle problematyki kultury', *Archaeologia Polski* 10: 42–71.

—— (1971) 'O przedmiocie archeologii i jej procesie poznawczym', *Acta Universitatis Wratislaviensis Studia Archeologiczne* 4: 5–69.

Urbańczyk, P. (1980) 'Some problems of formal methods and computer science application against the background of contemporary archaeological theory and methodology', *Archaeologia Polona* 19: 97–114.

—— (1981a) 'Archeologia współczesności?' *Archeologia Polski* 26: 49–63.

—— (1981b) 'O mozliwościach poznawczych archeologii', *Przeglad Archeologiczny* 29: 5–52.

—— (1983) 'Dyskusja nie na temat', *Przeglad Archeologiczny* 32:213–7.

Wartołowska, Z. (1964) 'Metoda dialektyczna w badaniach archeologicznych', *Swiatowit* 25: 213–25.

Wasilewski, J. S. (1980) 'Das symbolische Universum der mongolischen Jurte', *Etnologia Polona* 5 (1979): 115–34.

Wielowiejski, J. (1970) 'Przedmiot i zakres historii kultury materialnej', *Kwartalnik Historii Kultury Materialnej* 18: 183–91.

Wyszomirska, B. (1987) 'New approaches in Polish Stone Age research', *Norwegian Archaeological Review* 20: 11–30.

Zalizniak, A., Iwanow, W. and Toporow, W. (1977) 'O mozliwościach strukturalno-typologicznych badań semiotycznych', in E. Janus and M. R. Mayenowa (eds) *Semiotyka kultury*, Warsaw: PIW.

Żak, J. (1966) 'Historia pierwotna i jej wspołczesne metody', *Studia Metodologiczne* 2: 67–89.

—— (1968) 'Archeologia w systemie nauk historycznych', *Archeologia Polski* 13: 455–73.

—— (1973) 'W sprawie trudności badań nad etnogenezą Słowian', *Slavia Antiqua* 20: 47–8.

—— (1975) 'Teoretyczne uwagi o refleksji prahistorycznej', *Archeologia Polski* 20: 259–73.

—— (1977a) 'Migracje Słowian w kierunku zachodnim w V/VI-VII w. n.e.', *Studia Historica Slavo-Germanica* 6: 3–30.

—— (1977b) 'O studiach osadniczych', *Archeologia Polski* 22: 421–4.

—— (1981) 'Początki ujęć syntetyzujacych pradzieje społeczeństw zamieszkujących miedzyrzecze Odry i Renu', *Studia Historica Slavo-Germanica* 10: 3–30.

—— (1985) 'O kontynuacji i dyskontynuacji społecznej i kulturowej na ziemiach nadodrzańskich i nadwiślańskich w V-V/VI w.n.e.', *Folia Praehistorica Posnaniensia* 1 (1984): 85–108.

10

RECENT THEORETICAL ACHIEVEMENTS IN PREHISTORIC ARCHAEOLOGY IN CZECHOSLOVAKIA

Evžen Neustupný

It is rather difficult to talk about a theoretical debate in an archaeo-logical community where theoretical issues are rarely formulated other than in conjunction with practical questions. Yet, any kind of enquiry is always accompanied by some sort of theory and methodology, even if they are not expressed in theoretical works. Another aspect of the theoretical debate is connected with the interpretation of the concept of theory. There has been a tendency recently to narrow this concept down to the most general, more or less philosophical, level. My conception is much broader: archaeological theory is constituted by any set of general state-ments concerning any level of archaeological enquiry.[1]

Turning to Czechoslovakia, it might be useful to characterise in brief the situation in archaeological theory prior to the 1960s. The first half of this century was dominated by what I call typo-logical paradigms; more specifically, these took one of the follow-ing forms: either Montelius's typology, or the diffusionism derived from the Vienna culture-historical school, or Kossinna in a mild, non-aggressive form. Some archaeologists used an eclectic mixture of more than one variant of the typological paradigm (see Neus-tupný 1976).

Events of the 1940s had revolutionised the intellectual atmos-phere in Czechoslovakia. First, there was the war, which upset accepted values, and was followed by two years of rapid social development which inevitably affected archaeology. Archaeol-ogists were unanimous in the belief that their science was part of history, and that archaeological finds should bear on more questions than formal typological classification (e.g. Böhm 1953; Filip 1953). The typological paradigm, however, was far from being abandoned: new questions and new attitudes emerged, but nobody knew how to answer them on the basis of archaeological finds.

I should like to stress two other interesting facts. The first is that unlike most of their West European colleagues, Czechoslovak archaeologists have taken intensive philosophy courses. These university courses were compulsory, and comprised lectures in Marxist philosophy (including epistemology and what could be described as the most general level of theoretical sociology), detailed study of selected works by Marx and Engels, and further reading of philosophical literature, mainly in translation from Russian. Virtually every archaeologist of the middle and younger generations has undergone a similar training in political economy.

Another influence was the Soviet archaeological and ethnographical literature which was widely studied in Czechoslovakia in the 1950s. This literature, study of which was also compulsory, presented many questions concerning economics, social relations, prehistoric religion, etc. The solutions given were mostly deductions from the general theory but this made archaeologists aware that such questions could be asked, and some colleagues tried to make their own conclusions on the basis of their finds.

Thus, at the beginning of the 1960s, Czechoslovak archaeologists were equipped with several of the areas of the theoretical knowledge they would need to devise a new framework: the basics of philosophy, economics and epistemology, general sociological theory, and a new set of questions produced by this theory. This is not to say that everybody used their non-archaeological training when approaching their finds. One of the main reasons for this 'failure' was the fact that there was no acceptable theory on a level immediately applicable to archaeological finds. The general philosophical theory was conceptually too distant, and its applications almost exclusively concerned with modern history, a conceptually different field.

I will now discuss my personal way out of the typological paradigm since in my own case I can describe not only the results but perhaps also the motivation. I shall return to the attempts made by other Czechoslovak archaeologists later. In my thesis, 'The beginnings of patriarchy in Central Europe' (presented 1964, published 1967), I started from the question of what was the decisive development in the economy of the aeneolithic period (as opposed to the preceding neolithic). I asked how this development (which turned out to be the plough) influenced aeneolithic co-operation, various forms of the division of labour, exchange and ownership. Then I considered the problem of how the relations of production determined the concrete configuration of natural communities, local communities and patriarchy (the term I used to denote the social system of the prehistoric communities of Central Europe in the aeneolithic period). At the end of my thesis I traced the changes that had taken place in this social system during the succeeding Bronze Age and the beginning of the Iron Age. I used a modelling method which seemed to me the only one capable of bridging the gap between the dead, static system of the archaeological record on the one hand, and the dynamic system of the living prehistoric societies on the other. My work was well received and many later papers and books published in Czechoslovakia followed the same line of thought, at least in some areas (Pleslová-Štiková 1972; Pleiner and Rybová 1978; Základné 1978; Pleiner 1979; Bátora 1982; Oždáni 1986).

Prior to this work I published, together with my father Jiří Neustupný, a survey of the prehistory of Czechoslovakia, in the Peoples and Places series (Neustupný and Neustupný 1961). In a sense, and in some areas, it anticipated my 'Beginnings of patri-archy' but being based predominantly on records worked on within the typological paradigm, it appeared somewhat dogmatic in certain places. The impression of dogmatism was a consequence of the lack of the appropriate analytical and synthetical methods necessary to process archaeological records before they can be compared to the models. I therefore studied statistics and infor-mation theory intensively, feeling that mathematics was crucial in this task. At that time I was unaware of the advances in numerical taxonomy, seriation, matrix analysis, factor analysis and other multivariate methods. It was only in the late 1960s that I came across the early works of the New Archaeologists and the early papers by David Clarke and Colin Renfrew. I immediately realised that I had found what I was looking for. I learned how to pro-gramme computers, experimenting a lot with various multivariate methods, mainly from the factor analysis family (Neustupný 1973a, 1973b, 1973c, 1978a, 1978b, 1979, etc.). Although I soon noticed that these methods had their own problems, I still consider them to be appropriate in many instances for the recovery of the structure of the archaeological record.

I have so far concentrated mainly on my personal approach to archaeological theory and method. There were, however, other archaeologists in Czechoslovakia at the same time who were also trying to pose new questions and solve them by new methods. They often met with similar obstacles to mine: the methods available were not sufficient to tackle important problems and could provide only half instead of two-thirds of the solutions. A strong theory-conscious group concentrated around the Bylany project (B. Soudský, I Pavlů, M. Zápotocká, J. Rulf, M. Zápotocký) and many archaeologists in Prague and Nitra also tried their luck in the field of theory and method. I shall try to sort out their efforts according to the questions they were dealing with.

Interest in general problems of archaeological theory and method was not widespread (J. Neustupný et al. 1960; E. Neustupný 1971, 1986a; several authors in Základné 1978; Pleiner and Rybová 1978; Malina 1981). The first group of problems frequently discussed concerned prehistoric economy. It was recognised that agriculture had been of prime importance ever since the neolithic period, and that the study of agriculture could not be equated with the description of agricultural tools, remains of cultivated plants and bones of domestic animals. Patterns of land use and quantitative relations within prehistoric agriculture became equally, if not more, interesting. Following the pioneering papers by J. Kudrnáč (1958, 1961, 1962) there have been many other studies, some of them quite recent (E. Neustupný 1967, 1969b, 1985; Soudský and Pavlů 1972; Pleiner and Rybová 1978; Beranová 1980, 1986, 1987; Rulf 1981; Waldhauser and Holodňák 1984; Peške 1985, 1987; Peške and Tintěra 1985; Holodňák 1987). The problem of nutrition is closely related (J. Neustupný 1952; Rulf 1981; Beranová 1981; E. Neustupný and Dvořák 1983; Vencl 1985).

Prehistoric agriculture, however, cannot be effectively studied without some knowledge of the quantitative aspects of prehistoric communities and without taking into account the space in which prehistoric peasants lived and worked. Demographic interests appear natural in this context (Stloukal 1962, 1964, 1985; Buchvaldek 1974; Strouhal 1978; Čilinská and Wolska 1979; Waldhauser 1979; Rulf 1979; E. Neustupný 1981a, 1982, 1983a, 1983b; Furmánek and Stloukal 1985; Holodňák 1987), as well as studies of the natural environment (Pavúk 1976, 1982; Rulf 1979, 1983, 1986; Peške 1981; Bouzek 1982; Zápotocká 1982; E. Neustupný 1985). The latter topic, of course, cannot be confined to the problem of adaptation to the natural conditions of living; it also involves changes in these conditions brought by the activities of prehistoric people (Ložek 1981, 1982; Opravil 1983; E. Neustupný 1985, 1987). Structured exploitation of space by individual communities has recently emerged as an important point at issue not only theoretically (Soudský 1973; E. Neustupný 1986b) but also in connection with the study of selected microregions (Soudský and Pavlů 1972; Zápotocký 1982; Pavluå 1983; Waldhauser 1984; Smrž 1986, 1987; Velímský 1986; Kuna and Slabina 1988). On the one hand, the study has been made possible by the remarkable density of prehistoric sites in Czechoslovakia; on the other hand, it is the result of large-scale rescue excavations sometimes covering several square kilometres. Some of the extensive excavations of settlement sites made it possible to approximate their internal structure (Soudský and Pavlů 1972; Pavlů 1977, 1983; Pavlů et al. 1986; Turková and Kuna 1987; Pleinerová and Hrala 1988; Dreslerová-Turková 1988). The advances made in the fields described above were facilitated by the work of many natural scientists who have been studying, often for decades, various ecofacts from archaeological excavations.

Non-agricultural production also received much attention. Our study of the extraction of raw materials has made some progress. Prehistoric quarzite mines have been uncovered but so far unsatisfactorily published (E. Neustupný 1966; Žebera 1966; Fridrich 1972). Quarries yielding stone for neolithic bracelets and aeneolithic axes have been identified (Fridrich and Kovářík 1980; Zápotocká 1984), as have traces of the mining of copper ores in the mountains of Slovakia (Točík and Bublová 1985). Some evidence in this field has been obtained in Bohemia (Čujanová and Prokop 1968; Waldhauser 1985). Places for the extraction of the raw material for the production of querns have also been uncovered (Fridrich 1972; Waldhauser 1981).

Functional analysis of both the chipped and polished stone artefacts has been used (Vencl 1960, 1961, 1970; Svoboda 1985). Much effort has been devoted to the study of the technological aspects of iron production (Pleiner 1958, 1962, 1982) and sophisticated methods have been applied successfully to the study of prehistoric pottery (Pelikán 1961; Bareš and Lička 1976; Weber and Šebela 1976; Lička and Bareš 1979; Bareš *et al.* 1982; Šaldová 1981).

All the studies concerned with non-agricultural production are of considerable consequence. If they are to testify to the state of prehistoric societies, however, it is necessary to formulate the implications in the relations of production, i.e. to determine exactly how the changes in technology affected concrete forms of co-operation, division of labour, exchange and ownership. No innovation in the sphere of the production of material goods, agricultural or other, can have a direct impact on a prehistoric community; it is always through the relations of production that this impact occurs. These relations, however, and their patterning have rarely been discussed (E. Neustupný 1967; Furmánek 1973; Furmánek, Bánesz, S. Dušek, M. Dušek, Benadík, Miroššayová, and Demeterová in Základné 1978). This is not surprising considering that the direct connection between technology and social organisation was often believed to be natural within materialistically orientated archaeological theory.

It is, of course, possible to describe changes in prehistoric societies as they appear in the archaeological record or as they can be inferred from written documents. This method, a more or less inductive procedure, has often been used by Czechoslovak archaeologists, just as it is by their colleagues throughout the world. Their attention has concentrated on two highly suitable topics, hill-forts (J. Neustupný 1968; Šaldová 1977; Filip 1978; Motyková *et al.* 1984) and cemeteries (Pleinerová 1959; Zápotocký 1964; Bouzek *et al.* 1966; Koutecký 1968; Pavúk 1972; Dušeková 1973, 1977; Čižmář 1972; Furmánek 1973, 1977; Sankot 1978; Waldhauser 1978; E. Neustupný 1978a, 1978b; Bouzek and Koutecký 1980; Bujna 1982; Bátora 1982; Nevizánsky 1984, 1985a, 1985b; Gojda 1984; Oždáni 1986; Bouzek 1986; Matoušek 1987). Comparatively few archaeologists used finds from settlement sites for this purpose or combined more groups of records (E. Neustupný and J. Neustupný 1961; Mašek 1961; Soudský 1966; Pleiner and Rybová 1978; Pleiner 1979; Salaš 1985). The hill-forts have often been taken to imply some kind of 'higher' social organisation because of the communal work which must have been invested in the building of ramparts, ditches, etc. This is no doubt true but, at the same time, it is a very abstract model. Similarly, the cemeteries disclose social 'differentiation' as there are differences in the wealth of grave goods and the arrangement of mortuary monuments. It has been believed that 'logical' inference can lead to inductively built theory. However, because no strict induction is able to lead to non-formal solutions, one always has to use a stipulative model from which some measure of knowledge is deduced. The success of such descriptions then depends on which model has been used; if the model is abstract (i.e. poorly specified), then the knowledge generated by archaeological 'facts' will be equally poor.

From my point of view, archaeological artefacts (and the higher artefactual entities) express certain functions, meanings and significances which they had in the living prehistoric society (E. Neustupný 1986a). Most artefacts have at the same time both a function and a meaning and/or significance. Function can be defined as the relation of the individual to his or her natural environment. Meaning reflects the relation of one person to another (or a group of people to another group). The significance of an artefact reflects the relation of its producer or user to a segment of his or her consciousness. The latter aspect, i.e. significance, has rarely been studied in detail (Soudský and Pavlů 1966; Šalkovský 1980; Oliva 1985; Kuna 1986, 1988), but many remarks in literature show that it was not completely unknown (e.g. Zápotocký 1966 in relation to the aeneolithic battleaxes). Unusual forms of graves have often been explained as symbolising the outstanding position of the deceased within his or her community, neolithic figurines symbolised the importance of the idea of fertility, early La Tène non-geometrical style distinguished its proprietors from the rest of the society that still lived in the 'geometrical' world typical since the neolithic period (E. Neustupný and J. Neustupný 1961). All these, however, were marginal notes, not to be compared to what has become known as symbolic archaeology in the last decade or so.

It is rather difficult to discover theoretical innovations in the field of studies orientated historically, i.e. towards either the history of ethnic groups or the history of artefact types. The impact of tradition was very strong: migrationist and diffusionist approaches predominated. Detailed chronologies of the neolithic and aeneolithic periods, both relative and absolute, have already prepared the way for future change, and the same is now true for most other subperiods of prehistory. Like several other archaeologists, I have hardly missed an opportunity to argue against migrations. The demographic approach to migrations has now obtained its theoretical basis (E. Neustupný 1981a, 1982, 1983a) but a switch to new attitudes can hardly be made without more interest in explaining the change in artefacts in terms of social factors.

In the post-war period there was little interest in the Indo-European question, but at least two attempts have been made. One of them is a development of traditional views (Pleiner and Rybová 1978), the other has been based on the continuity/disconti-nuity model (E. Neustupný 1961; J. Neustupný 1966, 1968, 1976). This model does not try to equate languages and ethnic groups with specific archaeological culture groups or even with individual types of artefacts; what it attempts is to identify, on the basis of detailed knowledge of the past culture, periods of continuous development and periods of discontinuity. Cultural continuity over large areas can be explained in ethnic terms. There were, however, many attempts at solving particular problems within the Indo-European question by concentrating on the origin and later displacements of Celts, Scythians, Thracians, Dacians and Ger-manic tribes. Solutions proposed were mostly based on the con-sideration of art styles, religions (mainly grave rituals) and artefact typology. As these questions were not treated as theoretical, I do not consider it necessary to discuss them in any detail. True, there was an unexpressed, maybe even unconscious, theoretical basis ultimately going back to Kossinna but the form in which these 'theories' were proposed was pragmatic. It should perhaps be made clear at this point that Czechoslovak prehistoric archaeol-ogists (with very few exceptions) never indulged in the kind of speculation which tries to prove that one or another nation, ethnic or language group was 'original' somewhere, or even superior to somebody. Consequently, the crisis of Kossinna's paradigm was different in Czechoslovakia from other Central European coun-tries where it caused a general retreat from any theoretical topic. Yet concern with migrations as the only explanatory principle was generally taken for granted.

Discussions about methodological questions in the 1960s were still largely concerned with traditional problems such as the nature of typological change, the definition of traditional archaeological entities (phases, culture groups, cultures, etc.), the reconstruction of relative sequences, etc. (J. Neustupný 1960, 1961b; J. Neus-tupný et al. 1960). One group of archaeologists continued to take their work in this direction even in later years (see some of the contributions in Bouzek and Buchvaldek 1971, Pleiner and Rybová 1978, Točík 1978, etc.).

There was, however, an ever-growing interest in ecofacts and the natural properties of artefactual entities. Thus, for example, the very first calibration of archaeological radiocarbon dates was devised in Czechoslovakia (Bucha and Neustupný 1967; E. Neustupný 1968, 1969a). Interest in archaeomagnetic dating (Bucha 1965, 1967; Bucha and Neustupný 1969) and geochemical and geophysical prospecting also started early (Pelikán 1955; Linington 1970) and was widely applied later (see many contributions in the volume *Geofyzika a archeologie* 1983; Tirpák 1983; Bálek *et al.* 1986), sometimes with significant refinements (Majer 1984). Probabilistic sampling and planning of excavations on probabilistic grounds followed later (E. Neustupný 1973c, 1984a). There was also interest in archaeoastronomy (Pleslová *et al.* 1980; E. Neustupný 1984b). This did not, of course, mean any deep changes in archaeology from the theoretical point of view but it was often just in these spheres that new questions arose and helped to undermine the typological paradigm. At least, it became more and more difficult to ignore the existence of the many kinds of ecofacts and the existence of radiocarbon dates.

Several authors expressed their views on various transformations turning the living prehistoric culture into an archaeological record. In some cases the existence of transformations just satisfied the need to express the idea that 'nothing is as simple as you believe' but in others it served as the starting point for the archaeological method, i.e. it demonstrated the necessity of modelling (Vencl 1968; E. Neustupný 1981b, 1986a, 1987; Beneš 1989).

The problem of databases was tackled for the first time by B. Soudský at Bylany as early as the 1960s, and the work was continued by I. Pavlů so that a computerised database for that rich site has now become available. Theoretical considerations on the same problem were discussed by a group of archaeologists in Moravia (Podborský *et al.* 1977; Salaš 1984). A general purpose database for Slovakia is available on a computer in Nitra and other similar ventures are in preparation.

Another line of research in methodology was concerned with mathematical methods. These methods were viewed not only as a means of grasping the quantitative aspect of the archaeological record but mainly as procedures able to reveal the formal structure of finds. In addition to methods of mathematical statistics there were plenty of others, mostly of a multivariate nature, based on graph theory, linear algebra, probability theory, systems theory, etc. Many of them have been tried in Czechoslovakia in connection with concrete archaeological records and most of them successfully (Neustupný 1973a, 1973b, 1973c, 1978a, 1978b, 1979; Pavlů 1977; Pleinerová and Pavlů 1979; Eisler *et al.* 1981, O. Soudský 1981, 1986; Bialeková and Tirpáková 1983; Pavlů *et al.* 1986; Turková and Kuna 1987; Dreslerová-Turková 1988). The indisputable fact that their impact upon Czechoslovak archaeology as a whole has been small can be explained as follows: once the methods had been successfully applied in a limited number of cases, their possibilities remained unexploited by other specialists who either did not understand them properly and were not willing to use a 'black box', or just did not consider them necessary for solving their problems rooted in the typological paradigm.

Most mathematical procedures are exploited in the stage of the archaeological method which I denote as synthesis of formal structures. As soon as such structures are found (irrespective of what kind of procedures, traditional or mathematical, have been used), the stage of their interpretation or explanation follows. In my opinion, this should be done by modelling, i.e. by comparing the structures with archaeological models derived in the long run from some kind of living reality such as described by ethnography, history, etc. Although I applied modelling as early as 1964 (E. Neustupný 1967), its more detailed description has been made only recently (E. Neustupný 1986a). I believe that an archaeological model should take the form of a theory, but one that can be used to interpret archaeological structures. Consequently, a model can have several variants. If it proves only partially compatible with the structures, it can be supplemented or progressively modified until a better fit is achieved. Thus, a model is not just a collection of isolated hypotheses arrived at randomly, but an internally structured system of logically deduced theses. Only when successfully tested against the corresponding formal structures does it become part of the theory of a segment of prehistoric reality. Clearly, models differ from ethnographic analogies which are concrete, historically conditioned pieces of knowledge about ethnographic societies. Yet ethnographic or historical analogies still prevail in the attempts at interpreting archaeological finds in Czechoslovak archaeology (Beranová 1980, 1987; Vencl 1984, 1985; Bouzek and Koutecký 1980; Oliva 1985, etc.).

It should be noted, at least briefly, that apart from ethnography, history, ethno-archaeology, etc., experimental archaeology also provides material for building up models. It has found several adherents in Czechoslovakia (Pleiner 1961; Malina 1980; Beranová 1981, 1987; Peške and Tintěra 1985; Pleinerová 1986; Peške 1987; Pleinerová and Neustupný 1987). Quantitative aspects of models, whether synchronic or diachronic, have been studied by means of mathematical modelling – rather simple at the beginning of the period covered by this chapter but more complex in recent years. This is a field where much can be expected in the future. The first attempts at quantifying variables contained in models derived from ethnography and history have been connected with the study of prehistoric agriculture (Kudrnáč 1962; E. Neustupný 1967; Soudský and Pavlů 1972; Waldhauser and Holodňák 1984; Holodňák 1987; Peške 1987; etc.); prehistoric demography and related questions form another field of study where mathematical modelling had been used more or less successfully (e.g. E. Neustupný 1983b; Neustupný and Dvořák 1983; Holodňák 1987).

Summing up the achievements of Czechoslovak archaeologists in the theoretical and methodological fields during the last quarter of the century and especially in the last decade, I hope not to be overoptimistic in stating that a lot of work has been done. It may not yet constitute a complete break with the traditional typological paradigm (and it is doubtful whether such a break would be desirable), but we have certainly reached the take-off point.

The achievements, however, could not remain unaffected by the development of thinking in archaeology in other countries. The influences, or diffusion of ideas, bring about more or less the same kind of controversy as the influences and diffusion that some archaeologists discover in prehistory. No scientific community will accept ideas which it considers alien and/or unnecessary. There is probably one exception: this is the case when the community or part of it (such as the youngest generation) wants to break with earlier ideas at any cost, usually to challenge a group of colleagues. Such a situation has not been typical of Czechoslovakia in the last two decades.

External influences on archaeology in Czechoslovakia can be divided into three currents. The first of these is undoubtedly the so-called New Archaeology which appeared attractive mainly because of its endeavour to combine new questions with new methods. The second current is the so-called behavioural archaeology which has clearly formulated certain problems connected with the opposition of dead and living culture. Such problems were not previously unknown in Central Europe, but few archaeologists were able to formulate them as clearly as Schiffer did (Schiffer 1976). The third current is only beginning to impinge: it is the so-called structural archaeology formulated by some British colleagues. We have certainly not paid enough attention to the symbolic nature, or what I call the significance, of many artefacts.

It must be pointed out, however, that most Czechoslovak archaeologists have not studied the primary sources of the three theoretical currents – partly because of their inaccessibility – and have often been limited to secondhand sources. This is mirrored, among other things, in the scarcity of references to the works of Binford, Renfrew, Clarke, Schiffer, Hodder and their associates. It would be, however, an oversimplification to reduce the phenomenon of the non-acceptance of American and British theoretical currents in Czechoslovakia to the inaccessibility of publications by their representatives. If people really want a book, they usually find a way of getting it. In fact, not that many are needed as in many cases the ideas expressed by an author in one book tend to reappear later, so that the most recent work is usually enough to convey his or her principal views.

Other reasons why these authors have not been accepted certainly include language. Czech and Slovak archaeologists who entered the discipline in the middle of this century were still orientated towards German archaeology which logically brought about a preference for German. Although this is rapidly changing in favour of English, it is still difficult for many Czechoslovak archaeologists to read complicated English texts with any certainty of understanding them properly. The problem of insufficient knowledge of English is compounded by the historical fact that in the last five decades Czechoslovak archaeologists have not travelled to English-speaking countries and have few personal contacts with their colleagues living there.

Then, another closely related problem complicates the situation further. The Marxist philosophy, sociology, economics, ethnography and history in which Czechoslovak archaeologists have been trained operates within a system of concepts which is often quite different from that of their American and British colleagues. Thus the problem of understanding is not limited to language: not only the words but even the concepts differ. I will not discuss the ideological aspect of accepting a foreign theory.

Thus, it is certainly not the desire to be original that makes archaeologists in some countries appear reticent towards theoretical achievements in the English-speaking world. Most archaeologists in any case have no theoretical aspirations and a large proportion of those who have would probably prefer to join a ready-made trend rather than labour to create something different. This, I feel, is true in any archaeological community.

I have given a list of archaeologists of the English-speaking countries who are usually accepted as representatives of the post-typological paradigm or paradigms. It is widely acknowledged that they did not work in a vacuum; in fact, studying their works, including the notes and references, reveals a network of opponents, predecessors and followers, as well as persons who arrived at similar conclusions independently. The last-mentioned category is admittedly large in parts of the world where other languages are spoken, but its members rarely appear in the bibliographies of the 'mainstream'. This is another historical fact which has to be accepted.

In my view, none of the above-mentioned mainstream steps in the construction of a new archaeological paradigm is fully acceptable in its present form; nor do I believe these steps to be mutually exclusive to the extent that some of their proponents hold. But I may not be a typical Czechoslovak archaeologist.

Postscript 1990

At the beginning of 1990 Ian Hodder asked me to bring my original manuscript up to date. When I compiled it in 1987, Czechoslovakia still lived under a neo-Stalinist regime which would not have allowed a critical appraisal of the theoretical achievements of Czechoslovak archaeology. In spite of this, I decided not to rewrite my contribution in 1990 but to comment on it.

I did not write anything untrue in the original text which precedes, but I could not write everything I wanted to without running the risk of its being the last thing I would ever write.

I particularly regret that I could not discuss the content of individual theories. This was something reserved for the former archaeological bureaucratic elite which was supposed to make its judgements in conformity with Communist Party policy. My discussion of these problems would necessarily disclose the inadequacy of the theories concerned, and this would contradict the official claim of overall progress.

I stressed the ideological training that Czechoslovak archaeologists received in the 1950s and 1960s. Why has it had such a limited effect on archaeological theory? The answer may be that the training was on a rather general, often dogmatic, level which made it difficult to use in specific instances. Moreover, the official 'Marxism' of that time included many theses based on nineteenth-century ethnography (e.g. 'matriarchy' as a stage in the development of humankind) which were hardly acceptable to most archaeologists but could not be discarded while party ideology was in control.

Surprisingly, political ideology seems not to have influenced the development of theory, as very few archaeologists accepted Marxism as a *political* theory. Most of them, however, adopted it as the one social theory to which they knew no alternative. I remember that some of my colleagues were strongly opposed to communism as a political doctrine but accepted many of the Marxian philosophical theses. This situation lasted until the 1960s.

Everything changed drastically after the Russian invasion of Czechoslovakia in 1968. The state ideology ceased to rely on Marxism, which was replaced by a purely political doctrine supporting the party bureaucracy ideologically. Marxism was still taught in schools but nobody believed it any more, so ideological pressure was relaxed. This allowed a climate in which an anti-theoretical archaeology could flourish. Fortunately, the New Archaeology could begin to creep in at that time, although few people had the courage to defend it openly.

Because the new political situation deepened the economic crisis of the country, access to new western literature and 'archaeological science' became very difficult, if not impossible. The regime's tendency to isolate the population from the west put a stop to most of the personal contacts between Czechoslovak archaeologists and their western colleagues, as only a very special class of scientists was allowed to travel more frequently, and even for non-scientific reasons.

Many archaeologists, including the present author, ceased to write on theory, concentrating instead on non-theoretical topics: theory became dangerous, whether Marxian or not, as it could engender conflict with some segment of the currently valid ideological doctrine.

Some colleagues who have never experienced a totalitarian regime may form the impression that I have brought in politics unnecessarily. But I would be glad if this were my last contact with politics.

Notes

1. I am taking this opportunity to present a review of the main theoretical and methodological problems discussed by Czechoslovak archaeologists in the last thirty years. I have completely omitted not only medieval archaeology (which is not 'prehistoric') but palaeolithic studies as well. Also, I have concentrated on topics rather than solutions. This approach frees me of the need to evaluate individual contributions, many of which are just building bricks of an as yet unfinished edifice. This concentration on topics may give a factographic appearance to some parts of this chapter but it also allows an insight into the wealth of ways in which even a small community can approach its territory's prehistoric past. The number of archaeologists in any one community can have an important influence on its theoretical interests: because with a lot of work to be done outside pure theory, and a limited number of people involved, we cannot expect the field of enquiry to be covered densely (many significant questions will not be discussed at all, other problems will receive attention only from time to time). Moreover, archaeologists who consider themselves historians are usually reluctant to become theoreticians using their finds as examples instead of as sources of knowledge. There is also a clear dependence between the development of theory and the wealth of artefacts found during excavations. It may be no accident that major theoretical volumes often appear in countries whose archaeological record is one-sided and comparatively poor. People working in areas where prehistoric finds turn up in great quantities on any occasion are usually more inclined to become antiquarians, art historians and/or positivists. In respect of its wealth of archaeological evidence Czechoslovakia occupies a middle position between the north and north-west of Europe on the one side and the south-east of our subcontinent on the other.

References

Bálek, M., Hašek, V., Měřínský, Z. and Segeth, K. (1986), 'Metodický přínos – Aerial survey and geophysical methods in archaeological investigations in Moravia', *Archeologické rozhledy* 38: 550–74.

Bareš, M. and Lička, M. (1976) 'K exaktnímu studiu – The exact study of prehistoric pottery', *Sborník Národního muzea v Praze A*, 30(3–4): 137–244.

Bareš, M., Lička, M. and Růžičková, M. (1981) 'K technologii – On the technology of neolithic pottery I', *Sborník Národního muzea v Praze A*, 35: 137–228.

Bátora, J. (1982) 'Ekonomicko-sociálny vývoj – Sozialökonomische Entwicklung der Ostslowakei in der älteren Bronzezeit', *Slovenská archeológia* 30: 249–314.

Beneš, J. (1989) 'Reprezentativnost mobilní části – Representativity of the mobile component of archeological cultures in comparison with ethnographic sources', *Archeologické rozhledy* 41.

Beranová, M. (1980) *Zemědělství starých Slovanů – Die Landwirtschaft der alten Slawen*, Prague: Academia.

—— (1981) 'Zur Frage des Ernährungseiflusses auf den Gesundheitszustand der Bevölkerung', *Anthropologie* 19: 165–70.

—— (1986) 'Otázka velikosti – Die Ackergrösse im Verhältnis zur Ernährung eines Menschen, einer Familie und eines Dorfes bei den Slawen und in der Vorzeit', *Archaeologica Pragensia* 7: 151–70.

—— (1987) 'Zur Frage des Systems der Landwirtschaft im Neolithikum in Mitteleuropa', *Archeologické rozhledy* 39: 141–98.

Bialeková, D. and Tirpáková, A. (1983) 'Preukázatel nost – Nachweisbarkeit der Benützung römischer Masse bei der Anfertigung von slawischer Keramik', *Slovenská archeológia* 31: 121–48.

Böhm, J. (1953) 'Studie o periodizaci pravěkých dějin – Study about the periodization of the primeval history', *Památky archeologické* 44:1–32.

Bouzek, J. (1982) 'Climatic changes and central European prehistory', in A. F. Harding (ed.) *Climatic Changes in Later Prehistory*, Edinburgh.

—— (1986) 'Die Möglichkeiten der Erforschung der Gefolgschaft in der mitteleuropäischen Vor- und Frühgeschichte', *Slovenská archeológia* 34: 293–97.

Bouzek, J. and Buchvaldek, M. (eds) (1971) *Nové archeologické metody I*, Prague: Karlova univerzita.

Bouzek, J. and Koutecký, D. (1980) 'Mohylové a knovízské – Skelettbestattungen in Gruben der Knovízer und Hügelgräberkultur aus Nordwestböhmen', *Památky archeologické* 76: 360–432.

Bouzek, J., Koutecký, D. and Neustupný, E. (1966) *The Knovíz Settlement of North-west Bohemia*, Prague: Národní muzeum.

Bucha, V. (1965) 'Archeomagnetický výzkum – Die archäomagnetische Forschung und ihre Verwendung zur Bestimmung des Alters der archäologischen Objekte', *Archeologické rozhledy* 17: 198–239.

—— (1967) 'Intensity of the earth's magnetic field during archaeological times in Czechoslovakia', *Archaeometry* 10: 12–22.

Bucha, V. and Neustupný, E. (1967) 'Changes of the Earth's magnetic field and radiocarbon dating', *Nature* 215: 261–3.

—— (1969) 'Archäomagnetische Forschung in der Slowakei', *Slovenská archeológia* 17: 233–45.

Buchvaldek, M. (1974) 'Erwägungen zur Bevölkerungsdichte im jüngeren Aeneolithikum', *Musaica* 14: 17–22.

Bujna, J. (1982) 'Spiegelung der Sozialstruktur auf latènezeitlichen Gräberfeldern in Karpatenbecken', *Památky archeologické* 73: 312–431.

Čilinská, Z. and Wolska, W. (1979) 'Štrukturálna a demografická analýza

– Strukturelle und demographische Analyse des frühgeschichtlichen Gräberfeldes in Želovce', *Slovenská archeológia* 27: 139–66.

Čižmář, M. (1972) 'Společenská struktura – Die Gesellschaftsstruktur der Kelten in Mähren im Lichte der Erforschung von Gräberfeldern', *Časopis Moravského muzea* 57: 73–81.

Čujanová, E. and Prokop, R. (1968) 'Měděná ložiska – Kupfererzlager in Westböhmen als die vermutliche Rohstoffquelle in der Bronzezeit', *Archeologické rozhledy* 20: 312–29.

Dreslerová-Turková, D. (1988) 'Možnosti využití – Possibilities of use of cluster analysis on the Late Bronze Age settlement structures', *Archeologické rozhledy* 40.

Dušeková, S. (1973) 'K otázce – Zur Frage der militärischen Demokratie in der urgeschichtlichen Entwicklung der Slowakei', *Slovenská archeológia* 21: 409–22.

Dušek(ová), S. (1977), 'Zur chronologischen und soziologischen Auswertung der Gräberfelder von Chotín', *Slovenská archeológia* 25: 13–46.

Eisler, J., Smetánka, Z. and Durdík, T. (1981) 'Možnosti využití – The possibilities of utilisation of computerized drawings in archaeology', *Archeologické rozhledy* 33: 199–208.

Filip, J. (1953) 'Keltská společnost – La société celtique à l'époque de La Tène', *Archeologické rozhledy* 5: 205–33.

—— (1978) 'Keltská opevnění – Celtic strongholds as an indicator and reflection of the evolution and the structure of Celtic society', *Archeologické rozhledy* 30: 420–2.

Fridrich, J. (1972) 'Paleolitické osídlení – Eine paläolithische Besiedlung bei Bečov', *Archeologické rozhledy* 24: 249–59.

Fridrich, J. and Kovářík, J. (1980) 'Příspěvek k dobývání – Ein Beitrag zur Gewinnung und Bearbeitung steinerner Rohstoffe im Aeneolithikum', *Archaeologica Pragensia* 1: 39–54.

Furmánek, V. (1973) 'K některým – Zu einigen sozialökonomischen Problemen der Bronzezeit', *Slovenská archeológia* 21: 401–8.

—— (1977) 'Pilinyer Kultur', *Slovenská archeológia* 25: 251–370.

Furmánek V. and Stloukal, M. (1985) 'Jihovýchodní popelnicová pole – South-eastern úrnfields in the light of the anthropological analysis', *Slovenská archeológia* 33: 137–52.

Geofyzika a archeologie (1983) Prague: Archeologický ústav.

Gojda, M. (1984) 'K problematice – The problems of burials with arms in central European cemeteries of the Roman period', *Archeologické rozhledy* 36: 67–89.

Holodňák, P. (1987) 'Methodische Probleme bei der Bestimmung von Populationsgrösse in der Latènezeit', *Anthropologie* 25: 143–54.

Koutecký, D, (1968) 'Velké hroby – Grossgräber, ihre Konstruktion, Grabritus und soziale Struktur der Bevölkerung der Bylaner Kultur', *Památky archeologické* 59: 400–87.

Kudrnáč, J. (1958) 'Stroslovanské obilnářství – Die altslawische Getreidewirtschaft in den böhmischen Ländern', *Památky archeologické* 49: 478–98.

—— (1961) 'Rekonstrukce přirozené krajiny – Die Rekonstruktion der

PREHISTORIC ARCHAEOLOGY IN CZECHOSLOVAKIA

natürlichen Landschaft in der Umgebung der durchforschten Burgstätten und Gemeinden', *Památky archeologické* 52: 609–15.

—— (1962) 'Okázka velikosti – Die Frage der Grösse des Hinterlandes zur Ernährung des Menschen in der Burgwallzeit', *Archeologické rozhledy* 14: 693–7.

Kuna, M. (1986) 'Artifacts as tools and signs: on the interpretation of the earliest metallurgy of copper', in *Archaeological 'Objectivity' in Interpretation* vol. 2, Southampton: World Archaeological Congress.

—— (1988) 'Soziale und ökonomische Faktoren der Entwicklung der frühen Kupfermetallurgie in Südost – und Mitteleuropa', *Praehistorica* 15.

Kuna, M. and Slabina, M. (1988) 'Zur Problematik der Siedlungsareale', in *Archäologische Rettungstätigkeit in den Braunkohlengebieten*, Most: Archeologický ústav.

Lička, M. and Bareš, M. (1979) 'Antropomorfní nádoba – Das anthropomorphische Gefäss aus dem Objekt Nr. VI/30 aus Buštěhrad', *Sborník Národního Muzea v Praze A* 33 (2–3): 69–172.

Linington, R. (1970) 'Prospecting methods in archaeology', *Archeologické rozhledy* 22: 169–94.

Ložek, V. (1981) 'Změny krajiny – Der Landschaftswandel in Beziehung zur Besiedlung im Lichte malakologischer Befunde', *Archeologické rozhledy* 33: 176–88.

Ložek, V. (1982) *Faunengeschichtliche Grundlinien zur spät– und nacheiszeitlichen Entwicklung der Moluskenbestände in Mitteleuropa*, Rozpravy ČSAV 92/4, Prague: Academia.

Majer, A. (1984) 'Relativní metoda – The relative method of phosphate analysis of soil', *Archeologické rozhledy* 36: 297–313.

Malina, J. (1980) *Metody experimentu v archeologii*, Studie AÚ ČSAV v Brně VII/1F, Prague: Academia.

—— (1981) *Archeologie včera a dnes – Archaeology yesterday and today*, České Budějovice: Jihočeské muzeum.

Mašek, N. (1961) 'Příspěvek k poznání – Beitrag zum Veständnis der wirtschaftlichen und socialen Verhältnisse in der jüngeren Phase des Aeneolithikums in Böhmen', *Památky archeologické* 52: 124–31.

Matoušek, V. (1987) 'Příspěvek ke studiu – A contribution to the study of the late Aeneolithic burial rite in Bohemia', *Archeologické rozhledy* 39: 199–208.

Motyková, K., Drda, P. and Rybová, A. (1984) Opevnění – Fortification of the late Hallstatt and Early La Téne stronghold of Závist', *Památky archeologické* 75: 331–444.

Neustupný, E. (1966) 'L'exploitation néolithique et énéolithique du quarzite à Tušimice', in *Investigations archéologiques en Tchécoslovaquie*, Prague: Academia.

—— (1967) *K počátkům patriarchátu ve střední Evropě – The Beginnings of Patriarchy in Central Europe* (Rozpravy ČSAV 77/2), Prague: Academia.

—— (1968) 'Absolute chronology of the neolithic and aeneolithic periods in central Europe', *Slovenská archeológia* 16: 19–60.

—— (1969a) 'Absolute chronology of the neolithic and aeneolithic periods in central and south-east Europe II', *Archeologické rozhledy* 21: 783–810.

—— (1969b) 'Economy of the Corded Ware cultures', *Archeologické rozhledy* 21: 43–68.

—— (1971) 'Whither archaeology?' *Antiquity* 45: 34–9.

—— (1973a) 'Factors determining the variability of the Corded Ware culture', in C. Renfrew (ed.) *The Explanation of Culture Change*, London: Duckworth.

—— (1973b) 'Jednoduchá metoda – A simple method of archaeological analysis', *Památky archeologické* 44: 169–234.

—— (1973c) 'Sekvenční metoda – Archäologische Ausgrabungen nach dem Prinzip der Sequenzmethode', *Archeologické rozhledy* 25: 300–28.

—— (1976) 'Paradigm lost', in *Glockenbechersymposion Oberried 1974*, Bussum/Haarlem.

—— (1978a) 'Mathematics at Jenišův Újezd', in J. Waldhauser (ed.) *Das keltische Gräberfeld bei Jenišův Újezd in Böhmen* Bd. II, Teplice: Krajské muzeum.

—— (1978b) 'Mathematical analysis of an aeneolithic cemetery', *Studia Praehistorica* 1–2: 238–43.

—— (1979) 'Vektorová syntéza – Vector synthesis of finds from settlement sites', *Archeologické rozhledy* 31: 55–74.

—— (1981a) 'Mobilität der äneolithischen Populationen', *Slovenská archeológia* 29: 111–9.

—— (1981b) 'Zachování kostí – Destruction of bones in prehistoric sites', *Archeologické rozhledy* 33: 154–65.

—— (1982) 'Prehistoric migrations by infiltration', *Archeologické rozhledy* 34: 278–93.

—— (1983a) 'The demography of prehistoric cemeteries', *Památky archeologické* 74: 7–34.

—— (1983b) *Demografie pravěkých pohřebišť – The Demography of Prehistoric Cemeteries*, Prague: Archeologický ústav.

—— (1984a) 'Archeologická prospekce – Prospecting by means of probabilistic methods', in *Nové prospekční metody v archeologii*, Prague: Archeologický ústav.

—— (1984b) 'Poznámky – Notes on astronomical orientation of prehistoric features', *Archeologické rozhledy* 36: 59–66.

—— (1985) 'K holocénu – On the Holocene period in the Komořany lake area', *Památky archeologické* 76: 9–70.

—— (1986a) 'Nástin – An outline of an archaeological method', *Archeologické rozhledy* 38: 515–39.

—— (1986b) 'Sídelní areály – Settlement areas of prehistoric farmers', *Památky archeologické* 77: 226–34.

—— (1987) 'Pravěká eroze – Prehistoric erosion and accumulation in the Lužice brook basin', *Archeologické rozhledy* 39: 629–43.

Neustupný, E. and Neustupný, J. (1961) 'Czechoslovakia before the Slavs', London: Thames & Hudson.

Neustupný, E. and Dvořák, Z. (1983) 'Výživa – Nutrition of prehistoric farmers: a model', *Památky archeologické* 74: 224–57.

Neustupný, J. (1949) 'Nový pohled – Nouvelles vues sur la muséographie préhistorique', Archeologické rozhledy 1: 80–1.

—— (1952) 'Alliaceous plants in prehistory and history', Archiv orientální 20: 356–85.

—— (1960) 'Some suggestions concerning archaeologic records and archaeologic cultures', Światowit 23: 31–40.

—— (1961a) 'K otázce – Problème de la limite entre la préhistoire et l'histoire', Památky archeologické 52: 13–17.

—— (1961b) 'The classification of groups of prehistoric finds according to the activity of man', in Bericht über den V. Internationalen Kongress für Vor- und Frühgeschichte Hamburg 1958, Berlin.

—— (1966) 'From Indo-Europeans to prehistoric Celts in central Europe', Revista de Faculdade de Letras de Lisboa III (10): 3–32.

—— (1968) 'Otázky pravěkého osídlení – Some problems of the settlement of Cechoslovak territory in prehistory', Sborník Národního muzea v Praze A 22 (2): 61–119.

—— (1976) 'Archaeological comments to the Indo-European problem', Origini 10: 7–18.

Neustupný, J., Hásek, I., Hralová, J., Břeň, J. and Turek, R. (1960) Pravěk Československa, Prague: Orbis.

Nevizánsky, G. (1984) 'Sozialökonomische Verhältnisse in der Polgár-Kultur aufgrund der Gräberfeldanalyse', Slovenská archeológia 32: 263–310.

—— (1985a) 'Grabfunde und Überbauerscheinungen der Träger der Badener Kultur im zentralen Gebiet des Karpatenbeckens', Slovenská archeológia 33: 249–72.

—— (1985b) 'Grabfunde der äneolithischen Gruppen der Lengyelkultur als Quelle zum Studium von Überbauerscheinungen', Archeologické rozhledy 37: 58–82.

Oliva, M. (1985) 'Úvahy – Some thoughts on certain productional and social aspects connected with the prehistoric polished industry', Časopis Moravského muzea 70: 17–36.

Opravil, E. (1983) Údolní niva v době hradištní – Die Talaue in der Burgwallzeit, Studie AÚ ČSAV XI/2, Prague: Academia.

Oždáni, O. (1986) 'Zur Problematik der Entwicklung der Hügelgräberkulturen in der Südslowakei', Slovenská archeológia 34: 5–95.

Pavlů, I. (1977) 'K metodice – To the methods of Linear pottery settlement analysis', Památky archeologické 68: 5–55.

—— (1983) 'Die Entwicklung des Siedlungsareals Bylany 1', in Siedlungen der Kultur mit Linearkeramik in Europa, Nitra: Archeologický ústav.

Pavlů, I., Rulf, J. and Zápotocká, M. (1986) 'Theses on the neolithic site of Bylany', Památky archeologické 77: 288–412.

Pavúk, J. (1972) 'Neolithisches Gräberfeld in Nitra', Slovenská archeológia 20: 5–105.

—— (1976) 'Zu einigen Fragen der Entwicklung der neolithischen Besiedlung in der Westslowakei', Jahresschrift Halle 60: 331–42.

—— (1982) 'Die Hauptzüge der neolithischen Besiedlung in der Slowakei in Bezug zu Naturbedingungen', in Medodoligické problémy československé archeologie, Prague: Archeologický ústav.

Pelikán, J. (1955) 'Fosfátová – Analyse pédologique de phosphates', *Archeologické rozhledy* 7: 74–84.

—— (1961) 'Rentgenometrie – Roentgenometrische Analysen der vorgeschichtlichen Keramik', *Památky archeologické* 52: 117–21.

Peške, L. (1981) 'Ekologická interpretace – Oekologische Interpretation der Holozänavifauna in der Tschechoslowakei', *Archeologické rozhledy* 33: 142–3.

—— (1985) 'Osteologické nálezy – Bone finds of the Bell Beaker culture from the site of Holubice and notes on the harnessing of cattle in the Aeneolithic', *Archeologické rozhledy* 37: 428–40.

—— (1987) 'Žárové zemědělství – Das Brandwirtschaftssystem aus der Sicht des NPK-Kreislaufs im Boden und dessen Erschöpfung', *Archeologické rozhledy* 39: 317–33.

Peške, L. and Tintěra, L. (1985) 'Pěstování pšenice – Der Anbau zweikörnigen Weizen auf einem durch Brandrodung gewonnene Grundstück', *Archaeologica Pragensia* 6: 221–9.

Pleiner, R. (1958) *Základy slovanského železářského hutnictví v českých zemích – Die Grundlagen der slawischen Eisenindustrie in den böhmischen Ländern*, Prague: Nakladatelství ČSAV.

—— (1961) 'Experiment – Versuche in der Vorgeschichtswissenschaft', *Památky archeologické* 52: 616–22.

—— (1962) *Staré evropské kovářství – Alteuropäisches Schmiedehandwerk*, Prague: Academia.

—— (1979) *Otázka státu ve staré Galii – The Problem of State in Ancient Gaul*, Prague: Academia.

—— (1982) 'Untersuchungen zur Schmiedetechnik auf den keltischen Oppida', *Památky archeologické* 73: 86–173.

Pleiner, R. and Rybová, A. (ed) (1978) *Pravěké dějiny Čech*, Prague: Academia.

Pleinerová, I. (1959) 'Otázka skupinových – Die Frage der Gruppenfriedhöffe in der Unjetitzer Kultur', *Archeologické rozhledy* 11: 379–408.

—— (1986) 'Březno: Experiments with building Old Slavonic houses and living in them', *Památky archeologické* 77: 104–76.

Pleinerová, I. and Hrala, J. (1988) *Březno. Osada lidu knovízské kultury v SZ Čechách – Březno. Die Siedlung des Volkers mit der Knovízer Kultur in Nordwestböhmen*, Ústí: Severočeské naklad.

Pleinerová, I. and Neustupný, E. (1987) 'K otázce – On the preparation and consumption of food in the Early Middle Ages', *Archeologické rozhledy* 39: 90–101.

Pleinerová, I. and Pavlů, I. (1979) *Březno. Osada z mladší doby kamenné v severozápadních Čechách – Březno, ein jungsteinzeitliches Dorf in Nordwestböhmen*, Ústí: Severočeské naklad.

Pleslová-Štiková, E. (1972) 'Hospodářský – Die sozialökonomische Entwicklung des mitteleuropäischen Aeneolithikums', *Zprávy Čs. společnosti archeologické* 14: 30–102.

Pleslová, E., Marek, F. and Horský, Z. (1980) 'A square enclosure of the Funnel beaker culture (3500 BC) at Makotřasy (Central Bohemia): a palaeoastronomic structure', *Archeologické rozhledy* 32: 3–35.

Podborský, V., Kazdová, E., Košturík, P. and Weber, Z. (1977)

Numerický kód moravské malované keramiky – Numerical Code of Moravian Painted Ware, Brno.

Rulf, J. (1979) 'K relativní hustotě – To the relative density of the neolithic and eneolithic settlement in Bohemia', *Archeologické rozhledy* 31: 176–91.

—— (1981) 'Poznámky k zemědělství – Notes on the central European neolithic and eneolithic agriculture', *Archeologické rozhledy* 33: 123–32.

—— (1983) 'Přírodní prostředí – Naturmilieu und Kulturen des böhmischen Neolithikums und Aeneolithikums', *Památky archeologické* 74: 35–95.

—— (1986) 'Environment of the earliest agricultural settlements of Bohemia', in *Archaeology in Bohemia 1981–1985*, Prague: Archeologický ústav.

Salaš, M. (1984) 'Návrh – Entwurf einer numerischen Deskription der neolithischen geschliffenen Steinindustrie', *Sborník prací FFBU E29*: 67–107.

—— (1985) 'Metalurgická – Metallurgische Erzeugung auf der bronzezeitlichen Höhensiedlung bei Blučina', *Časopis Moravského muzea* 70: 37–56.

Šaldová, V. (1977) 'Sociálně-ekonomické podmínky – Die sozial-ökonomischen Bedingungen der Entstehung und Funktion der Spätbronzezeitlichen Höhensiedlungen in Westböhmen', *Památky archeologické* 68: 117–63.

—— (1981) 'Westböhmen in der späten Bronzezeit', Prague: Archeologický ústav.

Šalkovský, P. (1980) 'Špirálová ornamentika – Die Spiralornamentik der älteren Bronzezeit in Karpatenbecken und im unteren Donaugebiet', *Slovenská archeológia* 28: 287–312.

Sankot, P. (1978) 'Struktur des Latènezeitlichen Gräberfeldes', in J. Waldhauser (ed.) *Das keltische Gräberfeld bei Jenišův Újezd in Böhmen*, Teplice: Krajské muzeum.

Schiffer, M. (1976) *Behavioural Archaeology*, New York: Academic Press.

Smrž, Z. (1986) 'Lužický potok. Research project into a micro-region of the Late and Final Bronze Age in NW Bohemia', in *Archaeology in Bohemia*, Prague: Archeologický ústav.

—— (1987) 'Vývoj a struktura – The development and structure of settlement in the microregion of the stream Lužický-potok in the area of Kadaň', *Archeologické rozhledy* 39: 601–21.

Soudský, B. (1966) *Bylany, osada nejstarších zemědělců z mladší doby kamenné – Bylany, station des premiers agriculteurs de l'âge de la pierre polie*, Prague: Academia.

—— (1973) 'Higher level archaeological entities: models and reality', in C. Renfrew (ed.) *The Explanation of Culture Change: Models in Prehistory*, London: Duckworth.

Soudský, B. and Pavlů, I. (1966) 'Interprétation historique de l'ornament linéaire', *Památky archeologické* 57: 91–125.

—— (1972) 'The Linear pottery culture settlement patterns of Central Europe', in P. Ucko, R. Tringham and G. Dimbleby (eds) *Ma, Settlement and Urbanism*, London: Duckworth.

Soudský, O. (1981) 'Einige Möglichkeiten hypothetischer Wertung der Verhältnisse unter den Charakteristiken archäologischer Funde', *Archeologické rozhledy* 33: 544–50.

—— (1986) 'Test shody – A test of the equality of two samples from multinominal distributions', *Archeologické rozhledy* 38: 501–3.

Stloukal, M. (1962) 'Struktura obyvatelstva – Die Struktur der Bevölkerung von Mikulčice. Ein Beitrag zur Paläodemographie der Altslawen', *Archeologické rozhledy* 14: 61–83.

—— (1964) 'Rozdíly ve výbavě – Die Unterschiede in der Ausstattung der slawischen Männer– und Frauengräber', *Archeologické rozhledy* 16: 101–17.

—— (1985) 'Antropologický rozbor – Anthropologische Analyse der Skelette vom Gräberfeld in Holešov', in *Studie muzea Kroměřížska 85*, Kroměříž: Muzeum.

Strouhal, E. (1978) 'Demography of the Early Bronze Age cemetery at Výčapy-Opatovce', *Anthropologie* 16: 131–5.

Svoboda, J. (1985) 'Štípaná industrie – Spaltindustrie der Nitra-Gruppe vom Gräberfelt in Holešov', in *Studie muzea Kroměřížka 85*, Kroměříž: Muzeum.

Tirpák, J. (1983) 'Geofyzikálny prieskum – Geophysikalische Untersuchung archäologischer Fundstellen in der Slowakei', *Slovenská archeológia* 31: 149–72.

Točík, A. (1978) 'K metodickým a terminologickým otázkam archeológie na Slovensku', in *Základné metodologické problémy a marxistické kategórie v archeológii*, Nitra: Archeologický ústav.

Točík, A. and Bublová, J. (1985) 'Príspevok k výskumu – Beitrag zur Untersuchung des stillgelegten Kupferabbaues in der Slowakei', *Študijné zvesti* 21: 47–135.

Turková, D. and Kuna, M. (1987) 'Zur Mikrostruktur der bronzezeitlichen Siedlungen', in *Die Urnenfelderkulturen Mitteleuropas, Symposium Liblice 1985*, Prague: Archeologický ústav.

Velímský, T. (1986) 'Die archäologischen Ausgrabungen im nordböhmischen Braunkohlengebiet – Probleme, Ergebnisse und Perspektiven', *Arbeits- und Forschungsberichte Dresden* 30: 6–36.

Vencl, S. (1960) 'Kamenné nástroje – Les instruments lithiques des premiers agriculteurs en Europe Central', *Sborník Národního muzea v Praze* A 14: 1–91.

—— (1961) 'K otázce interpretace – Zur Frage der Interpretation der Funktion vorzeitlicher Gegenstände', *Archeologické rozhledy* 13: 678–93.

—— (1968) 'K otázce interpretace – Zur Frage der Deutung der urzeitlichen Bauten', *Archeologické rozhledy* 20: 490–510.

—— (1970) 'Zur Funktion des geschliffenen Steingeräts. Das Silexgerät', in M. Buchvaldek and D. Koutechý, *Vikletice. Ein schnurkeramisches Gräberfeld*, Prague: Univerzita Karlova.

—— (1984) 'Otázky poznávání vojenství v archeologii – Problems relating to the knowledge of warfare in archaeology', Prague: Archeologický ústav.

—— (1985) 'Žaludy – Acorns as food. Assessing the significance of food-gathering for prehistoric dietary habits', *Archeologické rozhledy* 37: 516–65.

Waldhauser, J. (1978) 'Zusammenfassende Auswertung des keltischen Gräberfeldes bei Jenišův Újezd', in J. Waldhauser (ed.) *Das keltische Gräberfeld bei Jenišův Újezd in Böhmen*, Bd. II, Teplice: Krajské muzeum.

—— (1979) 'Konfrontation der anthropologischen und archäologischen Ermittlung von Männer-, Frauen- und Kindergräbern auf keltischen Nekropolen in Böhmen', *Antropologie* 17: 55–62.

—— (1981) 'Keltské rotační mlýny – Keltische Drehmühlen in Böhmen', *Památky archeologické* 72: 153–221.

—— (1984) 'Mobilität und Stabilität der keltischen Besiedlung in Böhmen', in *Studien zu Siedlungsfragen der Latènezeit*, Marburg.

—— (1985) 'Získávání mědi a její tavba v keltských Čechách', *Studie z dějin hornictví* 16: 46–88.

Waldhauser, J. and Holodňák, P. (1984) 'Keltské sídliště – Keltische Siedlung und Gräberfeld bei Bílina Bez. Teplice', *Památky archeologické* 75: 181–216.

Weber, Z. and Šebebla, L. (1976) 'Některé fyzikální – Einige physikalische Parameter der neolithischen Keramik', *Sborník prací filozofické fakulty brněnské univerzity E* 20–1: 249–55.

Základné 1978, *Základné metodologické problémy a marxistické kategórie v archeológii. Zborník referátov Nové Vozokany 27.–29. mája 1974*, Nitra; Archeologický ústav.

Zápotocká, M. (1982) 'Zur Auswahl der Siedlungsregionen der Stichbandkeramik', in *Siedlungen der Kultur mit Linearkeramik in Europa*, Nitra: Archeologický ústav.

—— (1984) 'Armringe aus Marmor und anderen Rohstoffen im jüngeren Neolithikum Böhmens und Mitteleuropas', *Památky archeologické* 75: 50–130.

Zápotocký, M. (1964) 'Bylanské kostrové – Bylaner Skelettgräber im unteren Egergebiet', *Památky archeologické* 55: 156–77.

—— (1966) 'Streitäxte und Streitaxtkulturen', *Památky archeologické* 57: 172–209.

—— (1982) 'Lovosice a oblast – Lovosice und die Böhmische Pforte – frühbronzezeitliche Siedlungskonzentration mit Nachweisen für Metallgiesserei', *Archeologické rozhledy* 34: 361–405.

Žebera, K. (1966) 'Exploitation préhistorique du quarzite près de Bečov dans le "České středohoří" (Bohême)', in *Investigations archéologiques en Tchéchoslovaquie*, Prague: Academia.

11

ARCHAEOLOGICAL THEORY IN HUNGARY SINCE 1960: THEORIES WITHOUT THEORETICAL ARCHAEOLOGY

J. Laszlovsky and Cs. Siklódi

Introduction

This chapter attempts to offer an outline of the ideas that have influenced archaeological theory in Hungary in the past twenty-five years.[1] A fully satisfactory review must necessarily include all aspects of theoretical writing. It is therefore not enough to empha-sise the influence of the New Archaeology or other trends orig-inating in the USA. If we only examined this question it would suffice to review the academic careers of a few archaeologists, but this would definitely lead to one-sided conclusions, and we would surely omit important ideas and lose sight of other scholars who played a prominent role in Hungarian archaeology.

The link between political and historical changes in Hungary and archaeological theory must definitely be considered (Patterson 1986: 7–8; Harding 1982: 2–3). These wider social and political movements acted not only as background, but in many cases they had profound and lasting effects on the social sciences, limiting or widening the *Lebensraum* of academic life. This phenomenon is more obvious in Central and Eastern Europe than in the west (Szücs 1983: 178–81).

Scientific ideas at the theoretical level, especially in this part of the world, cannot be surveyed in a restricted way. In other words, the theories and conceptual frameworks of foreign academic cen-tres and their influence cannot be evaluated in themselves. It is impossible, for example, to analyse the influence of the neo-Marx-ist theories which have made their appearance alongside or in opposition to the New Archaeology without considering what kind of picture Hungarian archaeologists had of classical Marxism, or whether Marxism had or could ever have been the subject of scholarly debate. Similarly, any evaluation must also include a discussion of the role played by modern sociology in Hungarian archaeology; it must be pointed out that for political reasons sociology was exiled from the official scientific disciplines for a long time.

Thus we must go back to the 1950s, because only then can the effects of the political changes after 1956 be understood. The direct influence of politics on scientific research and on the writings and publications of almost every scholar can definitely be demonstrated for the dogmatic, Stalinistic period of the 1950s. However, the twists and turns of the political situation had their impact not only on archaeological theory, but also on the day-to-day life of scholarly research.

The premisses, ideas and theories of international scientific research can only hope to influence the scholarly thought and literature of a country if it is possible for scholars of that country to participate in international conferences, to study with the aid of scholarships in other countries and to have access to the newest literature. Therefore consideration must be given to whether Hungarian archaeologists have been able to establish international contacts of this kind in the past twenty-five years, and whether the New Archaeology or any other theory could in fact have reached and made an impact on Hungarian scholars at all.

Aside from these general considerations which are relevant not only to Hungary, it is also our purpose to examine other important aspects of Hungarian archaeology. The traditional archaeological schools of most European countries generally emerged around local museums or universities, and sooner or later they usually began to follow one particular methodological approach and theoretical framework: at the same time scientific discussions between these schools became one of the most important fields of scholarly life.

However, this was less significant in Hungary because scholarly debates generally tend to be among individuals rather than between long-standing scholarly centres. This state of affairs is also reflected in the university training of archaeologists. As a consequence, the ideas of leading archaeologists became authoritative in university courses, and their view on the New Archaeology, for example, shaped the outlook of a whole generation of archaeologists. This became even more conspicuous when the results of foreign research found their way to a wider circle of Hungarian archaeologists through exactly the same university lecturers. The archaeological and historical libraries in Hungary faced great financial difficulties in acquiring the newest scholarly literature, and thus the private libraries of prominent scholars built up. Thus international personal contacts played a significant, mediatory role in the spread and possible acceptance of new ideas.

Archaeological theory since the 1950s: the indigenous tradition

Hungarian archaeology has traditionally been strongly influenced by German schools. This can be observed both in the methodological literature and in the system of university training. There were signs of Hungarian archaeological schools between the two world wars, one in Budapest with a strong predilection towards Classical archaeology and the other in Szeged, with an emphasis on the excavation of prehistoric and medieval sites and archaeological minutiae in fieldwork (Banner 1961; Oroszlán 1966; Csorba 1969–70). From a theoretical point of view, however, both 'schools' shared an infatuation with typological studies and explanatory frameworks steeped in positivism and culture history (Tompa 1932).

A strong Soviet influence began to dominate the scene from the late 1940s and particularly from the 1950s, and this had little, if any, intellectual ancestry in Hungary. Following the fundamental political changes in the country after the Second World War, Marxism became the official ideology, and archaeological studies were affected. Marxism basically meant vulgar Marxism in the dogmatic Stalinist period of the 1950s, when the entire theory was reduced simply to the tenet of class struggle and the relationship between base and superstructure.

It must none the less be emphasised that only a small portion of archaeological works published during this period is characterised by this obligatory theorising. Most publications followed the theoretical principles of the former literature with some kind of ideological garnish. It was a general practice in archaeological articles written according to the traditional framework that Marxism only appeared in the form of periodic and mostly *non sequitur* quotes from Marx and Engels. Hungarian archaeologists hoped in this way to avoid the pitfalls of the officially controlled ideology, but this resulted, almost undetectably, in archaeological interpretation becoming extremely one-sided. Although Hungarian archaeology was not forced into the frame of the Russian type of 'history of material culture', archaeological materials were very often used to support the idea of a simplified evolutionary process in the social organisation.

This vulgar approach to history had yet another influence on archaeology, namely that theoretical issues were avoided and most studies were restricted to descriptions of excavations and catalogues of their finds. No archaeological book discussing theoretical questions has been published in Hungary in the past twenty-five or thirty years, and the *Régészeti Kézikönyv* ('Handbook of archaeology') published in 1954 is little more than a compendium of practical advice for would-be archaeologists lacking any kind of theoretical digressions (Banner *et al.* 1954). Only plans for the publication of a more theoretical series of archaeological handbooks, with each volume designed to cover a different period, have emerged so far. The volume on the paleolithic, also reviewing theoretical problems such as the concept and interpretation of archaeological cultures or the informative value of archaeological sources and methods appeared in 1965 (Vértes 1965). However, this book did not exert a profound influence on Hungarian archaeology because research on the palaeolithic period had always been isolated.

It would appear from the above that Hungarian archaeology could best be described as atheoretical and concerned only with practical and methodological problems. None the less, certain characteristic and important trends in the theoretical field which emerged in the course of an internal development can be pinpointed. Unfortunately, novel ideas or approaches never came to be published in comprehensive studies or articles, but were generally to be found in archaeological books written for the general public or tucked away in the fine print of archaeological articles.

Gyula László, András Mócsy and István Bóna, all three professors at the University of Budapest, communicated their theoretical ideas on archaeology in their university courses. However, these statements often formed a kind of *ars poetica* and so in Hungarian archaeological general knowledge their ideas appeared closely allied to the personal images of the scholars.

'Archaeological ethnography' introduced by Gyula László was a response to the inflexibility and closed system of the typological school. He first summarised his ideas in his book *A honfoglaló magyar nép élete* ('The life of the Hungarians in the Conquest period'), published in 1944 (László 1944), but these only gained a wider currency in the 1950s and 1960s. The book became, and was used, as a kind of Bible by generations of archaeologists, and after several decades of university lecturing he can regard almost all Hungarian archaeologists as his disciples. His personal charm and evocative style made him a well-known writer, as well as a TV and radio personality, who acquainted the general public with his ideas.

'Archaeological ethnography' drew its inspiration from several sources, most important among which was Hungarian ethnography, a discipline that had always been more important in Hungary than in the west. Another important source was culture history, a highly fashionable direction in Hungarian historiography during the 1930s and 1940s. These combined to create a theoretical framework in which the emphasis was not on typological sequences or chronological phases, but rather on the reanimation of the finds, on letting them speak for themselves. Besides describing the formal characteristics of the finds, he also laid emphasis on the analysis of their function and mode of manufacture, on the comparative analysis of various assemblages as well as their find context. It was understood that archaeology cannot do away with traditional methods, but it was politely suggested that archaeologists should look beyond the finds and attempt to catch sight of their makers, their everyday lives and their ideas (László 1944, 1970, 1984, 1990). On this basis László introduced a new approach to the analysis of cemeteries, in which he distinguished four phases, proceeding from the larger to the smaller units. In the first phase he mapped contemporaneous cemeteries which offered insights into settlement patterns and ethnic conditions. In the second, he distinguished grave groups within a given cemetery with the aid of artefact types and artefact assemblages, and drew conclusions concerning the social organisation and family structure of the given community. In the third phase he analysed individual graves that enabled the reconstruction of burial customs and burial rites, as well as of the beliefs concerning the netherworld. Only in the fourth phase did he turn to the examination of the artefacts themselves, a procedure that had formerly been the exclusive approach in cemetery analyses.

László also called attention to another important theoretical issue. Since most finds and artefacts can only be regarded as dim reflections of the past, important details of which have become irrevocably lost for archaeologists, only in a few exceptional cases can archaeology formulate absolute truths about the past, using archaeological methods. The terminology and categories used by archaeology can, at the most, only be technical devices whose value is relative. In the same way as 'the natural sciences are actually the sciences of our knowledge of nature and are by no means equal with nature', so too is archaeology a 'science dealing with the past, but it is by no means identical with the past' (László 1980: 112). 'One of the greatest pitfalls of history – and of archaeology – is that, intentionally or unintentionally, we tend to approach the past armed with our modern concepts' (László 1977: 56). These general problems led László to coin the phrase 'creative uncertainty' to describe the practical application of archaeological theories. Since our methods and tools are restricted, our conclusions cannot be absolute. Consequently there are no definitive solutions to scientific questions, and neither is there but one fruitful line of research. However, it must at the same time be emphasised that László always formulated his theories from a practical point of view and not as abstract, philosophical principles. He illustrated his points with ethnographical, archaeological and historical analogies.

Another clear, marked theoretical direction was historicity. According to this idea archaeology should, by recognising the pitfalls of traditional methods and archaeological categories, represent a higher level in the perception of historical reality.

Archaeology provides a compendium of historical sources that is assembled by its specific sampling techniques and analytical methods. However, the unity of the historical sciences cannot be subdivided into individual, special disciplines according to the nature of the sources and dealing with these specific fields, because in this case there would be no place for a synthetic discipline which alone could contest the right of historicism. Thus, archaeology can only become a historical discipline if it attains a level of historicity from where it can no longer hope to advance further with the help of its specific methods. While archaeology remains bogged down in its special problems and sources, it will be incapable of revealing the real historical truth.

(Csorba 1969–70)[2]

These ideas were formulated by András Mócsy, whose research centred on the historical problems of Roman Pannonia. At the same time he used the methods that turned out to be fruitful in the course of his investigation of this province for the study of the whole empire. The archaeological research of a small region was always embedded into the wider context of the empire (Mócsy 1974). The final guiding principle was always historicity, historiography in the classical sense which, however, does not merely involve the chronological sequence of historical events, but also an attempt to recapture the past in its entirety. Through a comparison of the names and the costume of the deceased depicted on grave reliefs, and the archaeological finds, he could reconstruct the level of Romanisation of the aboriginal population in various areas. Thus did the Roman inscriptions and excavated buildings become sources for social and economic studies.

A similar historicity can be observed in the academic *oeuvre* of István Bóna. He discussed a number of archaeological problems ranging from the neolithic to the Middle Ages in his works, but he interpreted the data as parts of a homogenous historical process, not as distinct, unrelated cultures, periods, horizons, which can be studied by archaeology. The categories, *Stufen*, used by archaeology as practical devices should in no way be identified with history, since the ultimate aim of archaeology cannot simply be the clarification of these problems alone (Bóna 1985: 223–36). This historicity was methodologically linked to a positivistic theory, with the complete collection of historical and archaeological evidence that would provide the basis for the reconstruction of historical processes (Bóna 1971, 1978, 1982–83, 1986b). This positivism can be observed not only in the collection of data but also in terms of theoretical issues. The ideas were originally incorporated into the interpretation of a given problem. One approach or theory can be used with good results in the solution of one specific problem, whereas another can be more fruitful in the next one. All ideas were subordinated to historicity as a final guiding principle.

His monograph on the Middle Bronze Age is not only a corpus of material excavated and published by a former generation of scholars or by the author, but also an attempt to outline the historical, chronological and cultural problems of the entire period for the first time (Bóna 1975a and b). The complex approach also called for a discussion of theoretical issues such as the concept and interpretation of the archaeological culture or period, etc. However, the work which for technical reasons was only published in 1975, fifteen years after its writing, does not reflect the research results of the second half of the 1970s. For example, because of the lack of C14 dates, its theoretical results remained, for the most part, inconclusive. He successfully combined in his work the characteristic research methods of former archaeological schools, adopting the general approach of the 'Budapest school' and the detailed analytical methods of the 'Banner school'. (J. Banner was a prominent scholar of the Szeged school, who later became professor at the University of Budapest; there he incorporated the results and principles of the Szeged school into his lectures.)

István Bóna's other main field of interest is the Migration period, and the influence of László on his outlook can be definitely felt, but with a stronger emphasis on historicity. In his own words,

I filled the historical framework worked out on the basis of written sources with the historical, economic and social data derived from archaeology. Or, to be more precise, not only with the data, but also with the results and tendencies suggested or implied by the sum of major data.

(Bóna 1986a: 565)

He then proceeded to refine this method and extended it also to other periods that lacked written sources in order 'to build history through the critical evaluation of the entire archaeological material from one region' (Bona 1986a: 565). A clearly crystallised form of this approach is to be found in his historical essay on the prehistory of Hungary (Bona 1984).

Historicity as a major theoretical trend obviously played a prominent role in medieval archaeology since the abundance of written sources pushed the archaeological research of this period into the background for a long time. However, the past three decades have witnessed resurgence in medieval archaeology: it grew into an independent research discipline (Fodor and Selmeczi 1985; Kubinyi 1985). This also means that, like other fields of archaeology, historicity became one of the numerous theoretical directions in medieval archaeology, instead of being dominant, as formerly (Hodges, 1982).

Large-scale excavations and corpus-type monographs rather than theoretical debates, dominated the scene during the 1960s and 1970s. New fields of archaeological research were discovered and colonised, reflected for instance in the new dimensions added to medieval archaeology. However, these new areas only generated methodological debates.

Significant changes can be noted in the organisation of archaeological research during this period. The Archaeological Institute of the Hungarian Academy of Sciences was founded, and several local museums in the provinces grew into independent research centres with a number of well-trained archaeologists. The increase and growth of fieldwork and the resulting rethinking of various archaeological problems led to questions beyond the scope of methodology from the mid 1970s. This development was closely allied to the gradual depletion of financial resources and also to the increasing cost of excavation work. Thus, it became more and more necessary to select which sites to excavate in terms of their archaeological, historical and educational value (Kovács 1980; Mócsy 1982). Similar problems were raised by a new general project of Hungarian archaeology: the Archaeological Topography of Hungary was organised with the aims of systematically surveying the entire country, of mapping sites and of assembling the relevant data from the archaeological literature (Torma 1969). The first general results of this project surfaced in this period. This kind of survey came to be extremely important in view of modern industrial, agricultural and building activities throughout the country that threatened a number of archaeological sites. The new large-scale rescue excavations called for a novel and rapid approach that, in turn, necessitated a clear picture of the number and types of sites.

At the same time, the results of this survey work enabled an assessment of the extent to which previous research on settlement history and settlement patterns of various periods could be considered representative. Since the first general conclusions clearly implied that whole periods and groups had remained undetected by former research, this problem attained a deeper theoretical dimension: to what extent is it possible to reconstruct all aspects of the past using current archaeological methods and theories (Jankovich 1985; Miklós 1985)? However, this problem, too, was mostly approached from a practical point of view and did not lead to more general formulations on the theoretical level.

At the same time beside works expressing modern theories of culture complexes (Bognár-Kutzián 1972), books and articles were still being published employing the traditional German typological method (Mozsolics 1973, 1985; Kemenczei 1984; Patek 1968; Patay 1974).

There were increasing possibilities for Hungarian scholars to participate more actively in international academic life. Chances for foreign travel and a larger influx of foreign archaeological literature made a discernible impact on Hungarian archaeological studies. From the mid 1970s numerous foreign scholars participated in Hungarian archaeological researches, and there were joint projects as well. However, this did not mean that widely debated foreign ideas and fashionable theories immediately found their way to the Hungarian scholars.

Another apparently unimportant, but highly significant factor influenced the discussion of theoretical issues. The most important books – such as the Bronze Age monograph by Bóna – were published with delays of six to ten years, for technical reasons. Thus, not only was the bibliographical database out of date by the time of publication, but so also were most of the theories based on the 'newest' research. The implications of this fact for theoretical issues cannot be emphasised strongly enough since any new monograph on an archaeological period or culture is always an important step forward in its research, regardless of when it is published. But the theoretical issues discussed in it are practically lost for research.

We must mention yet another important factor that affected the reception of the New Archaeology in Hungary, namely the impact of Gordon Childe's theories and, to a certain extent, his personal influence. This impact can be demonstrated for prehistory, but his theories also influenced wider circles of Hungarian research. Childe recognised that the results of prehistoric research in the Carpathian Basin played a crucial role in the reconstruction of European prehistoric development (Childe 1929, 1948, 1950, 1957). His visits to Hungary and his personal contacts enabled him to acquire a first-hand knowledge of Hungarian research results. He was of the opinion that 'all European archaeologists know the great wealth of prehistoric antiquities that have been collected in Hungary and appreciate the leading role that Hungary played in the development of civilizations throughout Europe in prehistoric and early historic times' (Banner 1958: 57). Only in the light of contemporary Hungarian history can his lasting influence on Hungarian archaeology be understood, since at the time of his visit to Hungary – 1955 – Hungarian archaeology was almost completely sealed off from international research and personal contact with outside archaeologists, because of the Stalinist politics of that period. The other reason for his tremendous impact is that one of his last theoretical articles came to be published in a Hungarian archaeological journal precisely during this closed period (Childe 1956). This largely explains why in the 1960s after the eclipse of vulgar-Marxist ideology, Childe's scientific *oeuvre* became a model for Hungarian archaeologists (Childe 1959, 1962, 1968; Makkay 1989).

The influence of the New Archaeology and other new theoretical directions in Hungary

It is extremely difficult to evaluate the effect of the New Archaeology on Hungarian scholars because the intellectual ferment of international scholarship characterising the latter half of the 1970s by-passed Hungary. Two main points must be discussed in this respect: the nature of the answers given to questions raised by the New Archaeology, and the introduction of new theories in university courses.

It is interesting and typical that the first article on the New Archaeology, as a new phenomenon in the archaeological world, was written by a scholar of culture history, not by an archaeologist. The article entitled 'Ujrégészet' ('New Archaeology') was published in a journal reviewing current topics of history, economy and social sciences – often with a theoretical slant – that enjoys currency not only among specialists of these sciences (Vekerdi 1976).

Its author pronounced the New Archaeology an omnipotent discipline on the basis of a handful of books that had favourably impressed him, which he also reviewed. At the same time he gently chided Hungarian archaeologists for being old-fashioned and not open to new ideas. This obvious provocation elicited an answer from two archaeologists. Nándor Kalicz is a scholar of international renown who plays a leading role in Hungarian neolithic studies, and therefore the issues raised by the New

Archaeology concerned him in a direct way. He is the author of several monographs that represent a crystallised form of the topological approach (Kalicz and Makkay 1977). On the other hand, his works show that he is always aware of recent developments in archaeological research and that he utilised these in his studies. Pál Raczky, the other archaeologist, had received a basically identical training, but he was unusually open-minded towards the new theories in Anglo-American archaeological studies. Their reply to the article 'Ujŕgészet' was written from one specific point of view: it challenged the novelty of the New Archaeology, as shown by their title, 'How new is the New Archaeology?' (Kalicz and Raczky 1977). They mostly avoided theoretical issues and concentrated on the questions of whether new data, such as C14 measurements, contradict traditional interpretations, and whether former approaches – particularly the theories proposed by Gordon Childe – are really as restricted and outdated as had been suggested by the author of the first article. Kalicz' and Raczky's defence of the traditional framework does not, however, imply the rejection of the New Archaeology, only a reluctance to the positioning of the New Archaeology against the 'Old Archaeology'.

One unfortunate consequence of this debate was that certain issues of the New Archaeology were overemphasised while other more general problems were relegated to the background. Many readers got the impression from the two articles that the entire debate was largely internal to Balkanic and Aegean neolithic research. At the same time it was not stressed strongly enough that some of the concepts and categories employed by traditional archaeology are unsuitable for describing historical processes, necessitating a rethinking of the possibilities and range of archaeological interpretation.

Following this debate this New Archaeology virtually disappeared from the Hungarian archaeological scene for quite a long time. Monographs and theoretical articles reflecting the imprint of the New Archaeology only began to be published from the early 1980s (Makkay 1982). One of the reasons why the New Archaeology began to influence Hungarian research at a rather late date is to be found in the opportunities for research. This can be demonstrated by the problems of chronology. The C14 method, and the chronological and historical questions allied to this dating technique, played a crucial role in the emergence of the New

Archaeology. In Hungary, however, there was an almost total lack of data of this kind and it was impossible to build up a coherent C14 sequence. Thus the small number of available dates were fitted into the already existing historical chronology (Kalicz and Raczky 1977).

One of the most crucial questions raised by the New Archaeology, the problem of whether contemporary or near-contemporary cultures emerged and developed indpendently and in parallel, or whether innovations spread like a chain reaction (Renfrew 1973, 1978), was irrelevant in terms of the neolithisation of the Carpathin Basin since it was fairly clear that the Körös culture, the earliest neolithic culture in Hungary, was a new arrival to this area without any local precursors. The same is true of the spread of metallurgy in this area. Thus, apart from a few exceptions (Makkay 1976), Hungarian archaeology remained a passive onlooker in the debate over various dating systems and theories. Theoretical articles reviewing these problems only began to be published after the controversy calmed down. The first purely theoretical study on this problem was written by J. Makkay, who was also the first to summarise the different chronological frameworks and to compare them with the Hungarian system (Makkay 1985a,b, 1987). There also appeared articles that discussed chronological questions with a basically new theoretical approach (Raczky 1987: 63–4, 1988, 1989; Bökönyi 1989).

By this late reaction, Hungarian archaeology managed to avoid the pitfalls of the absolutism of the C14 method but the advantages thus gained were diminished by a serious disadvantage, namely the lack of lively debate in the wake of a reassessment of issues and problems.

An up-to-date and thorough knowledge of the state of Near Eastern, Balkan and Aegean research became essential because of the strong links between the prehistoric cultures of these regions. This is clearly reflected in the bibliographies of some archaeological studies published in the late 1970s and 1980s. Interestingly enough, these studies showed that the New Archeology and other theories had a wholly different impact from what was to be expected, since the methodological approach, rather than the theoretical frameworks, were adopted. On the one hand, the new researches stimulated further investigations, but on the other hand the mechanical adoption of models based on research in the Near

East led to false conclusions (Makkay 1982; Horváth 1983). The mistake was soon realised once Hungarian archaeologists became better acquainted with new survey and sampling techniques, partly through participation in survey projects conducted by British and other teams in Hungary (Sherratt 1982, 1982–3, 1983).

The Anglo-Hungarian archaeological project, as well as the various studies of foreign scholars working on Hungarian material, employed different methods and theoretical models (Kosse 1979; Choyke 1982–3; Nacev-Skomal 1980; 1985). As one of these archaeologists pointedly remarked:

> As an archaeologist trained according to somewhat different principles I had lots of opportunities for interesting discussions. In this article I would like to review the most important phases of the field survey not from a better or fresher, but from simply another point of view.
>
> (Choyke 1981; 94–5)

The conclusions also differed, sometimes radically, from the ideas of Hungarian archaeologists. The works not only inspired a rethinking of oft-debated questions, but also proved the usefulness of new approaches and of novel survey and sampling techniques. The new theories and methods found their way to Hungarian archaeologists through their foreign colleagues with whom they worked on these projects, rather than through the actual publications that proved difficult to acquire. At the same time, the often patchy knowledge of the Hungarian archaeological material shown by foreign researchers gave rise to some very general conclusions indeed (Jarman *et al.* 1982), and some Hungarian archaeologists were inclined to reject not only the research results, but also their methods.

The appraisal and review of the New Archaeology as well as of various other historical and scientific theories in their original form gained wider currency in university training. This was in large part due to Géza Komoróczy, an Assyrologist who, in contrast to many, did not search for analogies for Hungarian prehistoric processes and archaeological artefacts, but studied the civilisations of the ancient Near East in themselves. The problem of establishing direct parallels between the Carpathian Basin and the ancient Near East had been a recurrent issue in Hungarian research (Makkay 1978). Because of Komoróczy's different approach to this problem he could point out the mistakes that were often made by archaeologists. His role in university training is also important because – given the lack of comprehensive reference books – he undertook the task of reviewing new directions and trends in archaeological, historical and scientific theory.

Similar problems were also discussed in detail by Miklós Szabó and his university lectures on Classical archaeology and Celtic research. In his introductory course on Greek archaeology and art history he too reviewed current theories and sampling techniques. As a member of several international projects and visiting professor at the Sorbonne, he carried out a personal enquiry on their applicability. The role of these international contacts can be seen as crucial, since visiting professorships did not exist in Hungary and the number of scholarships for study in foreign universities was limited. The university education system was inflexible. So not even visiting professors from the eastern block countries took part in teaching.

Pál Raczky in the 1980s also offered a survey of theoretical issues and trends in his university lectures. It can thus be said that from the latter half of the 1970s the results both of new archaeological theories such as the Anglo-American New Archaeology, as well as of the most fruitful and stimulating concepts of the 'local' theoretical directions – formulated by Gyula László, István Bóna, András Mócsy and others – were incorporated into Hungarian archaeological training, and this obviously enabled a comparison between the differeing theoretical systems. It must be noted that the 'local' theoretical directions or the theories raised in contradiction or parallel to the New Archaeology also touched upon some of the same questions.

First and foremost among these questions was the interpretation of the technical terms and categories used by archaeology. The pre- and photo-history of the Hungarian people, the Conquest period and the identification of the ethnic groups of the Migration period, provide examples. A group of archaeological assemblages originating from the tenth to eleventh centuries, long termed the Bielo Brdo culture, was alternately associated with the Slavic and with the Hungarian population (Sköke 1959, 1962; Bálint 1976). Similarly, basically identical finds of the Late Migration Period were linked to Slavic, Avar or Hungarian population groups (Bóna 1971). Most of the monographs and articles published on this subject revealed a strong ethnic interest and a preoccupation with the ethnic attribution of specific archaeological features, house types, tools, etc., with the obvious result that otherwise uncontroversial issues acquired a rather sharp edge in this corner of the world. This can basically be ascribed to the fact that the political boundaries drawn up in the course of the peace negotiations following the First World War did not coincide with ethnic boundaries, which in turn gave rise to strongly chauvinistic political views and arguments which often employed historical and archaeological data in order to prove their particular 'truths'.

Only after detailed studies and often heated debates could the problem of ethnic attribution be reviewed and revised, and only then could the first tentative steps be taken from specific archaeolgical problems towards broader issues of correlation between archaeological cultures, assemblages, language and ethnic groups. Similar problems had to be faced in the research of the prehistory and the original homeland of the Hungarian people (László 1961; Fodor 1977a, 1977b, 1982). A sensitivity to ethnic questions can also be noted in works on other periods, such as the Roman or medieval period (Mócsy 1959; Fodor and Selmeczi 1985; Pálóczi Horváth 1989).

Other problems of interpretation included the differences noted in the archaeological material between various types of grave goods, and their possible association with different population groups, i.e. the identification of social strata and groups. Questions of this type were always raised in connection with specific artefact types, and in connection with the definition of symbols of rank and power in a given period. Unfortunately, these analyses never involved the investigation of whether material culture is suitable for reconstructing social stratification at all. The complexity of this problem also derives from the fact that in the Marxist framework 'class' was the only accepted form for the description of social categories for a long time. Thus in Hungarian archaeology and historiography, new paradigms such as ranked or stratified societies only found their way into the interpretational framework from the second half of the 1970s (Laszlovszky in press; Nacev-Skomal 1985). Prior to this, Hungarian archaeologists attempted to clarify social questions on the basis of the archaeological material. For example, a wealth of data on social position was preserved in Roman inscriptions – as compared to archaeological finds – and this provided an excellent basis for the reconstruction of social groups. The anlaysis of these data clearly revealed that only through a detailed examination of the entire material can the pitfalls of drawing a schematic and simplified picture be avoided. At the same time, the quantity of material made analysis with traditional methods impossible, and thus statistical and computer approaches were experimented with (Mócsy *et al.* 1983; Mócsy 1985).

The role of analytical methods varied in Hungarian archaeology. There were no institutional possibilities for palaeobotanic, palynological, C14, climatic and provenence studies, and these could only gain prominence owing to the particular interest of a specific scholar. A case in point is palaeozoology, which developed into an independent discipline following the investigations by Sándor Bökönyi (Bökönyi 1974) and János Matolcsi (Matolcsi 1973). S. Bökönyi is regarded in international scientific circles as a prominent scholar of palaeozoology, who also takes an anthropological approach to osteological remains. He took part in the excavations and post-excavation works of several Near Eastern, south-east European, etc. sites, and as a result of these studies he suggested general, very often theoretical conclusions in the interpretation of the Hungarian materials. However, his studies gained a strong influence only in the research of some periods (neolithic, Copper Age, etc.) and had no visible impact on Hungarian general archaeological theory. At the same time, palaeobotanic studies (Hartyáni and Nováki 1975) or the analysis of soil samples (Laszlovszky 1982) mostly remained isolated experiments.

This one-sided interdisciplinary research was the main reason why analytical studies did not have an impact on Hungarian archaeology of the theoretical level. The growing need for the application of various analytical methods became obvious, but appendices of this kind inserted at the end of archaeological articles very often only gave a semblance of modernity. In the meantime, studies appeared which argued that the various analytical methods and statistical studies could not offer absolute, definitive conclusions because only a few aspects of the past, rather than the entire historical process itself, can be studied in a quantitative way (Bartosiewicz 1986).

Besides the analytical methods borrowed from the natural sciences, anthropology, sociology, human geography and palaeoeconomy also played an important role in recent developments. These often grew into independent disciplines. They brought a certain measure of renewal from a methodological point of view and at the same time also generated new theoretical thinking

(Bogucki 1985; Hodder 1982a; Hodges 1982). However, these disciplines primarily influenced Hungarian archaeology through ethnography.

In Hungary and in other countries of Central and Eastern Europe industrialisation began later than in western Europe. Thus, peasant society and its archaic cultivation techniques, tools, social phenomena, etc. survived into the twentieth century. Consequently, ethnography occupied a central place in Hungarian social science and in some periods these studies were strongly linked to political issues. For example, sociological studies on peasant society in Hungary were carried out not only for purely academic reasons, but also as part of a programme for the preparation of an agrarian reform or revolution.

Hungarian archaeologists traditionally turned to ethnographic analogies observed in the material and spiritual culture of local peasants, rather than to parallel phenomena in other parts of the world (Hodder 1982b, 1982c, 1982) in the reconstruction of social structures (e.g. kinship ties, family structure, etc.), in the interpretation of agrarian techniques or in the functional analysis of archaeological objects. They also felt more comfortable using parallels drawn from Hungarian ethnogrpahy since most archaeologists had a first-hand knowledge of these from their own everyday experience. Moreover, quite a number of archaeologists had also acquired an ethnographic training and a good part of their studies cannot be categorised as either purely archaeological or purely ethnographic, but rather represent a synthesis of these disciplines (Szabó 1938; Banner 1937; Csilléry 1982; Balassa 1985). Consequently, social anthropology made little impact on archaeological research and did not grow into an independent discipline; the 'anthropological' aspect of the New Archaeology appeared less attractive in Hungary.

Similarly, human geography was merely a research direction in ethnography. The methods used by human geography (spatial analysis, site catchment, etc.) and its framework of interpretation (central place theory, the use of Christaller's polygons, mapping methods) were based on deduction, with specific conclusions drawn from a set of general premises, obviously linked to empirical observations. In contrast, Hungarian ethnography investigated specific aspects of a settlement system or a settlement pattern in a given period and reached general conclusions through induction from a set of premises based mostly on field experience or empirical evidence. This strong empirical way of investigation was extremely useful in the solution of practical issues, but at the same time had the disadvantage of suggesting erroneous or false conclusions. For example, contemporary isolated farmsteads were cited as analogies for the similar dispersed settlement types of the Conquest period, which led to false conclusions concerning cultural continuity (Laszlovszky 1986). However, this approach does not mean that the inductive method should be wholly rejected since erroneous conclusions reached through deduction can also be cited.

As regards sociology, the situation is considerably more complex. A major sociological school emerged in the 1930s that maintained strong ties with ethnography and also contained a political line that attempted to offer a sociography of contemporary agrarian society. It must also be borne in mind that sociology, *sensu stricto*, was exiled from academic life as a 'bourgeois pseudo-discipline' that could not be reconciled with Marxism. It gradually began to be revived in the 1970s, but none the less, sociology only made an impact on research through 'archaeological ethnography' and thus did not cause a really major breakthrough.

It follows from the above that in terms of theoretical studies, archaeological research in the 1960s and 1970s mostly followed an internal, 'national' tradition. The traditions of Hungarian archaeology discussed here still form an integral part of research directions. Beginning with the late 1970s the impact of international projects and theoretical debates can be clearly felt in the organisation of archaeological studies. New, more problem-orientated excavations were begun in which the selection of sites was more conscious (Raczky *et al.* 1985). In the course of excavations and in the archaeological interpretation of the excavations the analytical methods borrowed from the natural sciences became equal partners, enabling the first tentative steps towards ecological and environmental archaeology (Jerem *et al.* 1984–5; Biro 1980). Emphasis was laid not so much on the quantity as on the quality of recovered information, and this enabled a widening of research horizons.

Conclusions

It has been shown that there were various archaeological theories and research directions in Hungarian archaeology, and also that theoretical ideas from the international literature have made some sort of impact in the past twenty-five years. What remains to be answered is why these were not summarised in general works, and why they did not generate theoretical debates.

The theories that had grown from local Hungarian traditions were strongly linked to individual scholars, particularly in the case of Gyula László, whose personal image and charm enhanced his influence on archaeologists. At the same time most theories were proposed as solutions to specific questions, to pratical archaeological problems. This strong empiricism can mostly be traced to a strong ethnographic influence.

The other basic reason why methodological and theoretical ideas were never set down in purely theoretical terms is that as long as methodological problems only were debated, the discussions remained internal to archaeology; a review of theoretical questions would have involved a rethinking of ideological issues as well. During most of the period surveyed in this chapter these issues remained taboo because ideology and philosophy were part and parcel of the institutionalised section of the political system (Harding 1982).

Finally we shall attempt briefly to outline possible future perspectives in Hungarian archaeological research. Given the present situation, wtih increasing opportunities for international contacts, we will undoubtedly witness the growing impact of foreign research which will most certainly lead to a polarisation in methodological and theoretical debates; and this, in turn, will undoubtedly enrich Hungarian archaeology. At the same time, the various 'local' theoretical directions mentioned above are, on the whole, fairly open to new paradigms and issues. And since there is no one 'safe' path, this will sooner or later lead to a theoretical chaos. This can only be avoided if the various theoretical views are clearly formulated. Any ensuing debate will undoubtedly stimulate further research but only if the most basic issues and questions can also be subjected to discussion without any kind of restrictions.

On the other hand, it is to be hoped that Hungarian archaeology will preserve its sensitivity to practical, empirical questions, the salient feature of archaeological ethnography and historicity. Only thus can we hope that Hungarian archaeology can loosen its ideological 'chains' – now that the country has literally lost its chains – and will be moving in a direction, where 'it is not the increase of tangible finds, but the refinement of observations that will enrich our archaeology and its perception of the past.' (László 1980: 153).

Notes

1 On the recent development of Hungarian archaeology, see Fülep 1987; on the archaeological publications of this period, Banner and Jakabbfy 1954, 1961, 1968, Jakabbfy 1981.
2 Translations of quotes are by the authors.

References

Balassa, M. I. (1985) *A parasztház évszázadai (A magyar lakóház közép-kori fejlödésének vázlata) Jahrhunderte des Bauernhauses (Eine Skizze der mittelalterliche Entwicklung des ungarischen Wohnhauses)*, Békéscsaba: Tevan Andor Szakközépiskola.

Bálint, Cs, (1976) 'A magyarság és az ub. Bielo-brdoi, kultura. Die Ungarn und die sogenannte Bielo-Brdo Kultur,' *Cumania* 4: 225–54.

Banner, J. (1937) 'Die Ethnologie der Köros-Kultur', *Dolgozatok* 13: 32–50.

—— (1958) 'Vere Gordon Childe 1892–1957', *Archaeologiai értesitö* 85: 56–8.

—— (1961) 'A budapest egyetem és a kolozsvári régészeti iskola. Die Budapester Universität und die archäologische Schule von Kolozsvar', *Dissertationers Archaeologicae* 3: 44–7.

Banner, J. and Jakabbfy, I. (1954) *A Közép-Dunamedence régészeti bibliográfiája. Archäologische Bibliographie des Mittel-Donau-Beckens*, Budapest: Akadémiai Kiadó.

—— (1961) *A Közép-Dunamedence régészeti bibliográfiája 1954–1959. Archäologische Bibliographie des Mittel-Donau-Beckens 1954–1959*, Budapest: Akadémiai Kiadó.

—— (1968) *A Közép-Dunamedence régészeti bibliográfiája 1960–1966. Archäologische Bibliographie des Mittel-Donau-Beckens 1960–1966*, Budapest: Akadémiai Kiadó.

Banner, J., László, Gy., Méri, I. and Radnóti, A. (1954) *Régészeti kézikönyv I*, Budapest: Akadémiai Kiadó.

Bartosiewicz, L. (1986) 'Multivariate methods in archaeozoology', *Acta Archeologica Academiae Scientiarium Hungaricae* 38: 279–94.

Biró, K. T. (1980) 'A Kárpát-medencei obszidiánok vizsgálata. Archaeometrical study of the Carpathian Obsidians', *Archaeologiai értesitö* 108: 194–205.

Bognár-Kutzián, I. (1972) *The Early Copper Age Tiszapolgár Culture in the Carpathian Basin*, Budapest: Akadémiai Kiadó.

Bogucki, P. (1985) 'Theoretical directions in European Archaeology', *American Antiquity* 50: 780–8.

Bóna, I. (1971) 'Ein Vierteljahrhundert Völkerwanderungszeitforschung in Ungarn (1945–1969)', *Acta Archaologica Academiae Scientiarum Hungaricae* 23: 265–336.

—— (1975a) 'Diskussionsthesen über die Frühbronzezeit Ungarns (Ethnische und chronologische Fragen der Ungarischen Gesellschaft für Archäologie und Kunstgeschichte)', *Acta Archaeologica Academiae Scientiarum Hungaricae* 27: 285–6.

—— (1975b) *Die Mittlere Bronzezeit Ungarns und Ihre südöstlichen Beziehungen*, Budapest: Akadémiai Kiadó.

—— (1978) 'Arpadenzeitliche Kirche und Kirchhof im südlichen Stadtgebiet von Dunaujváros', *Alba Regia* 16: 99–157.

—— (1982–3) 'A XIX. század nagy avar leletei. Die grossen Awarenfunde des 19. Jahrunderts', *Szolnok Megyei Muzeumok évkönyve* 81–160.

—— (1984) 'A nemzetségi és törzsi társadalom története Magyarországon. A népvándorláskor és a korai középkor története Magyarországon', in A. Bartha and Gy. Székely (eds) *Magyarország története (Elözményet és magyar történet 1242-iq)*, Budapest: Akadémiai Kiadó.

—— (1985) 'Arpadenzeitliche Dörfer, Kirche und Friedhof am Marosfluss (Kurt Horedt, Moresti. Band 2. Bonn 1984)', *Acta Archaeologica Academiae Scientiarum Hungaricae* 37: 223–36.

—— (1986a) 'Dáciától Erdöelvéig. A népvándorlás kora Erdélyben (271–896)', in B. Köpeczi (ed.) *Erdély története* vol. I, Budapest: Akadémiai Kiadó.

—— (1986b) 'Javarézkori aranyleletekröl. Fejezetek a magyar ösrégézet multszázadi-századeleji történetéböl', *Veszprém Megyei Muzeumok Közleményei* 18: 21–72.

Bökönyi, S. (1974) *History of Domestic Mammals in Central and Eastern Europe*, Budapest: Akadémiai Kiadó.

—— (ed. 1989) *Neolithic of Southeastern Europe and its Near Eastern Connections (International Conference 1987 Szolnok-Szeged)*, Varia Archaeologica Hungarica II, Budapest.

Childe, V. G. (1929) *The Danube in Prehistory*, Oxford: Clarendon Press.

—— (1948) 'The final bronze age in the Near East and in temperate Europe', *Proceedings of Prehistoric Society* 14: 177–95.

—— (1950) *Prehistoric Migrations in Europe*, Instituttet for Sammenlignende Kulturforskning, Serie A, Forelesninger XX, Oslo: Instituttet for Sammenlignende Kulturforskning.

—— (1956) 'Notes on the chronology of the Hungarian Bronze Age', *Acta Archaeologica Academiae Scientiarum Hungaricae* 7: 291–300.

—— (1957) *The Dawn of European Civilisation*, 6th edn, London: Routledge & Kegan Paul.

—— (1959) *A civilizáció bölcsöje* [= *What Happened in History*], Budapest: Gondolat Kiadó.

—— (1962) *Az európai társadalom östörténete* [=*The Prehistory of European Society*], Budapest: Gondolat Kiadó.

—— (1968) *Az ember önmaga alkotója* [= *Man Makes Himself*], Budapest: Kossuth Kiadó.

Choyke, A. M. (1981) 'Régészeti lelöhelyek módszeres felszini vizsgálata (Systematic Archaeological Survey)', *Archaeologiai értesitö* 108: 95–9.

—— (1982–3) 'An analysis of bone, antler and tooth tools from Bronze Age Hungary', *Mitteilungen des Archäologischen Instituts der Ungarischen Akademie der Wissenschaften* 12–13: 13–57.

ARCHAEOLOGICAL THEORY IN EUROPE

Csilléry, K. K. (1982) *A magyar népi lakáskultura kialakulásának kezdetei. Anfänge der ungarischen volkstümlichen Wohnkultur*, Budapest: Akadémiai Kiadó.
Csorba, Cs. (1969–70) 'Posta Béla kolozsvári régészeti iskolája és a "Dolgozatok". L'école archéologique de Béla Posta et les "Dolgozatok"(études)', *Debreceni Déri Muzeum évkönyve* 117–46.
Flannery, K. V. (1982) 'The Golden Marshalltown: a parable for archaeology of the 1980s', *American Anthropologist* 84: 265–78.
Fodor, I. (1977a) 'Altungarn, Bulgarotürken und Ostslawen in Südrussland (Archäologische Beiträge)', *Acta Antiqua et Archaeologica 20, Opuscula Byzantina* 4: 1–135.
—— (1977b) 'Der Ursprung der in Ungarn gefundenen Tonkessel', *Acta Archaeologica Academiae Scientiarum Hungaricae* 29: 323–49.
—— (1982) *In Search of a New Homeland. The Prehistory of the Hungarian People and the Conquest*, Budapest: Corvina Kiadó.
Fodor, I. and Selmeczi, L. (eds) (1985) *Oközépkori régészetünk újabb eredményei és idöszerü feladatai. Neuere Ergebnisse und aktuelle Fragen der Mittelalter-Archäologie in Ungarn*, Budapest: Magyar Nemzeti Museum.
Fülep, F. (1987) 'Recherches archéologiques', in B. Köpeczi (ed.) *Sciences sociales et humaines en Hongrie*, Budapest: Akademmiai Kiadó.
Harding, A. F. (1982) 'The Bronze Age in Central Europe: advances and prospects' in F. Wendorf and A. E. Close (eds) *Advances in World Archaeology* vol. 2, London: Academic Press.
Hartyáni, P. B. and Nováki, Gy (1975) 'Samen und Fruchtfunde in Ungarn', *Agrártörténeti Szemle, Supplementum* 17: 1–88.
Hodder, I. (ed.) (1982a) *Symbolic and Structural Archaeology*, New Directions in Archaeology, Cambridge: Cambridge: University Press.
—— (1982b) *Symbols in Action. Ethno-archaeological Studies of Material Culture*, Cambridge: Cambridge: University Press.
—— (1982c) *The Present Past. An Introduction to Anthropology for Arcaheologists*, London: B. T. Batsford Ltd.
Hodges, R. (1982) *Dark Age Economics*, London: Duckworth.
Horváth, F. (1983) 'A feilödes megtorpanása (Discontinuity in the development)', in Gy Kristó (ed.) *Szeged története (A history of Szeged)* vol. I, Szeged: Somogyi Könyvtár.
Horváth, F. and Trogmayer, O. (1985) 'A dél-alföldi ujkökori fejlödès kezdete és vége', *Tudomány* 1/2: 30–7.
Jakabbfy, I. (1981) *A Közép-Duna-medence régészeti bibliográfiaja 1967–1977. Archäologische Bibliographie des Mitteldonaubeckens 1967–1977*, Budapest: Adadémiai Kiadó.
Jankovich, D. (1985) 'Archaeological Topography, Theoretical and Practical Lessons', *Mitteleungen des Archäologischen Instituts der Ungarischen Akademie der Wissenschaften* 14: 283–92.
Jarman, M. R., Bailey, G. N. and Jarman, H. N. (1982) *Early European Agriculture (Its Foundation and Development)*, Cambridge: Cambridge University Press.
Jerem, E. *et al.* (1984–5) 'A Sopron-Krautackeren feltárt vaskori telep régészeti és környezetrekonstrukciós vizsgálata I-II [The archaeological

ARCHAEOLOGICAL THEORY IN HUNGARY SINCE 1960

and environmental investigation of the Iron Age settlement discovered
at Sopron-Krautacker]', *Archaeologiai Ertesitö* 111: 141–69; 112: 3–24.
Kalicz, N. and Makkay, J. (1977) *Die Linienbandkeramik im der Grossen
Ungarischen Tiefebene*, Budapest: Akadémiai Kiadó.
Kalicz, N. and Raczky, P. (1977) 'Uj-e az "Ujrégészet"?' *Valósáq* 6:
76–94.
Kemenczei, T. (1984) *Die Spätbronzezeit Nordostungarns*, Budapest: Akadémiai Kiadó.
Kosse, K. (1979) *Settlement Ecology of the Körös and Linear Pottery
Culture in Hungary*, British Archaeological Report S64. Oxford.
Kovács, T. (1980) 'Régészetünk néhány idöszerü kérdéséröl', *Archaeologiai értesitö* 107: 116.
Kubinyi, A. (1985) 'Die Rolle der Archäologie und der Urkunden bei
der Erforschung des Alltagsleben im Spätmittelalter', *Etudes Historiques
Hongroises*, Budapest: Akadémiai Kiadó.
László, Gy (1944) *A honfoglaló magyar nép élete*, Budapest: Magyar Élet
Kiadása.
—— (1961) *Östörténetünk legkorábbi szakaszai*, Budapest: Akadémiai
Kiadó.
—— (1970) *The Art of the Period of Great Migrations in Hungary*,
Budapest: Corvina Kiadó.
—— (1977) *Régészeti tanulmányok*, Budapest: Gondolat Kiadó.
—— (1980) *Régészeti levelek*, Szolnok: Damjanich János Muzeum.
—— (1984) *The Treasure of Nagyszentmiklos*, Budapest: Corvina Kiadó.
—— (1990) *Öseinkröl (Studies)*, Budapest: Gondolat Kiadó.
Laszlovszky, J. (1982) 'The Correls in the Villages of the Arpadian Age
(The employment of the phosphate analysis in the investigations of the
Settlement structure)', in *III. Internationale Archäologische Studentenkonferenz. Pécs*, Budapest: ELTE Universitätspresse.
—— (1986) 'Einzelhofsiedlungen in der Arpadenzeit', *Acta Archaeologica
Academiae Scientiarum Hungaricae* 38: 227–55.
—— (in press) 'Social stratification of the Hungarian rural population in
the 11–13th centuries. A reconstruction based on the archaeological
evidence', *Symposia Thracica*.
Makkay, J. (1976) 'Problems concerning Copper Age chronology in the
Carpathian Basin', *Acta Archaeologica Academiae Scientiarum Hungaricae* 28: 251–300.
—— (1978) 'A Szegvár-tüzkövesi ujkökori férfiszobor és a föld és èg
elválasztásának ösi mitosza. (The Neolithic Male Figurine from
Szegvár-Tüzköves and the ancient Myth of the Separation of Heaven
and Earth', *Archaeologiai értesitö* 105: 164–83.
—— (1982) *A magyarországi neolitikum kutatásának uj eredményei.
(New Results in the Research of the Hungarian Neolithic)*, Budapest:
Akadémiai Kiadó.
—— (1985a) 'The crisis of prehistoric chronology', *Mitteilungen des
Archäologischen Instituts der Ungarischen Akademie der Wissenschaften*
14: 53–70.
—— (1985b) 'Diffusionism, antidiffusionism and chronology: some gen-

eral remarks', *Acta Archaeologica Academiae Scientiarum Hungaricae* 37: 3–32.

—— (1987) 'Utószó', in S. Pigott, *Az európai civilizáció kezdetei*, Budapest: Gondolat kiadó.

—— (1989) 'V. G. Childe on chronological correlations between the Orient and Europe', in S. Bökönyi (ed.) *Neolithic of Southeastern Europe and its Near Eastern Connections (International Conference 1987 Szolnok-Szeged)* Varia Archaeologica Hungarica II, Budapest.

Matolcsi, J. (1973) *Domestikationsforschung und Geschichte der Haustiere, Internationales Symposion in Budapest 1971*, Budapest: Akadémiai Kiadó.

Miklós, Zs. (1985) 'Einige Fragen der mittelalterlichen Siedlungsgeschichte im Spiegel der archäologischen Topographie', *Mitteilungen des Archäologischen Instituts der Ungarischen Akademie der Wissenschaften* 14: 235–42.

Mócsy, A. (1959) *Die Bevölkerung von Pannonien bis zu den Markomannenkriegen*, Budapest: Akadémiai Kiadó.

—— (1974) *Pannonia and Upper Moesia. A History of the Middle Danube Provinces of the Roman Empire*, London: Routledge & Kegan Paul.

—— (1982) 'Provinciális régészetünk állásáról', *Archaeologiai értesitö* 109: 287–90.

—— (1985) *Beiträge zur Namenstatistik*, Dissertationes Pannonicae Ser. III, vol. 3, Budapest: ELTE Régészeti Tanszék.

Mócsy, A., Feldman, R., Marton, E. and Szilágyi, M. (1983) *Nomenclator provinciarum Europae Latinarum et Galliae Cisalpinae cum indice inverso*, Dissertationes Pannonicae. Ser. III vol. 1, Budapest: ELTE Régészeti Tanszék.

Mozsolics. A. (1973) *Bronze- und Goldfunde des Karpatenbeckens. Depothorizonte von Forró und Opályi*, Budapest: Akadémiai Kiadó.

—— (1985) *Bronzefunde aus Ungarn. Depothorizonte von Aranyos, Kurd und Gyermely*, Budapest: Akadémiai Kiadó.

Nacev-Skomal, S. (1980) 'The social organisation of the Tiszapolgár group at Basatanya', *The Journal of Indo-European Studies*, 8: 75–91.

—— (1985) 'A bronzkor elötti társadalmi rendszerek Európában (Pre-Bronze Age European Social Systems. A synthesis)', *Archaeologiai értesitö* 112: 119–27.

Oroszlán, Z. (1966) 'Egyetemünk Régészeti Tanszékeinek kialakulása és története', *Dissertationes Archaeologicae* 8: 55–7.

Pálóczi Horváth, András (1989) *Pechenegs, Cumans, Iasians (Steppe Peoples in Medieval Hungary)*, Budapest: Corvina Kiadó.

Patay, P. (1974) 'Die hochkupferzeitliche Bodrogkeresztur-Kultur', *Bericht der Römisch-Germanischen Komission* 55: 1–71.

Patek, E. (1968) *Die Urnenfelder-Kultur in Transdanubien*, Budapest: Akadémiai Kiadó.

Patterson, T. C. (1986) 'The last sixty years: towards a social history of Americanist archaeology in the United States', *American Anthropologist* 88: 7–26.

Raczky, P. (ed.) (1987) *The Late Neolithic of the Tisza Region. A Survey of Recent Excavations and Their Finding: Hodmezövásárhely-Gorzsa,*

Szegvár-Tüzköves, öcsöd-Kováshalom. Vésztö-Mágor. Berettyoujfalu-Heroály, Budapest Szolnok: Damjanich János Muzeum.

Raczky, P. (1988) *A Tisza-vidék kulturális és kronológiai kapcsolatai a Balkánnal és az Égeikummal a neolitikum, rézkor idöszakában*, Szolnok.

—— (1989) 'Chronological framework of the early and middle neolithic in the Tisza region', in S. Bökönyi (ed.) *Neolithic of Southeastern Europe nd its Near Eastern Connections (International Conference 1987 Szolnok-Szeged)*, Varia Archaeologica Hungarica II, Budapest.

Raczky, P. *et al.* (1985) 'Öcsöd-Kováschalom. The intensive topographical and archaeological investigation of a late neolithic site. Preliminary report', *Mitteilungen des Archäolgischen Instituts der Ungarishcen Akademie der Wissenschaften* 14: 251–78.

Renfrew, C. (1973) *Before Civilization*, London: Jonathan Cape.

—— (1978) 'Trajectory, discontinuity, and morphogenesis; the implications of catastrophe theory for archaeology', *American Antiquity* 43: 59–76.

—— (1979) *Problems in European Prehistory*, Edinburgh: University Press.

Sherratt, A. (1982) 'Mobile resources: settlement and exchange in early agricultural Europe', in C. Renfrew and S. Shennan (eds) *Ranking, Resource and Exchange. Aspects of the Archaeology of Early European Society*, Cambridge: Cambridge University Press.

—— (1982–3) 'The development of neolithic and Copper Age Settlement in the great Hungarian plain, Part I The regional setting, Part II Site surveys and Settlement dynamics', *Oxford Journal of Archaeology* 1: 287–316.; 2: 13–41.

—— (1983) 'Early agrarian settlement in the Körös region of the great Hungarian plain', *Acta Archaeologica Academiae Scientiarum Hungaricae* 35: 155–69.

Szabó, K. (1938) *Az alföldi magyar nép müvelödéstörténeti emlékei. (Kulturgeschichtliche Denkmäler der Ungarischen Tiefebene)*, Budapest: Országos Magyar Történeti Muzeum.

Szöke, B. (1959) 'A bjelobrdoi kulturárol. (Sur la civilisation de Bjelobrdo)', *Archaeologiai értesitö* 86: 32–47.

—— (1962) *A honfoglaló és kora Arpád-kori magyarsá régészeti emlékei*, Régészeti Tanulmányok I, Budapest: Akadémiai Kiadó.

Szücs, J. (1983) 'The Three Historical Regions of Europe', *Acta Historica Academiae Scientiarum Hungaricae* 28: 131–85.

Tompa, F. (1932) 'Régészet', in B. Hóman (ed.) *A magyar történetirás új útjai*, Budapest.

—— (1934–5) '25 Jahre Urgeschichtsforschung in Ungarn 1912–1936', *Bericht der Römische-Germanischen Komission* 24–5: 27–127.

Torma, I. (1969) 'A Veszprém megyei régészeti topográfiai kutatások öskori vonatkozásu eredményeiröl (Über vorgeschichtliche Ergebnisse der archäologischen Topographie auf dem Gebiet des Komitats Veszprém)', *Veszprém Megyei Muzeumok Közleményei* 8: 75–81.

Vekerdi, L. (1976) 'Ujrégészet', *Valóság* 11: 26–41.

Vértes, L. (1965) *Az öskökor és az átmeneti kökor emlékei Magyarországon*, Budapest: Akadémiai Kiadó.

INDEX